D1571122

Donald Davidson's Truth-Theoretic Semantics

Donald Davidson's Truth-Theoretic Semantics

Ernest Lepore
Kirk Ludwig

CLARENDON PRESS · OXFORD

OXFORD
UNIVERSITY PRESS

Great Clarendon Street, Oxford OX2 6DP

Oxford University Press is a department of the University of Oxford.
It furthers the University's objective of excellence in research, scholarship,
and education by publishing worldwide in

Oxford New York

Auckland Cape Town Dar es Salaam Hong Kong Karachi
Kuala Lumpur Madrid Melbourne Mexico City Nairobi
New Delhi Shanghai Taipei Toronto

With offices in

Argentina Austria Brazil Chile Czech Republic France Greece
Guatemala Hungary Italy Japan Poland Portugal Singapore
South Korea Switzerland Thailand Turkey Ukraine Vietnam

Oxford is a registered trademark of Oxford University Press
in the UK and in certain other countries

Published in the United States
by Oxford University Press Inc., New York

© Ernest Lepore and Kirk Ludwig 2007

The moral rights of the authors have been asserted
Database right Oxford University Press (maker)

Crown copyright material is reproduced under Class Licence
Number C01P0000148 with the permission of OPSI
and the Queen's Printer for Scotland

First published 2007

British Library Cataloguing in Publication Data
Data available

Library of Congress Cataloging in Publication Data
Data Available

Typeset by Laserwords Private Limited, Chennai, India
Printed in Great Britain
on acid-free paper by
Biddles Ltd, King's Lynn, Norfolk

ISBN 978–0–19–929093–2

1 3 5 7 9 10 8 6 4 2

For 林世嫺

K. L.

For Peter Klein and Jesse Rosenthal
two good friends who have watched over me
for the past quarter of a century

E. L.

Preface

This is the second of two books on Donald Davidson's central philosophical project. The first, *Donald Davidson: Meaning, Truth, Language and Reality* (Oxford: Oxford University Press, 2005), dealt with the basic framework of Davidson's truth-theoretic approach to providing a meaning theory for a natural language, and then with his development of his general project in the philosophy of language and theory of meaning by way of the analysis of the empirical confirmation of a meaning theory for a speaker, from the stance of the radial interpreter, that is, the interpreter who starts out without any detailed knowledge of the speakers' meanings or attitudes. Much of the first book concentrated on the larger philosophical themes of Davidson's work, how to understand meaning and thought and its relation to the world, and the implications of that project for the extent of our knowledge of our own minds, of the minds of others, and of the external world, the possibility of alternative conceptual schemes, the extent of indeterminacy of meaning, the role of conventions in communication, and the role of language as the basis for the capacity for thought. This book turns to the development of details of Davidson's semantic program, specifically, the pursuit of the project of providing a compositional semantic theory for natural languages by making strategic use of an appropriately adapted Tarski-style axiomatic truth theory. Such a theory aims to provide a specification of the truth conditions of any felicitous utterance of a natural language sentence which serves to interpret it, and exhibits in the proof of the theorem that gives the truth conditions the compositional structure of the sentence and how its truth depends on its context of utterance. This project can be separated from the more ambitious themes of Davidson's work and pursued independently. The basic idea of the approach was given in Part I of the first book in the context of a historical introduction to Davidson's project. We begin this book with a condensed presentation of the core ideas of the program, and then extend the basic framework to a language with quantifiers, and pursue a variety of issues about natural language semantics in this framework. Part I of the first book provides more of the philosophical motivation for the approach, and though we will provide a sketch at the outset, the reader in search of a fuller understanding should turn to that.

This book and its previously published companion have been long in preparation, far longer than the authors had anticipated, and it is perhaps with some relief that we release it finally, though also with the regret that comes from parting with an engaging companion. It is, we are aware, far from the state of perfection or completion which we would like for it to be in, but that is a vanishing ideal, and so we offer it as a stage in what is a larger and longer range project pursued collectively and from many different points of view, the advance of our understanding of the nature of language, meaning, and communication. We have learned an enormous amount in the process writing these books, and we hope that some of the excitement we have felt and the sense of adventure with which we have pursued the project will be communicated to the reader. Davidson's program in truth-theoretic semantics provides the most philosophically sophisticated approach to natural language semantics available. By this we mean to endorse not any specific proposal pursued within the framework but the framework itself, which, we argue, provides as much as can be hoped for by way of a compositional meaning theory specifically, and with a minimum of ontological resources, at least so far as the basic framework is concerned. We hope this book will serve as a clarification of the project as well as a contribution to its program in various specific areas.

We have been aided by many people in the work that is represented here, too many to make proper acknowledgments to everyone whose advice or comments have made this a better book than it would otherwise have been. We apologise here to any whom we should mention but fail to. Special thanks go to Ana Maria Andrei, Emil Badici, Barry Loewer, Christopher Lubbers, Ellen Macarrone, Robert May, Paul Pietroski, Greg Ray, Ivana Simić, and several anonymous reviewers for Oxford University Press. We extend thanks also to our students in seminars and discussion groups over the years at Rutgers and the University of Florida, and to Elka Shortsleeve for preparing the index. We wish to thank Peter Momtchiloff, our editor at Oxford University Press, for his help, advice, and patience with this project, and to thank also Catherine Berry at OUP who saw it through production, and our copy-editor at OUP for both this and the last book, Jane Robson. Of course, our primary thanks go to Donald Davidson to whose inspiration this book owes whatever merit it has.

Contents

Detailed Table of Contents

Note on In-Text Citations

The author–date citation method is used in the text. When the citation is to a reprinted essay, the format of the citation is as follows, where 'n' is a placeholder for the page or pages cited, if any.

(Author Date-of-Collection (Original-Publication-Date): n)

This allows a reader to keep track of the original publication date of material cited, which is relevant to understanding the development of Davidson's work and many interpretive issues. In the Bibliography, the references are ordered by author, date of collection, and then original publication date. Where further distinctions are required, '*a*', '*b*', etc. are appended to the date of collection, and works are further ordered alphabetically by title. For example, the following citation

(Davidson 2001*b* (1969): 38)

would be sorted first by the author's last name, 'Davidson', then by the date of publication of collection from which page numbers are cited, 2001, and then by the original date of publication. The '*b*' appended to '2001' indicates that there are at least two entries which share these features. They will be listed in order in the bibliography. Original publication information follows the main entry. Thus, for example, the portion of the bibliography corresponding to the above is:

[Davidson] (2001*a* (1969)). The Individuation of Events. *Essays on Actions and Events* (2nd edn., pp. 163–80). New York: Clarendon Press. Originally published in N. Rescher (ed.), *Essays in Honor of Carl G. Hempel.* Dordrecht: D. Reidel.

―――(2001*b* (1969)). True to the Facts, *Inquiries into Truth and Interpretation* (2nd edn., pp. 37–54). New York: Clarendon Press. Originally published in *Journal of Philosophy*, 66 (1969), 748–64.

Introduction

1. Background and General Motivation

This book is an examination of the foundations and applications of the program of truth-theoretic semantics for natural languages introduced in 1967 by Donald Davidson in his classic paper "Truth and Meaning." It began as one part of a larger project on Davidson's philosophical work in the theory of meaning and philosophy of language, and a set of interrelated arguments and conclusions in epistemology, philosophy of mind, and metaphysics founded on that work. In the end it became clear that this relatively more technical portion of the project should be separated into a stand-alone treatment of truth-theoretic semantics.

A philosophical theory of meaning is concerned with the nature of meaning. It seeks to understand meaning at a level that abstracts away from contingent features of actual human languages. But no philosophical theory of meaning can gain any traction without careful attention to the workings of actual human languages within which philosophical theorizing is done. They are our primary objects of study. It is through understanding them, and seeing what in them is essential and accidental, that we come to that general understanding of the nature of language and meaning which is the object of the philosophical study of language. Thus, any realistic philosophical theory of meaning needs to come to grips with what it is for words in human languages to mean what they do.

One of the starting points, and a keynote, of Davidson's work in the theory of meaning is the observation that natural languages are compositional, in the sense that they contain a division of expressions into the semantically complex and primitive, and that, being finite beings, we must understand the infinity of nonsynonymous sentences of the languages we speak on the basis of understanding a finite number of primitives and rules for their combination that enable us to understand the complex expressions that can be grammatically formed from them.[1] This places important constraints on an account of meaning and language, and on the analysis of various ranges of discourse of interest independently to philosophers. No analysis of a construction of natural language is acceptable if it implies that there is an infinity of semantical primitives in the language.

Two examples of analyses of indirect discourse which have this consequence will suffice to drive home the point, and the importance of the requirement. Take as an example the sentence, 'Voltaire said that one feels like crawling on all fours after reading Rousseau's work'. Israel Scheffler (1954) proposed an analysis of sentences of indirect discourse that treats them as making claims about particular utterances, with the complement sentence functioning as a predicate of the utterance. Thus, our sample sentence would receive the following analysis:

> Voltaire spoke a that-one-feels-like-crawling-on-all-fours-after-reading-Rousseau's-work utterance.

The hyphens indicate that the complement is to be treated as a primitive predicate of the utterance. Scheffler's proposal neatly evades an objection which Alonzo Church had made to Carnap's analysis of indirect discourse as a relation to a sentence. Carnap's analysis failed what is called Church's translation test. For example, the translation into German of *the analysis* of a sentence of English should be *the analysis in German* of the translation into German of the original English sentence. But Carnap's analysis makes an English report of indirect discourse *about an English sentence*, and likewise a German report of indirect discourse *about a German sentence*, and so the translation of the analysis in English is not the analysis in German of the translation of the original English sentence. Scheffler's proposal avoids this problem because it contains no reference to the complement sentence. But the cost is too high, for there is no limit to the number of distinct sentences which may grammatically appear in the complement of a sentence of indirect discourse, which immediately implies an infinity of semantical primitives on Scheffler's account, which there cannot be.

A second example is provided by at least one reading of Frege's famous proposal that in sentences of indirect discourse the words that appear do not

---

[1] See Lepore and Ludwig (2005: ch. 2), for further discussion.

have their usual function, but serve instead to refer to indirect senses.[2] Our example above would be treated as a relation between Voltaire and the sense of the sentence 'one feels like crawling on all fours after reading Rousseau's work' when it is used (in English) by itself—its customary sense. The motivation for this is that in indirect discourse we are concerned not with the words someone used to say something but with the sense of what he said. However, when we apply this motivation to the sentence, 'Rousseau said that Voltaire said that <u>one feels like crawling on all fours after reading Rousseau's work</u>', it would seem that we want the underlined sentence to refer not to its customary sense but to the sense it has when spoken in 'Voltaire said that one feels like crawling on all fours after reading Rousseau's work'. It seems, then, that each such sentence would shift its sense upon a further embedding, and since Frege held that the sense of a sentence was composed out of the senses of its components, each word in such a sentence would be infinitely ambiguous, assuming no senses are modes of presentation of themselves. Each word taken with a distinct sense is a semantical primitive. Each of the senses of 'band', for example, must be learned independently. This would therefore require us to understand an infinity of semantical primitives to understand the language, which is impossible.

Truth-theoretic semantics is concerned with this compositional aspect of meaning, with how we understand complex expressions on the basis of their contained primitives and mode of combination. This is one part of a more general project in the theory of meaning, which can be expressed with the question, 'What is it for words to mean what they do?' This more general project has two parts. One is how complexes are understood on the basis of their primitive parts. The other is concerned with what it is for the primitives to have the meanings that they do. For terminological clarity we will reserve 'theory of meaning' for the more general project, and use 'meaning theory' for a compositional meaning theory.

The second project is the concern of Davidson's work on the project of *radical interpretation*. Radical interpretation involves constructing a theory of interpretation of a speaker on the basis of his observable interaction with the environment in the absence of any knowledge of the meanings of his words or any detailed knowledge of the contents of his propositional attitudes. The

---

[2] It has been disputed that Frege's theory (1997 (1892)) commits him to this. See, e.g. Parsons (1981), but also Boisvert and Lubbers (2003) for the contrary view. For purposes of illustration of the force of the finitivity requirement it is not necessary to enter into the dispute about the interpretation of Frege.

3

goal is not to provide an analysis of the concept of meaning, or an analysis piecemeal of particular words or what it is for someone to understand them, but to illuminate as a whole the set of concepts deployed in understanding other speakers by considering how one could confirm such a theory on the basis of evidence described without appeal to those concepts (Davidson 2001*b* (1973): 137). The two projects are interconnected, for Davidson conceives of the task of the radical interpreter as in part that of confirming a compositional meaning theory—which takes the form of an interpretive truth theory (more on this below)—of his subject.

We have considered the second project in Lepore and Ludwig 2005 (esp. part II). In this book, we are concerned solely with the first project. What this means is that we may take for granted knowledge of the meanings of primitive expressions in seeking to understand how complex expressions are understood on their basis. Thus, it is no part of the project of providing a compositional meaning theory for a natural language that it explain what it is to understand primitive expressions or grasp the concepts which they express. Its goal is to illuminate one central aspect of meaning, not every aspect of meaning.

What is distinctive about truth-theoretic semantics is the form in which it casts a compositional meaning theory for a natural language. The proposal is to use an axiomatic truth theory for the language, which meets certain constraints, to serve the goals of a compositional meaning theory for the language. An axiomatic truth theory states conditions under which each sentence of the object language—the language for which it is a theory—is true in the metalanguage—the language of the theory—in the form of a biconditional, of which (*T*) will serve as an illustration (abbreviating 'if, and only if,' as 'iff').

> (*T*)   *s* is true iff *p*

A structural description of an object language sentence as constructed out of its significant parts replaces '*s*', and '*p*' is replaced by a metalanguage sentence that provides conditions under which *s* is true. Truth is not meaning, and stating conditions under which a sentence is true is not to state what it means. However, the key idea of truth-theoretic semantics is that placing certain constraints on an axiomatic truth theory will nonetheless put us in a position, knowing that the theory meets the constraints, to use it to interpret object language sentences and to see how understanding of them depends on an understanding of their parts and mode of combination. One, but not the only constraint, is that the theory meet Tarski's Convention *T*, or an analog for natural languages. Convention *T* requires in part that an adequate theory of truth for a language has as theorems all instances of (*T*) (or some analog) in which '*p*' is replaced by a sentence in the metalanguage that translates the object language sentence. In this case, we know that 'is true iff' can be replaced with 'means that' to yield a true sentence. This was Davidson's key insight about how a truth theory could be employed to forward the goal of providing a compositional meaning theory.[3] We discuss the constraints required in more detail in Chapter 1 below, as well as how to adapt the central idea to a context-sensitive language.

There are a number of motivations for pursuing a compositional meaning theory in this indirect way. One is that the connection between meaning and truth is laid bare, albeit indirectly. It is a plausible constraint on any compositional meaning theory that it reveal what conditions have to be met for a sentence of the language of study to be true in virtue of what it means. A second is that it achieves the ends of a compositional meaning theory with a minimum of resources. Any compositional meaning theory must have the resources to identify an adequate truth theory for the language. If identifying an adequate truth theory for the language meeting certain constraints suffices, then we have achieved the end with a minimum of commitments. In particular, we need no more ontology than is required by, in effect, the theory of reference, and, in particular, we do not need to quantify over meanings, senses, properties, relations, propositions, denoting complexes, or the like. This ontology is shown to be superfluous from the point of view of the meaning theory. And where an ontology which may be thought to be essential is shown to be superfluous, we gain a deeper understanding of our subject matter.

Of course, where our sentences employ referring terms or descriptions which, if they refer to or denote anything at all, refer to meanings, properties, relations, propositions, or possibilia of various sorts, we are committed to there being such things to the extent to which we are committed to holding those sentences true. The present point though is that the commitment to such entities does not fall out of the commitment to giving a theory of meaning, the recursive work of which is accomplished by an absolute truth theory in the style Davidson suggests. For example, the statement of the truth conditions for 'The possible fat man in the doorway is asleep' are given in the form of a biconditional which only asserts an equivalence, which will be true even if

---

[3] Church (1951: 102) is the first person we are aware of who notes explicitly that a Tarski-style truth theory puts one in a position to understand the object language.

there is no possible fat man in the doorway because there are no possibilia. Even in the case of the suggestion that an adequate semantics for indirect discourse or attitude sentences requires terms that refer to propositions, the truth theory itself may remain neutral on whether there are propositions, for if anything refers to them, it is a certain sort of complement clause, and its reference conditions can be given conditionally. Take as an example a sentential complement formed from 'that' and a sentence: for any x, if x is the proposition expressed by 'p', then the referent of 'that p'$= x$. (See Ch. 11 for further discussion.) The same point applies to possible worlds analyses of modal statements. The truth theory itself is not committed to there being possible worlds even if a theorist decides that the best analysis of modal statements represents them as quantifying over possible worlds. This can be represented in the truth theory by restricted quantification or a special style of variable which can be treated as a definitional abbreviation of restricted quantification. The truth theory is no more committed to possible worlds by giving such a semantics for modal statements than it is by giving truth conditions for 'Some unicorns have red heads'.

A third motivation is that when we examine theories of meaning that aim to achieve the recursion needed to provide a statement of meanings for every object language sentence by quantifying over meanings, we can see that the meanings quantified over drop out as irrelevant to the approach's achieving its ends, which it does by apt choice of metalanguage terms for meanings, which enables a matching of object and metalanguage expression alike in meaning. In other words, the meanings qua entities are neither necessary nor sufficient for achieving the ends of a meaning theory.[4]

The project aims for philosophical illumination, but at a number of different levels. It aims to illuminate the nature of meaning by illuminating one central aspect of meaning, the systematic role of words in contributing to what different sentences in which they appear mean. It does this, however, not by abstraction but by considering how to develop in detail a working theory for actual natural languages. It is through the detailed investigation of the actual workings of languages that we build up a picture of the richness and range of devices which we employ in representing and talking and the ways in which the atoms of meaning can be combined.

We learn by this process how resourceful we can be with a few fundamental devices: predicates, referring terms, quantifiers, and logical connectives. We

---

[4] These points are closely related to Davidson's recent brilliant discussion of the problem of predication (2005: chs. 4–7).

learn what role context plays in interpreting what we mean, and how much information we exploit in interpreting what people say. We see how more fundamental tiers of language are exploited in extensions of our ability to talk about things. Thus, we move from talking about the world to talking about our talking and thinking about it, and from stating what is so to telling people what to do, asking questions, making promises, offering congratulations, and so on. We see also what the different options are in developing a range of devices for getting the work of language done, roads that could have been taken but were not.

We gain insight into how to adjudicate between rival hypotheses about the logico-semantic form of natural language constructions (see Ch. 13). There is enormous resolving power in putting these questions in the context of a systematic and comprehensive theory for the whole language. A particular hypothesis about logical form will have implications for our interpretation of many constructions which will not have been in view in the initial hypothesis. A simple example is the suggestion that the logical form of 'All philosophers are rich' is the same as 'For all x, if x is a philosopher, then x is rich'. On the plausible assumption that 'Most men are mortal' has the same logico-semantic form as 'All philosophers are rich', we find that the proposal has unacceptable consequences, since there is no equivalent paraphrase of 'Most philosophers are rich' using unrestricted quantifiers. 'For most x, if x is a philosopher, then x is rich' is true since most things are not philosophers, but the original is false. Paraphrasing 'Most F are G' as 'Most x are such that x is F and x is G' likewise fails in this case since it is not the case that most things are philosophers and rich. No other paraphrase using unrestricted quantifiers provides an adequate interpretation (see Ch. 2, §3 for more discussion).

The work of putting together an adequate interpretive truth theory for a natural language bears on the traditional task of philosophical analysis in the following way. In any analysis of a range of discourse of interest in a philosophical investigation, there are two separable stages. The first is that of determining the logical form of the sentences of interest in the relevant range of discourse. The second is that of analyzing the key terms, ideally into a set of illuminating necessary and sufficient conditions, or, falling short of that, at least by way of tracing out analytic connections between them and other terms. An interpretive truth theory will reveal logico-semantic form, and so provide an answer to questions proposed at the first stage, relative to an adequate account of the logic of the metalanguage. It will also help to distinguish the two stages by distinguishing what contributions to truth conditions are due to the structure of a sentence and what are due to the contributions of the primitives in it. Sometimes it will show that there is hidden structure which bears on questions of ontology, and help to isolate the underlying relations expressed. An example of this is found in Davidson's well-known analysis of action sentences as involving an implicit quantifier over events to provide a compositional way of handling adverbial modification. From (1) we can infer (3)–(4) on the basis of form alone, and it is clear that 'shot' means the same in each of these sentences. The challenge to a compositional meaning theory is to show how to understand the logico-semantic form of (1) so as to secure this result. Davidson proposed treating the verb as introducing an implicit quantifier over events, and treating the adverbs as predicates whose argument places were bound by the quantifier introduced by the verb, as in (5).

(1)   Shem shot Shaun with a gun in the park
(2)   Shem shot Shaun with a gun
(3)   Shem shot Shaun in the park
(4)   Shem shot Shaun
(5) $(\exists e)(\text{Shot}(e, \text{Shem}, \text{Shaun}) \ \& \ \text{with}(e, \text{a gun}) \ \& \ \text{in}(e, \text{the park}))$

On the pattern of analysis given in (5), (2)–(4) are seen to follow from (1) by conjunction elimination. The analysis incidentally has the consequence of showing in ordinary action sentences a commitment to the existence of events, and so showing a commitment of our common sense ontology to changes. (In line with the discussion above, any commitment to events arises from holding such sentences to be true, not from holding the event analysis itself to be true.) Settling issues of logical form leaves open, however, how to understand the three-place relation expressed by 'shot' and the two place relations expressed by 'with' and 'in'. Yet the account of logical form bears on the analysis of 'shot', for example, by showing it to be a three-place rather than a two-place relation, or a four-place relation, as might be suggested by (1). Arguably further analysis is required to account for 'Shem did something' following from 'Shem shot Shaun'. See Chapter 7 for further discussion.

Thus, the project of truth-theoretic semantics has a direct bearing on questions of analysis in most fields of philosophy through providing illumination about the logico-semantic structure of particular ranges of discourse which philosophers have been interested in, which may, as we have just seen, reveal ontological, or other commitments, not immediately apparent. More generally, through seeing how a detailed picture of the workings of language is developed through an interpretive truth theory for it, we see what the combinatorial aspects of meaning come to, and what their fundamental components are. The mechanics of meaning are laid bare. We gain thereby insight into the complex practical ability which is mastery of a language, for corresponding to each word is a disposition to use it in accordance with its type, and in accordance with its content. Mastery of a language or a portion of a language consists in a set of interlocking dispositions attaching to its vocabulary. This is directly reflected in the axioms of a suitably formulated truth theory for the language.

A more general and subtle lesson of the project is that illumination of the combinatorial aspects of meaning is not advanced by the introduction of meanings, and that the attempt to state straightforwardly how we understand complex expressions on the basis of their primitives must fail. An interpretive truth theory shows how we understand complex expressions on the basis of understanding their significant components. But, as we have said, it does not state how we do it. For the illumination for a particular language presupposes grasp of another language, the metalanguage, in which the theory is given. It is through our already gasping a language which is at least equal in expressive power to the object language, and in some respects greater (the object language need not have the resources to give its own truth theory), that we are able to see in detail how the semantic combinatorics of the object language work. This should not come as a surprise. For there is no question of a standpoint for understanding meaning that is outside of language altogether. And the most fundamental and powerful devices for representation can obviously not be explicated without the use of just those devices. We can then at best show how they work by showing how they systematically contribute to how we understand sentences in which they appear. And there will be no way to do this that does not mirror the structure of the sentences whose structure we seek to illuminate.

We said above that a compositional meaning theory does not attempt to say what it is for someone to understand the primitive expressions in a language. But it is not completely unconnected with the question what it is for the primitive expressions to mean what they do. For the meaning of a primitive expression in a language which can combine with others to form complex meaningful expressions is exhausted by its potential contribution to the meanings of any sentence in which it appears. In knowing this, we know all there is to know about the meaning of the primitive expression. And knowing the right things about a truth theory puts us in a position to understand each of the primitive expressions of the language and how it combines with other expressions to determine the interpretive truth conditions of declarative sentences—and this insight can be extended to non-declarative sentences as well (see Ch. 12).

Still, this is not to provide analyses of primitive expressions in other terms, or to state anything explicitly about meaning connections between semantical primitives, even to the extent of stating anything about meaning connections between logical connectives. Thus, it falls short of providing an account of word meaning. For example, it will not tell us that if something satisfies 'is an uncle' then it must also satisfy 'has a niece or nephew', or that '*A* is colored' and '*A* is not blue' follow from '*A* is red'. Nor does this tell us under what stimulus conditions we should apply terms to objects around us, that is, it does not tell us how to apply expressions on the basis of how they look, or smell, or taste, or feel, etc. It will not tell us, for example, that a competent speaker will be disposed to apply 'red' to an object that looks red to him in what he believes to be normal light.

This does not mean that a truth theory will not have anything to say about the structure of word meanings. A truth theory will delve as deeply into word meaning, but only as deeply, as is required to account for entailments that are based on form. Thus, a truth theory will pay attention to inflection for tense and to at least some affixes. In some cases, reading non-explicit structure into a word and sentences in which it is used is required, though there is no overt marker for it. An illustration of this is the event analysis of adverbial modification of action sentences sketched above. Other examples that may call for recognition of structure is the relation between the transitive use of, say, 'boiled' and the intransitive use, and between a verb and its progressive form. From 'John boiled the water' it follows that 'The water boiled', though it does not follow from the latter that someone boiled the water. Similarly, from 'John left' it follows that 'John was leaving', but not vice versa. In each of these cases, these sentences seem to reflect a pattern of inference we recognize as valid independently of the specific meaning of the verbs. From 'A V-ed B' we infer 'B V-ed', and from 'A V-ed' we infer 'A was V-ing' where 'V' stands in for an event verb. These patterns plausibly fall in the scope of the compositional meaning theory, and so must be represented in a truth theory used in its pursuit.

2. Overview

In the following, our primary aim is to illustrate the promise of the truth-theoretic approach by laying out the philosophical foundations of it, and then sketching and discussing applications to a range of important natural language constructions. A subsidiary aim is to clarify the concept of the logical or logico-semantic form of a natural language sentence, and its relation to a compositional meaning theory whose aim is to uncover semantic structure in complex expressions. The applications to specific natural language constructions provide illustrations of the techniques for revealing and investigating logical form. A discussion of the concept of logical form is reserved for Chapter 13.

Chapter 1 lays out the philosophical foundations of the program of truth-theoretic semantics. In Chapters 2–9, we consider a variety of topics in natural language semantics: quantifiers (2–3), referring terms and quotation (4–6), adverbial and adjectival modification (7), tense (8–10), opaque contexts (11), and non-declarative sentences, that is, imperatives and interrogatives (12). In Chapter 13, against the backdrop of these discussions, we take up the question of how we can characterize fully generally the concept of sameness of logical form between any two sentences in any two languages. In the final chapter, Chapter 14, we take up the discussion of the concept of truth employed in the semantic theory, and, in particular, its relation to the correspondence theory of truth. These treatments are intended to illustrate the sorts of resources we must invoke within a broadly Davidsonian framework in order to provide a compositional semantic theory, and to illustrate the sorts of obstacles we naturally encounter and must overcome in pursuing our overall project. We consider, where appropriate, Davidson's own suggestions for how to deal with the constructions we consider, but often offer a different or modified account to deal with problems that arise in trying to carry out Davidson's suggestions.

Before providing a more detailed overview of the book, a word on its limitations is in order. We do not take ourselves to have provided in the following an exhaustive or final treatment of any of the subjects we discuss, nor to have discussed, by any means, all of the topics which properly fall in the scope of semantics of natural languages (for example, modality). Any of the topics we discuss could, and, for complete treatment of the issues that arise involving them, should be explored at much greater length. But even that would be the task not of one but of many books. Nor have we attempted to provide a systematic comparison with other approaches to the semantics of natural languages, as valuable as that would be. Indeed, it would be particularly valuable to examine in a detailed way the relation between the model-theoretic approach to semantics and the Davidsonian program. (Some remarks on the relation between the programs can be found in Lepore 1983.) Yet this must also be left for another day, or another set of hands, for it would be an enormous project in its own right. It is not the project we have set ourselves here. Our project grows out of, and is centered on, our interest in Donald Davidson's philosophical program, of which his program in the theory of meaning is one aspect. It is a project of clarification, evaluation, and amplification, from within the program, and is intended to help provide a foundation for further work and comparisons with other approaches. We hope that it can serve this purpose, though there will be lacunae in its treatments even of the topics it takes up. It is perhaps worth remarking also, even at the risk of belaboring the obvious, that what we see as the virtues of the truth-theoretic approach to semantics, as developed in Davidson's work, do not depend upon the correctness of any account of particular ranges of discourse to be found in the following pages. The framework for providing a semantical theory is one thing, the accounts within that framework of particular ranges of discourse are another. The proposals made about particular natural language constructions in English are of course empirical. They are subject to revision and refutation in the light of further evidence, and considerations of theoretical coherence, and of course the delicate business of drawing the line between the semantics of what we say and our capacity for using that to convey more than what is literally said.

We turn now to a more detailed account of the work of each chapter.

Chapter 1 introduces and motivates the compositionality requirement on natural language semantics. It is this requirement that led Davidson to the proposal to make use of a truth theory in pursuing a meaning theory in the light of the difficulties that accrue to more traditional approaches. We discuss the problems that arise for attempts to do the work needed by quantifying over meanings, arguing that they are neither necessary nor sufficient, and that what is required shows that the meanings do no work at all. We then discuss Tarski's Convention T and how it gives rise to the proposal to use a truth theory to give a meaning theory. We introduce a simple non-context-sensitive language in illustration, and introduce a requirement on the axioms of the truth theory parallel to the requirement that Convention T imposes on its theorems, arguing that this is both necessary and sufficient, relative to an adequate logic in the metalanguage, to use a truth theory in pursuit of a compositional meaning theory. We also introduce the crucial notion of a canonical proof, which is intuitively a proof drawing only on the content of the axioms, and is required to select the T-form sentences which enable interpretation of the object language sentences. We turn next to how this account must be modified to handle sentences with context sensitive elements, introduce an analog of Convention T for natural languages, which we call Davidson's Convention T, and show how to adapt the truth theory we provide to handle context sensitive expressions. We then given an explicit statement of the meaning theory, and draw out some of its consequences in responding to some objections. The discussion of the rest of the book is then developed against this background.

We begin with a discussion of quantifiers in Chapters 2 and 3. This requires the introduction of the satisfaction relation (or some technical device which achieves the same work), which relates an open sentence to objects associated with its argument places. The truth of closed sentences is then defined in terms of the notion of satisfaction. We consider the motivation for the modification in the classical treatment of unrestricted quantifiers, such as 'everything' and 'something', and then show how to extend the treatment to restricted quantifiers, such as 'most students' and 'many politicians'. A small informal theory is introduced in illustration in Chapter 3. The discussion in subsequent chapters takes place, then, in this new framework in which the axioms of the theory are either reference axioms or satisfaction axioms (apart from axioms for our theory of functions from variables to objects, which we choose as formula satisfiers).

Chapter 4 then takes up a variety of referring devices and issues that arise in discussing their semantics: proper names (such as 'Socrates' and 'Plato'), indexicals (such as 'I') and simple demonstratives ('this', 'that', 'these', and 'those'). We argue that the framework itself is not committed to any particular theory about the functioning of proper names, and that it is flexible enough to accommodate both direct reference theories of proper names and Fregean or neo-Fregean accounts. We consider in more generality what modifications are required to accommodate context-sensitive referring terms in the truth theory when we turn to indexicals and demonstratives.[5] Chapter 5 focuses specifically on complex demonstratives, constructed from a demonstrative and a nominal, such as 'that man', or 'that politician'. We argue that, in fact, these expressions should be understood as quantified noun phrases in which a simple demonstrative appears in the restricting predicate, roughly, 'that man' is treated as equivalent to 'the man who is identical to that'. Finally, Chapter 6 takes up a topic Davidson has discussed (2001*b* (1979)), the semantic character of quotation devices. We discuss in some detail Davidson's proposal for handling quotation, some difficulties that arise for the proposal, and, briefly, a simpler alternative which at least one of the authors (Ludwig) thinks will satisfy the desiderata on a successful account.

---

[5] This account corrects some problems noted with the simpler account introduced for preliminary illustration in Lepore and Ludwig (2005).

In Chapter 7, we consider how adjectival and adverbial modification can be handled in a compositional meaning theory. The basic approach in each case is to treat the modifiers as contributing a predicate to the satisfaction conditions of the sentence in which they appear. As already noted, in the case of adverbs, following Davidson (2001*b* (1967)), this forces the introduction of a suppressed quantifier into the account of the logical form of most sentences. (Independently of this, the treatment of tense also motivates the introduction of a temporal quantifier: in Chapter 9, §5, we combine the two accounts.) We consider also how modifiers which interact with the noun or verb that they modify may be handled in the framework (as in 'Beavers are large rodents' and 'John drank slowly').

We take up the topic of tense in Chapters 8–10. We treat tense as introducing a restricted indexical quantifier over times which binds an implicit argument place in tensed verbs (Ch. 8). Given the requirement that our semantic theory be context-insensitive, the prevalence of tense in English and other natural languages shows that the metalanguage in which the semantic theory is given must extend the object language by the inclusion of context-insensitive verbs relating things to times, which are not present in the object language. We consider the interaction of tense with a variety of temporal modifiers, relations, and temporal referring terms (Ch. 9). The account enables us to explain dependence relations between tenses in main and subordinate clauses as involving quantifier binding, and we discuss in particular the relation between the main verb and complement verbs in attitude reports (Ch. 10). We show also how the account which we give of the basic tenses, past, present, and future, may be extended to handle the perfect tenses (Ch. 10).

In Chapter 11, we turn to consider the treatment of opaque contexts, with Davidson's well-known paratactic treatment of indirect discourse as our starting point (2001 (1968)). We consider difficulties for this treatment and suggest some responses to the difficulties for Davidson's account, as well as some alternatives still in the spirit of his suggestion. We consider how these accounts may be extended to other opaque contexts, including attitude sentences and modal contexts.

We turn in Chapter 12 to the question how to integrate into the truth-theoretic approach sentences such as imperatives and interrogatives, whose uses do not appear on the face of it to be truth evaluable. We evaluate Davidson's attempt to fit these sentences into the mold of a truth-theoretic semantics (Davidson 2001*a* (1979)). We raise some difficulties, and discuss alternative ways of accommodating imperatives and interrogatives in the framework of truth-theoretic semantics, including a proposal for a generalization of the truth-theoretic framework, which employs a generalized notion of satisfaction conditions and the notion of fulfillment conditions; the notions of satisfaction and truth conditions employed in the core theory are treated as varieties of the generalized notions. On this account declarative sentences are assigned truth conditions as in the core theory. Imperatives and interrogatives are assigned compliance conditions, which are recursively specified in terms of the truth conditions of declarative sentences, without, however, reducing imperatives and interrogatives to varieties of declarative sentences.[6]

In Chapter 13, we turn to a consideration of how to give a general characterization of the notion of logical form in the light of the truth-theoretic, and then generalized fulfillment-theoretic, approach to natural language semantics. We are interested in the notion of logical form as semantic form, and take as basic the relation of a sentence s in a language L being the same in logical form as a sentence s' in a language L'. We explicate the notion of sameness of logical form by making use of the idea of corresponding canonical proofs of T-sentences (or, for the generalized theory, F-sentences) for the sentences in interpretive truth or fulfillment theories for their languages. We discuss also briefly the issue of the identification of logical constants in the language in the light of the semantic framework we employ, and some issues having to do with the extension of the notion of logical validity and logical consequence to natural languages.

The final chapter, Chapter 14, departs from the program of applying the framework to questions about natural language semantics to take up the question what light Tarski's work on truth sheds on our concept of truth. We are primarily concerned to explain Davidson's conception of the place of the concept of truth in the program, and, in particular, its relation to the traditional correspondence conception of truth. The chapter depends on the previous chapters in the sense that it presupposes some knowledge of the details of the development of a Tarski-style theory for a language, which requires the introduction of the satisfaction relation, or something equivalent.

---

[6] This approach is favored by one of the authors (Ludwig), but is viewed more cautiously by the other (Lepore).

1

Truth-Theoretic Semantics: Basic Framework

I think both linguists and philosophers interested in natural languages have missed the key importance of the theory of truth partly because they have not realized that a theory of truth gives a precise, profound, and testable answer to the question how finite resources suffice to explain the infinite semantic capacities of language, and partly because they have exaggerated the difficulties in the way of giving a formal theory of truth for a natural language.

(Davidson 2001*c* (1970): 55)

The foundations for Davidson's semantic program are laid in "Theories of Meaning and Learnable Languages" (1966) and "Truth and Meaning" (1967). In this chapter, we provide a condensed account of the philosophical foundations of the program, and discuss some standard objections, and provide responses to them. A fuller defense and discussion of the history of responses to the program can be found in part I of Lepore and Ludwig (2005).

Davidson's program is developed from two starting points. The first is the insistence that a meaning theory for a natural language be cast as a compositional meaning theory. This is the main theme of "Theories of Meaning and Learnable Languages." The second is the proposal, first put forward in "Truth and Meaning," that the most philosophically perspicuous way of doing this is by adapting a Tarski-style axiomatic truth theory for the purpose. We will elaborate and defend both of these proposals in this chapter. We henceforth call this project 'Truth-Theoretic Semantics'.

In the following, we begin in §1 discussing the compositionality requirement. In §2 we develop the argument against the utility of meanings in
responding to the compositionality requirement. In §3 we introduce Davidson's suggestion that we can employ a axiomatic truth theory to pursue the
goals of a compositional meaning theory, and provide a sample theory in §4.
In §5 we introduce a requirement on the axioms of a truth theory analogous to
Convention *T*, and explain the role played by canonical proofs in identifying
the theorems of the theory that aid us in interpreting object language sentences
and understanding their compositional structure. In §6, we introduce context
sensitivity, and discuss various options for modifying a truth theory to handle
this, opting for relativizing the semantic predicates to speaker and time. In §7
we introduce a modified convention for the adequacy of a truth theory for
a context-sensitive language which we call Davidson's Convention T. In §8
we show how to adapt our sample truth theory for the addition of context
sensitive features, and in §9 we give an explicit meaning theory. §10 reviews
some objections to providing a truth or meaning theory for natural languages
and shows how they can be met, and §11 provides a brief summary of the
chapter.

1. The Compositionality Requirement

In "Theories of Meaning and Learnable Languages," Davidson introduces a
requirement on any acceptable meaning theory for a natural language.

> I propose what seems to me clearly to be a necessary feature of a learnable language: it
> must be possible to give a constructive account of the meaning of the sentences in the
> language. Such an account I call a theory of meaning for the language, and I suggest
> that a theory of meaning that conflicts with this condition, whether put forward by
> philosopher, linguist, or psychologist, cannot be a theory of a natural language; and
> if it ignores this condition, it fails to deal with something central to the concept of a
> language. (Davidson 2001 (1966): 3)

What Davidson calls 'a constructive account of the meaning of the sentences
in the language' we will call a compositional meaning theory. The requirement on an adequate meaning theory for a natural language is that it be a
compositional meaning theory, that is, that it give a constructive account of
the meanings of the sentences of the language.

What is it to give a constructive account of the meaning of sentences in
the language? As Davidson intends it, the account must (1) define a predicate
that applies to all and only grammatical sentences of the language, and,

(2) enable us "to specify, in a way that depends effectively and solely on formal considerations, what every sentence means" (2001 (1966): 8). By 'specifying the meaning of a sentence' Davidson intends that the theory put someone who understands it in a position to understand any sentence of the language for which it is a theory. But his requirement is stronger than this suggests. For he requires that we specify what each sentence means in a way that enables us to understand it on the basis of understanding its significant parts. The theory will therefore provide a division of terms into semantically primitive and semantically complex terms. A term is a 'semantical primitive' if the "rules which give the meaning for the sentences in which it does not appear do not suffice to determine the meaning of the sentences in which it does appear" (Davidson 2001 (1966): 9). The theory then will provide an account of the meaning of the complexes on the basis of the semantical primitives in a way that enable anyone who understands it to understand the meaning of the complex. We will state this canonically in [*CM*]

> [*CM*] A compositional meaning theory for a language *L* is a formal the-
> ory that enables anyone who understands the language in which
> the theory is stated to understand the primitive expressions of *L*
> and the complex expressions of *L* on the basis of understanding
> the primitive ones.

This compositionality requirement is imposed on an adequate meaning theory for a natural language because, while we are finite beings, our competence encompasses the whole of the language, which contains an infinite number of nonsynonymous sentences. Thus, our understanding of a natural language must rest on our understanding a finite number of semantical primitives and rules for their combination, which enable us to understand every sentence of the language.[7]

Semantical primitives will divide into different types, for example, into *referring terms*, such as *proper names* ('John Bull') and *demonstratives* ('this' and 'that'), *monadic* and *relational predicates* ('talk', 'hit'), *sentential connectives* ('and', 'or', 'not', 'since', 'because'), and *quantifiers* ('some', 'all'). The competence that attaches to a semantical primitive will typically have two components. One has to do with the category into which the term falls. This determines how it can combine meaningfully with other terms given their categories, and the manner of its contribution to the meaning of grammatical expressions

---

[7] See Lepore and Ludwig (2005: ch. 2, §2) for a detailed discussion of Davidson's learnability argument.

including it. The other has to do with that aspect of its meaning which distinguishes it from other terms in the same category.

To take an example, 'is red' and 'is round' are both monadic predicates, and in virtue of this combine in the same ways with terms in other categories. Thus, we may form a sentence with either by prefacing them with a referring term, as in 'John Bull is red' and 'John Bull is round', and in each case this is to predicate what is expressed by the monadic predicate of the referent of the subject term. That this aspect of our competence in using these terms attaches to their category is shown by our knowing how to interpret such sentences schematically without knowing more than the categories of the terms in them. If someone uses a monadic predicate we do not understand, perhaps, 'is a phasmid', and a name whose referent we don't know, 'Quentle Quezal', we nonetheless know the form of what is said. Another aspect of our competence, which distinguishes the meanings of these two terms in the same category, is expressed in our applying them to things on the basis of different features of them. We apply 'is red' to things we recognize or think are red, and we apply 'is round' to things we recognize or think are round.

A compositional meaning theory aims to capture the structure of our competence in speaking a language. Thus, in [*CM*] the requirement that knowing the theory put one who understands it in a position to understand the primitives and to understand the complexes on their basis is supposed to impose a requirement that will reveal the structure of the competence of a speaker of the language. Thus, we understand 'on the basis of understanding the primitive ones' in [*CM*] to require that the theory contain in it information sufficient to recover the rules for understanding complex expressions in the language on the basis of their primitive components and combinations that are expressed in the structured dispositions of competent speakers of the language. This will then include both information attaching to the categories of terms that determine how they can be meaningfully combined with other terms and the manner of their contribution to the meaning of the complex expressions in which they can grammatically appear, and information about the meaning of primitive expressions.

While a correct compositional meaning theory will capture, in the sense just indicated, the rules for understanding complex expressions on the basis of semantical primitives in a language, there is no suggestion here that it is or must be a theory which speakers of the language know, explicitly or implicitly. A compositional meaning theory in the sense discussed above is formulated by the theorist, and is about the competence of a speaker of the language for which it is a theory in the sense that it aims to capture the structure of the dispositions of the speaker which constitute her competence in speaking and understanding speech in the language.

Speakers typically have some propositional knowledge of rules of language. It is plausible to suppose that all speakers of English know that 'red' applies to or is true of red things, and the like. However, it is doubtful that their whole competence should be modeled on knowledge of a fully explicit meaning theory. If speakers know such a theory, it is not accessible to conscious reflection. Consequently, it would have to be some form of implicit propositional knowledge. Yet there seems no more reason a priori to suppose that linguistic competence is realized by implicit propositional knowledge of a meaning theory than to suppose that competence in riding a bicycle is realized by implicit propositional knowledge of how to move one's body to propel the bicycle forward and maintain one's balance. There are also questions that can be raised about the coherence of the hypothesis that linguistic competence is realized by implicit knowledge of a compositional meaning theory.[8]

Therefore, for the purposes of the discussion in this book, it should be understood that the aim of formulating a compositional meaning theory is to capture the structure of a complex practical ability, but not to be formulating a theory which speakers of the language are supposed to know in any sense.[9]

2. Problems for Meanings

To understand Davidson's proposal about how to provide a compositional meaning theory for a natural language, it is important to understand his criticisms of approaches that appeal to meanings. When we talk of approaches that appeal to meanings here, we have in mind approaches to providing a meaning theory of a natural language which assign to meaningful expressions of the language entities which are called meanings or intensions (or the like), and which attempt to provide an account of the meanings of complex expressions on the basis of constructing a complex meaning out of the meanings assigned to the component expressions in accordance with a rule which is based on the mode of combination of the primitive expressions in the complex expression.

---

[8] See Ludwig (1996a) for a discussion of parallel difficulties for unconscious inference theories of perceptual accomplishment.

[9] Thus, this project is to be distinguished from that in Larson and Segal (1995), which explicitly aims at an account of the supposed implicit propositional knowledge that speakers of a language possess in virtue of being competent speakers of it. See also Lepore (1997).

The appeal to meanings in the meaning theory is attractive, but its explanatory power is illusory. Its attractiveness derives from two sources.

The first is the verbal utility of introducing an entity to assign to things to serve as a proxy for equivalence classes of them derived from some equivalence relation. For example, 'is as long as' expresses an equivalence relation, since it is reflexive, that is, any x is as along as x, symmetric, that is, for any x, y, if x is as long as y, then y is as long as x, and transitive, that is, for any x, y, z, if x is as long as y, and y is as long as z, then x is as long as z. Given this, we can introduce a count noun, 'is a length', and assign an entity, a length, to every object (along every spatial dimension of it, but let us suppress this for present purposes). We will then say that two objects have the same length, that is, the length of the one is the same as the length of the other, iff the first is as long as the second. The length of one object is greater than the length of another iff the one is longer than the other. And so on. In this way, talk of lengths can be systematically interchanged with talk of being as long as, being longer than, etc. This provides an economy of expression particularly when used in conjunction with a system of measurement. We introduce a unit of measure by reference to a standard. For example, we say that an object which is as long as a certain bar under certain conditions is one meter long. Operationally, then, to say that x is one meter long is to say that it is as long as the relevant bar in the standard conditions. It is more convenient to say instead that its length is one meter. In addition, we can talk of lengths of objects without having any particular objects in mind, and so say such things as every physical object has some length, which would otherwise have to be expressed as every physical object is such that there is a physical object which is such that it is as long as, longer than, or neither as long as nor longer than it. Since the relation of synonymy is likewise an equivalence relation, we can introduce an entity assigned to any meaningful expression on its basis to go proxy for talk about the synonymy of expressions in a language, and we can extend this then across languages as well. We may then replace 'x is synonymous with y' with 'the meaning of x is the same as the meaning of y' or 'x and y have the same meaning'. Then, as in the case of talk of lengths, we can talk about the meanings of expressions independently of having particular expressions in mind, and so achieve considerable economy in abstract claims about meaning, such as that the meaning of any expression is determined by the meanings of its significant parts and their modes of combination. This would otherwise have to be expressed in the following fashion (which itself exploits various forms of reification on the basis of equivalence relations):

two complex expressions are synonymous iff they have the same number of significant parts and there is a correlation between the significant parts such that if in one a significant part combines in the whole in a certain way, the part corresponding to it in the other combines in the whole in the same way, and the semantical rule attaching to the one is the same as the semantical rule attaching to the other, and corresponding significant parts are synonymous.

The forms of talk we use which are derived from reification on the basis of an equivalence relation are in principle eliminable. They can be treated as a façon de parler, a verbal convenience, and such talk is harmless as long as we keep in mind what the shorthand is a shorthand for. This would not be the basis of a serious use of meanings in the meaning theory.

But the second source of the attractiveness of introducing meanings is also supposed to be the source of its genuine utility in the meaning theory. To give a constructive account of the meanings of complex expressions in a language on the basis of meanings of its significant parts and their mode of combination requires giving an account that says something about the meanings of semantical primitives and generates an assignment of meanings to sentences. It is natural to think that it should aim to produce theorems of the form (M) with the requirement that 's' is replaced by a description of an object language sentence in terms of the semantical primitives used in it, and 'p' is replaced by a metalanguage sentence that is the same in meaning as the object language sentence.

(M) s means in L that p

Knowing that, for example, 'Les fleurs sont rouge' in French means that the flowers are red suffices to tell us what 'Les fleurs sont rouge' means in French. If the theory were able to produce such a theorem for each sentence of the object language in a way that captured the structure of the practical ability which constitutes mastery of it, then it would have done everything that we want out of a compositional meaning theory. But how is a theory to do this?

Evidently, it must do so by way of axioms that attach to primitive expressions. Some of these will in some sense give the meaning of the primitive expressions. This will be the sort of axiom that attaches to predicates and referring terms. And some will give or express rules for determining the meanings of complex expressions. This will be the sort that attaches to sentential connectives and to quantifiers. We will derive from the theory sentences of the form M by applying rules of both sorts to s, which is described in terms of its semantically primitive elements. If we think of meanings as entities assigned to expressions, and the meanings of complex expressions as functions of or composed out of the meanings assigned to their primitive components, then a natural route to this goal suggests itself.

To see the nature of the strategy, let us first consider a simple theory of reference (this example is take from "Truth and Meaning," and Davidson uses it to the same purpose). Take a fragment of a natural language, a functor, 'The father of x', and some proper names, 'Cassius', 'Brutus', 'Octavio', 'Caesar'. A referring term is a proper name or 'The father of' concatenated with a referring term. This generates an infinite number of referring terms. We need then a rule for assigning referents to the infinity of expressions on the basis of referents assigned to the proper names and their concatenation with 'The father of'. A simple rule suffices:

> For any proper name N, 'The father of'⌒N refers to the father of the referent of N.

Together with axioms for the proper names, 'Cassius' refers to Cassius, 'Brutus' refers to Brutus, 'Octavio' refers to Octavio, and 'Caesar' refers to Caesar, this provides us with a way of assigning to any referring term in the language a referent. The adequacy condition for such a theory of reference is that it entail for each referring term t of the language a sentence of the form

> t refers to x

where 't' is replaced by a structural description of the object language term and 'x' is replaced by a metalanguage term that refers to the same thing. Clearly our toy theory meets the adequacy condition. For example, for 'The father of the father of Octavio' we can derive

> 'The father of'⌒'the father of'⌒'Octavio' refers to the father of the father of Octavio.

In this case, it can be noted that 'refers to' may be replaced with 'means' while preserving truth. Thus, we have as well a backdoor meaning theory for these referring terms.

We will return to this observation, but the immediate interest of the exercise is what it suggests about the treatment of sentences. Frege's assimilation of all open expressions to functional expressions suggests a way of extending the strategy used in this simple reference theory to a meaning theory, provided that we take expressions to refer to their meanings. (This is not Frege's view, but an adaptation of it, since Frege took terms to express their senses, and to refer to objects if they were proper names (in which he included definite descriptions), or functions if they were open expressions (an expression obtained from a complete expression by replacing a significant term in it with a variable). For the sake of simplicity, let us take proper names to have their referents as their meanings. Then we will take predicates to have functions as their meanings, and we may suppose that these are individuated so that two predicates denote the same function iff they are synonymous. We will take them to be functions from arguments to the meanings of the sentences formed from them by putting in their argument places terms that refer to those arguments. Let us retain the names we have introduced above and add the predicates 'is honorable' and 'is wise'. Then we can introduce axioms for these, namely,

> 'is honorable' means *is honorable*
> 'is wise' means *is wise*

where we take the right-hand sides to be terms that denote the functions. Then we say

> For any name N, for any predicate P, $N^\frown P$ means the referent of P given the referent of N as argument.

We add that the value of a function denoted by a predicate given an argument is denoted by the predicate with an argument term in its argument place which refers to that argument. Given this, we can derive from our axioms (where we underline 'Brutus is honorable' to indicate that as a unit it is to be taken as a referring term)

> 'Brutus'$^\frown$'is honorable' means <u>Brutus is honorable</u>.

This treatment may be extended to connectives treated as functions from sentence meanings to sentence meanings, and quantifiers treated as functions from functions to sentence meanings, and, it may be hoped, to full range of constructions and semantic devices found in natural languages.

This then looks to hold out the hope of providing a theory that assigns to every sentence of the language a meaning on the basis of axioms attaching to the primitive expressions. It should be noted that there are various other ways of representing the same general idea. We could, for example, have talked not of expressions *referring* to their meanings but of *expressing* them, and said that a sentence expresses a proposition which is a structured entity containing the meanings of its component expressions. We might then represent the proposition expressed by 'Brutus is honorable' as <Brutus, honorableness>, and have written as our canonical theorem:

'Brutus'⌒'is honorable' expresses the proposition <Brutus, honorable-ness>.

This bit of notation, of course, understood as intended, enables us to state explicitly that 'Brutus is honorable' means that Brutus is honorable. It is that fact that gives the notation sense, rather than the other way around. Thus do meanings as entities seem to pay their way in a compositional meaning theory. But, as we said above, this appearance is illusory.

There are two connected difficulties.[10] The first is that the introduction of meanings does no work in helping us to understand the expression to which they are assigned. The meaning is an object, and as an object it may be picked out in various ways. We may call the meaning of 'is honorable' *Harry*. We could equally well pick it out using a definite description, such as 'the meaning of "is honorable" '. In saying that 'is honorable' means Harry or 'is honorable' means the meaning of 'is honorable', we have specified the meaning so far as saying what object is the meaning just as well as in saying, as above, that 'is honorable' means *is honorable*. There is a difference between these ways of specifying the meaning of 'is honorable'. But it does not lie in what object it is that we say is the meaning. It lies in the fact that in the last way of specifying the meaning we use an expression in the metalanguage which is the same in meaning, and understood to be the same in meaning, as the object language expression it is being used to give the meaning of. The fact that we treat the expressions as referring to, or being assigned, a meaning, is not what enables understanding. It is prior understanding of the expressions in the metalanguage which are chosen because they are the same in meaning as the object language terms. This is true as well of approaches which assign properties or relations to predicates and propositions to sentences. The properties are identified using predicates synonymous with the predicates whose meanings are being given ('being red' for 'red', etc.), and the propositions are represented using ordered n-tuples of items specified using terms that are the same in meaning as object language

---

[10] Davidson raises a number of difficulties for the appeal to meanings. A famous objection is that an argument deriving ultimately from Frege, through Alonzo Church, shows that, on the assumption that sentences refer to their meanings, all sentences alike in truth value must have the same meaning. We do not think this argument is successful. See Lepore and Ludwig (2005: ch. 3, §4) for a detailed discussion of this argument. We concentrate instead on developing another objection which is sketched in "Truth and Meaning," which, if successful, shows that the ontology of meanings is neither necessary nor sufficient for accomplishing the aims of a compositional meaning theory.

terms, and whose structure is understood in accordance with a rule that enables us to produce a metalanguage sentence alike in meaning to the object language sentence the proposition expressed by which is thereby represented. The whole effect is achieved by contriving a mechanical way of matching a metalanguage sentence alike in meaning to an object language sentence. Since it is the mechanical matching of object language sentences with metalanguage sentences we understand that does the work, the appeal to meanings as entities is not necessary. Since assigning the meanings does not itself guarantee that we assign them in ways that generates such a mapping, the appeal to meanings is not sufficient either. Thus, the ontology of meanings in the meaning theory is neither necessary nor sufficient for producing a theory which will generate an *M*-sentence for each object language sentence.

The second difficulty is that this way of matching object language with metalanguage sentences alike in meaning, even if it can be carried through in full generality, does not reveal to us the semantic functions of the com-binations of terms. It is at best a mechanical way of producing a sentence in the metalanguage that we understand which translates the object language sentence. It does not exhibit what the semantic functions of the component parts are. It does not exhibit, for example, how they contribute to fixing under what conditions the sentences are true, which is a cental aspect of the contributions of their meanings to the complexes in which they appear. It does not, therefore, satisfy the constraint that we placed on a composi-tional meaning theory, namely, that "the theory contain in it information sufficient to recover the rules for understanding complex expressions in the language on the basis of their primitive components and combinations that are expressed in the structured dispositions of competent speakers of the language."[11]

---

[11] For further discussion of these issues, see Lepore and Ludwig (2005: ch. 3) and also Davidson (2005: chs. 4–7). The difficulties for finding a genuine explanatory role for meanings to play in the theory of meaning is closely connected with the problem of predication, where they likewise fail to advance our understanding. Predication is the most basic semantic operation, essential to the possibility of stating anything, and understanding it is fundamental to understanding the compositional character of natural languages (of any language). It is here that we see the most basic failure of the appeal to meanings. Assignment of meanings to the parts of a sentence cannot tell us how the parts function together to say what they say, for after the assignment we must still be told why we have more than a list. When properties, universals, relations, concepts, and meanings are introduced and assigned to expressions, as referents or otherwise, terms involving them can still play two distinct roles in sentences, that of predicate and that of referring term. That each may have the same object, the universal, etc., associated with it, shows that the associated object plays no explanatory role. The difference in semantic function remains to be explained (ibid., esp. 145–6).

3. Convention T and the Proposal to Use a Truth Theory as a Vehicle for a Meaning Theory

We have found two difficulties with the attempt to provide a compositional meaning theory by way of assigning meanings to expressions. The ontology is neither necessary nor sufficient and, in any case, something crucial is left out of the sort of method which emerges: any account of the semantic contribution of the component expressions to our understanding of the complexes in which they appear. It is against this discouraging record that the proposal is made to use an axiomatic truth theory modeled after Tarski's pioneering work on truth theories for formal languages to do the work of a compositional meaning theory. The key insight is contained in this passage in "Truth and Meaning," which occurs after a brief consideration of treating the context after 'means that' as intensional rather than taking terms that refer to meanings.

The only way I know to deal with this difficulty [of dealing with the "logic of the apparently non-extensional 'means that'"] is simple, and radical. Anxiety that we are enmeshed in the intensional springs from using the words 'means that' as filling between description of sentence and sentence, but it may be that the success of our venture depends not on the filling but on what it fills. The theory will have done its work if it provides, for every sentence s in the language under study, a matching sentence (to replace 'p') that, in some way yet to be made clear, 'gives the meaning' of s. One obvious candidate for matching sentence is just s itself, if the object language is contained in the metalanguage; otherwise a translation of s in the metalanguage. As a final bold step, let us try treating the position occupied by 'p' extensionally: to implement this, sweep away the obscure 'means that', provide the sentence that replaces 'p' with a proper sentential connective, and supply the description that replaces 's' with its own predicate. The plausible result is

(T) s is T if and only if p.

What we require of a theory of meaning for a language L is that without appeal to any (further) semantical notions it place enough restrictions on the predicate 'is T' to entail all sentences got from schema T when 's' is replaced by a structural description of a sentence of L and 'p' by that sentence.

Any two predicates satisfying this condition have the same extension, so if the metalanguage is rich enough, nothing stands in the way of putting what I am calling a theory of meaning into the form of an explicit definition of a predicate 'is T'. But whether explicitly defined or recursively characterized, it is clear that the sentences to which the predicate 'is T' applies will be just the true sentences of L, for the condition we placed on satisfactory theories of meaning is in essence Tarski's Convention T that tests the adequacy of a formal semantical definition of truth. (Davidson 2001*c* (1967): 22–3)

We have seen above that the real achievement of a theory which assigns meanings to expressions comes to no more than that they match object language sentences with metalanguage sentences alike in meaning. Davidson's suggestion was that this could be achieved without meanings by noticing that a truth theory which meets Tarski's Convention T achieves the same result. Tarski's Convention T requires that an adequate theory of truth for a formal language have as theorems all sentences of the form (T) above in which 's' is replaced by a structural description of an object language sentence, a description of it as formed out of its primitive meaningful components, and in which 'p' is replaced by a metalanguage sentence that translates it. If we know that a sentence of the form (T) is one of these theorems, then we can replace 'is T iff' with 'means that' to yield a true M-sentence. Thus, if

'Snow is white' is T iff snow is white

is one of the theorems required by Convention T, we may replace 'is T iff' with 'means that' to yield the correct

'Snow is white' means that snow is white.

Thus, provided that we have a mechanical way of identifying the theorems which satisfy the condition that the sentence that replaces 'p' in (T) translate the sentence that 's' describes, we have a way of generating a true M-sentence for each object language sentence. (This, it will noticed, is exactly parallel to the backdoor theory of meaning mentioned in connection with the theory of reference for 'the father of x' above. It is no accident that Davidson began his discussion with this example.) We thus achieve everything that the approach that appeals to meanings achieves.

But we have more than this. For a correct truth theory, relative to an appropriate choice of axioms, about which we will say more below, will also give us information about the semantic contribution of expressions to our understanding of complex expressions of which they are part, and, in particular, about their contributions to the truth conditions of the sentences in which they appear. As we noted, this is something which the approach that appeals to meanings leaves out of the picture.

4. A Sample Theory

To illustrate and make these points clearer, we introduce a simple axiomatic truth theory for a non-context-sensitive language modeled on English, which we will call 'Simple English$_0$'.[12]

Simple symbols include predicates, names, and logical constants. Simple English$_0$ does not have quantifiers or variables. Including these would introduce additional complications in the formulation of the truth theory (the introduction of the satisfaction relation and either sequences or functions from variables to objects as satisfiers) which are irrelevant to understanding the role a truth theory can play in pursuing the goal of a compositional meaning theory. We take up quantifiers in Chapters 2 and 3 below. To keep clear the distinction between the symbols of Simple English$_0$ and our informal metalanguage, Simple English$_0$ appears in a different typeface. Simple English$_0$ has one (untensed) predicate, 'is ambitious', two names, 'Brutus' and 'Caesar', which we will also call singular terms, three logical constants, 'and', 'or' and 'Not:', left and right parentheses, '(' and ')', and the space ' '. *Expressions* in Simple English$_0$ are finite strings of the above symbols. *Atomic formulas* are expressions consisting of a name followed by a space followed by a predicate. For example:

```
Caesar is ambitious
Brutus is ambitious
```

Molecular formulas are built up out of atomic formulas using the logical connectives in accordance with rules (i)–(ii) below (illustrations are provided after each). A formula is an expression that is either an atomic or molecular formula. We use corner quotation marks, '⌜' and '⌝', to form descriptions of expressions. For example, '⌜(ϕ and ψ)⌝' is read as ' ('⌢ϕ⌢' '⌢'and'⌢' '⌢ψ⌢')' where 'ϕ' and 'ψ' are metalinguistic variables and '⌢' is read as 'concatenated with'.

(i) If ϕ is a formula, then its negation, ⌜Not:ϕ⌝, is a formula.

```
Not: Caesar is ambitious
```

(ii) If ϕ and ψ are formulas, then their conjunction, ⌜(ϕ and ψ)⌝, and disjunction, ⌜(ϕ or ψ)⌝, are formulas.

---

[12] We used this simple theory in illustration also in Lepore and Ludwig (2005: ch. 4).

```
(Caesar is ambitious and Brutus is ambitious)
(Brutus is ambitious or Caesar is ambitious)
```

All formulas of Simple English$_0$ are sentences; atomic formulas are atomic sentences and molecular formulas are molecular sentences.

Our informal truth theory for Simple English$_0$, TRUTH$_0$, will exploit what we know about the intended meanings of its terms. They are intended to mean what they would in English, but for the elimination of any context-sensitive features. That Simple English$_0$ is context-insensitive requires that our metalanguage be as well. Thus, we will treat the metalanguage predicates used in the axioms as tenseless. We will suppose, for the purposes of discussion, that an untensed predicate is true of an individual iff the corresponding tensed predicate in English is true of the individual at some time. Thus, for example, 'x is ambitious' in the metalanguage used below will be interpreted to be true of an object iff for some time t, that object is ambitious at t. In another departure from English, we will introduce parentheses in the metalanguage to indicate the scope of the sentential connectives, where appropriate.

That the axioms we provide for Simple English$_0$ use expressions which translate the object language expressions is, as we will see, the condition we will impose below on its serving as an appropriate vehicle for a compositional meaning theory.

The axioms of TRUTH$_0$ divide into different categories, according to their different functions. Base axioms assign reference conditions to names and truth conditions to atomic sentences. Recursive axioms assign truth conditions to molecular sentences in terms of the truth conditions of their constituent sentences. By this device, the truth conditions of molecular sentences are ultimately reduced to those of atomic sentences. Explanatory remarks follow the axioms in each category.

1. Base Axioms

1 Reference$_0$ axioms

For any singular referring term α, we treat $\ulcorner\text{Ref}_0(\alpha)\urcorner$ as a function from α to its referent in Simple English$_0$. We treat functional expressions (functors supplied with an argument term) as contributing only their value to what is meant by sentences in which they are used (see Ch. 4, §2).

R1. Ref$_0$('Caesar') = Caesar
R2. Ref$_0$('Brutus') = Brutus

Reference axioms assign referents to names; they tell us what each proper name refers to.

2 Truth$_0$ axioms for atomic formulas

We will abbreviate 'is true in Simple English$_0$' as 'is true$_0$'.

> B1. For all names α, $\ulcorner\alpha$ is ambitious$\urcorner$ is true$_0$ iff Ref$_0(\alpha)$ is ambitious.

The base axioms R1–R2 and B1 assign reference and truth conditions to expressions of the language which do not function recursively to generate more complex expressions out of simpler ones. What this contrast comes to is best understood by comparing the axioms with the recursive axioms below.

2. Recursive axioms for truth$_0$ for molecular formulas

> RC1. For all formula ϕ, $\ulcorner$Not$:\phi\urcorner$ is true$_0$ iff it is not the case that ϕ is true$_0$.
>
> RC2. For all formulas ϕ, ψ, $\ulcorner(\phi$ and $\psi)\urcorner$ is true$_0$ iff (ϕ is true$_0$ and ψ is true$_0$).
>
> RC3. For all formulas ϕ, ψ, $\ulcorner(\phi$ or $\psi)\urcorner$ is true$_0$ iff (ϕ is true$_0$ or ψ is true$_0$).

The recursive axioms[13] give truth$_0$ conditions for formulas devised from simpler formulas by the syntactical rules (i) and (ii) above. They do this for the infinitely many expressions devisable using them by giving truth$_0$ conditions of complex terms in terms of truth$_0$ conditions of the parts from which they are constructed. By continued application of the recursive axioms, one reaches parts whose truth$_0$ conditions issue from the base axioms, which eliminate the truth predicate.

Now let us consider an illustration of applying the axioms of TRUTH$_0$ to spell out informally the conditions under which 'is true$_0$' applies to some sentence of Simple English$_0$, for example, $\ulcorner$(Brutus is ambitious or Not:Caesar is ambitious)$\urcorner$. We want to apply the axioms to this sample sentence to yield a biconditional which reveals in the metalanguage

---

[13] These are called 'recursive axioms' because, in giving truth conditions for formulas, they employ the predicate 'truth$_0$' as applied to simpler formulas out of which the complex one is constructed

under just what conditions this sentence is true$_0$, according to TRUTH$_0$. We do this by constructing an informal proof (1)–(7). The proof does this by appealing to axioms at each point which provide reference$_0$ or truth$_0$ conditions in the metalanguage for object language names or sentences which use terms which translate the object language terms.

To state the three rules of inference we employ here, we introduce some notation. 'UQUANT(ϕ, v)' means 'the universal quantification of ϕ with respect to v'. 'Inst(ϕ, v, β)' means 'the result of replacing all instances of the free variable v in ϕ with the singular term β'. Note that we count structural descriptions of object language terms as singular terms. 'EQ(ϕ, ψ)' means 'the biconditional linking ϕ with ψ (in that order)'. 'S(x)' stands for a sentence containing the grammatical unit x, which may be a word, phrase, or sentence. 'IDENT(α, β)' means 'the identity sentence linking α with β (in that order)'. This allows us to state the rules of inference as applying to sentences in certain categories without having to define the syntax precisely.

> *Universal Quantifier Instantiation*: For any sentence ϕ, variable v, singular term β: Inst(ϕ, v, β) may be inferred from UQUANT(ϕ, v).
>
> *Replacement*: For any sentences ϕ, ψ, S(ϕ): S(ψ) may be inferred from EQ(ϕ, ψ) and S(ϕ).
>
> *Substitution*: For any singular terms α, β, sentence S(α): S(β) may be inferred from S(α) and IDENT(α, β).

(1) ⌜(Brutus is ambitious or Not:Caesar is ambitious)⌝ is true$_0$

    if and only if

   ⌜Brutus is ambitious⌝ is true$_0$ or ⌜Not: Caesar is ambitious⌝ is true$_0$. [From RC3 by two applications of Universal Quantifier Instantiation]

(2) ⌜Not: Caesar is ambitious⌝ is true$_0$ iff it is not the case that ⌜Caesar is ambitious⌝ is true$_0$. [From RC1 by Universal Quantifier Instantiation]

(3) ⌜(Brutus is ambitious or Not: Caesar is ambitious)⌝ is true$_0$

    if and only if

   ⌜Brutus is ambitious⌝ is true$_0$ or it is not the case that ⌜Caesar is ambitious⌝ is true$_0$. [From (1) and (2) by Replacement]

(4) ⌜Brutus is ambitious⌝ is true$_0$ iff Ref$_0$('Brutus') is ambitious. [From B1 by Universal Quantifier Instantiation]

(5) ⌜Caesar is ambitious⌝ is $true_0$ iff Ref_0('Caesar') is ambitious. [From B1 by Universal Quantifier Instantiation]

(6) ⌜(Brutus is ambitious or Not: Caesar is ambitious)⌝ is $true_0$

> if and only if
>
> Ref_0('Brutus') is ambitious or it is not the case that Ref_0('Caesar') is ambitious. [From (3) and (4) and (5) by two applications of Replacement]

(7) ⌜(Brutus is ambitious or Not: Caesar is ambitious)⌝ is $true_0$

> if and only if
>
> Brutus is ambitious or it is not the case that Caesar is ambitious. [From (6), R1 and R2 by two applications of Substitution]

Note that our (informal) proof (1)–(7) is a string of biconditionals. We invoked only three rules of inference, Universal Quantifier Instantiation, Replacement Schema, and Substitution of Identicals. The proof proceeds by applying these rules to the axioms of the theory and previous lines of the proof.

We have so far laid out the form of what we have called a truth theory of Simple $English_0$, but we have not said much about why one should consider the predicate '$true_0$', whose extension is characterized by $TRUTH_0$, to have anything to do with truth, or to have all and only true object language sentences in its extension. $TRUTH_0$ may be said to be a truth theory in virtue of its form, but this does not yet guarantee that its "truth predicate" has anything to do with the intuitive notion of truth. It is at this point that Tarski's Convention T enters the picture. One of Tarski's great insights was to see how to provide a criterion for determining what he called the *material adequacy* of a recursive definition like that above, a criterion which if met guarantees that 'is $true_0$' has all and only the true sentences of the object language in its extension. The criterion in application to $TRUTH_0$ is that the theory has as theorems all sentences of the form $[T]$ (a T-form sentence),

$$[T] \quad s \text{ is } true_0 \text{ iff } p,$$

in which 's' is replaced by a structural description of an object language sentence, and 'p' is replaced by a sentence of the metalanguage which translates the object language sentence.[14] We call such instances of $[T]$ 'T-sentences'.[15]

---

[14] See Tarski (1983 (1935): 187–8).

[15] That is, we distinguish a T-form sentence from a T-sentence. The latter on our use is a T-form sentence in which the right-hand side translates or interprets the sentence mentioned on

Material adequacy guarantees that any sentence to which 'is true$_0$' applies is true iff the sentence used in the metalanguage is true, because the meaning of a sentence determines (relative to the world) its truth value, that is, whether it is true or false. Two sentences alike in meaning, then, must be alike in truth value. Thus, the sentence used on the right hand side of a T-sentence must agree in truth value with the sentence mentioned on the left, of which it is a translation. Thus, if TRUTH$_0$ meets Tarski's Convention T, then 'is true$_0$' has in its extension all and only true sentences of Simple English$_0$. In light of the intention that the truth theory should meet Tarski's Convention T in characterizing the extension of true$_0$, we may plausibly say that it expresses a restriction of the intuitive concept of truth to Simple English$_0$.

5. Interpretive Axioms and Canonical Proofs

It is evident that TRUTH$_0$ meets the requirement of Tarski's Convention T that it have among its theorems all sentences of the form $[T]$,

    $[T]$ s is true$_0$ iff p,

in which 's' is replaced by a structural description of an object language sentence, and 'p' is replaced by a sentence of the metalanguage which translates the object language sentence, that is, all T-sentences for the object language. This is guaranteed by the fact that the object language expressions are assigned truth conditions using terms which translate them. Thus, for proper names in the object language, we use proper names in the metalanguage which translate them. If the proper names are simply directly referring terms, then we use a proper name in the metalanguage which is a directly referring term that has the same referent. If there is more to the meaning of proper names, we use a proper name in the metalanguage alike in meaning to the proper name in the object language to give its referent (see Chapter 4 for further discussion). For predicates, we give the truth conditions, as illustrated in B1, with a metalanguage predicate the same in meaning as the object language predicate. For a "truth-functional" connective we use a truth-functional connective in the metalanguage alike in meaning to that in the object language, in the manner illustrated in RC1–RC3. An axiom which in the way indicated gives the reference or truth conditions for an object language term using a metalanguage term that translates it we will call *interpretive*. In Chapter 3,

---

the left-hand side. This use of 'T-sentence' corresponds to Tarski's use of 'equivalence of the form (T)' in Tarski (1944: 344).

we will illustrate how to make this intuitive requirement more precise for a language which contains quantifiers and context-sensitive expressions. It can be seen that a formally adequate truth theory with interpretive axioms, and a rich enough logic, will meet Convention T.

Consider the effect of this first for the truth$_0$ conditions for an atomic sentence. If we prove a T-sentence using just applications of Universal Quantifier Instantiation and Substitution, the expressions being substituted on the right-hand side of the biconditional translate those on the left, and we preserve the semantic form of the sentence. This ensures that the sentence used to give truth conditions (i) translates the object language sentence and (ii) is constructed from parts which translate the parts of the object language sentence, and are used in the same way in the metalanguage sentence as the corresponding object language terms are used in it. We see in the proof, then, relative to the knowledge that the axioms provide translations of the singular terms and predicate in the object language sentence, how the meaning of the whole depends on the meanings of the parts and their mode of combination.

This point carries over to the proofs of T-sentences for molecular sentences. For example, when we apply Universal Quantifier Instantiation to RC2, the effect is to specify truth conditions of the object language sentence in terms of a metalanguage sentence whose main connective translates the main connective of the object language sentence. Further applications of the axioms to the two conjuncts on the right-hand side will by stages provide translations of them, until the final result is a metalanguage sentence that translates the object language sentence whose truth conditions it specifies, derived from axioms that translate the object language terms they apply to, and reproduce the structure of the object language sentence at each step. Thus, the proof of the T-sentence from interpretive axioms which relies only on their content will show how our understanding of the sentence depends on our understanding of the parts and their mode of combination. We will call a truth theory with interpretive axioms an *interpretive truth theory*. It is important to note that this requires more than just that the theory meet Convention T, which does not impose the requirement that the axioms be interpretive. This requirement suffices, together with a strong enough metalanguage logic to meet Convention T, but not vice versa.[16]

The form of the proof by which we generate a T-sentence is important to the question whether it shows how its components combine to determine

---

[16] For example, the theory provided in Larson and Segal (1995) meets Convention T but is not interpretive in our sense.

the meaning of the object language sentence. If we restrict inference rules in such proofs to those employed above, and require that they be employed in application to the axioms and sentences derived from them, then it is intuitively clear that any proof ending in a T-form sentence that has eliminated the semantic vocabulary introduced by the theory will be a T-sentence, and that the structure of the proof will reveal how the component words combine to determine the meaning of the object language sentence. Formalizing our truth theory would then enable us to provide a strictly syntactic criterion for a T-form sentence being a T-sentence. Let us call a 'canonical proof' a proof characterized formally which is designed so as to draw only on the content of the axioms of the theory to prove T-form sentences in which we have eliminated the semantic vocabulary introduced by the theory. This will result in T-form sentences which assign truth conditions to sentences by using only sentences synonymous with those for which they fix truth conditions. Let us call any T-form sentence resulting from a canonical proof a *canonical theorem* of the theory. We can be confident that any canonical theorem of the theory is a T-sentence, provided that the axioms of the theory are interpretive.

Let us now illustrate relatively informally how to effect this sort of strategy for characterizing a canonical proof for the theory TRUTH$_0$. The T-sentences for TRUTH$_0$ will be easily identified if the axioms are interpretive, as we will assume they are. The T-sentences are all and only the instances of the schema $[T]$, where 'p' is replaced by an English sentence with the same string of symbols that constitute the sentence denoted by the structural description replacing 's'.

$[T]$ s is true$_0$ iff p.

It is easy enough to characterize the constraints on a proof that guarantee that it draws solely on the content of the axioms, and so yields all and only the T-sentences for the theory. A *canonical proof* for TRUTH$_0$ is, we suggest:

(a) a finite sequence of sentences of our metalanguage for TRUTH$_0$ the last of which is a T-form sentence (as above) containing no semantic vocabulary introduced by the theory on the right-hand side;

(b) each member of which is either (i) an axiom, or (ii) derived from earlier members by *Universal Quantifier Instantiation*, *Substitution*, or *Replacement* as defined in §4, repeated here for reference.

Universal Quantifier Instantiation: For any sentence ϕ, variable v, singular term β: Inst(ϕ, v, β) may be inferred from UQUANT(ϕ, v).

Substitution: For any singular terms α, β, sentence $S(\alpha)$: $S(\beta)$ may be inferred from $S(\alpha)$ and IDENT(α, β).
Replacement: For any sentences ϕ, ψ, $S(\phi)$: $S(\psi)$ may be inferred from EQ(ϕ, ψ) and $S(\phi)$.

A canonical theorem of TRUTH$_0$ is a canonically provable T-form theorem of TRUTH$_0$. The T-sentences will be all and only the canonical theorems of TRUTH$_0$. All that stands in the way of a completely formal characterization is a formal characterization of our metalanguage.

Why should we be so confident that proofs proceeding in accordance with (a) and (b) yield all and only T-sentences? TRUTH$_0$ is by hypothesis interpretive. It is evident that the rules we can appeal to prohibit the introduction of logical truths at any stage in a proof. They can operate only on earlier members of the proof. The only sentences that can enter into a proof without being derived from earlier members are axioms. All the axioms are universally quantified, and to derive anything from them one must first use Universal Quantifier Instantiation on object language expressions. This yields sentences from which further sentences can be derived only by replacement either of singular terms in the sentences on the right-hand sides, if appropriate, or of the sentence on the right-hand side by another which appears on the right-hand side of a biconditional with the first sentence on the left. Arriving at an appropriate T-form sentence requires eliminating the semantic vocabulary from the right-hand side of a sentence derived from one of the sentential axioms. The only means of doing so results in the replacement of semantic predicates of object language expressions by metalanguage expressions, which by hypothesis translate their object language counterparts. The end result is a T-form sentence whose right-hand side translates the object language sentence denoted on the left, that is, the end result is a T-sentence.

We have illustrated this here for the very simple truth theory TRUTH$_0$, but there is no reason to doubt that we can formulate acceptable characterizations of canonical proofs which meet our intuitive requirement for more complex theories. This problem is technical, rather than conceptual.

A syntactical characterization of the class of canonical proofs gives us a syntactical characterization of the class of canonical theorems, and so, relative to the assumption that a theory is interpretive, of the theory's T-sentences. The importance of this emerges when we ask what it is that a theorist is required to know in order to be in a position to use the theory for interpretation.

If we can specify a canonical procedure for proving T-form sentences, we can show how the meanings of complex expressions are understood on the basis of the meanings of their parts, if we have an interpretive truth theory. We can make explicit this connection between a truth theory and our original project in the following way:

[1] For every sentence *s*, language *L*, *s* in *L* means that *p* iff a canonical theorem of an interpretive truth theory for *L* uses a sentence that translates '*p*' on its right hand side.

As exhibited, [1] is a schema with respect to '*p*'. Thus, an interpretive truth theory, plus a procedure for identifying the *T*-sentences among its theorems, seems to provide all we need to be able to say what every sentence in the object language means, ignoring for the moment difficulties associated with applying Tarski's method to natural languages instead of the more circumscribed language given in illustration above.[17] What we wanted was a (formal) theory which, from a finite number of rules and semantical primitives, issued in a specification of the meaning of every sentence of the language. It was not part of the "bargain also to give the meanings of the atomic parts," as Davidson says (2001*c* (1967): 18). Thus, it looks as if we have all the resources we need in TRUTH$_0$ *if* the axioms of TRUTH$_0$ are interpretive.

Thus, more generally, if we know an interpretive truth theory (we will expand on what this comes to below) and a canonical proof procedure, we are in a position to interpret every object language sentence on the basis of understanding their significant parts and modes of combination.

At this point, Davidson's own approach differs from ours. Davidson did not impose the condition on a truth theory that it be interpretive if it is to be used as a compositional meaning theory. The reason he did not was that he had a larger goal in mind than just to provide a compositional meaning theory, namely, to illuminate more generally what it is for words to mean what they do by considering what substantive conditions could be placed on a truth theory for a language that would guarantee that it could be used to interpret a speaker's language. More specifically, he suggested that taking up the question how one could empirically confirm a truth theory for a speaker in the light of certain general constraints would enable us to provide more substantive constraints on a truth theory the meeting of which would suffice for it to be used to interpret object language sentences. In terms of the notion of an interpretive truth theory we have introduced above, the aim was to state substantive conditions on a truth theory the meeting of which would suffice for

---

[17] Church (1951: 102) seems to have had essentially this insight. This was brought to our attention by Wallace (1978: 54).

it to be an interpretive truth theory. This extended project is not be our concern in this book; we discuss it at length in part II of Lepore and Ludwing (2005). Our concern in this book is with the project of providing a compositional meaning theory for a language, one which aims to illuminate the meanings of complex expressions in terms of the meanings of their significant parts. For this purpose, it is not necessary to inquire into the conditions under which the primitive expressions get what meanings they have.

6. Context Sensitivity

We have so far sketched how a truth theory for a context-insensitive language may be used to promote the aims of a compositional meaning theory. To apply the technique to natural languages, which contain context-sensitive referring terms and devices like tense, we must make some modifications to the truth theory to accommodate the relativity of truth to occasion of utterance. There are two basic approaches. On the first, we relativize the truth predicate to features of context which serve as input to rules for determining the contribution of context-sensitive expressions to what the expressions in which they occur mean as used in the context. On the second, we apply a monadic truth predicate to utterances of sentences. We illustrate both approaches with respect to the use of the first person pronoun 'I' and the present tense of 'stand'.

On the first approach, we will relativize the truth predicate to the speaker and the time of the utterance. We represent the relativized truth predicate as 'true(S, t)' where 'S' is a variable that ranges over speakers and t is a variable that ranges over time intervals, of which an instant is a limiting case. We likewise relativize reference to speaker and time, and represent our reference function as a relation between speaker, time, and referring term, written as 'Ref(S, t, x)'. The reference clause for 'I' then would be

For any S, t, Ref$(S, t,$ 'I'$) = S$.

For convenience, we would rewrite all the reference axioms so that the reference function is relativized to speaker and time, even for context-insensitive referring terms like proper names. The axiom for 'stands' on this approach is:

For any referring term α, for any speaker S, any time t, $\alpha ^\frown$ 'stands' is true(S, t) iff Ref(S, t, α) stands(t).

Several clarificatory remarks are in order. First, we treat the reference function as contributing only its value to the statement of the truth conditions for sentences (see Ch. 4, §2). Second, in giving the contribution of 'stands' to fixing the truth conditions of sentences containing it we have employed in the metalanguage a non-context-sensitive verb which includes an explicit argument place for time interval. A condition on stating in general the truth conditions of sentences relative to context is that the theory that states them does not itself contain any context-sensitive expressions. Therefore, the metalanguage must replace context-sensitive expressions with expressions which contain variables that are bound by the quantifiers over features of context relevant to their contribution. (We will discuss these issues involving tense at greater length in Chs. 8–10.) Third, there is the question of the interpretation of the relativized truth predicate. It would be a mistake to interpret this counterfactually, as saying that if one were to utter the relevant sentence, it would be true. For we can evaluate a sentence such as 'I am not speaking' as true relative to a speaker and a time when the speaker is not speaking at that time, but an utterance of that sentence by that speaker at that time would not be true. The intent of the relativization is to evaluate the truth of the sentence relative to its interpretation given the contextual parameters as input to the rules that provide the contribution of its context-sensitive elements relative to context. That is to say, we wish to ask after the truth of the sentence interpreted as if uttered but not as uttered.[18]

The alternative approach makes use of a monadic truth predicate and conditionalizes on utterances of sentences in contexts.[19] This approach must also quantify over the features of context relevant to interpreting the sentence. We may retain the same reference axioms, but provide the following axiom for 'stands'.

For any referring term α, for any speaker S, any time t, any utterance u, if u is an utterance of $\alpha \frown$ 'stands' by S at t, then u is true iff Ref(S, t, α) stands(t).

It is clear from this that the two approaches encode the same information about the interpretation of uses of sentences. The statement of the truth conditions is exactly the same. The difference lies in whether the truth predicate is relativized to contextual parameters or applied directly to a variable for utterances restricted to the sentence relative to a context type fixed by the

---

[18] See Lepore and Ludwig (2005: 81–2) for further discussion.
[19] For a precise development, though different from the approach sketched here, for a simple language with a single demonstrative, see Weinstein (1974).

same contextual parameters. We adopt the first approach in the following development in part because it issues in deliverances about sentences rather than speech acts, and so delivers in the end pronouncements about what sentences mean (see §7).

With respect to the first approach, there are different options for which features of context to quantify over. One could include in addition to speaker and time, also location, and demonstrata to handle demonstratives. We believe that where a context-sensitive term is used to determine a location, it can be determined relative to the speaker and time of utterance. In the case of demonstratives, speaker and time do not by themselves determine the object the demonstrative refers to. But they can be used to state a rule that determines relative to a context of use what the demonstratum is, roughly, the object the speaker refers to using the demonstrative on that occasion of use in his speech act. (See Chs. 4 and 5 below for further discussion.) In the other direction, a more minimal use of contextual features would be quantifying over the speech act the speaker performs. This suffices to fix the speaker and time by description—the speaker of *u* and the time of *u*. This has certain advantages from a technical point of view, and other virtues that emerge when we consider non-declarative sentences, but we will develop the approach initially at least by using speaker and time as the contextual parameters (we will introduce a quantifier over speech acts in the discussion of demonstratives to accommodate dual uses of token demonstratives—Ch. 4, §5). We choose speaker and time partly because we wish the truth theory to represent the structure of speaker's dispositions in speaking and understanding a language, and we believe that this represents better the information which speakers actually use in interpreting utterances.

7. Davidson's Convention *T*

We now state a requirement of adequacy on a truth theory for a context-sensitive language analogous to Convention *T* for a context-insensitive language. We call this Davidson's Convention *T*.

To show how to do this, we first restate Convention *T* in a form which will make the generalization to a context-sensitive language transparent. Convention *T* requires that a truth theory have among its theorems all sentences of the form (*T*) in which '*s*' is replaced by a structural description of an object language sentence and '*p*' is replaced by a sentence that translates it. We observed that in these circumstances one can replace 'is *T* iff' with 'means that' and preserve truth, for that is just the condition for an instance of (*M*) to be true.

(*T*)   *s* is *T* iff *p*
(*M*)   *s* means that *p*

Thus, we can state Convention *T* as follows:

> An adequate truth theory for a context-insensitive language must be formally correct and have as theorems all sentences of the form (*T*) where '*s*' is replaced by a structural description of an object language sentence and '*p*' is replaced by an object language sentence such that the corresponding sentence of the form (M) is true.

The corresponding sentence of the form (*M*) is the result of replacing 'is *T* iff' with 'means that'.

To state a corresponding condition on a truth theory for a context-sensitive language we need only specify the corresponding form of a context relativized statement of the meaning of a sentence. This requires only that we introduce a relativized meaning predicate, 'means(*S*, *t*)', interpreted as 'means taken as if uttered by *S* at *t*'. Davidson's Convention *T* can then be stated in terms of (*TC*) and (*MC*).

(*TC*)   For all *S*, *t*, *s* is true(*S*, *t*) iff *p*
(*MC*)   For all *S*, *t*, *s* means(*S*, *t*) that *p*

by replacing (*T*) and (*M*) in the above formulation with (*TC*) and (*MC*) and replacing 'insensitive' with 'sensitive'.

> An adequate truth theory for a context-sensitive language must be formally correct and have as theorems all sentences of the form (*TC*) where '*s*' is replaced by a structural description of an object language sentence and '*p*' is replaced by an object language sentence such that the corresponding sentence of the form (*MC*) is true.

8. Adapting the Truth Theory

We now illustrate the extension of Tarski's techniques to a simple context-sensitive language which is an extension of Simple English$_0$, which we call 'Simple English$_1$'. We will also discuss what it is for axioms of a truth theory for a context-sensitive language to be interpretive in the light of our sample theory.

We start with the vocabulary of Simple English$_0$. We add the singular terms 'I' and 'that', which we will suppose are synonymous with 'I' and 'that' in English. We will group names, indexicals, and demonstratives together under the heading 'singular referring terms'. We will treat predicates of the form $\ulcorner$ is $\phi\urcorner$ as present tense predicates, and suppose that, for each present tense predicate in the language, there is a past tense predicate of the form $\ulcorner$ was $\phi\urcorner$ in the simple past. We will give a fuller treatment of context-sensitive singular terms in Chapter 4, as well as accommodate problems that arise for modifications suggested here when we consider the ramifications throughout the fragment treated; we give a fuller treatment of tense in Chapters 8–10.

Aside from tense, the context sensitivity in sentences with terms like 'I' and 'that' attaches to referring terms. We therefore, as above, incorporate context sensitivity for these terms into the reference axioms. This also turns out to be more economical.

Since 'I' and 'that' refer only relative to occasions of use, reference axioms for these terms are universally quantified over speakers and times. We introduce a reference function, expressed by 'Ref$_1(S, t, \alpha)$'; and we stipulate that for any S, t, α, Ref$_1(S, t, \alpha) =$ the referent of α for S at t in Simple English$_1$. The rule that governs the referent of 'I' in English is that it refers to the person using it. The rule that governs 'that' in English (to a first approximation) is that it refers to the object the speaker demonstrates when using it.[20] Our Simple English$_1$ terms are to mean the same, so we give the following axioms for 'I' and 'that':

> I1.   For any speaker S, any time t, Ref$_1(S, t,$ 'I'$) = S$.
> I2.   For any speaker S, any time t, for any x, if $x =$ the object demonstrated by S at t, then Ref$_1(S, t,$ 'that'$) = x$.

Having introduced a reference relation relativized to a speaker and a time, it will be convenient to revise the original reference axioms R1–2 using the new reference relation; though with a proper name the same referent is assigned for each speaker and time. The advantage of using the same reference relation is that it allows us to state more economically the truth conditions for singular terms concatenated with predicates. For this reason, we will rewrite R1–2 using the reference relation relativized to a speaker and time.

---

[20] This treatment is inadequate as a general treatment because it will not always yield the correct results for two-place predicates whose argument places are both occupied by the same demonstrative; e.g. 'That is bigger than that'. See Ch. 4 below for refinements needed to accommodate the truth theory to all the complexities demonstratives introduced in natural language.

R1. For any speaker S, time t, $\text{Ref}_1(S, t, \text{'Caesar'}) = \text{Caesar}$

R2. For any speaker S, time t, $\text{Ref}_1(S, t, \text{'Brutus'}) = \text{Brutus}$

Now we turn to axioms for sentences of Simple English$_1$. We relativize the truth predicate to a speaker and time, as discussed above. We now rewrite B1 and add an axiom for 'was ambitious'.

B1. For any speaker S, time t, singular term α, $\ulcorner\alpha$ is ambitious$\urcorner$ is true$_1(S, t)$ iff $\text{Ref}_1(S, t, \alpha)$ is ambitious at t.

B2. For any speaker S, time t, singular term α, $\ulcorner\alpha$ was ambitious$\urcorner$ is true$_1(S, t)$ iff $\text{Ref}_1(S, t, \alpha)$ is ambitious at some $t' < t$.

The modifications illustrated above distribute throughout the theory initially introduced. We would rewrite RC1 as follows:

RC1. For any speaker S, time t, formula ϕ, $\ulcorner\text{Not}:\phi\urcorner$ is true$_1(S, t)$ iff it is not the case that ϕ is true$_1(S, t)$.

And similarly for RC2 and RC3.

In addition, our understanding of what it is for axioms to be interpretive must be modified slightly when moving to a language with context-sensitive expressions, in a way similar to the way Tarski's Convention T must be modified for truth theories for natural languages. We want to say that an axiom for a referring term or predicate is interpretive if—in the context of the axiom—it *interprets* the object language term. For a referring term, we require that the axiom give the right referent relative to the contextual parameters. For a predicate such as 'is ambitious', what we want of its axiom B1 is that every sentence B1* derived from it by instantiating the meta-linguistic variable to a singular term '*a*' be such that the corresponding sentence M1 is true:[21]

B1*. For any speaker S, time t, $\ulcorner a$ is ambitious$\urcorner$ is true$_1(S, t)$ iff $\text{Ref}(\text{'}a\text{'}, S, t)$ is ambitious at t,

---

[21] As we noted above, when we instantiate 'S' and 't' to a particular speaker and time, the contribution of '$\text{Ref}(x, S, t)$' to what is meant by a sentence is just the value of the function for those arguments. This is to assume that the only contribution of names and other referring terms in our simple language to what we understand by an utterance of a sentence in which they are used is what they refer to, relative to the speaker and time. If more is required for other languages, such as matching of a Fregean sense of a name in the object language with a Fregean sense of a name in the metalanguage, this can be incorporated into the requirement on the axioms. As we have mentioned, there are additional complications in the case of demonstratives. See Ch. 4 for discussion of these issues.

M1.   For any speaker S, time t, $\ulcorner a$ is ambitious$\urcorner$ means$_1(S, t)$ that Ref('a', S, t) is ambitious at t.

Suppose, for example, that 'a' is replaced by 'I'; then we require that M1^a be true as a condition on B1 being interpretive, where for any S, t, Ref('I', S, t) $= S$:

M1^a.   For any speaker S, time t, $\ulcorner$I am ambitious$\urcorner$ means$_1(S, t)$ that Ref('I', S, t) is ambitious at t.

This is equivalent to M1^b.

M1^b.   For any speaker S, time t, $\ulcorner$I am ambitious$\urcorner$ means$_1(S, t)$ that S is ambitious at t.

Now take the case of a proper name. Suppose 'a' is 'Caesar'. Then we have for M1, M1^c, where for any S, t, Ref('Caesar', S, t) $=$ Caesar.

M1^c.   For any speaker S, time t, $\ulcorner$Caesar is ambitious$\urcorner$ means$_1$ (S, t) that Ref('Caesar', S, t) is ambitious at t.

'Ref('Caesar', S, t)' contributes only its value to what is meant by sentences in which it appears, so we may replace it with 'Caesar'. So, the effect of this is to require that M1^d be true as a condition on B1 being interpretive:

M1^d.   For any speaker S, time t, $\ulcorner$Caesar is ambitious$\urcorner$ means$_1(S, t)$ that Caesar is ambitious at t.

This requirement is readily generalizable by replacing object and metalanguage predicates in B1* and M1 with schematic letters. Modifying the requirement for recursive axioms is not necessary, since the connectives we have introduced are not context-sensitive. As before, we will say that a truth theory for a context-sensitive language is interpretive provided that its axioms are interpretive. This will suffice, relative to an adequate logic, for it to have as theorems all the T-sentences for the object language.

9. A Formulation of an Explicit Meaning Theory

An interpretive truth theory, for a context-insensitive or a context-sensitive language, otherwise formally adequate, meets Convention T for a context-insensitive language and Davidson's Convention T for a context-sensitive language. A canonical proof procedure allows us to produce a T-sentence for each sentence of the object language via a proof that reveals its compositional structure. The *T*-sentence can be converted into an explicit statement of the meaning of the object language sentence. (Similarly for the axioms of the theory.) But an interpretive truth theory does not state that it is an interpretive truth theory, and so knowledge of an interpretive truth theory does not amount to knowledge sufficient to interpret its object language. To interpret the object language, we need to know things about the truth theory.

A compositional meaning theory, as we have characterized it above, is a theory knowledge of which puts one in a position to interpret every sentence of the object language on the basis of knowledge of the meanings of their significant constituents and mode of combination. To see clearly the connection between an interpretive truth theory and the goal of pursuing a compositional meaning theory we need to state what knowledge about the truth theory suffices to interpret every object language sentence on the basis of knowledge of its parts and their mode of combination. A statement of this will constitute a statement of the content of the compositional meaning theory as opposed to the content of an interpretive truth theory.

An explicit compositional meaning theory allows us to derive for each sentence of the object language an appropriate *M*-sentence, [*M*].

> [*M*]   For all speakers *S*, times *t, s* means for *S* at *t* in *L* that *p*.

The connection between an interpretive truth theory and a meaning theory is that if we have an interpretive truth theory, then the right-hand sides of its canonical theorems provide *interpretations* of the sentences denoted on the left. And this we have *defined* in terms of their corresponding *M*-sentences being true. Thus, if we know this for a particular *T*-sentence of the form,

> [*T*]   For all speakers *S*, times *t, s* for *S* at *t* is true in *L* iff *p*

we know that the sentence that replaces '*p*' in [*T*] can be substituted for '*p*' in [*M*] to yield a true sentence. Thus, our explicit meaning theory will state that a truth theory is interpretive, it will state what the theory is, and since understanding the theory is crucial to being able to deploy it to interpret object language sentences, it will state what each axiom of the theory means in a way that enables someone who grasps the meaning theory to understand the truth theory, and since we must be able to pick out the *T*-sentence, the theory will also state a canonical proof procedure for the truth theory and state that it is a canonical proof procedure. Putting this together, we can give an outline of the form of a compositional meaning theory for a language *L* as follows.

> [1]   Every instance of the following schema is true:

For all speakers S, times t, s for S at t in L means that p iff it is canonically provable on the basis of the axioms of an interpretive truth theory T for L that for all speakers S, times t, s for S at t is true in L iff p.[22]

[2] $\mathcal{T}$ is an interpretive truth theory for L whose axioms are . . .

[3] Axiom . . . of $\mathcal{T}$ means that . . .

Axiom . . . of $\mathcal{T}$ means that . . .

. . .

[4] A canonical proof in $\mathcal{T}$ is . . .

[1] simply states Davidson's Convention T, making precise the role a truth theory is to play in a compositional meaning theory for a natural language. [2] introduces the interpretive truth theory as a syntactical object. [3] states what its theorems mean; this is required because otherwise what one knows would not put one in a position to interpret object language sentences. [4] states a canonical proof procedure and that it is a canonical proof procedure.[23] It is an interesting feature of the form of a meaning theory which makes reference to an interpretive truth theory that it does not itself state what the truth theory states. As we will show in the next section, this means that the compositional meaning theory is not subject to some objections that can be lodged against a interpretive truth theory for the language.

10. A Brief Review of Some Objections

We treat briefly in this section four objections to the approach outlined above in application to natural languages.[24] The first is that natural languages do not

---

[22] Two worries might arise about this from the standpoint of the next section in which it is claimed that the meaning theory is not committed to the truth of the truth theory. The first is that 'it is canonically provable that p' implies 'p'. But this is not a requirement. Being canonically provable is a syntactic notion, not a semantic one. What is true is that if all the premises of a proof are semantically complete and consistent, then that 'p' is canonically provable will imply that 'p' is true. Second, there is the worry that if 'p' is replaced by a sentence with a vague predicate that is applied to a borderline case, the 'it is canonically provable that p' will be neither true nor false. But again there is no pressure to construe 'it is canonically provable that p' as requiring even that 'p' be truth valued. See Ch. 11 for an account of sentential complements which shows how this can be so.

[23] At the end of "Reply to Foster" (Davidson 2001 (1976): 178–9), Davidson gives a reason for thinking, given his paratactic account of intensional contexts, that this would not be a theory in the formal sense. For on the paratactic account, the axioms stating what axioms of the truth theory mean would contain a demonstrative element, and so would not have a content apart from context. See Ch. 11 for further discussion.

[24] See Lepore and Ludwig (2005: ch. 9) for a fuller discussion of these issues.

have a precise syntax, and so are not suited for treatment in a formal theory. The second is that lexical and structural ambiguity undermine the application of a truth theory to natural languages. The third is that the semantic paradoxes undercut the possibility of formulating a truth theory for natural languages. The fourth is that truth value gaps due to vague terms in the language show that no correct truth theory can be formulated for a natural language.

While natural languages do not have a precise syntax because they are constantly changing, and because at any given time there will be difficult questions that arise about what expressions in the language count in the community as grammatical or not, this is not an obstacle to formulating a truth theory for at least a large portion of natural language. Furthermore, if successful for those relatively stable portions of the language, we will know how to extend it to the other portions relative to various ways in which the unclarities that attend them are sorted out.

The problem of ambiguity is that the theorems of the truth theory, and therefore of the meaning theory, will not provide unambiguous deliverances about the truth conditions or meaning of the object language sentences. A *T*-theorem such as [1] and [2] can be read in different ways.

1. 'The army charged the navy' is true(S, t) iff (for some $t' < t$) (the army charges(t') the navy).
2. 'I shot an elephant in my pajamas' is true(S, t) iff S shot(t) an elephant in S's pajamas.

This is problematic for two reasons. First, we want a theory that delivers unambiguous verdicts. Second, we cannot admit structural ambiguity in a formal metalanguage whose proofs of *T*-sentences we want to reveal the compositional structure of the object language sentence for which they give truth conditions.

The solution is to formulate the truth theory for a disambiguated version of the object language which subscripts expressions with distinct senses, and which excludes structurally ambiguous constructions, but has the same expressive power as the object language. Then we assign truth conditions to a sentence of the object language as uttered by deciding in the context which of the unambiguous sentences of its disambiguated cousin it is synonymous with, and assign it the form and truth conditions of that sentence.

The problem with the semantic paradoxes is that Convention T will require that for a sentence such as (L) we prove (TL). Since in the metalanguage 'L' refers to 'L is not true', we derive a contradiction in (TL^*).

(L)   *L* is not true

(TL)   '*L* is not true' is true iff *L* is not true.

(TL*)   *L* is true iff *L* is not true.

One reasonable response to this difficulty would be to limit the project to providing a truth and meaning theory for that portion of the language which did not include any semantic terms. This would not undercut the utility of the project, and it might be urged that every theory will have to make some sort of special provision in handling semantic terms which cover their own language. However, there is another option open to us once we have distinguished between the truth theory for the language and the compositional meaning theory, as we have done in the last section. For we saw in that section that the meaning theory does not state what the truth theory does, and, in particular, the axioms of the truth theory are not axioms of the meaning theory. The meaning theory will have (*TM*) as a theorem, but not (*TL*).

(*TM*)   '*L* is not true' means that *L* is not true.

While (*TL*) leads to contradiction, in contrast (*TM*) does not. (*TM*) is not and does not entail a logical contradiction. In particular, it does not entail that *L* is not true. Thus, the semantic paradoxes are not a threat to the deliverances of the compositional meaning theory as opposed to the truth theory.

A similar response is available to the threat posed by vague expressions in the object language. It is generally agreed that vague expressions create truth value gaps.[25] Since the truth theory will be required to produce *T*-sentences for sentences which on this view lack a truth value, those *T*-sentences will lack a truth value as well.[26] Thus, for example, if 'Mr Visible Pate' refers to a borderline case for 'bald', the *T*-sentence for 'Mr Visible Pate is bald' would be [TB].

[TB]   'Mr Visible Pate is bald' is true iff Mr Visible Pate is bald.

Yet if 'Mr Visible Pate is bald' translates 'Mr Visible Pate is bald', then as the latter is a sentence about a borderline case which is neither true nor false, so must be the former, and the biconditional cannot be true. However, once we have distinguished the compositional meaning theory from the interpretive truth theory, we can see that this need not be an obstacle to

---

[25] Ludwig and Ray (2002) argue that no sentences which use vague predicates are truth valued.

[26] If one uses a three-value logic to model this, this is not to assign a third truth value to the sentence, but to assign it a letter that signifies its lacking a truth value.

providing a compositional meaning theory using the recursive machinery of a interpretive truth theory. For the corresponding theorem of the meaning theory is [MB].

> [MB] 'Mr Visible Pate is bald' means that Mr Visible Pate is bald.

[MB] is not committed to the truth of 'Mr Visible Pate is bald', and can be true even if that sentence lacks a truth value. [MB] specifies precisely what the vague sentence of the object language means provided that 'Mr Visible Pate is bald' translates 'Mr Visible Pate is bald'.[27]

11. Summary

This chapter has laid the philosophical foundations for truth-theoretic semantics. The motivation for truth-theoretic semantics derives from two sources. The first is the observation that natural languages are compositional in the sense that they divided into semantically primitive and complex expressions, the latter of which are understood on the basis of understanding the former and rules for their combination. The second is the difficulty of how to tackle the problem of giving an account of how we understand complex expressions on the basis of understanding their primitive components and mode of combination by appeal to a 'means' or 'means that' locution in the axioms which does the work we expect of a compositional meaning theory. The difficulty here is not so much that one might not manage by liberal quantification over intensional entities (meanings, intensions, properties, relations, propositions, and the like) to match object language expressions with metalanguage expressions alike in meaning, but that the theory would succeed in doing this only by judicious choice of metalanguage terms for meanings, namely, a choice which uses metalanguage terms to refer to meanings, etc., assigned to object language expressions which are understood to be alike in meaning to the object language expressions. This shows that the work is being done by the choice of expressions rather than what they are supposed to refer to. Furthermore, the matching would fail to exhibit something of crucial importance in understanding the meaning of object language sentences,

---

[27] We leave unexplicated here the logical form of '*x* means that *p*'. See Ch. 11 for discussion of the semantics of sentential complements. The ability of these constructions to accommodate sentences about borderline cases, which presumably do not express propositions, raises a problem for traditional views according to which 'that *p*' refers to the proposition expressed by '*p*'.

namely, how their parts contribute to fixing the conditions under which the sentences are true. Davidson's response was to urge a novel employment of a truth theory for a language. The key insight is to see that an axiomatic truth theory for a language of the right sort contains all the information that we need to meet the goals of providing a compositional meaning theory for a language. Davidson suggested that Tarski's requirement, Convention T, on an adequate truth definition for a formal language can be adapted to natural languages. Convention T requires, inter alia, that the theory have as theorems instances of the T-schema, 's is T iff p', in which s is translated by the sentence in the metalanguage, 'p', that is used to specify its truth conditions. Thus, if we identify a theorem in which this condition is met, we may replace 'is T iff' with 'means that' *salva veritate*. We have illustrated this with a sample theory for a non-context-sensitive language modeled after a fragment of English. We introduced a convention on the axioms of the theory, analogous to the requirement that Convention T places on theorems, which is required for it to serve the aims of a compositional meaning theory, namely, that the axioms use metalanguage terms that translate, or, for a context-sensitive language, interpret, the object language terms for which they give reference and truth conditions. This ensures that the theory meets Convention T, and at the same time ensures that proofs of T-sentences, which draw only on the content of the axioms (canonical proofs), reveal how understanding of the primitives contributes to understanding the complexes, and exhibit how the primitives and their mode of combination contribute to fixing the truth conditions of the object language sentences. We called such a theory an interpretive truth theory. We next extended this basic framework to context-sensitive languages. We introduced semantic predicates relativized to speaker and time ('means(S, t)', 'is true(S, t)', 'Ref(x, S, t)') to take into account features of context relevant to interpreting utterances of sentences, and modified Convention T to what we called Davidson's Convention T using these predicates. The parallel requirement on the theorems is that the truth theory have among its theorems all sentences of the form 'For every S, t, s is true(S, t) iff p' whose corresponding M-sentence, 'For every S, t, s means(S, t) iff p', is true. In parallel with our treatment of a context-insensitive language, we require of the truth theory for a context-sensitive language that its axioms meet an analog of Davidson's Convention T. We illustrated these modifications by modifying our sample theory to accommodate context-sensitive terms. In light of this discussion, we identified the meaning theory with what it is that we have to know to use a truth theory to interpret an object language, and provided an outline of the content of the meaning theory, which has four main components. It must state the connection between the canonical theorems of an interpretive truth theory and an explicit statement of the meaning of sentences in the object language. It must include a specification of an interpretive truth theory for the object language and state that it is an interpretive truth theory. It must further state what each axiom of the theory means, and it must specify a canonical proof procedure. An interesting upshot is that the meaning theory itself does not embed any axioms of the truth theory. We considered some standard objections to the project of providing a truth theory for a natural language, the objection that natural languages do not have a precise syntax, that they contain structural and lexical ambiguity, that they contain their own semantic predicates, and so will generate inconsistent T-sentences, and that they contains vague terms which will give rise to truth value gaps in the truth theory. The first problem at most shows that we must take a snapshot of a fairly stable portion of the language as our subject of study. The issues here are not different than in the theory of syntax. The second must be dealt with by providing a truth theory for a regimented language without ambiguity, and mapping a sentence used in a context onto a disambiguated sentence in the language's regimented cousin. The third and fourth problems were shown not to be inherited by the meaning theory because it does not embed the truth theory, and the problems that the semantic paradoxes and vague terms represent for T-theorems are not problems for M-theorems.

2

Quantifiers

Tarski taught us to appreciate the problem and he gave an ingenious solution. The solution depends on first characterizing a relation called *satisfaction* and then defining truth by means of it.

(Davidson 2001*b* (1969): 47)

The first topic we take up is the treatment of quantifiers and quantified noun phrases in natural languages. Before we can begin a serious treatment of natural language expressions in a truth-theoretic framework, we must consider the changes that including quantifiers requires, and, in particular, the need to introduce a satisfaction relation (or an equivalent device) that applies to open sentences (the result of replacing one or more noun phrases in a sentence with variables, for example, '$x < y$').

In this chapter, we will first consider *un*restricted quantifiers as illustrated in sentences like '*Everything* is fallow' and '*Something* is quick', and then restricted quantifiers, as illustrated in sentences like '*All men* are mortal', '*Some administrators* are honest', '*Most politicians* are ambitious', and '*Two students* are waiting'. Quantifier words like 'most', 'few', and 'many' are of particular interest because sentences with them cannot be paraphrased into a (first order) language with only unrestricted quantifiers and truth-functional connectives. This indicates, we will argue, that even those sentences containing quantifier phrases such as 'all men', 'some women', 'the king', 'both dogs', 'neither cat', and 'the three coins', *inter alia*, which have logically equivalent classical paraphrases, are not properly represented by them. However, in prelude to the treatment these latter quantifiers receive, we must first consider the classical treatment of unrestricted quantification.

It will not be our intention in this chapter to discuss all quantifier phenomena in natural languages. That would be at least a book length project by itself. Our aim is to lay out the basic framework for handling quantifiers in the Davidsonian truth-theoretic framework, and show how it can be extended to handle restricted quantifiers in particular.

The discussion in this chapter will be relatively informal. We will introduce and illustrate the basic modifications needed to treat quantifiers in a truth theory. In the next chapter, we illustrate how to incorporate these changes systematically into a truth theory for an expansion of Simple English₁ which includes unrestricted and restricted quantifiers.

1. Unrestricted Quantifiers

We begin with reasons why the techniques in Chapter 1 cannot extend straightforwardly to quantified sentences. Troubles arise because quantified sentences can have *internal* structure involving predicates or open sentences to which the concept of sentence truth is inapplicable. In this case, we cannot straightforwardly recursively treat quantified sentences using 'is true'.

To see how difficulties arise, consider a simple fragment of English with one-place predicates, 'is coming to dinner' and 'is bringing wine', the existential quantifier 'someone' and a conjunction, 'and', to be used in particular for predicate conjunction, as in 'is coming to dinner and is bringing wine'. (To keep the discussion simple, we will omit explicit relativization of the truth predicate to the language and contextual variables. Appropriate relativization will be reintroduced later.) The inclusion of predicate conjunction immediately gives us an infinite number of sentences, and so we must provide a recursive theory. The recursion required, however, must operate not on complete sentences, but on predicates, and, more generally, on open sentences. This forces us to give up the straightforward approach of Chapter 1, where we were able to perform recursion using the truth predicate because we were dealing with closed sentences.

To see the importance of the internal structure of the predicates, contrast [1] with [2].

[1]   Someone is coming to dinner and is bringing wine.
[2]   Someone is coming to dinner and someone is bringing wine.

[2] could be true even if no one both comes to dinner and brings wine (a delivery man may bring the wine without staying for dinner). [1] is true only if a dinner guest *also* brings wine. Thus, unlike a proper name, a quantifier

like 'someone' does not distribute across predicate conjunction; this is because its function is not to designate a particular individual, so that 'α is coming to dinner and bringing wine' could function as a shorthand for 'α is coming to dinner and α is bringing wine'. Rather, in [1], 'Someone' applies to both argument places of the predicates at the same time, but *not independently* of the application to the other, and, thus, it is not equivalent to a conjunction of two sentences formed from the complex predicate with 'someone' in the subject position in each conjunct (i.e. [2]).

In a regimented notation, this function of the quantifier in [1] is usually represented by introducing a variable with the quantifier and placing it in each of the argument places in the following predicate which the quantifier 'binds', as represented in [1'] (read as 'someone, x, is such that x is coming to dinner and . . .').[28]

[1'] (Someone x)(x is coming to dinner and x is bringing wine).

We will henceforth adopt this representation of the form of a quantified sentence, which will simplify exposition.

The importance of the contrast between [1] and [2] is that it shows that there is internal structure in [1] to which 'Someone' applies, namely, the conjunction of the two predicates in 'x is coming to dinner and x is bringing wine'. In virtue of this, the truth conditions of [1] cannot be straightforwardly explained recursively via the truth conditions of its components, since these, 'x is coming to dinner' and 'x is bringing wine', not being full sentences, do not *have* truth conditions.

If truth cannot be predicated directly of components of a complex quantified sentence, such as [1], it is natural to suggest we evaluate the sentence by appeal to the truth conditions for sentences constructed from those components. This would provide the greatest continuity with our earlier approach. The most straightforward application of this idea will not work, however.

The most natural extension is to treat quantifiers as if they were used to say of the open sentences following them that, for some or every name (in the language), as the case may be, when substituted in the appropriate places, the resulting sentence is true. Thus, with [1], the suggestion would be that it is true just in case for some name, α, ⌜α is coming to dinner and α is bringing wine⌝ is true. That is, we might try axiom [3] for a sentence of the form [1].

---

[28] See Quine (1980: 22–3) for a lucid discussion of predicate abstraction by 'such that'.

[3] 'Someone is coming to dinner and is bringing wine' is true iff some name α is such that $\ulcorner\alpha$ is coming to dinner and α is bringing wine$\urcorner$ is true.[29]

The proposal founders, however, for it requires that there be a distinct name in the language for every object. Quantifiers in the object language range over all objects. To mirror the effect of this by quantifying over names, we need a name for each object. Since the truth predicate is implicitly relativized to the object language, this requires a name in the object language itself for every object. And this will not in general be the case, and, indeed, no language which beings with our limitations could learn could have names for even a very large number of objects. The effect of the proposal is to say that, for example, everything is tall just in case every named thing (in the language) is tall; and even if that were true, it might not be that everything is tall. Similarly, the proposal requires that something is F just in case some named thing (in the language) is F, and it could at best be a happy accident if a thing that is F is named. The oddity of this is highlighted by reflecting that, on this approach, 'Someone lacks a name' could never turn out to be true.

There are at least two ways that the suggestion might be repaired. These are given in Appendix A. At present, however, we turn to the standard approach to extending a truth theory to a language with quantifiers, which introduces a relation of satisfaction between open sentences and sequences of objects or functions from variables to objects. This will be the technique which we adopt in the following chapters, because of its familiarity. The alternatives we discuss in Appendix A, if we are right that they are also adequate to the task, could easily be used in the place of the standard approach.

2. Truth and Satisfaction

The standard approach attempts to find a more indirect way to explain under what conditions quantified sentences are true that makes use of their internal structure. What is right about the failed suggestion is that the import of [1] is that the complex predicate 'x is coming to dinner and x is bringing wine' is true *of* some object, which comes out in the idea that we should look for some name of an object to put in each argument place in the predicate. This gives us a relation between an open sentence and an object, which we will be able to use to work with the internal structure of such sentences. We show how to

---

[29] For the moment, we proceed as if 'someone' were not restricted to persons.

give axioms for this relation for the simplest open sentences. We then show how to give recursive axioms for its application to complex sentences, both open and closed. Finally, we show how to define sentence truth in terms of it.

Consider a simple atomic open sentence with no quantifiers, that is, an open sentence with no logical constants, such as 'x is coming to dinner'. We can think of this as true of an object as assigned to its variable, or, somewhat artificially, as true of an assignment of an object to its variable. Reversing the order, and introducing a predicate to express this inverse relation, we can say that an assignment of an object to its variable *satisfies* the open sentence. When we consider relational predicates, such as 'x brought y to the party', we must speak more generally of assignments of objects to its variables. In the general case, then, we take assignments of objects to variables, or, in other terms, *functions* from variables to objects, as our basic satisfiers. (In Appendix B, we compare this approach with Tarski's, which employs sequences of objects as satisfiers. The differences are not significant.)

Since we will want to consider satisfaction of open formulas with an arbitrarily large number of distinct variables, for simplicity, we will take as our domain all total functions from variables used to represent argument places in the object language to objects, that is, all functions f that assign an object to every object language variable (of which there will be in the general case an infinite number).[30] Representing the object a function f assigns to a variable v as $\ulcorner f(v) \urcorner$, we would give, for example, the following forms of axioms for 'x is coming to dinner' and 'x brought y to the party'.

[5] For all functions f, f satisfies 'x is coming to dinner' iff $f('x')$ is coming to dinner.

[6] For all functions f, f satisfies 'x brought y to the party' iff $f('x')$ brought $f('y')$ to the party.

In [5] and [6], we use in our metalanguage a predicate the same in meaning as the object language predicate (the same one, here, of course, though in the general case the metalanguage and object language may be different) as we did for atomic sentences in Chapter 1. Indeed, it is clear that our functions from variables to objects serve the same role as our reference function from names to objects did in Chapter 1. The variables are being treated, as it were, as names relative to a function.

---

[30] Specifically, representing functions as sets of ordered pairs, if **D** is the domain of objects and **V** the set of variables, then the domain of functions $\mathbf{F} = \{S: \text{ for all } v \in \mathbf{V}, \text{ there is a } d \in \mathbf{D}, <v,d> \in S\}$.

The notion of satisfaction extends trivially to sentences with names. Let us suppose that Ref('Bud') = Bud, and Ref('Pearl') = Pearl. Then, in the case of the predicate 'is coming to dinner', we have [7], and similarly for other predicates.

> [7] For all functions f, for all names α, f satisfies ⌜α is coming to dinner⌝ iff Ref(α) is coming to dinner.[31]

When we have an account of the satisfaction conditions for the simplest forms of open sentences, we explain the satisfaction of complex open and closed sentences recursively on the basis of satisfaction conditions for their parts. For complex molecular sentences, whether open or closed, we use basically the same recursive clauses employed in Chapter 1, except that we replace the truth predicate with the satisfaction relation. Thus, for example, for predicate conjunction, we would introduce an axiom like [8].

> [8] For all functions f, all formulas ϕ, ψ, f satisfies ⌜ϕ and ψ⌝ iff f satisfies ϕ *and* f satisfies ψ.

The same pattern will extend to the other truth-functional sentential connectives.

Now we must turn to satisfaction conditions for quantified sentences. For simple quantified sentences such as 'Someone is coming to dinner' and 'Everyone is bringing wine', or their regimented cousins, we might try satisfaction conditions of the forms illustrated in [9] and [10].

> [9]   For all functions f, f satisfies '(Someone x)(x is coming to dinner)' iff some function f satisfies 'x is coming to dinner'.
>
> [10] For all functions f, f satisfies '(Everyone x)(x is bringing wine)' iff every function f satisfies 'x is bringing wine'.

It's clear that if some function f satisfies 'x is coming to dinner', '(Someone x)(x is coming to dinner)' is true. *Mutatis mutandis* for the satisfaction condition given in [10]. However, these satisfaction conditions will not suffice generally. To see why, consider a sentence such a [11], with two quantifiers.

---

[31] Some technical convenience would be gained by extending our functions to assignments of referents to names: every function would assign the same referents to every name. Then separate satisfaction axioms for formulas containing names would not be needed. However, representing the reference axioms separately serves a valuable heuristic function, and, as we will see later on in Ch. 4, having separate reference axioms turns out to be particularly useful when we are considering context-sensitive terms and referring terms, which we might wish to say have some descriptive content attached to them, though the content does not enter into the propositions expressed by sentences in which the terms are used.

[11]   Everyone is bringing someone to the party.

[11] is ambiguous between two readings. On the first of them, we read it as 'Everyone is such that there is someone he is bringing to the party'; on the other, we read it as 'Someone is such that everyone is bringing him to the party'. We will focus on the first reading. We represent it as in [12], with the order of quantifiers representing which we take first in order of evaluation (read 'everyone, x, is such that someone, y, is such that . . . ').

[12]   (Everyone x)(Someone y)(x is bringing y to the party).

Now suppose we apply the satisfaction condition illustrated in [10] to [12]; then we get [13].

[13]   For all functions f, f satisfies '(Everyone x)(Someone y)(x is bringing y to the party)' iff every function f satisfies '(Someone y)(x is bringing y to the party)'.

Our trouble now is that we need to know what it is for a function to satisfy '(Someone y)(x is bringing y to the party)', but we have made no provision for the free variable in '(Someone y)(x is bringing y to the party)'. It would obviously be a mistake to say a function satisfies it if some function satisfies 'x is bringing y to the party', for then the right-hand side of [13] would be equivalent to 'some function f satisfies "x is bringing y to the party"', and it would suffice for that to be true if *someone* brought someone to the party. We want to consider whether some function f' satisfies 'x is bringing y to the party', while keeping fixed the assignment made by f to 'x', because we want to consider for every function that assigns something to 'x', whether some object relative to that assignment satisfies 'x is bringing y to the party'. We can do this by considering whether some function f' which does not differ from f with respect to the assignment to 'x' satisfies 'x is bringing y to the party'. What we say here about when a function satisfies an existentially quantified sentence, of course, applies as well to a universally quantified sentence, with 'every' replacing 'some'. The point generalizes. For a formula ϕ with an arbitrary number of free variables, in considering whether a function f satisfies $\ulcorner(Q\,v)(\phi)\urcorner$, where '$Q$' stands in for a universal or existential quantifier, we must consider functions f' which differ from f at most with respect to the assignment to the variable v that the quantifier binds. For if we have a sentence with n quantifiers binding n variables, as we work through them in order of evaluation, at each stage, for each subsequent one, we will want to keep fixed the previous assignments of objects to the formula's free variables.

This puts us in a position to introduce general satisfaction clauses for unrestricted universal and existential quantifiers. Before doing so, it will be useful to introduce the following shorthand.

> Def.   For any functions f, g, any variable v, f is a v-variant of g iff f differs from g at most in what it assigns to v.

Now we proceed to give our satisfaction clauses for universal and existential quantifiers as in [14] and [15], representing the universal quantification of ϕ with respect to a variable v as UQUANT(ϕ, v) and the existential quantification of ϕ with respect to a variable v as EQUANT(ϕ, v).

> [14]   For all functions f, all formulas ϕ, f satisfies UQUANT(ϕ, v) iff every v-variant f' of f is such that f' satisfies ϕ.
>
> [15]   For all functions f, all formulas ϕ, f satisfies EQUANT(ϕ, v) iff some v-variant f' of f is such that f' satisfies ϕ.

(For an alternative formulation due to David Wiggins see Appendix B.)

We have yet to connect satisfaction with truth. In terms of satisfaction of a sentence by functions, when is the sentence true? First, notice that whether a function satisfies an open sentence ϕ depends only on its assignments to the free variables in ϕ. For a sentence ϕ with no free variables, whether a function satisfies ϕ cannot depend on what it assigns to any variable. So either every function will satisfy ϕ, or none will. If we consider the conditions under which a function satisfies a simple non-compound sentence, such as 'Jack is tall', it is clear that those are just the conditions under which we think it is true (namely, the referent of 'Jack' is tall); similarly, for compound sentences formed out of such sentences. For closed quantified sentences, we can see from [14] and [15] that the satisfaction conditions obtain for sentences with one universal (or existential) quantifier just when everything (or something) is whatever is expressed by the relevant open sentence, which is just when the object language sentences are true. With each additional quantifier, the effect is the same. Quantification over functions assigning objects to variables just mimics quantification over the objects assigned by the functions to the variables. Thus the satisfaction conditions for quantified sentences effectively determine their truth conditions. In general, then, satisfaction conditions for closed sentences are their truth conditions, and we can say that a sentence ϕ is true just in case every function satisfies ϕ; otherwise it is false, as represented in [16].

> [16]   For any sentence ϕ, ϕ is true iff for all functions f, f satisfies ϕ.

3. Restricted Quantifiers

Expressions like 'everything' and 'something' are unrestricted quantifiers in English. Most natural language quantifiers, however, are restricted rather than unrestricted quantifiers. An example is 'All men' in 'All men are mortal'. In 'All men', 'men' functions as if it were a variable restricted to taking on as values only men, in contrast to 'All things', where 'things' functions as a variable which can take on anything as a value. We have, in fact, used, in some of our examples, restricted quantifiers while pretending that they are unrestricted, specifically, 'someone' and 'everyone', which are understood to range over people, and not things generally. It is not surprising that most natural language quantifiers include some restriction, since most often we are interested in saying something about things in a restricted domain. These include all complex quantified noun phrases which consist of a quantificational determiner concatenated with a nominal which is not true of everything. Examples are 'few philosophers', 'most politicians', 'all Greeks', 'every drunk', 'anytime', 'three boats', 'many books', 'some dogs', 'both candidates', and so on. In these examples the nominal restriction is a simple noun, but these positions are productive in the sense that they may take a nominal of arbitrary complexity, for example, 'politicians from the South who are elected to national office before they are forty' may be conjoined with any quantificational determiner to form a quantified noun phrase. A semantic account, then, needs to exhibit the truth conditions of sentences involving restricted quantifiers recursively in part in terms of the satisfaction conditions for their nominals.

The standard procedure for paraphrasing sentences such as 'All men are mortal' and 'Some administrators are honest' into a form representable in first order logic is to treat them as involving unrestricted quantification over a conditional and a conjunction, respectively, as in [17] and [18].

[17]   All x are such that if x is a man, then x is mortal.
[18]   Some x are such that x is an administrator and x is honest.

Since we already know how to provide a recursive semantics for unrestricted quantifiers, if these are equivalent to the originals, we have thereby solved the problem of extending our semantics to restricted quantifiers. However, from the perspective of a semantic theory for natural languages, this looks unpromising, because there are no connectives in the target object language sentences. Prima facie we would like to incorporate sentences involving

61

restricted quantifiers into a truth theory without reading truth-functional structure into these sentences in virtue of their restricted quantifiers.

A more powerful reason for an alternative treatment is that the paraphrase strategy falters when applied to restricted quantifiers with quantifier words like 'most', 'few', and 'many'. For a sentence like 'Most administrators are honest', the paraphrase strategy would recommend treating it as equivalent to [19].

[19] Most x are such that if x is an administrator, then x is honest.

But [19] will be true if most things are not administrators, whether or not most administrators are honest. It is clear that the strategy recommended by [18] would also fail, since it is false that most things are both administrators and honest. In fact, there is no truth-functional connective that will do the job.[32]

The problem is that the predicate from which the nominal following a quantifier word is derived functions to restrict its domain of quantification for purposes of evaluating the quantifier with respect to an open sentence obtained by removing the quantifier expression from the sentence. This cannot be effected by conditionalizing on the predicate that restricts the domain, because the effect of this is not to evaluate the target open sentence relative to the restricted domain, but to evaluate a conditional with respect to an unrestricted domain. We get the same effect, in the case of 'most', only if most things satisfy the predicate that effects the domain restriction. But this of course will not in general hold. So, we should abandon any attempt to represent quantified sentences of the form 'Most F are G', 'Many F are G', and the like, as quantified conditionals.

If we reject the paraphrase strategy here, however, we should reject it quite generally for sentences of the form 'QF are G', whether or not corresponding paraphrases agree in truth value with the original, or are logically equivalent to them, for each of these structures functions alike. That is, the predicate F restricts the domain of quantification for the purpose of evaluating the quantifier Q with respect to the open sentence 'x are G'.

The effect we want would be achieved if we restrict the functions with respect to which 'x are G' is evaluated to only those functions f such that $f('x')$ satisfies 'x is F'. Consider a regimented version of 'Most politicians are ambitious': 'Most x such that x is a politician are such that x is ambitious'. In effect, we want to evaluate 'x is ambitious' with respect to most functions which satisfy 'x is a politician'. We can say, then, that any function f satisfies 'Most x such that x is a politician is such that x is ambitious' just in case most

[32] See Altham and Tennant (1975); Rescher (1962); Wiggins (1980).

functions f' that differ from f at most in what they assign to 'x' and which satisfy 'x is a politician' satisfy 'x is ambitious' as well.

Let us define a ϕ/v-variant of a function f relative to a language L.

> Def. For any functions f, f', f' is a ϕ/v-variant of f iff$_{def}$ f' satisfies ϕ and f' is a v-variant of f.

Note that since 'satisfies' will be defined recursively over formulas of the language, 'ϕ/v-variant' is also. Then, in accordance with the above, we give the satisfaction conditions in [20] for 'Most x such that x is a politician are such that x is ambitious':

> [20] For all functions f, f satisfies 'Most x such that x is a politician are such that x is ambitious' iff most 'x is a politician'/'x'-variants f' of f are such that f' satisfies 'x is ambitious'.

It should be noticed that, in effect, we are using a restricted quantifier in the metalanguage to give the satisfaction conditions for the object language restricted quantifier. (We used a restricted quantifier in the metalanguage also when giving satisfaction conditions for unrestricted object language quantifiers; for restricted quantifiers we add an additional condition to the restriction on the quantifier.) Thus, all we have done in [20] is to mimic the behavior of the object language quantifier by restricting the functions we quantify over to those which satisfy the nominal.

To give a general form for satisfaction axioms for restricted quantification, it will be convenient to introduce a special notation to represent restricted quantification. Let us represent a restricted quantifier, such as 'All men', as '[All x: x is a man]', read 'all x such that x is a man are such that'. Thus, as for unrestricted quantifiers, we introduce explicitly a variable associated with the quantifier, but include as part of the quantifier also explicitly a predicate restriction at least one of whose argument places must be occupied by the variable associated with the quantifier. In general, the form of a restricted quantifier can be represented as '$[Qx: \phi(x)]$'. We will suppose we are working with a language in which quantified sentences are built up by adding a quantifier at the front of a formula enclosed in parentheses, as for example in '[All x: x is a man](x is mortal)'. We can then give the general form for axioms for regimented restricted quantifier sentences, where 'Q' goes proxy for any quantifier word, as in [21].

> [21] For all functions f, predicates $\phi(x)$, formulas ψ, f satisfies $\ulcorner[Qx: \phi(x)](\psi)\urcorner$ iff $[Qf': f'$ is a $\phi('x')/'x'$-variant(s) of $f]$(f' satisfies ψ).

This completes the introduction of the tools needed to extend a truth theory to a language containing quantifiers. We incorporate them into a truth theory for an extension of Simple English₁ which includes quantifiers in the next chapter.

Appendix A. Quantification without Satisfaction

We outline here two approaches to extending a truth theory to a language with quantifiers that build on the idea that truth conditions for quantified sentences can be understood in terms of truth conditions of unquantified sentences. The first approach considers the truth of a sentence in a given language in an extension of the language, which, it is claimed, contains names for all objects.[33] The second approach also considers extended languages, but quantifies effectively over interpretations of names by quantifying over minimal name variants of the object language.[34]

(1) An extension of the object language with names for all objects

The objection we considered above to giving truth conditions by quantifying over names ran aground on the fact that languages typically do not have names for all the objects there are, so that we can be guaranteed to be mimicking the effect of quantifying over objects by quantifying over names. If a language had names for every object, then this objection would disappear. This suggests evaluating the truth of a quantified sentence not in the object language, if it does not have names for all objects, but in an extension of the object language that has distinct names for all the objects that the language itself lacks names for (we assume throughout there is no ambiguity in the languages we are considering).[35] Thus, we could give truth conditions for universal and existential quantification as in [1] and [2].

---

[33] See Davies (1981: ch. 6) and Dummett (1973).

[34] The approach is adapted from Benson Mates's model theory in Mates (1972). Dummett (1973: 18) essentially suggests the same approach, as a way of avoiding an objection he raises to the first. It is also discussed in Evans (1977) and in Davies (1981). Baldwin (1979) discusses Mates's model theory and other proposals in the context of Wallace's argument that substitutional quantification must be construed as a variant of objectual quantification, if it is to serve certain explanatory purposes.

[35] The assumption of no ambiguity is important in extending the approach to cardinality quantifiers, 'few cars', 'most philosophers', 'three men', etc., for it ensures that each object has no more than one name. We can get the wrong results for cardinality quantifiers if there are more names of objects of various kinds than there are things of the kind. With the restriction lifted we could still get the right result by evaluating truth with respect to a language which removes ambiguity in the original and include just one name for each object.

[1] For all formulas ϕ, UQUANT(ϕ, ν) is true in L iff for every name **v** in L^+, ϕ **v**/ν is true in L^+.

[2] For all formulas ϕ, EQUANT(ϕ, ν) is true in L iff for some **v** in L^+, ϕ **v**/ν is true in L^+.

Here 'ϕ**v**/ν' is the result of "replacing" all free instances of 'ν' in ϕ with '**v**', and L^+ is a language that extends L at most in having a distinct name not already in L for each object which is not named in L. (One can think of these as functional terms, which can in turn be treated as directly referring terms by the techniques discussed in Chapter 4.) Note here that we have a standard method for matching metalanguage variables over names with object language variables over objects, namely, using boldface for the metalanguage variable over names in place of the italic object language variable over objects, associating thus distinct metalanguage variables over names with distinct object language variables over objects. Consider in illustration the application of [1] and [2] to [3]. Applying [1] first, we get [4], and applying then [2], we get [5]. Invoking a reference function for English$^+$, and the axiom for 'loves' in a truth theory for English, which will be the same in English$^+$, we get [6] from [5]. From [6] we can infer [7], given that we assume every name we are quantifying over in English$^+$ has a referent.[36] (Note the shifts between bold and italicized variables, which correspond to the shifts between metalinguistic and objectual variables.)

[3] (Everything x)(Something y)(x loves y).

[4] For every name **x** in English$^+$, $\ulcorner$(Something y)(**x** loves y)$\urcorner$ is true in English$^+$.

[5] For every name **x** in English$^+$, some name **y** in English$^+$, $\ulcorner$(**x** loves **y**)$\urcorner$ is true in English$^+$.

[6] For every name **x** in English$^+$, some name **y** in English$^+$, Ref$_{E+}$ (**x**) loves Ref$_{E+}$ (**y**).

[7] For every x, for some y, x loves y.

Thus we get the following T-sentence, [8], for [3].

[8] '(Everything x)(Something y)(x loves y)' is true in English iff for every x, for some y, x loves y.

We achieve this result in a particularly straightforward way, invoking only a truth predicate and a reference function, and without appeal to a relation of

---

[36] This assumption does not mean by itself that we cannot allow vacuous names in a language, for we can always restrict the quantifiers to non-vacuous names.

satisfaction between predicates and sequences or functions. This technique can obviously be extended to restricted quantifiers given their treatment above.[37]

This approach requires that it be possible to add names for every object. It might be objected that this is not possible because there cannot be an uncountably infinite number of names, though there are an uncountably infinite number of things, for example, the real numbers.[38] This objection might be supported by the suggestion that names are finite strings of symbols and in principle can be exhaustively listed. If all names can be placed on a list, then they can be put in one to one correspondence with the natural numbers or a subset of them, and, hence, there are a denumerable infinity of them at most.

There is no reason, however, that we should require that all names be finite in length. If we allow names which are infinite in length and constructed from two or more distinct symbols, then it follows trivially from Cantor's diagonal proof that there can be a non-denumerable infinity of them. The real numerals, like the real numbers which they denote, are non-denumerable: Cantor's diagonal proof exploits that fact. For the simplest case, suppose we have just two distinct symbols, 'a' and 'b'. Consider all the infinite strings of these two symbols. Now consider an infinite list of strings so constructed.

aaba...
baba...
bbba...
aaab...

We can always construct a string not on the list by taking the string got from the diagonal, 'aabb...', in this case, and changing each of the members, in this case, for example, to 'bbaa...'. The resulting string differs from the first in our list by its first element, from the second by the second, from the third

---

[37] When Davies (1981: 118) suggests that it does not, he does not have in mind using the technique illustrated in the last section of the chapter above.

[38] Dummett makes this claim (1973: 17). In his discussion of this approach, Davies (1981), though he cites Dummett's chapter, does not respond to this objection that Dummett raises. In an early paper which considers an approach like this, which, however, uses conjunctions and disjunctions in the metalanguage to give truth conditions in place of quantifiers, J. C. C. McKinsey also rejects this approach for uncountably infinite domains on the grounds that "it is only in some Pickwickian sense that we could ever say that we had at hand an uncountable infinity of constants" (McKinsey 1948: 431). It is not quite clear whether McKinsey would think the difficulty applies to the present approach, which does not require that we have these constants in hand, but only that there be an extended language that contains them, since all we need to do is quantify over them. This problem is also mentioned in Baldwin (1979: 224–5) with references to other discussions.

by the third, and so on, and so is not on the list. Since for any list of strings of symbols we can construct by this method a string is not in it, no list can contain all infinite strings of symbols.

This approach requires only that there be an extension of the object language containing names for all objects. It does not require that we produce all the names, and it does not require that the extended language with names for everything be learnable or graspable by us. It obviously would not be learnable by us, since it would contain an infinite number of semantic primitives. However, the technique employed merely quantifies over all the names, which no more requires our knowing what they are than quantifying over all objects requires us knowing what they are.

One might still feel some discomfort with this approach because, while we have defused an objection to the claim that there are enough names to go around, namely, the objection that there are at most a denumerable infinity of names, we have not given a proof that there are enough names for all objects.

Moreover, Quine (1947) has argued that Cantor's proof that the classes of any kind of objects cannot be paired off with those objects shows that there are more objects than there could be expressions, and, hence, more objects than there could be names. Consider, specifically, the class of all names, N. Suppose there is some correlation of the names in N with subclasses of N, so that every name in N is correlated with one and at most one subclass of N. Let $H = \{x: x \in N$ and $\sim (x \in$ the subclass of N with which x is correlated)$\}$. Clearly, H is a non-empty subclass of N, since some subclasses of N will contain more than one name. Suppose for a reductio that there is some name n which is correlated with H. Now, $n \in H$ iff $n \in N$ and $\sim (n \in$ the subclass of N with which n is correlated) iff $n \in N$ and $\sim (n \in H)$. Since $n \in H$ only if $n \in N$, this gives us $n \in H$ iff $\sim (n \in H)$, which is a formal contradiction. Consequently, there is no name n correlated with H, though H is a subclass of the class of names. Hence, there are not enough names to be correlated with every object.[39]

---

[39] Although this is a standard proof, one might have some reservations about it. Its application here assumes that there is a class of all names. This might be rejected: just as there are classes but no class of all classes, it might be said there are names but no class of all names. One might also feel some discomfort with the way 'H' is introduced, since it is introduced in terms which appear to presuppose the prior individuation of the class of subclasses of N, but is itself supposed to refer to a subclass of N. Thus, the way we have introduced it in the text appears to violate the set-theoretic vicious-circle principle, since the specification of 'H' is impredicative. See (Chihara 1973: ch. 1). However, in this case, it appears to be possible, as Greg Ray has pointed out to us, to provide a proof which avoids this objection by constructing the set H in a way that avoids the charge of circularity. Let $\{n_i\}_{i \in I}$ be a fixed well-ordering on N with index set I. (The existence

One option here may be simply to allow everything, or, at least, everything over which our quantifiers can range, and which do not already have names in the object language, to count as a name for itself. And if there are more things than these (as we can try to put it), then we still will not be missing anything which we could talk about anyway.[40] This may cause some discomfort in turn, on the grounds that not just anything can count as a name. However, for the technical purposes for which we introduce an extended language with names for everything, it does not matter whether the objects we correlate with things are really names, as long as there is a function from them to anything which can be a value of a variable, and a truth predicate can be defined for sequences of them and formulas of English. Thus, consider again [1], repeated here.

[1]   For all formulas ϕ, UQUANT(ϕ, v) is true in L iff for every name **v** in L^+, ϕ **v**/v is true in L^+.

We allow the term 'name' to have a technical meaning that includes in its extension everything in the domain of the "reference" function for L^+. The reference function for L^+ pairs the names of L with the objects they name, and pairs each other object with itself. Then we interpret 'ϕ **v**/v' as the formula that is the result of replacing v with **v** when **v** is a name of L, and as the ordered triple $<$**v**, $v, \phi>$ *otherwise* (an ordered triple since we wish systematically to associate **v** with the position(s) of v in ϕ**).** Since we could, if we chose, represent sentences as ordered triples of names, variables, and open formulas, it is clear that our concept of truth can be extended so as to cover sentences in this extended sense. Obviously, there are details that need to be filled in, but this appears to show the way to implementing this approach despite worries about there not being enough names to go around.

However, the next approach we consider will allow us to remove whatever residual worries there might be about this first approach on the grounds

---

of this presupposes the axiom of choice.) For each $i \in I$, let $N_i = \{n_j\}_{j \leq i}$, i.e. the set of all $n \in N$ in the ordering up to and including that for the index i. Clearly, $N = \cup_{i \in I} N_i$, i.e., the union of all the N_i. For each $i \in I$, let f_i = the restriction of the correlation f of names to subclasses of N to N_i (where $f_i(x)$ = the subclass of N correlated with x). Let H_0 = the empty set. For each $i \in I$, let $H_{i+1} = H_i$ if $n_{i+1} \in f_{i+1}(n_{i+1})$ and let $H_{i+1} = H_i \cup f_{i+1}(n_{i+1})$ if $n_{i+1} \notin f_{i+1}(n_{i+1})$. Now let $H = \cup_{i \in I} H_i$. Intuitively, this is the set of all names in N which are correlated with a subset of N that does not include that name, but we have introduced it by a construction which at no point involves appeal to all subclasses of N. Clearly, for any $x, x \in H$ iff $x \in N$ and for all $i, n_i, x \notin f(n_i)$, i.e., iff $x \in N$ and $x \notin f(x)$. Then on the supposition that there is an n such that $f(n) = H$, we obtain a contradiction, as before.

[40]   This has the effect of denying the assumption of the proof just discussed that there is a class of all names, on the assumption that our quantifiers can range over everything. At the least, this guarantees that whatever our quantifiers can range over, we will have names for.

that there are not enough names to name every object, since it does not require an extension of the object language that contains names for every object.

(2) Extensions of the object language which differ from it at most in what they assign to some name

The second proposal is to consider extensions of the object language which differ from it at most in what they assign to some name, and then to treat each quantifier in the metalanguage by introducing a quantifier of the same sort over names in such a language. This gets around the difficulty of the object language not having names for everything, and will avoid also worries about whether any language could contain names for everything. Let us introduce some terminology for convenience.

>   Def. L' is an α-variant of L iff L' differs from L at most in that (a) L' assigns a referent to α while L does not, or (b) $\mathrm{Ref}_{L'}(\alpha) \neq \mathrm{Ref}_L(\alpha)$.

Now we can get around the difficulty about the object language not having enough names by considering an α-variant of it. We give the general clauses in [9] and [10].

>   [9]   For all formulas ϕ, UQUANT(ϕ, v) is true in L iff for every name **v** (not in ϕ), language L', such that L' is a **v**-variant of L, ϕ **v**/v is true in L'.
>
>   [10] For all formulas ϕ, EQUANT(ϕ, v) is true in L iff for some **v** (not in ϕ), language L', such that L' is a **v**-variant of L, ϕ **v**/v is true in L'.

Consider now the application of [10] in [11] (for convenience, we will simply understand the restriction to names not in the object language sentence).

>   [11] '(Someone x)(x is old and x is tired)' is true in L iff for some **x**, L', such that L' is an **x**-variant of L, ⌜(**x** is old and **x** is tired)⌝ is true in L'.

And from [11], we can infer first [12], and then [13].

>   [12] '(Someone x)(x is old and x is tired)' is true in L iff for some **x**, L', such that L' is an **x**-variant of L, ⌜**x** is old⌝ is true in L' and ⌜**x** is tired⌝ is true in L'.
>
>   [13] '(Someone x)(x is old and x is tired)' is true in L iff for some **x**, L', such that L' is an **x**-variant of L, $\mathrm{Ref}_{L'}(\mathbf{x})$ is old and $\mathrm{Ref}_{L'}(\mathbf{x})$ is tired.

69

Quantifiers

And given that we know [14] and [15], we can infer (from in this case [14]) [16].

[14]   For some **x**, L', such that L' is an **x**-variant of L, $S(\mathrm{Ref}_{L'}(\mathbf{x}))$ iff for some x, $S(x)$.

[15]   For every **x**, L', such that L' is an **x**-variant of L, $S(\mathrm{Ref}_{L'}(\mathbf{x}))$ iff for every x, $S(x)$.

[16]   '(Someone x)(x is old and x is tired)' is true in L iff some x is such that x is old and x is tired.

Now let us consider how well the approach works with multiple quantifiers, as in [17]. Again, we unpack them in two stages in [18] and [19]. We reduce this further to [20], and then, by [14] and [15], to [21].

[17]   (Everyone x)(someone y)(x loves y)

[18]   '(Everyone x)(someone y)(x loves y)' is true in L iff for every **x**, L', such that L' is an **x**-variant of L, $\ulcorner$(someone y)(**x** loves y)$\urcorner$ is true in L'.

[19]   '(Everyone x)(someone y)(x loves y)' is true in L iff for every **x**, L', such that L' is an **x**-variant of L, for some **y**, L'', such that L'' is a **y**-variant of L', $\ulcorner$**x** loves **y**$\urcorner$ is true in L''.

[20]   '(Everyone x)(someone y)(x loves y)' is true in L iff for every **x**, L', such that L' is an **x**-variant of L, for some **y**, L'', such that L'' is a **y**-variant of L', $\mathrm{Ref}_{L''}(\mathbf{x})$ loves $\mathrm{Ref}_{L''}(\mathbf{y})$.

[21]   '(Everyone x)(someone y)(x loves y)' is true in L iff for every x, for some y, x loves y.

What difficulties might arise on this approach? It is technically satisfactory. One worry might be that, in order to derive T-sentences, we will have to introduce additional axioms for each new variant, and this would be unworkable. But we cannot do this anyway, since we do not know what names in what languages to consider. However, all we need for the required reasoning are some principles about languages that guarantee that, for every name and every object, in some language that is a minimal extension of any given language, that name *names* that object, and that, for every language L, there is an interpretive truth theory, and an axiom in it, for every name α of the language, of the form $\mathrm{Ref}_L(\alpha) = a$.[41] That should be enough to license inferences like that between [22] and [23].

[41] These assumptions are similar to those we need for functions in order for them to do the work they need to do on the standard approach. Cf. E1 and E2 in §2 of Ch. 3.

[22] $S(\ulcorner \alpha_2 \text{ loves } \alpha_1 \urcorner \text{ is true in } L)$.

[23] $S(\text{Ref}_L(\alpha_2) \text{ loves } \text{Ref}_L(\alpha_1))$.

There might be some qualms about quantifying over languages, if these are thought of as intensional entities, since they have to be individuated by the meanings of expressions in addition to the expressions themselves. But this does not really introduce a new element, since we had already introduced names for languages understood to be fixed in that way. We can avoid that, if we wish, by treating the relativization to a language as involving a rigid description of how expressions are understood relative to some actual speech community, and then of how they would be understood, were conventions to have differed in certain ways. This would introduce a modal element, but not in a way that would introduce difficulties in proofs.

How different is this approach and the one considered in the text? They can be made to look very similar by the following device. Suppose that, instead of introducing a satisfaction relation, we retain a truth predicate holding between a sentence and language (we continue to ignore context-sensitive elements for simplicity of exposition), and we introduce functions from variables to objects. But now we think of evaluating a sentence containing a quantifier by evaluating the formula we get from removing the quantifier with respect to a language thought of as extended by the variable bound by the quantifier as a name, with a reference function that assigns to the variable what the function assigns to it. Then, for an axiom such as [24], we can substitute [25].

[24] For all functions f, f satisfies in L 'S(something)' iff some 'x'-variant f' of f satisfies in L '$S(x)$'.

[25] 'S(something)' is true in L iff for some $f('x')$-variant of L, L', '$S(x)$' is true in L'.

Def. L' is an $f(v)$-variant of L iff L' differs from L at most in that L' contains the name v and $\text{Ref}_{L'}(v) = f(v)$.

This makes more transparent the sense in which these two approaches do the same work. The variables to which objects are assigned by functions in fact simply function as names whose referents are assigned by functions, and considering different functions is a way of considering different assignments of referents to the names.

We have then at least three ways of extending a truth theory for a language without quantifiers to one with. We can introduce, as Tarski did, a predicate relating functions or sequences and open sentences, and languages, in the general case. Alternatively, by either one of the two methods, we can get by with just a truth predicate that relates sentences and languages, but appeal to extensions of the object language in which to discharge the role of the quantifiers. The second of these two, just reviewed, in particular, looks as if it does exactly the same work as that done on the standard approach. This raises a question about a claim sometimes made on behalf of Tarski's approach (by Davidson, for example, as in the epigraph to this chapter), that it shows how to *define* the notion of truth in terms of the notion of satisfaction. In light of the above, this looks rather less convincing. The satisfaction predicate takes on more the appearance of merely a technical device that accomplishes a goal which could be accomplished without it, and our understanding of which is parasitic on our understanding of the truth predicate. All of these approaches, however, share something in common, namely, they treat our understanding of the conditions under which sentences are true as involving our thinking of sentences as consisting of predicates with argument places, and the evaluation of a sentence semantically as a matter of evaluating the predicate with respect to objects associated with the argument places. This, of course, is true of even simple languages without quantifiers, but in the case of such languages, it would be possible not to let this come out by employing the brute force method of giving a separate axiom for every primitive sentence formed with predicates and names. Quantification forces us to represent in the truth theory this difference in function between predicates and referring devices. It does not force us to introduce a relation of satisfaction to do the recursion required for quantifiers.

Appendix B. An Alternative Formulation of the Satisfaction Clauses

The account of satisfaction given in §2 treats functions from object language variables to objects as satisfiers. In his pioneering work, Tarski originally employed sequences of objects directly as satisfiers (Tarski 1983 (1935): 171). Tarski defined sequences as one-many relations whose counter domain is the class of all natural numbers, excluding zero. Thus, each object is mapped onto a single number. This is a way of representing the ordering of the objects in the sequence. Suppose that 'xRy' expresses a one-many relation whose domain, the set of values 'x' can take on, is the universe of objects, and whose counter-domain, the set of objects 'y' can take on as values, is the set of natural numbers excluding zero. This sequence can be represented set-theoretically as a set of ordered pairs, $\sigma = \{< x, y >: \ xRy\}$. The second member of each pair will be a natural number greater than zero. The number with which an object is paired in a sequence will be said to be its index, and we will say that the index gives the place of the object in the sequence, so that if the index is i for an object x in a sequence σ, x will be said to occupy the ith place in σ, or to be the ith element of σ. Now, since we use variables to keep track of which argument places are to be evaluated with respect to which objects, to use sequences as satisfiers, we need to correlate variables with places in sequences, and then give satisfaction conditions in terms of the objects in the sequences correlated with the variables. Thus, if we have a standard list of variables, $v_1, v_2, v_3, \ldots, v_i, \ldots$, we can let $\sigma(v_i)$ denote the ith element of σ. Then we will say a sequence σ satisfies an open formula $\ulcorner v_i$ is $F \urcorner$ iff $\sigma(v_i)$ is F (where, in this case, the metalanguage embeds the object language; in the general case, of course, we require a translation in the metalanguage of the object language predicate on the right-hand side). For quantifiers, we consider appropriate variants of a given sequence, that is, ones which vary with respect to the place associated with the variable with respect to which a formula is being evaluated. We introduce some notation for convenience. Let '$\sigma' \approx_i \sigma$' abbreviate 'σ' differs from σ at most in the ith place'. Let us take $\ulcorner$(Every v_i)(v_i is fallow)$\urcorner$ as an example. The satisfaction clause would be given as follows:

> For all sequences σ, σ satisfies $\ulcorner$(Every v_i)(v_i is fallow)$\urcorner$ iff for all $\sigma' \approx_i \sigma, \sigma'$ satisfies $\ulcorner v_i$ is fallow$\urcorner$.

The essential role that sequences play, then, is mediated by their association with variables. We have chosen functions as satisfiers as a more direct expression of this mechanism, but the entire framework can be recast, of course, in terms of sequences as satisfiers.

One alternative to this approach is worth mentioning, introduced originally, so far as we know, by Wiggins (1980: 325). It is a feature both of the approach in the text and of the above that sequences or functions are quantified over in giving satisfaction conditions for quantified sentences. It is possible to quantify directly over objects and restrict them to objects which are identical with appropriate objects in sequences or assigned by functions to variables in giving satisfaction conditions for quantified sentences, to give the appearance of mimicking more closely the object language construction. Thus, for the example above, we could give the satisfaction conditions:

> For all functions f, f satisfies '(Every x)(x is fallow)' iff for every y, the 'x'-variant f' of f such that f' ('x') $= y$, is such that f' satisfies 'x is fallow'.

The technique can be extended straightforwardly to restricted quantification.

Wiggins gives two reasons to favor this formulation. The first is that it is not as unnatural as the standard approach. This conveys no technical advantage on the approach, however, and whether it seems more natural is evidently a subjective matter. The second reason is that the standard approach is supposed to be unworkable for quantifiers like 'most' because the number of sequences or functions is non-denumerable, and Wiggins suggests that we cannot make good sense of the application of 'most' to a non-denumerable domain (Wiggins 1980: 425–6). (It is not clear why the same problem is not supposed to attach to a denumerable infinite domain.)

It may well be that the practice of using proportionality quantifiers in everyday life does not determine their application to infinite domains, so that some decision about how to extend their application is required.[42] However, even if that is so, it is not clear why we should say that we *cannot* make good sense of 'most' and other proportionality quantifiers in application to infinite domains, including non-denumerable domains. We evidently do have some intuitions about their application to guide us. For example, prima facie, it makes sense to say, and it is true to say, that most positive real numbers are greater than 5.

To avoid the complications introduced by the vagueness of 'most', let us shift to a non-vague proportionality quantifier, such as 'more than half'. If we can make good sense of this as applied to an infinite domain, 'most' will not introduce any difficulties on that account. Consider then the claim that 'More than half the real numbers are greater than 5'. This is intuitively true, even though there are non-denumerably many reals. What facts about the reals and 5 make it true? For finite extensions, 'More than half the Fs are G' is true just in case the cardinality of the intersection of the extensions of 'F' and 'G' is greater than the cardinality of the intersection of the extension of 'F' and the complement of the extension of 'G' (the set of things 'G' is not true of)—that is, just in case there are more things that are F and G than are F and not G. This way of explicating the truth grounds for a claim of the form 'More than half of the Fs are G' extends straightforwardly to infinite domains, and appears to get the truth conditions intuitively right, where we have clear intuitions at all. Thus, clearly there are more things that are real numbers and greater than 5 than are real numbers and not greater than 5. Moreover, this gives clear truth conditions where our intuitions, accustomed or trained to

---

[42] We are indebted to helpful discussion with Emil Badici and Christopher Lubbers in the following.

finite domains, may give out. For example, 'Most natural numbers are not divisible by 17' is false, for there are as many natural numbers divisible by 17 as not divisible by 17; similarly, 'More than half the reals are not integers' turns out true, since there are only denumerably many integers, but the reals that are not integers are non-denumerable.

Plausibly, truth grounds for their application to infinite domains can also be given straightforwardly for strict proportionality quantifiers, like 'Half the *F*s are *G*s', which are modeled on truth grounds which make sense for their application to finite domains. In general, 'One-n^{th} of the *F*s are *G*' will be true just in case the cardinality of the extension of '*F*' is *n* times the cardinality of the intersection of the extension of '*F*' and that of '*G*'. In this case, it turns out that 'Half the positive integers are even' is false, since there are just as many positive integers as there are even integers.

In any case, since the domain for an unrestricted use of 'most' is plausibly everything, the worry that Wiggins raises is not avoided by shifting to his formulation of the satisfaction clauses. For 'Most things are fallow', the clause on Wiggins's approach would be:

For all functions f, f satisfies '(Most x)(x is fallow)' iff for most y, the 'x'-variant f' of f such that $f'('x') = y$, is such that f' satisfies 'x is fallow'.

We conclude that there is no technical or philosophical advantage to this approach.

3

Implementation of the Extension of the Truth Theory to Quantifiers

In this chapter, we show how to implement for an extension of Simple English$_1$, which we will call 'Simple English$_2$', the devices used for extending a truth theory to a language with quantifiers that were discussed in Chapter 2. The purpose of this is to illustrate in some detail, for a simple quantified language, how a truth theory may be given and used to derive T-sentences and M-sentences. Subsequent chapters discuss more informally the treatment of various natural language constructions in truth-theoretic semantics, and readers may skip this chapter, if they wish, without detriment to understanding subsequent chapters. In the following, we first discuss the additions to the syntax of Simple English$_1$ (§1), then reformulate the truth theory in terms of satisfaction axioms, first with respect to unrestricted quantifiers, and then with respect to restricted quantifiers (§2). In doing this, we also introduce explicit relativization of the satisfaction predicate introduced to speaker and time. We provide some examples of proofs of T-sentences using the axioms of the truth theory we introduce (§3), and review Convention T and the relation to an explicit meaning theory (§4). We discuss also some issues having to do with how to apply these devices to natural languages, particularly with regard to the use of regimented versions of natural language sentences which aid in the presentation of a formal theory for the language (§5).

1. Additions to the Syntax of Simple English₁

Simple English₂ is an extension of Simple English₁, but it will be useful to provide a complete description of its vocabulary and grammar. We do so in terms of the grammatical categories into which the terms fall.

Grouping elements. Parentheses. ' (', ') ' *Square brackets.* ' [', ']'

Colon. ' : '

Proper names. 'Brutus', 'Caesar'

Indexicals. 'I'

Demonstratives. 'that'

Proper names, indexicals and demonstratives will be called *referring terms.*

Variables. 'x', 'y', 'z', 'x_1', 'x_2', ...

Count nouns. 'man', 'tyrant'

Adjectives. 'honorable', 'ambitious', 'quick'

Verbs. 'stabs' (present tense), 'stabbed' (past tense)

Quantificational Determiners (Q-determiners). 'Some', 'all', 'the', 'few', 'most'

Copulas. 'is' (present tense), 'was' (past tense) ('am' will be treated as a variant of 'is' to be used in place of 'is' when 'I' is concatenated with a predicate formed with 'is')

Indefinite Article. 'a'

Connectives. 'and', 'or', 'not'

Predicates. (i) For any variables u, v, for any verb ξ, $\ulcorner u\frown\xi\frown v\urcorner$ is a predicate. A predicate is said to be in the present or past tense if the verb from which it is formed is. (ii) Any concatenation of a variable with a copula concatenated in turn with an adjective or with the concatenation of an indefinite article with a count noun is a predicate. A predicate formed with 'is' ('am') is in the present tense, one formed with 'was' in the past tense. (iii) Any conjunction or disjunction of predicates or any negation of a predicate is a (complex) predicate. A conjunction of predicates ϕ and ψ is $\ulcorner(\phi$ and $\psi)\urcorner$; a disjunction $\ulcorner(\phi$ or $\psi)\urcorner$; the negation of a predicate ϕ is $\ulcorner$not : $\phi\urcorner$. (iv) No expression that does not meet one of these conditions is a predicate. Examples. 'x is honorable', 'y is a man', 'x stabs y', '(x is honorable or x is a man)', '(x is honorable or y was ambitious)'. A predicate that meets condition (i) or (ii) is a simple predicate.

Quantifiers. An *unrestricted* quantifier is the result of enclosing the concatenation of a Q-determiner with a space and a variable in parentheses. Examples. '(Some x)', '(few x)'. A *restricted* quantifier is the result of enclosing in

square brackets a *Q*-determiner followed by a space, a variable *v*, a colon
':', a space and a predicate (other than a first person predicate) containing *v*.
Examples. '[Some x: x is a man]', '[Most y: (y is ambitious
or x is honorable)]'.

Formulas. An atomic formula is a simple predicate, or a simple predicate in
which one or more variables have been replaced with a proper name, indexical
or demonstrative, enclosed in parentheses. A formula is an atomic formula or
is built up by a finite number of applications of the following rules.

(i)   If ϕ is a formula, then ⌜not: ϕ⌝ is a formula.
(ii) If ϕ and ψ are formulas, then ⌜(ϕ and ψ)⌝ and ⌜(ϕ or ψ)⌝ are
      formulas.
(iii) If ϕ is a formula, $\sum$ is quantifier, then ⌜$\sum \phi$⌝ is a formula.

An occurrence of a variable *v* in a formula ϕ is bound if it is within an
occurrence in ϕ of a formula of the form ⌜(Q v) ψ⌝ or ⌜[Q v: P]ψ⌝, for any
Q-determiner *Q* and predicate *P*; otherwise it is free.

Sentences. A sentence is a formula in which no variable occurs free.

Conventions. We adopt the convention of capitalizing the first letter of a
formula. This will be treated as an alternate spelling of the word.

2. A Truth Theory for Simple English$_2$

We now give axioms for our extension of Simple English$_1$. Earlier we relativized truth conditions to speaker and time to accommodate indexicals,
demonstratives, and tense (Chapter 1). The same point carries over to recursion on satisfaction, that is, we must relativize the satisfaction predicate to
speakers and times to accommodate tense and context-relative referring terms.
We will call this truth theory 'TRUTH$_2$'.

To begin, we need axioms concerning the existence of the sorts of functions
that will serve as satisfiers in the truth theory.

1. Existence axioms

E1. There is at least one function f that assigns to every variable an
     object.

E2. For all functions f that assign to every variable an object, for all
     variables *v*, and all objects *x*, there is a function f', such that f'
     differs from f at most in that it assigns *x* to *v*.

E1–E2 constitute a theory of functions. They guarantee that the functions we quantify over will have the properties necessary to fix truth and satisfaction conditions for any of the infinitude of sentences of Simple English$_2$. E1 ensures that some function assigns to each of the infinitely many variables in Simple English$_2$ an object. This is needed, given the role of functions in the semantic theory, as will be seen below, because there is no upper limit on the number of distinct variables which may occur in a sentence of Simple English$_2$. E2 also plays a crucial role, since for the axioms for quantifiers to do the work they are intended to do, we must be sure that the functions we quantify over include every function from variables to objects in the domain. Adding E2 to E1 ensures this. E2 tells us that for an arbitrary function f, and any variable v, and any object x, there is a function f' that assigns x to v; and that otherwise f' makes the same assignments of objects to variables f does. This is true in turn of this f', and so on, so that every possible pairing of variables with objects is represented among the functions that we quantify over. And this allows us to consider whether a open sentence is satisfied by every object at places marked by a given variable, holding fixed the objects assigned to other variables in the sentence.

The base axioms are the same as before for proper names, indexicals, and demonstratives. (We postpone discussing difficulties with the treatment of demonstratives until Chapter 4.)

1 Reference axioms

'Ref$_2(S, t, \alpha)$' expresses a function whose value is the referent of α for S at t (see Chapter 4, §2, for discussion).

> R1. For any speaker S, any time t, Ref$_2(S, t,$ 'Caesar') = Caesar
> R2. For any speaker S, any time t, Ref$_2(S, t,$ 'Brutus') = Brutus
> I1. For any speaker S, any time t, Ref$_2(S, t,$ 'I') = S
> I2. For any speaker S, any time t, for any x, if $x =$ the object S demonstrates at t, then Ref$_2(S, t,$ 'that') = x.

2 Satisfaction axioms

We abbreviate 'satisfies in Simple English$_2$ understood as if spoken by S at t' as 'satisfies$_2(S, t)$'.

(A) Satisfaction axioms for atomic sentences. (We will revisit the treatment of tense in Chapter 8, where we will introduce some modifications to this simple sketch.) '<' will be used to mean 'is earlier than'. We take the metalanguage

verbs, for example, 'is ambitious at *t*', to be tenseless. Where repetition would be pointless, we describe rather than give the full form of the appropriate axioms. For convenience, we suppress explicit quantifiers over speaker and time in the following axioms, but they should be understood to be universally quantified over the variables '*S*' and '*t*', that is, any axiom presented below with variables '*S*' and '*t*' appearing in it, $\phi(S, t)$, should be understood to be equivalent to ⌜For any speaker *S*, time *t*, $\phi(S, t)$⌝.

A1.   (*a*) For all functions f, and all referring terms α, f satisfies$_2(S, t)$ ⌜(α is ambitious)⌝ iff Ref$_2(S, t, \alpha)$ is ambitious at t.
   (*b*) For all functions f, and all referring terms α, f satisfies$_2(S, t)$ ⌜(α was ambitious)⌝ iff Ref$_2(S, t, \alpha)$ is ambitious at some $t' < t$.

A2(*a/b*)–A4(*a/b*) are the corresponding axioms for formulas of the form, ⌜(α is honorable)⌝, ⌜(α was honorable)⌝, ⌜(α is a man)⌝, ⌜(α was a man)⌝, ⌜(α is a tyrant)⌝, ⌜(α was a tyrant)⌝, respectively.

A5.   (*a*) For all functions f, and all referring terms α, β, f satisfies$_2(S, t)$ ⌜(α stabs β)⌝ iff Ref$_2(S, t, \alpha)$ stabs Ref$_2(S, t, \beta)$ at t.
   (*b*) For all functions f, and all referring terms α, β, f satisfies$_2(S, t)$ ⌜(α stabbed β)⌝ iff Ref$_2(S, t, \alpha)$ stabs Ref$_2(S, t, \beta)$ at some time $t' < t$.

(B) Satisfaction axioms for open atomic formulas.

F1.   (*a*) For all functions f, and all variables v, f satisfies$_2(S, t)$ ⌜(v is ambitious)⌝ iff $f(v)$ is ambitious at t.
   (*b*) For all functions f, and all variables v, f satisfies$_2(S, t)$ ⌜(v was ambitious)⌝ iff $f(v)$ is ambitious at some time $t' < t$.

F2(*a/b*)–F4(*a/b*) are the corresponding axioms for the present and past tense predicates formed from 'honorable', 'man', and 'tyrant'.

F5.   (*a*) For all functions f, and all variables v, χ, f satisfies$_2(S, t)$ ⌜(v stabbed χ)⌝ iff $f(v)$ stabs $f(\chi)$ at some time $t' < t$.
   (*b*) etc.
F7.   (*a*) For all functions f, singular referring terms α, variables v, f satisfies$_2(S, t)$ ⌜(v stabbed α)⌝ iff $f(v)$ stabs Ref$_2(S, t, \alpha)$ at some time $t' < t$.
   (*b*) etc.

F8.   (*a*) For all functions f, singular referring terms α, variables v, f
      satisfies$_2$(S, t) $\ulcorner$ (α stabbed v) $\urcorner$ iff Ref$_2$(S, t, α) stabs $f(v)$ at some
      time $t' < t$.
      (*b*) etc.

3 Recursive axioms

(A) Recursive axioms for logical connectives.

RC1.   For all functions f, and all formulas ϕ, f satisfies$_2$(S, t) $\ulcorner$ not: ϕ $\urcorner$
       iff f does not satisfy$_2$(S, t) ϕ.
RC2.   For all functions f, and all formulas ϕ, ψ, f satisfies$_2$(S, t) $\ulcorner$ (ϕ
       and ψ) $\urcorner$ iff f satisfies$_2$(S, t) ϕ and f satisfies$_2$(S, t) ψ.
RC3.   For all functions f, and all formulas ϕ, ψ, f satisfies$_2$(S, t) $\ulcorner$ (ϕ or
       ψ) $\urcorner$ iff f satisfies$_2$(S, t) ϕ or f satisfies$_2$(S, t) ψ.

(B) Recursive axioms for quantifiers.
We define the expressions 'f' is a v-variant of f' and 'f' is a ϕ/v-variant of f'.

Def1.   For any functions f, f', variable v, f' is a v-variant of f iff f' and
        f differ at most in what they assign to v.
Def2.   For any functions f, f', variable v, speaker S, time t, f' is a
        ϕ/v-variant of f iff f' is a v-variant of f and satisfies$_2$(S, t) ϕ.

Unrestricted quantifiers: In the following 'Q v-variant of f, f', satisfies$_2$(S, t)
ϕ' abbreviates 'Q f' such that f' is a v-variant of f is such that f' satisfies$_2$(S, t)
ϕ', where 'Q' stands in for a quantificational determiner.

Q1.   For all functions f, and all variables v, and all formulas ϕ, f satisfies$_2$
      (S, t) $\ulcorner$ (All v) ϕ $\urcorner$ iff *every* v-variant of f, f', satisfies$_2$(S, t) ϕ.
Q2.   For all functions f, and all variables v, and all formulas ϕ, f satisfies$_2$
      (S, t) $\ulcorner$ (Some v) ϕ $\urcorner$ iff *some* v-variant of f, f', satisfies$_2$(S, t) ϕ.
Q3.   For all functions f, and all variables v, and all formulas ϕ, f satisfies$_2$
      (S, t) $\ulcorner$ (The v) ϕ $\urcorner$ iff *the* v-variant of f, f', satisfies$_2$(S, t) ϕ.[43]

Restricted quantifiers: Q4 and Q5 are the corresponding axioms for 'few' and
'most'. In the following, 'Q ψ/v-variant of f, f', satisfies$_2$(S, t)ϕ' is abbreviates
'Q f' such that f' is a ψ/v-variant of f is such that f' satisfies$_2$(S, t)ϕ', where

---

[43] In this case, since there is always more than one v-variant of any function f, the truth
conditions for sentences of this form secure that they are all false. The determiner 'the' has a
point only in restricted quantification.

'Q' stands in for a quantificational determiner; similarly for 'Q ψ/v-variant of f,f', satisfy$_2$(S, t) ϕ'. We also introduce the function *form(x)*, which yields as value the formula corresponding to a predicate supplied as argument. Complex predicates are already atomic formulas; however, simple predicates must be enclosed in parentheses to yield formulas. Thus, form (x) is the identity map for complex predicates, but yields as value the result of enclosing the predicate in parentheses for simple predicates. Examples. Form ('x is ambitious') = '(x is ambitious)', form (' (x is a man or y is a tyrant) ') = '(x is a man or y is a tyrant)'.

RQ1. For all functions f, variables v, formulas ϕ, predicates P containing v,f satisfies$_2$(S, t) $\ulcorner$[All v: P] $\phi$$\urcorner$ iff *every* form(P)/v-variant of f,f', satisfies$_2$(S, t) ϕ.

RQ2–5 are the corresponding axioms for 'some', 'the', 'few' and 'most', for example,

RQ5. For all functions f, variables v, formulas ϕ, predicates P containing v,f satisfies$_2$(S, t) $\ulcorner$[Most v: P] $\phi$$\urcorner$ iff *most* form (P)/v-variants of f,f', satisfy$_2$(S, t) ϕ.

4 Truth

Finally, we characterize truth in terms of satisfaction.

T. For all Simple English$_2$ sentences ϕ, ϕ is true$_2$(S, t) iff for all functions f,f satisfies$_2$(S, t) ϕ.

3. Proofs of T-Sentences

It will be useful to examine some proofs of *T*-sentences for Simple English$_2$. We begin with the existentially quantified sentence '(Some x)'$\frown$'(x stabbed Caesar)'. The rules used in the proof are given in Appendix A of this chapter. The proofs given here are intuitively canonical proofs, and are in accordance with the canonical proof procedure described in Appendix B.

(1) '(Some x)'$\frown$'(x stabbed Caesar)' is true$_2$(S, t)
      if and only if
      for all functions f,f satisfies$_2$(S, t) '(Some x)'$\frown$'(x stabbed Caesar)'. [From T by Universal Quantifier Instantiation (UI)]

(2) For all functions f,f satisfies$_2$(S, t) '(Some x)'$\frown$'(x stabbed Caesar)' iff *some* f' such that f' is an 'x'-variant of f is such

that f' satisfies$_2(S, t)$ '(x stabbed Caesar)'. [From Q2 by two applications of UI]

(3) '(Some x)'⌒'(x stabbed Caesar)' is true$_2(S, t)$

if and only if

for all functions f, some f' such that f' is an 'x'-variant of f is such that f' satisfies$_2(S, t)$ '(x stabbed Caesar)'. [From (2), (1) by Replacement (Rpl)]

(4) For all functions f, f satisfies$_2(S, t)$ 'x stabbed Caesar' iff $f('x')$ stabs Ref$_2(S, t,$ 'Caesar') at some time $t' < t$. [From F7 by two applications of UI]

(5) '(Some x)'⌒'(x stabbed Caesar)' is true$_2(S, t)$

if and only if

for all functions f, some f' such that f' is an 'x'-variant of f is such that $f'('x')$ stabs Ref$_2(S, t,$'Caesar') at some time $t' < t$. [From (3), (4) by Rpl]

(6) '(Some x)'⌒'(x stabbed Caesar)' is true$_2(S, t)$

if and only if

for all functions f, some f' such that f' is an 'x'-variant of f is such that $f'('x')$ stabs Caesar at some time $t' < t$. [From (5) and R1 by Substitution (Sub)]

(7) '(Some x)'⌒'(x stabbed Caesar)' is true$_2(S, t)$

if and only if

some x is such that x stabbed Caesar at some time $t' < t$. [From (6) and Function Elimination (FE)]

Now let us consider a proof of a *T*-sentence for 'I'⌒'am ambitious'.

(1) 'I'⌒'am ambitious' is true$_2(S, t)$

if and only if

for all functions f, f satisfies$_2(S, t)$ 'I'⌒'am ambitious'. [From T by UI]

(2) For all functions f, f satisfies$_2(S, t)$ 'I'⌒'am ambitious' iff Ref$_2(S, t,$ 'I') is ambitious at t. [From A1 by UI]

(3) 'I'⌒'am ambitious' is true$_2(S, t)$

if and only if

for all functions f, Ref$_2(S, t,$ 'I') is ambitious at t. [From (1), (2) by Rpl]

(4) 'I'⌒'am ambitious' is true$_2(S, t)$

if and only if

for all functions f, S is ambitious at t. [From (3) and I1 by Sub]

(5) 'I'⌢'am ambitious' is true$_2(S, t)$
     if and only if
     S is ambitious at t. [From (4) by Quantifier Dropping (QD)]

Let us consider a proof of a *T*-sentence for a simple sentence using a restricted quantifier, '[Most x: x is a man]'⌢'(x is ambitious)'.

(1) '[Most x: x is a man]'⌢'(x is ambitious)' is true$_2(S, t)$
     if and only if
     for all functions f, f satisfies$_2(S, t)$ '[Most x: x is a man]'⌢'(x is ambitious)'. [From T by UI]

(2) For all functions f, f satisfies$_2(S, t)$ '[Most x: x is a man]'⌢'(x is ambitious)' iff most f' such that f' is an '(x is a man)'/'x'-variant of f are such that f' satisfies$_2(S, t)$ '(x is ambitious)'. [From RQ5 and two applications of UI]

(3) '[Most x: x is a man]'⌢'(x is ambitious)' is true$_2(S, t)$
     if and only if
     for all functions f, most f' such that f' is an '(x is a man)'/'x'-variant of f are such that f' satisfies$_2(S, t)$ '(x is ambitious)'. [From (1), (2) by Rpl]

(4) '[Most x: x is a man]'⌢'(x is ambitious)' is true$_2(S, t)$
     if and only if
     for all functions f, most f' such that f' is an '(x is a man)'/'x'-variant of f are such that $f'(`x`)$ is ambitious at t. [From (3) and F1, by two applications of UI to F1, and by Rpl]

(5) '[Most x: x is a man]'⌢'(x is ambitious)' is true$_2(S, t)$
     if and only if
     for all functions f, most f' such that f' is an 'x'-variant of f, and f' satisfies '(x is a man)', are such that $f'(`x`)$ is ambitious at t. [From (4) by Def2]

(6) '[Most x: x is a man]'⌢'(x is ambitious)' is true$_2(S, t)$
     if and only if
     for all functions f, most f' such that f' is an 'x'-variant of f, and $f'(`x`)$ is a man at t, are such that $f'(`x`)$ is ambitious at t. [From (5) and F3 by two applications of UI, and by Rpl]

(7) '[Most x: x is a man]'⌢'(x is ambitious)' is true$_2(S, t)$
     if and only if
     most x such that x is a man at t are such that x is ambitious at t. [From (6) and FE]

4. Convention T Revisited

Let us revisit Convention T and the connection between a truth theory and a meaning theory briefly. Recall that in Chapter 1 we generalized the form of Tarski's Convention T to context-sensitive languages. The generalization relied on the observation that Tarski's Convention T for a context-insensitive language L and a truth predicate for L, 'is true$_L$', can be restated as follows:

> A truth theory $\mathcal{T}$ is adequate if it is formally correct and entails all instances of schema (T)
>
> (T) s is true$_L$ iff p
>
> where 's' is replaced by a structural description of an object language sentence such that the corresponding M-sentence is true.

The M-sentence corresponding to an instance of (T) is the corresponding instance of (M).

> (M) s means that p.

The generalization of Convention T is achieved by replacing the unrelativized semantic predicates in this characterization with relativized semantic predicates. We provide the instance of the Convention appropriate for Simple English$_2$.

> [CT_2]   A truth theory $\mathcal{T}$ is adequate if it is formally correct and entails all instances of schema (T_2)
>
> (T_2) s is true$_2(S, t)$ iff p,
>
> where 's' is replaced by a structural description of an object language sentence, such that the corresponding M-sentence is true.

The M-sentence corresponding to an instance of (T_2) in [CT_2] is (M_2).

> (M_2) s means$_2(S, t)$ that p.

As we noted in Chapter 1, it is important to place an additional requirement on the truth theory, if it is to illuminate the compositional semantic structure of object language sentences. This requirement is that the axioms of the theory themselves satisfy what is in effect an analog of Convention T. We call this Convention S. We will say that Convention S is a condition on S-adequacy of a theory. A theory which meets Convention S and for which there is available a suitably powerful logic will also meet Convention T.

85

Informally, what Convention S requires is that the satisfaction conditions for object language expressions be given using expressions in the metalanguage which translate them, or uses of them relative to occasions of use, barring such defects as failure of reference of demonstrative terms. What is meant here can be easily seen from considering the axioms given for Simple English$_2$.

Let us consider a more precise specification of Convention S. We start with a context-*in*sensitive language, which uses a satisfaction relation. We suppose we have a truth theory whose axioms can be divided into reference axioms, satisfaction axioms for predicates (predicate axioms, we will say), and recursion axioms, for connectives and for quantifiers, the latter both unrestricted and restricted. Each primitive term of the language receives an axiom in the theory. The axioms of will be conceived of as having a standard form. For concreteness, we will suppose the forms of the axioms of the theory conform to the following.

Reference Axioms

$\text{Ref}(\alpha) = a$

[where 'α' is replaced by a quotation name of an object language proper name and 'a' by a metalanguage proper name]

Predicate Axioms

For all functions f, variables $v_1, v_2, \ldots, v_n, f$ satisfies$_L$ $\phi(v_1, v_2, \ldots, v_n)$ iff $\phi^*(f(v_1), f(v_2), \ldots, f(v_n))$

[where '$\phi(v_1, v_2, \ldots, v_n)$' is replaced by *a structural description of* an object language predicate containing variables $v_1, v_2, \ldots, v_n$, and '$\phi^*(f(v_1), f(v_2), \ldots, f(v_n))$' by *a metalanguage predicate* with the same number of argument places as ϕ occupied respectively by '$f(v_1)$', '$f(v_2)$', $\ldots$, '$f(v_n)$'.]

Recursive Axioms

Connectives. For all functions f, for all formulas $\phi_1, \phi_2, \ldots, \phi_n, f$ satisfies$_L$ $\text{CON}(\delta, \phi_1, \phi_2, \ldots, \phi_n)$ iff con(δ^*, f satisfies$_L$ ϕ_1, f satisfies$_L$ $\phi_2, \ldots, f$ satisfies$_L$ ϕ_n)

[where '$\text{CON}(\delta, \phi_1, \phi_2, \ldots, \phi_n)$' is replaced by a structural description of an object language formula whose main connective is δ, and whose immediate subcomponents are $\phi_1, \phi_2, \ldots, \phi_n$ and 'con(δ^*, f satisfies$_L$ ϕ_1, f satisfies$_L$

$\phi_2, \ldots, f$ satisfies$_L$ ϕ_n)' by a metalanguage formula whose main connective is δ^*, and which combines the same number of sentences as δ, and whose immediate subcomponents are 'f satisfies$_L$'$^\frown\phi_1$, 'f satisfies$_L$'$^\frown\phi_2$, ..., 'f satisfies$_L$'$^\frown\phi_n$.]

Unrestricted Quantifiers. For all functions f, variables v, f satisfies$_L$ URQ(Q, v, ϕ) iff Q^* f' such that f' is a v-variant of f are such that f' satisfies$_L$ ϕ

[where 'URQ(Q, v, ϕ)' is replaced by an object language quantified formula involving an unrestricted quantifier constructed from the quantificational determiner Q with respect to an object language variable v and formula ϕ (e.g. '(Some x)(x is ambitious)'), and 'Q^*' is replaced by a metalanguage quantificational determiner.]

Restricted Quantifiers. For all functions f, variables v, f satisfies$_L$ RQ(Q, v, ϕ, ψ) iff Q^* f' such that f' is a ϕ/v-variant of f are such that f' satisfies$_L$ ψ

[where 'RQ(Q, v, ϕ, ψ)' is replaced by an object language formula involving a restricted quantifier constructed from the quantificational determiner Q with respect to an object language variable v, with ϕ as the object language predicate restriction and ψ as the object language formula to which it is applied, and 'Q^*' is replaced by a metalanguage quantificational determiner.]

Other than the axioms of the theory of functions, these will exhaust the axioms of the theory. In general, when we use 'truth theory', we have in mind a theory specified in this general way (i.e. a theory minimal in the sense that it has axioms for the theory of functions and for each primitive expression in the language, but no others, and whose axioms for primitive expressions are either assignments of referents to singular terms or quantified biconditionals whose quantifiers range only over functions, contextual parameters, and object language expressions).

We will specify Convention S in terms of what is required of each sort of axiom. Clearly, this statement of Convention S is relative to the forms of expressions found in the object language. For a completely general specification, we would need to canvass all possible forms of expressions in languages, and specify the requirements relative to languages constructed using various subsets of the total set of expressive resources possible. In practice, it is easy enough to see how to do it for a given language. For a truth theory with axioms of the above forms, we can specify Convention S, with reference to the above, as follows.

A truth theory $\mathcal{T}$ (for Simple English$_2$) is S-adequate if it is formally correct, and its axioms meet the following conditions.

(i) For reference axioms: '*a*' translates α (this requires minimally that they have the same referent, but extends to anything else that may be required for sameness of meaning—see the next chapter for further discussion).

(ii) For predicate axioms: '$\phi^*(v_1, v_2, \ldots, v_n)$' translates $\phi(v_1, v_2, \ldots, v_n)$, with $v_1, v_2, \ldots, v_n$ occupying corresponding argument places (i.e., argument places with the same semantic function).

(iii) For recursive axioms for connectives. δ translates δ^*, and $\phi_1, \phi_2, \ldots, \phi_n$ and 'f satisfies$_L$'$\frown \phi_1$, 'f satisfies$_L$'$\frown \phi_2$, ..., 'f satisfies$_L$'$\frown \phi_n$ occupy corresponding places.

(iv) For recursive axioms for quantifiers: Q^* translates Q.

A relatively minor modification is required to extend this to a context-sensitive language. First, we must replace our semantic relation 'satisfies$_L$' with one relativized to contextual parameters, speaker and time, following our practice, as in 'satisfies$_L(S, t)$'. Second, we must make provision for context-sensitive referring terms and context-sensitive predicates. For context-sensitive referring terms, we can look for illustration to the form of the axioms for Simple English$_2$. As we will see in subsequent chapters, the axiom for demonstratives will need to be modified, and other context-sensitive referring terms may also have other forms, but these will serve for purposes of illustration. We will restrict attention to context sensitivity introduced by tense for predicates. For predicates then, we characterize the form of the axioms as follows (restricting attention to present and past tenses—the extension to other tenses is straightforward).

Reference Axioms

(a) $\text{Ref}(S, t, \zeta) = D(S, t)$

(b) For any x if $x = D(S, t)$, then $\text{Ref}(S, t, \zeta) = x$[44]

[where 'ζ' is replaced by an object language referring term, and '$D(S, t)$' is replaced by a metalanguage proper name, variable, or formula containing as variables 'S', or 'S' and 't'.]

---

[44] As before, we suppress the quantifiers binding 'S' and 't' throughout. Thus, '$\text{Ref}(S, t, \zeta) = D(S, t)$' is short for 'For any S, t, $\text{Ref}(S, t, \zeta) = D(S, t)$' and 'For any x if $x = D(S, t)$, then $\text{Ref}(S, t, \zeta) = x$' is short for 'For any S, t, for any x if $x = D(S, t)$, then $\text{Ref}(S, t, \zeta) = x$'.

Predicate Axioms

For all functions f, variables $v_1, v_2, \ldots, v_n, f$ satisfies$_L(S, t)$ Present$[\phi(v_1, v_2, \ldots, v_n)]$ iff $\phi^*(f(v_1), f(v_2), \ldots, f(v_n), t)$

For all functions f, variables $v_1, v_2, \ldots, v_n, f$ satisfies$_L(S, t)$ Past$[\phi(v_1, v_2, \ldots, v_n)]$ iff $\phi^*(f(v_1), f(v_2), \ldots, f(v_n),$ some $t' < t)$

> [where 'Past$[\phi(v_1, v_2, \ldots, v_n)]$'/'Present$[\phi(v_1, v_2, \ldots, v_n)]$' is replaced by a structural description of a past/present tense object language predicate containing variables $v_1, v_2, \ldots, v_n$, and '$\phi^*(f(v_1), f(v_2), \ldots, f(v_n), t)$'/'$\phi^*(f(v_1), f(v_2), \ldots, f(v_n),$ some $t' < t)$' by a metalanguage predicate with $n +$ 1 argument places occupied respectively by '$f(v_1)$', '$f(v_2)$', $\ldots$, '$f(v_n)$', 't'/'some $t' < t$', where 't'/'some $t' < t$' occupies a temporal argument place.]

For now we will suppose that no modifications will be required for recursive axioms aside from those required to relativize the satisfaction predicate to contextual parameters. As we will see in Chapter 8, the interaction of tense with connectives in natural languages will force some additional complexity here. No modifications will be needed for the recursive axioms for quantified sentences. Thus, in specifying how to extend Convention S to a context sensitive language whose axioms take the forms indicated, we need merely show how to modify clauses (i) and (ii) above.

(i)   For reference axioms. (a) Either '$D(S, t)$' is a proper name that translates ζ, or '$D(S, t)$' is a variable or function whose value, relative to a specification of values for 'S' and 't', is what ζ refers to; (b) $D(S, t)$ is a description whose denotation, if it has one, is the referent of ζ, relative to a specification of values for 'S' and 't'.

(ii) For predicate axioms. The result of replacing 'satisfies$_L(S, t)$ Present $[\phi(v_1, v_2, \ldots,)]$ iff' in (a) with 'Present$[\phi(v_1, v_2, \ldots,)]$ means$_L(S, t, f)$ that' yields a true sentence; the result of replacing 'f satisfies$_L(S, t)$ Past$[\phi(v_1, v_2, \ldots,)]$ iff' in (b) with 'Past$[\phi(v_1, v_2, \ldots,)]$ means$_L(S, t, f)$ that' yields a true sentence.

(a) For all functions f, variables $v_1, v_2, \ldots, f$ satisfies$_L(S, t)$ Present $[\phi(v_1, v_2, \ldots,)]$ iff $\phi^*(f(v_1), f(v_2), \ldots, t)$

(b) For all functions f, variables $v_1, v_2, \ldots, f$ satisfies$_L(S, t)$ Past $[\phi(v_1, v_2, \ldots,)]$ iff $\phi^*(f(v_1), f(v_2), \ldots,$ some $t' < t)$

Comments

In the case of the clause for reference axioms, the guiding idea is that for context-sensitive referring terms, we use a reference axiom which employs a rule that correctly specifies the referent of a term relative to the contextually relevant parameters. In the case of the clause for predicates, it should be noted that the meaning relation we have introduced has an extra argument place for a function. To understand its purpose, one can take the extra argument place for a function to add to the specification of the language the variables as proper names and the function as the reference function for the additions. Otherwise, we understand it as explained in Chapter 1.

If a truth theory meets Convention *S*, then it will meet Convention *T*, if it has a logic powerful enough to formulate a canonical proof procedure. And the canonical *T*-theorems of the theory with an adequate logic will be *T*-sentences. We will say that a truth theory that meets Convention *S* is an interpretive truth theory.

We can then recall from Chapter 1 the explicit form of a meaning theory that uses an interpretive truth theory.

[1]   Every instance of the following schema is true:
      For all speakers *S*, times *t*, *s* means$_L$ (S, t) that *p* iff it is canonically
      provable on the basis of the axioms of an interpretive truth theory
      for *L* that for all speakers *S*, times *t*, *s* is true$_L$ (S, t) iff *p*.[45]
[2] $\mathcal{T}$ is an interpretive truth theory for *L* whose axioms are . . .
[3]   Axiom . . . of $\mathcal{T}$ means that . . .
      Axiom . . . of $\mathcal{T}$ means that . . .
[4]   A canonical proof in $\mathcal{T}$ is . . .

We have now completed our illustration of how to extend the discussion of Chapter 1 to a context-sensitive object language with quantifiers. In subsequent chapters, we will discuss more informally how to incorporate treatments of various natural language constructions into the general kind of framework outlined here, but will not explicitly revise our sample language to

---

[45] In Ch. 1, it was suggested that for the purposes of providing a compositional meaning theory, the theorems of the truth theory need not be true in the case of sentences containing vague predicates or in case of semantic paradoxes, on the assumption that this prevents them from having a truth value. It might be thought that, in the light of this, we should not be committed to the claim expressed in [1]. However, that is so only if 'it is canonically provable that *p*' can be true only if '*p*' has a truth value. Clearly, there is no difficulty in saying what it is for a sentence of this form to be true even in the case in which '*p*' does not have a truth value, namely, '*p*' can be derived from the axioms of an interpretive truth theory.

reflect these changes. It should be clear how to modify this basic framework to include the needed modifications in the light of the informal discussion, since, if we are right, the basic resources needed have already been discussed.

5. Regimentation and Natural Language

In presenting the modifications to a truth theory required to extend it to a language with quantifiers, and in illustrating these modifications in a simple artificial language, we introduced variables and grouping devices which enable us to provide an unambiguous interpretation of sentence structure. Natural languages are often lazy in these respects: they lack these devices, or do not always employ them, if they have them. It may well be asked, then, how the techniques discussed above are relevant to providing a semantic theory for natural languages, when many sentences in natural languages lack the devices needed to apply these techniques to them.

Consider, for example, simple restricted quantifier sentences in natural languages, such as 'Most men are ambitious'. Since there are no variables in this sentence, it is not clear immediately how we are to apply a truth theory of the form we have outlined to a language which contains such a sentence. Consider also a sentence such as 'Everyone brought someone to the party'. This has two different readings, depending on whether we understand 'everyone' to take priority over 'someone' or vice versa. The sort of satisfaction clause we have considered so far has no provision for this, but which we evaluate first makes a significant difference to the structure of a proof of a *T*-sentence and to the interpretation of the semantic form of the sentence.

Let us consider the problem of variables first. The function of variables is twofold. First, they mark argument places in predicates. Second, by their association with both argument places and quantifiers, together with devices for indicating scope, they show which quantifiers are to be associated with which argument places in a sentence. Of course, this information, ambiguity aside, must also be recoverable, for speaker and interpreter alike, from the surface structure of sentences in natural languages. In the case of 'Most men are ambitious', it is clear how this is so. 'Men' introduces a one-place predicate, as does 'are ambitious'. 'Most' introduces a device for binding argument places. The structure dictates that 'most' must bind an argument place in the nominal and in the verb phrase. There is only one in each, so no additional information is needed. Similar remarks apply to 'Someone is coming to dinner and bringing wine'. Forms of speech in natural language are selected. Where additional elements are not needed to recover the sense, compression is the order of the day. Another device employed is the location of the quantifier in the argument place that it is to bind, as in 'Everyone brought wine to the party'. This device is also employed, of course, in 'Most men are ambitious', as 'Most men' occupies the argument place in '___ are ambitious'. Additional resources are employed, such as pronouns of cross-reference, as needed, as in 'Someone lost his luggage on every trip he took'.

If the information is there in the forms of expression we utter or write, then it is possible to exploit it in giving a systematic truth theory for the language. It can be cumbersome, however, and once it is clear what sorts of techniques can be employed to achieve this, there is little point to carrying out discussions of natural language semantics in direct application to the apparent forms of sentences (apparent in the sense of the form offered in speech or writing for interpretation). We can facilitate discussion by offering regimented versions of natural language sentences as capturing their form, and then formulate the truth theory with greater economy and perspicacity in application to the regimented version.

If we suppose the language itself has the resources to formulate a regimented version with variables, such as 'Most x such that x is a man are such that x is ambitious', we can provide rules for translating the original into the regimented version and then apply the truth theory to it, assigning its truth conditions also to the original. If the language does not contain the resources needed to formulate the regimented version to which we can apply the truth theory directly, the simplest device is to evaluate its truth and satisfaction conditions with respect to a regimented version of the language that includes the devices needed, and then repeat the procedure already indicated. The truth theory, then, would apply not to actual sentences of the object language, but rather to their regimented versions, and then truth conditions would be assigned to actual sentences by a mechanical procedure for mapping them onto sentences for which *T*-sentences are generated.[46] For example, 'Some men are honest' in L might be mapped onto 'Some x such that x is a man are such that x is honest' in L^R, a regimented version of L, and the truth

---

[46] This is the procedure linguists follow in effect in producing structural representations of English sentences which aim to encode their semantically relevant structural features. The picture in linguistics is complicated by the fact that linguists think of these representations as the actual sentences of the language, and of speakers as having an internalized theory about these sentences, which undergo syntactic transformations between actual speech and semantic interpretation. Whatever one thinks of the psychological component, commitment to it is certainly unnecessary for the project of representing semantic structure in natural languages.

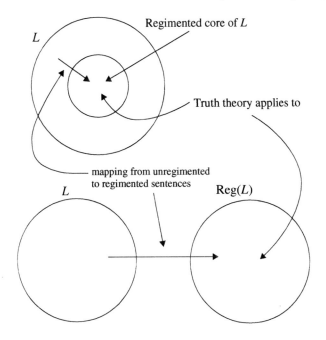

Figure 1

conditions generated for the latter would be assigned to the former. These cases are illustrated in Figure 1.

This technique could also be applied directly to the object language sentences in the truth theory. We illustrate this for 'Most men are ambitious' in [Q]. Let 'fresh(v, ϕ)' abbreviate 'v is a variable that does not appear in ϕ'. Let 'form(v, ϕ)' designate the formula of L^R formed by introducing v into the unoccupied argument place in ϕ, if ϕ is a verb phrase, and, if ϕ is a noun, designate the formula of L^R formed by mapping ϕ onto the predicate it is derived from, and introducing v into the unoccupied argument place in it. For example, form('x', 'men') = 'x is a man', form('x', 'are ambitious') = 'x is ambitious'.

> [Q] For all functions f, nominals ϕ, verb phrases ψ, f satisfies$_L(S, t)$ 'Most'$^\frown \phi^\frown \psi$ iff for some v such that fresh(v, 'Most'$^\frown \phi^\frown \psi$), most f' such that f' is a v-variant of f, and f' satisfies$_{LR}(S, t)$ form(v, ϕ), are such that f' satisfies$_{LR}(S, t)$ form(v, ψ).

However, since the same effect is achieved, with greater simplicity, by separating the task of mapping object language sentences onto regimented versions, and providing a truth theory for the regimented version, we will adopt that procedure instead.

For ambiguity, as we have discussed previously (Ch. 1, §9), there are two basic strategies. The first is to provide for each ambiguous sentence a set of disambiguated versions, one for each different possible reading of the original. In line with the discussion of the previous paragraph, we can suppose these to be in a regimented version of the language, if needed. For example, the two readings of 'Most men stabbed some tyrant' would be represented by distinct sentences. We use a standard regimented notation in Simple English₂ which could be used to represent the two readings, namely, '[Most x: x is a man][some y: y is a tyrant] (x stabbed y)' and '[Some y: y is a tyrant][most x: x is a man] (x stabbed y)'. This again yields considerable simplification when it comes to giving the truth theory for the regimented versions. To employ the truth theory, then, to interpret actual speech, one must decide on the basis of contextual factors which interpretation an ambiguous sentence should be assigned, and assign to its use on that occasion the truth conditions appropriate for the regimented version representing that interpretation. This slightly complicates our picture of the relation between the target language and its regimented cousin. When we set aside ambiguity, we can suppose that for every sentence of the target language there is a unique sentence of the regimented language it is mapped onto. When the target language includes ambiguous sentences, particularly sentences with structural ambiguity, then we will have a one to many mapping from the sentences of the target language to the sentences of the regimented language.

The second strategy is to relativize the interpretation to the speaker's intentions by conditionalizing on the speaker's intentions about the order in which the quantifiers are to be evaluated. The suggestion would be that the satisfaction axiom for, for example, 'Most men stabbed some tyrant', be given as in [A].

[A] For all functions f, f satisfies$_L$ (S, t) 'Most men stabbed some tyrant' iff

if S intends at t 'most' to be evaluated before 'some' in S's utterance at t of 'Most men stabbed some tyrant', then f satisfies$_{LR}(S, t)$ '[Most x: x is a man][some y: y is a tyrant](x stabbed y)',

and if S intends at t 'some' to be evaluated before 'most' in S's utterance at t of 'Most men stabbed some tyrant', then f satisfies$_{LR}(S, t)$ '[Some y: y is a tyrant][most x: x is a man](x stabbed y)'

A drawback to this approach is that some *T*-theorems will be assigned more complicated forms since their right-hand sides will be conjunctions of conditionals. This would require also refining Conventions *T* and *S*. In application to speech, one would first have to determine a speaker's intention before being able to use the theorem for interpretation. Since there are no technical or philosophical advantages to pursuing the second strategy, which is more cumbersome, we will henceforth adhere to the first.

In general, then, our strategy in subsequent chapters will be to consider proposals for the semantic forms of natural language sentences and expressions in the form of regimented versions of the sentences and expressions which make explicit their predicate and quantificational structure. Since we will henceforth be concerned with illustrating the approach with respect to English, we will also omit any explicit relativization to language in using semantic predicates.

Appendix A. Rules Used in Proofs

Our metalanguage is not a formally specified language. The example proofs we give are not meant to be formal proofs, but to provide a guide to how formal proofs could be given. In particular, when we speak of formulas of certain forms, we will allow slightly different syntactical forms which express the same thing to count as "of the same form".

It should be noted also that these rules of inference do not constitute a complete system of logic. They are less general than the rules one would introduce for a complete natural deduction system. However, our aim is not to provide a complete logic, but rather to provide inference rules adequate for the proofs we need. This is also helpful in specifying a canonical proof procedure. It reduces the amount of "mischief" that can be done using the rules in proofs.

Each of these rules could be justified in terms of a more basic set of inference rules which are provably sound.

We employ notation introduced in Chapter 1 with some additions and amendments. 'UQUANT($\phi, \nu_1, \nu_2, \ldots, \nu_n$)' means 'the universal quantification of ϕ with respect to $\nu_1, \nu_2, \ldots, \nu_n$'. Since the ordering of universal quantifiers in front of a formula is truth-conditionally irrelevant, we treat any sentence of the form $\ulcorner Q\nu\ Q\nu' \ldots \phi \urcorner$, where $Q\nu$, $Q\nu'$, etc. are universal quantifiers with respect to the variables ν, ν', etc., for each of the variables ν_i, as the universal quantification of ϕ with respect to ν_i. 'Inst(ϕ, ν, β)' means 'the result of replacing all instances of the free variable ν in ϕ with the singular term β'. We count structural descriptions of object language terms as singular terms. 'EQ(ϕ, ψ)' means 'the biconditional linking ϕ with ψ (in that order)'; 'UEQ (ϕ, ψ, v_1, v_2, ..., v_n)' means 'the universal quantification with respect to v_1, v_2, ..., v_n of the biconditional linking ϕ with ψ (in that order)'. 'S(x)' stands for a sentence containing the grammatical unit x, which may be a word, phrase, or sentence.

Universal Quantifier Instantiation (UI): For any sentence ϕ, variable v, singular term β: Inst(ϕ, v, β) may be inferred from UQUANT(ϕ, v).

Replacement (Rpl): For any sentences ϕ, ψ, S(ϕ): (a) S(ψ) may be inferred from EQ(ϕ, ψ) and S(ϕ); (b) for any formula ϕ with free variables v_1', v_2', ..., v_n', any formula ψ with free variables v_1'', v_2'', ..., v_n'', any sentences S(ϕ): S(ψ) may be inferred from UEQ(ϕ, ψ, v_1, v_2, ..., v_n) and S(ϕ).

Substitution (Sub): $\ulcorner$S(β(S(t)))$\urcorner$ may be inferred from $\ulcorner$S(Ref(S, t, α))$\urcorner$ and $\ulcorner$Ref(S, t, α) = β(S, t)$\urcorner$. (Here, as in the main text, we assume 'S' and 't' to be bound by universal quantifiers taking wide scope.) 'α' denotes an object language referring term; 'β(S, t)' is a metalanguage term that may contain variables 'S' and 't'.

Quantifier Dropping (QD). Provided that ψ contains no free instance of v, from any formula of the form S(for all v, ψ), a formula of the form S(ψ) may be inferred.

For our last inference rule, we will introduce additional terminology. A function quantifier chain is a series of quantifiers with respect to function variables such that (a) the first is a universal quantifier, 'for all functions f', (b) each subsequent one is either of form (i) or (ii),

(i) Qf' such that f' is a v-variant of f are such that
(ii) Qf' such that f' is a v-variant of f and S(f'(v)) are such that,

where 'Q' is replaced by a quantificational determiner (for our current purposes we can give a list, 'every', 'some', 'the', 'few', 'most'), and, in each, 'v' is replaced by a quotation name of an object language variable distinct from each of the others, and S(f'(v)) contains only f' as a free variable, and (c) for each of these, the variable that replaces 'f' is bound by the quantifier immediately to the left of it. For example, 'For all functions f, most f' such that f' is an 'x'-variant of f, and f('x') is a man, are such that every f'' such that f'' is a 'y'-variant of f' is such that'. Consider an (open or closed) sentence consisting of a function quantifier chain consisting of n quantifiers followed by an open sentence of the form

$$S(f^*(v_1), f^*(v_2), \ldots, f^*(v_n)),$$

where $v_1, v_2, \ldots, v_n$ are the object language variables mentioned in order from right to left in the function quantifier chain, and the only free function variable is that represented by 'f^*', and, in the sentence in which it appears, that variable is bound by the quantifier immediately to its left. Call this a *proxy sentence*. We say that a transform of a quantifier of the form (i) is (iii), and of (ii), (iv),

(iii) $Q\, x$ are such that,
(iv) $Q\, x$ such that $S(x)$ are such that,

where 'x' is a place holder for a metalanguage variable. A *replacement* of a proxy sentence is the result of (1) removing the leftmost quantifier, (2) replacing each subsequent quantifier with a transform of it employing a distinct metalanguage variable in the place of 'x', while (3) replacing each of '$f^*(v_1)$', '$f^*(v_2)$', ..., '$f^*(v_n)$' in 'S$(f^*(v_1), f^*(v_2), \ldots, f^*(v_n))$' with the variable used in the transform of the quantifier in which the variable it assigns a value to is mentioned.

Function Elimination (FE). If ϕ is a proxy sentence and ψ a transform of it, S(ψ) may be inferred from S(ϕ).

A word on the justification of this last rule of inference is in order. E1 and E2 together ensure that the domain of functions includes all functions that assign objects to all variables of the object language. Thus, the effect of considering whether Q functions f' such that f' is a v-variant of f are such that S$(f'(v))$ is to consider whether 'S(x)' is satisfied for Q values of 'x'. Similarly, when we consider whether Q functions f' such that f' is a v-variant of f and S$(f'(v))$ are such that S'$(f'(v))$, it is clear that we are in effect considering whether 'S'(x)' is true of Q values of 'x', y, such that S(y). Quantification over functions then, when argument places are occupied by terms denoting what the functions assign to variables, is a proxy for quantifying over the objects assigned to the variables. The effect of chaining the function quantifiers is simply to make each subsequent set of functions we quantify over respect the requirement imposed by previous quantifiers in the chain on other variables.

Appendix B. A Canonical Proof Procedure

A *canonical proof* for TRUTH$_2$ is a finite sequence of sentences of our metalanguage for TRUTH$_2$

(*a*) the last sentence of which is a *T*-form sentence, i.e., a biconditional in which 'is true$_2(S, t)$' is predicated of a structural description of an object language sentence on the left hand side, and the right hand side is a sentence which involves (i) no quantification over functions, and (ii) no semantic vocabulary of the metalanguage (i.e. 'Ref(...)', 'satisfies$_2$(S, t)', 'f(...)'); and

(b) each member of which is either (i) an axiom or (ii) derived from earlier members by *Universal Quantifier Instantiation, Substitution, Replacement, Quantifier Dropping*, or *Function Elimination*.

A *canonical theorem* of TRUTH$_2$ is a canonically provable T-form theorem of TRUTH$_2$. The T-sentences will be all and only the canonical theorems of TRUTH$_2$.

4

Proper Names, Indexicals, and Simple Demonstratives

> To thus accommodate the indexical, or demonstrative, elements in a natural language is to accept a radical conceptual change in the way truth can be defined, as will be appreciated by reflection on how Convention T must be revised to make truth sensitive to context. But the change need not mean a departure from formality.
>
> (Davidson 2001c (1970): 58)

In this chapter, we consider in more detail the treatment of some referring terms in truth-theoretic semantics. We consider briefly some issues that arise in thinking about the correct treatment of proper names, particularly the question whether truth-theoretic semantics can accommodate a Fregean view of proper names, according to which they have a sense as well as a referent, and some connected issues having to do with how competence in the use of certain specialized referring terms such as numerals, '0', '1', '2', etc., function terms, such as '$f(x)$', and complex date names, such as 'December 7, 1941', can be represented in a truth theory. Then we turn to some complications that arise in thinking about reference clauses for demonstratives and indexicals, which we have so far overlooked for the sake of keeping our initial presentation of the framework simple. We take up two additional topics in the subsequent two chapters, the semantics of so-called 'complex demonstratives', which are often, though we will argue wrongly, classified as referring terms, and the semantics of quotation.

1. Proper Names

Our principal thesis in this section is that no particular philosophical theory about how proper names function in natural language will present a difficulty for carrying out the truth-theoretic approach.

Philosophical theories of proper names may be classified along two dimensions. The first is how their referent is determined. The second is what proper names contribute to the propositions expressed by the sentences in which they appear (perhaps relative to an occasion of use).

A proper name may have associated with it as a matter of the conventions of the language a sense, thought of broadly as a semantic property of the name that determines its referent, perhaps relative to the way the world is (for example, a definite description), in a manner analogous to the way in which the sense or meaning of a predicate determines what its extension is, that is, that set of things it is true of.[47] In saying this, we do not intend to restrict what can count as the sense of a proper name, and, in particular, we do not intend to require that the sense of a proper name be expressible as a description or perhaps explicitly in words at all. If an account of proper names holds that proper names (or some category of proper name) have senses so characterized we will call it a sense theory of proper names (or the relevant category of proper name). Alternatively, a proper name may simply be given a referent, with there being no semantic property of it in the language (apart from its having what it does as its referent) that determines its referent. We will call accounts that hold that proper names function in this way (or some category of proper name) direct reference theories of proper names.

Direct reference theories of proper names hold that the contribution the name makes to the proposition expressed by a use of a sentence containing it is simply its referent. The name introduces an object into the proposition, and the proposition is then called a singular proposition and is individuated with respect to the name's referent. On traditional sense theories of proper names understanding of the proposition expressed by a use of a sentence containing such a name requires grasp of the sense of the proper name, and the sense of the proper names figures in the individuation of the proposition as shown by the behavior of the sentence in what have been traditionally called oblique or opaque contexts, such as modal contexts, and the sentential complements of verbs of indirect discourse and propositional attitudes, and following, in

---

[47] The *locus classicus* is Frege's seminal "Über Sinn und Bedeutung" (Frege 1997 (1892)).

particular, 'means(S, t) that'. This is view which Frege (1997 (1892)) took of the role of senses in the proposition expressed by a sentence containing a proper name. However, this is not a necessary feature of a sense theory as we have characterized them. One may hold that a proper name has a semantic property that determines its referent, but that only its referent is introduced into the proposition expressed by a use of a sentence containing it. This would be shown in the fact that the semantic property that determines its referent would not be relevant to the behavior of the sentence in modal or opaque contexts. Intermediate positions would also be possible.[48]

A direct reference theory of proper names presents no difficulty for a truth-theoretic semantics. In a truth theory for a language, the only semantic property assigned to a proper name is a referent. If assigning a referent to the proper name exhausts its semantic content, then a correct truth theory says all that needs to be said about the contribution of proper names to both the truth conditions and meaning of sentences in which they occur.

However, it has been alleged that there is a serious difficulty when we turn to sense theories of proper names, no matter how sense is characterized. A sense theory allows that distinct proper names with the same referent can have different senses. However, since all a truth theory for a language tracks is the referent of the name, it would seem that a truth theory would be neutral between axioms R and R*:

R.   'Samuel Clemens' refers to Samuel Clemens.
R*.   'Samuel Clemens' refers to Mark Twain.

Since Samuel Clemens is Mark Twain, R and R* both correctly assign a referent to 'Samuel Clemens'. However, if 'Mark Twain' and 'Samuel Clemens' differ in sense, and the sense is held to contribute to the proposition expressed by a sentence in which they appear, they cannot be intersubstituted in any sentential contexts while preserving sentential meaning. Thus, a truth theory which incorporates R* rather than R will, relative to the same canonical proof procedure, not assign the same interpretive truth conditions to those theorems we identify as *T*-sentences relative to the proof procedure. Thus, at least one theory must be incorrect.

It should be noted, first of all, that insofar as the truth and meaning theory aim to say what is meant by a use of a sentence, a sense theory that holds that

---

[48] For example, one might hold that some proper names have an associated sense that makes a difference in some contexts but not in others which have traditionally been treated as contexts in which propositions are referred to, eg. in modal contexts but not indirect discourse or attitude contexts, or vice versa.

a proper name contributes only its referent to individuating what is meant by a sentence would not face this difficulty. The difficulty arises only for sense theories that hold that the sense individuates what is meant by a use of a sentence.

However, even in this case, the difficulty is easily resolved. We take our cue from our proposed solution to the original problem of how to ensure that, relative to a canonical proof procedure, a theory generates and identifies correct *T*-sentences: we required that the axioms of the theory be interpretive. Earlier, we focused on what this required for predicates, namely, that satisfaction conditions of predicates use a term or expression which interprets the expression for which it gives satisfaction conditions. This guarantees, relative to an appropriate canonical proof procedure, that the *T*-form sentence provable on its basis will be interpretive. The problem is not different in kind for proper names. Our requirement is simply that the reference axioms for proper names assign referents to names using a name the same in sense as the name for which a referent is being specified.[49] (We anticipated this solution in specifying Convention *S* in the previous chapter.) This will guarantee, relative to the appropriate canonical proof procedure, that provable *T*-form sentences will be interpretive. If we find in a target language a proper name for which there is no name in the metalanguage the same in sense, we must, as in the parallel case of predicates or other parts of speech, introduce into the metalanguage a term the same in sense as the object language term. Thus, we need not say explicitly in the truth theory what the sense of a proper name is, or when two proper names differ in sense, any more than we do in the case of predicates, but rather we display it by using distinct axioms for proper names when they differ in sense, even if they have the same referent.

We need not here take any stand on whether a sense or direct reference theory of proper names is correct. Our view is that, no matter which theory is correct, it can be incorporated into a truth-theoretic semantics, and the success of the program does not depend on the outcome of this debate. The relation between the outcome of this debate about proper names and the success of the truth-theoretic approach to semantics for natural language illustrates, we believe, a relation that holds in general between debates about how particular expressions function in natural languages and possible success for the truth-theoretic approach. The success of the truth-theoretic approach does not depend upon the outcome of the debates about the semantics

---

[49] See Dummett (1973: 227); Evans (1982: 35); McDowell (1977).

of particular expressions. This is as it should be, since the truth-theoretic approach represents itself as a general method for giving meaning theories for natural languages. Insofar as any consistent theory about the semantics of a natural language expression could be true for some expression in some possible language, the truth-theoretic approach should be able to accommodate it.

2. Numerals, Complex Date Names, Function Terms

We turn now to discuss some specialized referring terms, namely, numerals, complex date names, and function terms. For ordinary proper names like 'William Coady' or 'Martha Jane Burk' (a.k.a. 'Calamity Jane'), it is plausible that competence in their use does not require grasp of any particular way of picking out the referent of the name; it suffices for competence that one knows that these are names, and knows what the referents are, at least in the sense that, for some substitution for 'F', one knows, for example, that the referent of 'William Coady' is the F (this may also involve borrowed reference, for example, the description may be 'The person referred to by so and so on such and such an occasion using "William Coady" ', or even 'The person "William Coady" refers to in the usage of whomever I may have originally got it from'). If this is correct, these would be in the terminology of the previous section directly referring terms. This is not so plausible in the case of numerals or complex date names. (We will come to function terms shortly.) Someone who knows only that '1' refers in English to the last object mentioned by Bob would hardly be counted competent in its use in English. Likewise, someone who knows only that 'December 7, 1941' refers to the first day Franklin Delano Roosevelt mentioned in his speech before Congress on December 8, 1941, would not be counted as competent in English.

One response to this would be to treat these terms as forms of definite descriptions, and then to provide standard paraphrases for sentences in which they appear in which they are replaced by appropriate quantified noun phrases. However, it would be preferable to find a way to explain the requirement on competence without treating these expressions as disguised definite descriptions. First, on the face of it, they appear to be singular referring terms. Second, they do not apparently exhibit the sort of scope ambiguities we would expect of quantified noun phrases in English.[50] Third, they cannot

---

[50] This is not entirely uncontroversial. We give here briefly some considerations in favor of denying that date names exhibit the kind of scope phenomena which would be expected of

enter generally into the sort of interactions with other grammatical elements that one would expect of quantified noun phrases. For example, one cannot bind the year position in a date name with a quantifier; there is no provision in English for a sentence such as '*Some year* is such that February 22 *it* is George Washington's birthday'. None of these considerations is decisive, of course, but they do suggest that if we can explain the phenomenon without treating these sorts of terms as disguised descriptions, we will have no reason to so treat them, and this condition can be met by the method we now describe.

We suggest following the treatment. These terms function as referring terms, and contribute to propositions expressed by sentences in which they appear only their referents, but nonetheless they have associated with them, as a matter of their semantic role in the language, a special reference-fixing description. It is in this way that they differ from ordinary proper names, competence in whose use does not require knowledge of any specific reference-fixing description, but only of some reference fixing description for the name. This difference can be represented in the truth theory by giving different reference clauses for the two classes of referring terms. We will call referring terms such as the numerals and complex date names 'description names'.[51] The content of this label, it should be noted, is to be exhausted by

quantified noun phrases, without, however, attempting to survey all the data which bear on the question. Suppose, then, we treat structured temporal designators such as 'December 25, 1941' as semantically equivalent to definite descriptions, e.g. 'the 25th day of the 12th month of the 1,940th year after ϕ', where 'ϕ' is replaced by a term that picks out an anchor time for the date system. For concreteness, let us suppose that 'the birth of Christ' can serve as the anchor description (more accurately, it is 'the year thought to be the year of Christ's birth by Dionysius Exiguus', which picks out a year which is thought to be four or five years after the birth of the historical Christ). The first trouble is that, intuitively, 'Necessarily, the birth of Christ was 1,940 years before December 25, 1941' is false. Christ could have been born earlier or later than he was (recall we are assuming that, as a matter of fact, Christ was born 1,940 years before December 25, 1941). If 'December 25, 1941' were equivalent to 'the 25th day of the 12th month 1,940 years after the birth of Christ', it would be true. But the narrow scope reading of the original (with respect to 'the birth of Christ') is not true. We might rigidify the anchor description, as in 'the time of the actual birth of Christ', but this seems *ad hoc*. (These considerations do not seem to us to be altered by choosing some other substitution for 'ϕ'.)

[51] Evans (1982) introduces a notion of a descriptive name. It is not, however, the same as the notion introduced here. They have in common the idea that it is a matter of convention that the name's referent is fixed by a certain description, and that someone competent in its use knows this and what the reference-fixing description is. However, Evans treats description names as contributing their "sense" to propositions expressed by sentences in which they appear; description names as we use the term contribute only their referent. In addition, Evans's description names can take wide or narrow scope over other elements in a sentence, such as negation. Thus, in effect, Evans's description names function like abbreviations of rigidified definite descriptions.

the facts about them we represent in the reference clauses of the truth theory by providing a description to fix their referents, and our remarking that this represents something competence in the use of the term requires knowledge of. We illustrate this first for the complex date name 'December 7, 1941'.

[1]   For any x, if x is day 7 of the month of December of the year $1,940$[52] years after the year of Christ's birth, then $Ref(S,\ t,\ \text{'December 7, 1941'})=x$.

More generally, we would give the following sort of reference axiom for complex date names.

[2]   For any speaker S, time t, numerals n_1, n_2, month designator M, for any x, if x satisfies $\ulcorner$is day n_1 of the month of M n_2-1 years after the year of Christ's birth$\urcorner$, then $Ref(S, t, \ulcorner n_1 M n_2 \urcorner)=x$.[53]

Let us turn now to the numerals. For purposes of illustration, we will assume a specific set-theoretic interpretation of the numerals. This is, however, only for the purposes of illustration. Nothing in the general approach depends on the particular interpretation we choose. The form of the account would be the same for any interpretation. With this proviso, then, we give the following complex reference clause for the numerals.

[3]   For any numeral n, if
       [a] $n=\text{'0'}$, then the x such that x is the set of all y such that $y \neq y$ is such that $Ref(\text{'}n\text{'})=x$.

---

[52] The anchor year being year 1, 1941 will be 1,940 years after.

[53] We conditionalize on there being a time interval which satisfies the associated description because some date names can fail to have a referent, e.g. 'February 29, 2002'. We treat 'December' as a general noun, and so as contributing a predicate to the description picking out the date; day of the week designators, 'Monday', etc., would be treated similarly. This makes best sense of their use in the nominal restriction of quantified noun phrases like 'Every December' and 'Some Mondays'. For further discussion about date names, see J. King (2001). In connection with vacuous date names, we can mention a potential objection to the claim that date names are directly referring terms. A test of this is whether 'John believes that his birthday is February 29, 2001' has a *literally* true reading, on which John has a false belief. If so, then, since on our account 'February 29, 2001' is a vacuous referring term, either something must be wrong with our account, or we need an account of the semantics of attitude reports that does not require every referring term in the complement to have a referent in order for it to express a proposition. This problem is not, however, specific to date names, since it occurs in the case of a vacuous term such as 'Santa Claus' as well. We face the same puzzle with respect to 'John believes that Santa Claus lives at the North Pole'. In both cases, we would argue that we use a sentence which does not express a proposition as a lazy way to express that John is committed to the truth of the sentence we use in the complement clause. In any case, though, there are no special problems for date names here.

[*b*] *n* = '1', then the *x* such that *x* is the successor of 0 is such that Ref('*n*') = *x*.

. . .

[*k*] *n* ≠ '0', . . . , '9', then for all *j*, if *L*(*n*, *j*), then the *x* such that *x* = SUM(0, *j*, Ref(*n_i*) × 10^i) is such that Ref(*n*) = *x*.

In clause (*k*), '*L*(*n*, *j*)' is read as '*n* is composed of a string of numerals of length *j*', and 'SUM(0, *j*, Ref(*n_i*) × 10^i)' is read as 'the sum of Ref(n_0) × 10 to the 0th power, Ref(n_1) × 10 to the first power, . . . , Ref(n_j) × 10 to the jth power', where n_0 is the rightmost numeral in *n*, n_1 to its left, and so on.

In this way, we can represent in the truth theory the special status that associated descriptions have for certain classes of referring terms, but without treating the referring terms as semantically equivalent to definite descriptions. We accommodate, therefore, both the thought that our understanding of these referring terms involves some descriptive content, and the thought that they function semantically just to introduce their referents into the proposition expressed by a use of a sentence in which they appear.

In terms of our taxonomy of views in the previous section, this is a sense theory of numerals and date names, but one which does not represent the sense as being contributed to the proposition expressed by a use of the sentence containing the name.[54] It is therefore not a Fregean sense theory of these referring terms.

We turn finally to function terms, such as '*f*(*x*)' or '*x* + *y*'. Function terms are typically treated as introducing only their referents into the propositions expressed by uses of sentences containing them, and yet it is clear also that they are systematic referring terms, in the sense that for a given function *f* which has been introduced, we know that each of the terms '*f*(*a*)', '*f*(*b*)', etc., refers to a potentially distinct item, and that it is determined by the function in question, so that, semantically, we understand the referent for terms of this form to be determined by two elements, the designation of the function and the argument term. So to use a function term for reference, we must know what the function is, that is, full competence in the use of the range of referring

---

[54] We put this in terms of talk of propositions expressed by sentences as used, but we can equally put it in terms of what is meant by a use of a sentence, where this need not commit us to propositions (see Ch. 11). The key question is what is required to understand what is meant by a use of a sentence, and sentences with words with different meanings in the broad sense may be used to mean the same thing in use. Thus, 'That is tall' and 'Bob is tall' may be used to mean the same thing in this sense, though they contain subject terms that are not the same in meaning, one being a demonstrative which can be used to refer to different things on different occasions, the other being a proper name which has a fixed referent.

terms requires knowing what function is involved. Evidently, the notion of a description name is made for this class of terms. We give, in illustration, the following reference clause for the functor '$x + y$'. We let 'α_1' and 'α_2' range over both numerals and function terms such as '$f('x')$'. Letting 'α_1', 'α_2' range over function terms allows [4] to be extended to quantification into functors.

[4]   For all α_1, α_2, the x such that x is the sum of Ref(α_1) and Ref(α_2) is such that Ref($\ulcorner \alpha_1 + \alpha_2 \urcorner$)$=x$.

We adopt this account for the use of function terms in our semantic theories as well. Clearly, this allows us also to assign referents to function terms with free variables in their argument places relative to an assignment of values to their variables, and so allows us to make sense of quantifying into what are semantically singular terms.

3. Complex Referring Noun Phrases

Some brief remarks are in order about noun phrases formed using logical connectives, as in 'Bud and Pearl went to the party', 'Sue, Bill, and Helen ate dinner together' and 'Bud or Bill but not Mary purchased lottery tickets'.

There is considerable pressure to treat noun phrases formed using logical connectives in the same way we treat verb phrases so formed, since the same terms appear and seem obviously to have the same basic function. This would recommend giving the following sort of axiom for a sentence such as 'Bud and Pearl went to the party',

[5]   For all functions f, f satisfies(S, t) 'Bud and Pearl went to the party' iff f satisfies(S, t) 'Bud went to the party', and f satisfies(S, t) 'Pearl went to the party'.

That is, we treat the connective as functioning basically as a sentential connective, and the sentence as a kind of abbreviation of a sentence in which the connective is more obviously serving to combine two sentences.

Certain sentences, however, resist treatment in this way. An example is the second sentence mentioned above, 'Sue, Bill, and Helen ate dinner together'. The difficulty lies in handling the adverb 'together'. If Sue, Bill, and Helen ate dinner together, then they all participated jointly in an act of dining. There is evidently no binary relation we can treat 'together' as introducing which would allow us to decompose the sentence into a conjunction of sentences which gets the truth conditions right, as in 'Sue ate dinner with Bill and Bill

107

ate dinner with Helen, and Sue ate dinner with Helen', for this cannot insure that all three were together for dinner. Nor can we plausibly treat 'together' as introducing a predicate which has any particular number of argument places, since it is clear there is no upper bound on the complexity of the subject term it can be used with. One radical solution would be to abandon the attempt to treat 'and' in such sentences as playing the role of a sentential connective, and treat it as a *sui generis* connective for referring terms, and then treat 'ate dinner' and 'together' as applying to plural subjects.[55] Roughly, and this is to anticipate the discussion of adverbs in Chapter 7, we would treat on this account 'Sue, Bill, and Helen ate dinner together' as meaning 'there is an eating of dinner e, and together(e, Sue, Bill, and Helen)'. Here 'together' is treated as a two-place relation, but the second place is occupied by a plural referring term, which refers to a plurality, the number of whose members can vary. On this approach, we would introduce axioms for referring terms like [6].

[6] For any referring terms α, β, Ref($S, t, \ulcorner\alpha$ and $\beta\urcorner$)=Ref(S, t, α) and Ref(S, t, β).

This can be extended to handle quantification into such contexts as well.

We mention this difficulty here and this alternative approach to illustrate how the resources of truth-theoretic semantics can be deployed to represent it. We do not, however, endorse this account of these complex noun phrases. It would be, to our minds, incredible that the connective 'and' functioned differently in noun phrases than in verb phrases. Moreover, it seems clear that 'and' would be special in this regard. Surely we do not want to treat 'Mary or Jane, but not Sue ate dinner at home last night' as involving a reference to a subject *Mary or Jane but not Sue*. Similarly for 'Bill and Sue or Judy ate dinner together last night'. What would it mean to say we are here talking of the plural subject *Bill and Sue or Judy*? In these cases, clearly we want to treat the connective 'or' at least as a sentential connective, but it functions grammatically in the complex noun phrase in the same way as 'and'. Our tentative conclusion is that 'and' in these noun phrases should be represented in the truth theory as a sentential connective. This leaves the problem of how to treat the adverb 'together' (and other similar adverbs and verbs such as 'cooperate'), but we will postpone further discussion of this until after we have discussed in more detail the logical role of adverbs (see Ch. 7).

---

[55] The suggestion to treat such terms as primitive plural referring terms is made in Yi (1999).

4. Indexicals

The term 'indexical' is often used for any referring term whose referent varies from context to context. Each context is thought to have different "indexes," and each different sort of term takes as its value its index for the context. We will use the term in a slightly narrower sense, for those context-sensitive referring terms whose values relative to a context of utterance can be determined strictly by a rule given in terms of features shared in all contexts, such as that there is a speaker of the term and a time at which he speaks. We treat separately demonstratives, whose referents cannot be predicted just from knowledge of features which any contexts must share.

Having said this, it is necessary to remark that there are relatively few basic pure indexicals in natural languages, and perhaps this is not surprising. Standard candidates are 'I' (and its cases), 'today', 'yesterday', 'tomorrow', 'now', and 'here'.[56] In fact there are reasons to think the latter two are not pure indexicals. It is natural to assign reference clauses for 'I', 'now', and 'here' as in [7]–[9].

[7] $\text{Ref}(S, t, \text{'I'}) = S$

[8] $\text{Ref}(S, t, \text{'now'}) = t$

[9]   The x such that x is the place at which S is located at t is such that $\text{Ref}(S, t, \text{'here'}) = x$.[57]

If these clauses are right, then the referent of each of these terms can be determined from features which any context of utterance must share, since each context of utterance will have a speaker and must occur at some time. However, there are uses of both 'now' and 'here' which do not conform to the reference clauses given in [8] and [9].

Thus, while treating 'now' as indexing the time of utterance is standard, it is inadequate for many of its uses. Here are two examples: 'Do it now, not later', 'Now I have a lot more time to do what I am interested in'.[58] Speakers

---

[56] From the basic indexicals complex indexical terms can of course be formed, e.g. 'two days from now', 'my hat', 'three days before yesterday', and so on.

[57] As in Ch. 1, rather than introduce quantification over places, we use speaker and time to fix in a context the referent of 'here'.

[58] In addition, there are uses of 'now' in narratives in which it appears intended to pick out a time which does not overlap with the presumed time of utterance, e.g. 'He finally completed the raft. He could now attempt the passage to the next island.' In the second sentence, 'now' functions as if bound by the temporal quantifier introduced by the past shifted modal 'can'. In this, it would be similar to other terms which have a demonstrative use. The pronouns 'it', 'he',

using such sentences would not intend to be interpreted as referring only to the time of their utterances. Someone who says, 'Do it now, not later', would not be thought to have commanded the impossible. One might insist that we should treat these uses as creating conversational implicatures, but they are so routine we are inclined to suggest that 'now' has a demonstrative as well as an indexical element. While a use of 'now' refers to a time which includes the utterance time, it can also refer to time extending beyond, and perhaps before, it. For example, "Years ago, we spent a week by the ocean every summer. Now we go much less frequently." Arguably, in the second sentence, 'now' is intended to cover an interval that includes some years prior to the time of utterance as well as the time of utterance. To accommodate these uses, we can modify [8] as in [10].

> [10]   For any t_1, (*a*) if t_1 is the interval including t referred to by S at t
> using 'now', Ref(S, t, 'now')$=t_1$; (*b*) if S does not at t intend to refer
> to a time interval including t in using 'now', Ref(S, t, 'now')$=t$.

Clause (*b*) yields the utterance time as the default referent, if the speaker lacks any referential intentions appropriate to extending the interval around the time of utterance.[59]

Some complications arise when we consider sentences such as 'Now you see it, and now you don't' or 'Now is not now'. To handle these we need to keep track in the truth theory, in the time interval in which the sentence as a whole is uttered, of the times of utterance of distinct uses of 'now'. The same problem arises with respect to uses of the same demonstrative more than once in a sentence. A solution to this problem is offered in §6.

In the case of 'here' we find a similar phenomenon. Consider these cases. (i) A speaker says, 'It's raining here at the moment', intending to convey that it is raining in, say, Jacksonville, Florida, where he is located. (ii) A speaker points to an object on the desk and says, 'The paper you were looking for is here'. (iii) A speaker points to a place on a map (which represents a location other than where the speaker is located) and says, 'They arrive here tomorrow; be sure to be there to pick them up.' (iv) Finally, consider the case in which someone asks, 'Where are you?', and someone replies, 'I am here'. It is only

---

'she', 'they', etc., which often function as bound variables, can also be used demonstratively. And the demonstratives 'this' and 'that' can in turn have uses as bound variables.

[59] An alternative is to hold that 'now' is ambiguous between a pure indexical use and an anchored demonstrative use. Unless there are some data which can't be handled on the view that they have a univocal sense, it seems best to avoid postulating an ambiguity.

the last of these cases that conforms to the rule given in [9]. Figuring out what 'here' refers to in the other cases requires some additional knowledge of the context and the speaker's intentions. Case (i) suggests treating 'here' as referring to a location centered around the speaker, in a spatial parallel to the function of 'now', but this obviously does not accommodate cases (ii) and (iii), so it appears that, while there is a default assumption that 'here' picks out a location centered around the speaker, it evidently can also be used in a more purely demonstrative fashion. We will postpone treatment of it, then, until the next section, in which we discuss demonstratives more generally.

Some other pure indexicals are provided by the array of descriptive indexical devices for referring to times or time intervals related specifically to the present, for example, 'today', 'tomorrow', 'tonight', 'yesterday', 'last month', 'next year', and so on. The pattern of treatment can be illustrated with two examples, as in [11] and [12].

[11]   For any times t_1 such that $t_1 =$ the night of t, Ref(S, t, 'tonight')$= t_1$.
[12]   For any times t_1 such that $t_1 =$ the day before t, Ref(S, t, 'yester-day')$= t_1$.

In assigning these reference clauses to temporal indexicals, we treat them as terms that introduce only their referents into propositions expressed by sentences containing them. In T-sentences derived from axioms like [11] and [12], the descriptive material does not contribute to truth conditions. The T-sentence for 'Tonight is the night', instantiated to speaker S' and time t', where t'' is the night of t', would be [13] (we ignore the contribution of tense for the time being, here and throughout this chapter).

[13]   'Tonight is the night' is true(S', t') iff t'' is the night.

Treating descriptive indexicals like these as contributing only their referents to propositions expressed by the use of sentences in which they occur is required because co-referring descriptive indexicals can be interchanged *salva veritate*. We can report your assertion *yesterday* of 'Today is Sunday' by saying *today* that you said that *yesterday* was Sunday (note also the shift in tense: we will discuss tense sequencing in complement clauses in Ch. 10).

This explains why temporal indexicals index to the time of the speaker even when embedded in sentences which otherwise are interpreted relative to a time distinct from the present, as in 'John said that Mary had believed that Bill would be here by now'. Difficulties introduced by such terms led to two-dimensional tense logics (see Kamp 1971). In the truth-conditional approach, we can provide a simple and natural explanation of this behavior by treating such terms as singular referring terms, and assigning them reference axioms which determine referents relative to the time of a speaker's use. This cuts through the difficulties Dowty (1982: see esp. §4.4.5–6) encounters working in another framework.

There are some cases of use of these indexicals in which it appears that they do not refer to the times predicted by the above reference clauses. Consider this passage from *The Two Towers* (Tolkien 1965: 412):

'What's the time? Is it today or tomorrow?'
   'It's tomorrow', said Gollum, 'or this was tomorrow when hobbits went to sleep . . . '
   ' . . . Gollum's come back, Mr. Frodo, and he says it's tomorrow.'

But this is a self-consciously literary effect. The semantically confused question is used to suggest the confusion of the state of mind of the speaker (and we could imagine someone so speaking without having to suppose he is using his language correctly). We have no more difficulty in understanding what is intended here than when someone says 'Show me the way and I will precede'. Again, also for literary effect, we can imagine someone writing,

It had been a long day, and they had made little progress. He thought that tomorrow, surely would be a better day, or the day after, they couldn't go on like this, at any rate.

This exhibits a mixing of direct and indirect reporting: the future modal is past shifted, 'would', but 'tomorrow' is intended to be interpreted relative to the time of the thought, as if we were listening in on the subject's verbal stream of consciousness. This is, though, also a self-consciously literary device, and it would be a mistake to take such experimentation with language for literary effect as a model for the semantics of indexicals such as 'yesterday' and 'tomorrow'. The same effect can be achieved with 'now', and even with simple demonstratives. Flouting usage for effect is a familiar device. When Macbeth says, "Tomorrow and tomorrow and tomorrow creeps in this petty pace from day to day to the last syllable of recorded time, and all our yesterdays have lighted fools the way to dusty death," the literary effect is achieved by the repetition of a word that in each use (assuming midnight does not pass in the middle of the utterance) literally refers to the same day—and pressing into use 'yesterday' as a count noun for effect gives us no more pause than does being told that "life's but a walking shadow," or "a tale told by an idiot," all misuses for effect.

Another sort of case is the use of the historical present, in which we can find uses of 'yesterday', 'today', and 'tomorrow' that pick out times relative to the time of the narrative given in the historical present:

It is July 5, 1685. The Duke of Monmouth gathers today his peasant army in Somerset. Tomorrow the field of Sedgemoor will be sown with its dead.

These cases seem best accommodated as uses of language in which the speaker pretends the past is the present for the sake of a more vivid narrative.

5. Simple Demonstratives

We now return to the discussion in Chapter 5 of demonstratives to consider additional issues that arise in incorporating them into a truth theory which is to serve as a meaning theory for a natural language.[60] Our procedure will be to work through a number of difficulties with an initial simple approach, making changes to accommodate each one of them, until we reach the final form of the account.

We begin with a very simple proposal, namely, that a simple demonstrative can be given a reference clause as illustrated in [14].

[14]   Ref(S, t, 'that')=the object demonstrated[61] by S at t.

It is not an objection to [14] that 'that' does not mean the same as any description, for [14] is simply giving the referent of 'that', and is not represented as providing an interpretation of it. Were we to treat 'that' as synonymous with a description, a recursive clause would be required, since this would be to treat it as a quantifier expression. Nonetheless, there are some difficulties to which the use of the description on the right side of the identity sign in [14] gives rise.

---

[60] Material in this and the next section is drawn from Lepore and Ludwig (2000).

[61] We use 'demonstration' in the sense of 'act of referring'; we do not assume a demonstration must involve a pointing, or be of a salient object in the perceptual environment, or, indeed, be of any object in the present environment. It is quite obvious that one may use a demonstrative to refer to anything one can refer to oneself, and that it need not be an object which is perceptually salient in the environment, nor an object which one is pointing to, or even could in principle point to. We can, e.g. refer to future events using demonstratives, or abstract objects. Consider these possible conversations (the first taking place in 1999): (1) A: That will be the last big party of the millennium. B: What? A: The New Year's eve party on December 31, 2001. (2) A: That's my favorite number. B: What? A: The number I'm thinking of. B: Okay, what number is that? It would be fatuous to claim that A does not succeed in referring with his uses of demonstratives in these exchanges. We can use a pure demonstrative to refer to anything; we can be successful in communicating using a demonstrative if we can get our audience to understand what it is that we are referring to. That is why we so often use demonstratives to refer to salient objects in the environment, or point to objects when using demonstratives, but these features of the typical use of demonstratives are clearly incidental, despite the attention which they have received in the philosophical literature. For some discussion, see Burge (1974: 209) and McGinn (1981: 162).

A first difficulty is that there may be no unique object demonstrated by a speaker at a time, since he may, for example, be demonstrating something in sign language in a conversation with one interlocutor and demonstrating something else in English in a conversation with another. Thus, it looks as if we should relativize the demonstration to the use of the demonstrative, as in [15].

> [15] Ref(S, t, 'that')=the object demonstrated by S at t using 'that'.

But even with this repair we face another problem, namely, that while 'that' is used rigidly, the description on the right-hand side of [15] is not rigid, and this will (potentially) create problems when dealing with sentences in which demonstratives are used in modal contexts. We can repair this by invoking a rigidified description, as in [16].[62]

> [16] Ref(S, t, 'that')=the object *actually* demonstrated by S at t using 'that'.

This solves one problem, but it looks as if another one is that [16] is simply false for most speakers and times, since for most speakers and most times, there is no object the speaker is demonstrating at the time.[63] To avoid this problem, we might appeal to the notion of a speaker's potentially demonstrating an object at a time, as in [17].

> [17] Ref(S, t, 'that')=the x that S potentially demonstrates at t using 'that'.

But [17] is problematic because it is not clear that there is a unique object which a speaker potentially demonstrates at a time. It seems that at any time any speaker might potentially demonstrate any number of objects, this chair, that lamp, those books, and so on. In addition, all of these suggestions will result in non-interpretive T-theorems. This is because for a sentence form like 'That is F', taking [17] as our input axiom for the demonstrative, we

---

[62] See Neale (1993: 108).

[63] We are assuming here and throughout our discussion a quantificational analysis of definite descriptions. Although this informs our discussion, it will become clear that it plays no essential role in motivating the final account we reach. Even if we adopted a Fregean view of definite descriptions, we would encounter the difficulty mentioned in connection with [17] of generating non-interpretive T-sentences. And where we assume, in making proposals, that the definite description is quantificational, one can focus on the formal representations, which are explicitly quantificational, for the purposes of the discussion and argument. For the case *for* Russell's analysis of definite descriptions as quantificational, see Neale (1990*a*).

will derive a *T*-form sentence of the form [18] (assuming the object language embedded in the metalanguage).

[18]   'That is *F*' is true(*S*, *t*) iff the object potentially demonstrated by *S* at *t* using 'that' is *F*.

However, since there is no definite description in 'That is *F*', but there is one on the right-hand side of [17], it fails to meet Davidson's Convention *T*. A consequence of this is that, when no object is demonstrated, 'That is *F*' turns out to be false according to [17], rather than, as it should be, without truth value.

To solve these problems, we need to conditionalize on a speaker's demonstrating an object at a time in giving a reference clause for demonstratives.[64] This is illustrated in [19].

[19]   For any object *x*, if *S* demonstrates *x* at *t* using 'that', then Ref(*S*, *t*, 'that')=*x*.

The cost, though a necessary one, is that we cannot discharge the appearances of 'Ref(*S*, *t*, 'that')' in our *T*-theorems until we can discharge the antecedent of [19]. But this simply reflects the fact that demonstratives have a referent only when used successfully in a speech act.

[19] is still not adequate. It will not yield the right results *if* a speaker performs more than one demonstrative act at the same time in two speech acts using the same token demonstrative in each to refer to different things. This could happen if a speaker performed ambiguously two speech acts using a single demonstrative sentence. One might, for example, point with one hand to a book, and with another to a chair, looking at two people, one closer to the book, the other closer to the chair, and say 'Bring me that', intending each to understand one to be directing a different order to him than the other, involving a different demonstrated object. To accommodate this possibility, we must conditionalize on speech acts, and relativize the reference relation to speakers, times, and speech acts, as in [20].

[20]   For all speech acts *u*, and objects *x*, if *s* demonstrates *x* at *t* using 'that' in *u*, then Ref(*S*, *t*, *u*, 'that')=*x*.

To say that "*s* demonstrates *x* at *t* using 'that' in *u*" is to say that "*s* uses 'that' in his performance of speech act *u* to demonstrate *x*". This means

---

[64] Without explaining the reasons why, this is what we did in Ch. 1.

also that satisfaction clauses for sentences with demonstratives must quantify over speech acts, as, for example, in [21]. T-theorems likewise must then be relativized to speech acts employing sentences.

[21]   For all functions f, speech acts u employing 'That is thin', f satisfies(S, t, u) 'That is thin' iff Ref(S, t, u, 'that') is thin.

Here 'satisfies(S, t, u)' is understood as 'satisfies understood relative to S at t as used in u'. Henceforth, for convenience, we will often drop the explicit quantifier over speech acts using sentences, and assume a convention similar to that we have adopted for 'S' and 't', with this difference: that the quantifier over speech acts is to be understood to restrict the speech act to an utterance of the sentence or formula, or a sentence constructed from it, for which satisfaction conditions are being given. Thus, we would abbreviate [21] as

For all functions f, f satisfies(S, t, u) 'That is thin' iff Ref(S, t, u, 'that') is thin.

The relativization to speech acts is needed to associate with the sentence for which satisfaction conditions are being given, and, indeed, its utterance, the appropriate referent for the demonstrative it contains. The satisfaction predicate too must be relativized to the speech act because if the same sentence is used to perform two speech acts at the same time with different truth conditions, what must be evaluated is not the sentence as uttered at that time, since there is only one, but what differs in content, which is the speech act. [20] will assign a referent to 'that' only when speaker S uses 'that' in a speech act u to demonstrate an object. A consequence is that the truth theory will issue in T-sentences for sentences containing demonstratives only when we can marshal information about the use of sentences in speech acts to assign a referent to the demonstrative as used by a speaker at a time in accordance with [20]. This shows that, for sentences with demonstratives, truth conditions can be assigned only relative to a speaker's use of the sentence in a particular speech act. There is, then, a sense in which the ultimate bearer of truth and falsity for such sentences must be seen as the speech act in which the sentence is used. In relativizing the satisfaction predicate to a speech act, in addition to speaker and time, we must also relativize our truth predicate to a speech act.

A brief aside is in order on the topic of the interpretation of inscriptions. In the above discussion, we have taken verbal speech acts as our model. The interpretation of inscriptions introduces some additional complications. Signs, for example, are intended to be interpreted relative to the context in which they are read, rather than the context in which they are written or posted. A sign posted on the lawn saying 'Keep off the grass' is interpreted relative to the time at which it is read, rather than the time at which the sign was posted, or the instruction would not prohibit the person reading it from walking on the grass. A bumper sticker which says 'If you can read this, you are too close to my car', provided it is read while on the road, is interpreted relative to the time at which it is read, and who 'you', and even 'my', picks out, can differ depending on features of the context of its reading. This phenomena can occur with pure demonstratives as well. A school teacher who puts a sign above her door that says 'This is the first day of the rest of your life' intends each person who reads it, on each occasion on which that person reads it, to interpret 'this' to refer to the day of that occasion of reading. Similarly in instruction manuals and in many other contexts. It seems clear that, in these cases, the intention in posting the sign, or writing the instruction, and so on, in anticipation that it will be read later, is that each person reading it should interpret it as if spoken (by the original author or perhaps by some contextually salient person) on that occasion. Thus, the semantics given here may be straightforwardly applied to yield the intended interpretation, even though no new speech act has been performed.

Before we bring this initial section to a close, there are two more matters we should make brief mention of.

The first is the difference in the conventional use of 'this' and 'that'. Though both are demonstratives used to denote something relative to a context, one will typically use 'this' when the object to be denoted is near or under immediate observation, and use 'that' otherwise. The question is whether, and if so how, to incorporate this difference in use into a truth theory that is to serve as a meaning theory. Our response to this is that this difference in usage should not be written into the truth theory, since a stand-alone use of 'this' can refer to anything. This difference in conventional usage can be flouted without failure of reference, and so it should be treated as not relevant to what is traditionally thought of as propositional meaning. In this respect, it may be treated as analogous to the difference between 'and' and 'but'.

The second is the question of how to extend the treatment above of singular pronouns and demonstratives to *plural* pronouns and demonstratives. The extension is straightforward. While plural referring terms like 'they', 'those', 'these', 'we', and 'you', used in the plural, raise puzzles about what is being referred to, they do not present a special problem for an interpretive truth theory. To give reference clauses for them, we employ *plural variables*, as opposed to singular variables. In natural languages, the plural pronouns do the work of plural variables: *the girls* liked the boys *they* met at the dance. Thus, for example, for 'they', used as a demonstrative pronoun, we can give the following reference clause: for all speech acts u, for all x's, if S demonstrates x's at t using 'they' in u, then $\text{Ref}(S, t, u, \text{'they'}) = x$'s. The case of 'we' is of special interest because it involves both an indexical and a demonstrative component. Someone who uses 'we' includes himself in the group he talks about, but who else is in the group is determined by his intentions in the context. In this case, we can give the axiom: for all speech acts u, for all x's, y's, if S indicates x's at t using 'we' in u and each of the x's is one of the y's and S is one of the y's and nothing else is one of the y's, then $\text{Ref}(S, t, u, \text{'they'}) = y$'s.

6. Multiple Demonstratives

We now turn to a different problem for incorporating demonstratives into a truth-theoretic semantics. The problem becomes apparent as soon as we consider sentences with two or more tokens of the same demonstrative type. Thus, consider [22] and [23].

[22]   That is next to that.
[23]   That is tall and that is thin.

The trouble is that in evaluating the reference clause for each demonstrative in [22] and [23], it looks as if we will evaluate them with respect to the same time. But we know that any use of [22] or [23] will involve two demonstrations using 'that', not one. So it looks as if the antecedent of our reference clause will never be satisfied, since it will require a unique demonstration by the speaker at the time of utterance using 'that'.

One solution is to give the truth theory not for English but for a language, say, English*, with indexes for demonstratives which syntactically individuate them, so that one can track the different demonstrations by attaching them to different demonstratives.[65] This is similar to the regimentation of English sentences necessary to handle scope ambiguity. The satisfaction clauses for

---

[65] Most formal treatments of multiple demonstratives have resorted to subscripting the demonstratives in a formal representation. See e.g., Burge (1974); Kaplan (1989: 587); Larson and Segal (1995: 203); Lewis (1975*b*: appendix).

[22] and [23] could then be given as in [24] and [25], respectively. We would then give [26] as the reference axiom for English*.

[24] For all functions f, f satisfies*(S, t, u) 'That$_1$ is next to that$_2$' iff Ref*$(S, t, u,$ 'that$_1$') is next to Ref*$(S, t, u,$ 'that$_2$').

[25] For all functions f, f satisfies*(S, t, u) 'That$_1$ is tall and that$_2$ is thin' iff f satisfies*(S, t, u) 'That$_1$ is tall' and f satisfies*(S, t, u) 'That$_2$ is thin'.

[26] For all numerals i, objects x, if S demonstrates x in u at t using $\ulcorner$that$_i\urcorner$, then Ref*$(S, t, u, \ulcorner$that$_i\urcorner) = x$.

However, there are two problems with this approach. First, it gives a semantics for sentences containing multiple demonstratives by mapping them onto sentences in a regimented language for which we can give a semantics. This should be avoided if we can find a way to give the semantics for these sentences directly. For the sentences are not ambiguous, and English speakers do not use any syntactic differences between different appearances of demonstratives in understanding sentences containing them other than where they appear. An approach which hewed closer to the surface syntax of English would also hew more closely to how we actually are able to understand them. The second objection is that the antecedent of [26] is false for English speakers at all times, since they do not utter sentences containing demonstratives with numerical subscripts.

This last difficulty might be avoided with some additional maneuvering. In particular, in our reference axiom, we might conditionalize not on a use of a subscripted demonstrative, but rather on the use of an unsubscripted demonstrative occurring in a certain order in the utterance, which corresponds with a subscript on a demonstrative in our regimented language. The suggestion is spelled out in [27].

[27] For all numerals i, speech acts u, objects x, if S demonstrates x at t with a use of 'that' in u which is the ith use of 'that' in u, then Ref*$(S, t, u, \ulcorner$that$_i\urcorner) = x$.

The regimented language would have to have rules of formation that guaranteed that subscripted demonstratives appeared in the sentence in strict order: 'that$_1$', 'that$_2$', and so on. The reference clause would then provide the right referent assignments for the subscripted demonstratives. We will, however, in the end suggest a different approach which keeps track of uses of 'that' by the order in which they are uttered in a containing utterance.

An approach sometimes adopted[66] is to relativize satisfaction and truth to sequences of demonstrata. Let 'σ' be a variable ranging over sequences of (potential) demonstrata, and let 'σ_1' denote the first member of σ, 'σ_2' denote the second member of σ, and so on. Relativizing satisfaction to a sequence, we can give satisfaction conditions for a sentence such as 'That is next to that' as in [28].

> [28] For all functions f, sequences σ, f satisfies(S, t, σ) 'That is next to that' iff σ_1 is next to σ_2.

This will yield T-theorems of the form [29].

> [29] For all sequences σ, 'That is next to that' is true(S, t, σ) iff σ_1 is next to σ_2.

However, [29] has the undesirable feature of not determining when a speaker has uttered a true sentence with a demonstrative. To connect [28] and [29] with speakers' utterances of sentences, we need something like [30].

> [30] For all sequences σ, if u is a speech act by S at t of 'that is next to that', and the first x S demonstrates at t in u using 'that' is σ_1, and the second xS demonstrates at t in u using 'that' is σ_2, then 'That is next to that' is true(S, t, u) iff 'That is next to that' is true (S, t, σ).

In light of this, it seems preferable to skip introduction of sequences of demonstrata, and make use directly of information about the ordering of uses of demonstratives in sentences in assigning satisfaction conditions to sentences containing multiple demonstratives.

We propose then to track the different uses of demonstratives in a sentence with multiple demonstratives by using information available to speakers when they actually interpret sentences with multiple demonstratives, in particular, that the demonstratives are uttered at different times, and therefore ordered in time. (This is true of course also of speech acts that produce inscriptions, though in their case there is also the spatial ordering which can be exploited.)[67] This requires only a minor modification of the satisfaction conditions for [22] and [23]. Intuitively, what we want is to relativize employment of the reference

---

[66] For example, Taylor (1980) and Larson and Segal (1995). See also Lewis (1975*b*: appendix), for a general discussion of the indices approach to handling context sensitivity.

[67] Another approach which relies on ordering can be found in Lepore and Ludwig (2000*a* n. 38).

clauses for each demonstrative that occurs in a sentence to a different time. But of course the times must be related appropriately to the time interval during which the sentence is uttered, that is, in evaluating a sentence relative to a speaker and time of utterance t, which contains more than one demonstrative expression, we wish to evaluate the demonstratives relative to different times within the interval during which the sentence is uttered, and in the order in which they are uttered. For this purpose, let us define a (family of) predicate(s) '$\Delta(\dots)$' as follows.[68]

Def. $\Delta(t, t_1, \ldots, t_n, \xi, \xi_1, \ldots, \xi_n, S, u)$ iff $t_1 < t_2 < \ldots t_n$ and $t_1, \ldots,$ t_n occur in t, and $\xi, \xi_1, \ldots, \xi_n$ are uttered by S at $t, t_1, \ldots, t_n$, respectively, in performing u.

Here 't', 't_1', etc. are variables taking on time intervals as values, '$<$' represents 'is (strictly) before', 'ξ', 'ξ_1', etc., are variables taking on expressions as values, and 'S' is restricted to speakers, and 'u' to speech acts.

We now add quantifiers over as many subintervals of time as needed for the number of subexpressions in an expression that we need to keep track of, and restrict them using 'Δ'. This leads to the revision of our satisfaction axioms as in [31] and [32], making here fully explicit all the quantifiers needed.

[31] For all speakers S, functions f, speech acts u, times t, t_1, t_2 such that $\Delta(t, t_1, t_2,$ 'That is next to that', 'that', 'that', $S, u)$, f satisfies(S, t, u) 'That is next to that' iff Ref$(S, t_1, u,$ 'that') is next to Ref$(S, t_2, u,$ 'that').

[32] For all functions f, times t_1, t_2, such that $\Delta(t, t_1, t_2,$ 'That is tall and that is thin', 'That is tall', 'That is thin', $S, u)$, f satisfies(S, t, u) 'That is tall and that is thin' iff f satisfies(S, t_1, u) 'That is tall' and f satisfies(S, t_2, u) 'That is thin'.

Clearly, this strategy can be generalized to predicates with an arbitrary (but finite) number of places, and to other recursive sentential connectives. By evaluating each appearance of 'that' in a sentence at a different time, we avoid the difficulties reviewed above.[69] Again, we can introduce abbreviatory conventions, rewriting [31] and [32] as [33] and [34], respectively.

---

[68] This represents a change from the treatment given in Lepore and Ludwig (2000), which did not restrict the times to times of utterances of the subformulas by the speaker in the speech act. These further restrictions are needed, however, in the case of molecular sentences, to ensure the axioms do not have false instances.

[69] An alternative approach to giving truth theories for natural languages, as we mentioned in Ch. 1, is to give them not for sentences using a truth predicate relativized to speakers and times (minimally), but to give them for utterances, or, more properly, as we now see, speech acts. This

[33] For all functions f, f satisfies(S, t, u) 'That is next to that' iff Ref$(S, t_1, u,$ 'that') is next to Ref$(S, t_2, u,$ 'that').

[34] For all functions f, f satisfies(S, t, u) 'That is tall and that is thin' iff f satisfies(S, t_1, u) 'That is tall' and f satisfies(S, t_2, u) 'That is thin'.

It is clear that the treatment we have given for dealing with multiple demonstratives extends straightforwardly to other demonstrative terms, as in two or more uses of, for example, 'you' in the same sentence that refer to different persons ('I want you and you to work together'; 'I want you to work with me and I want you to work with me'). This proposal also solves the problem presented by sentences such as 'Now is not now', and 'Now you see it and now you don't', and even, once we take into account tense explicitly, 'You see it and you don't see it'.

The relativization to speech acts introduces some complications in the project of giving truth conditions for natural language sentences in a regimented language which introduces variables, and otherwise cleans up the original to make it more amenable to formal treatment. The difficulty is that, in the theory for the regimented language, the speech act variable will be restricted to utterances of the sentences and subsentential expressions of the regimented language, rather than the language for which it is a regimentation. And the speakers of the unregimented language do not use those expressions. For any speech act u in a language L for which there is a regimented language L^R, there will be a correspondence between the sentence used to perform u, and its components, and the sentence in L^R, which is its regimentation, for the purposes of giving truth conditions for the original sentence as used in u. Let us represent this generally as '$C(u, e, e')$' where e is an expression used in performing u and e' is what corresponds to it. We can then handle the case in which we are giving truth conditions in a regimented language by redefining '$\Delta(\ldots)$' as follows. 'Def. $\Delta(t, t_1, \ldots, t_n, \xi, \xi_1, \ldots, \xi_n, S, u)$ iff $t_1 < t_2 < \ldots t_n$ and $t_1, \ldots, t_n$ occur in t, and there are $e, e_1, \ldots, e_n$ such that $e, e_1, \ldots, e_n$ are uttered by S at $t, t_1, \ldots, t_n$, respectively, in performing u and $C(u, e, \xi)$, $C(u, e_1, \xi_1)$, $\ldots$, $C(u, e_n, \xi_n)$.' The satisfaction relation now needs some additional explanation, since it relates a speaker and time and speech act to a sentence or sentence component which is not part of the sentence used in the speech act. But the idea is relatively straightforward. A function, f, satisfies a regimentation of a sentence component, ϕ, relative to a speaker

---

has some advantages, especially in light of the fact that we must in any case conditionalize on speech acts to accommodate demonstratives properly.

and time and speech act, iff (i) if ϕ is an atomic formula, then what f assigns to its free variables are such that the component to which ϕ corresponds expresses a predicate true of those objects in corresponding argument places, and terms are interpreted otherwise as they would be in the original; (ii) if it is a conjunction, then it satisfies each conjunct, etc.

5

Complex Demonstratives[70]

We have treated simple demonstratives as if they always function like rigid singular terms whose referents are determined only relative to contexts. However, unlike proper names, demonstratives can combine with nominals to form complex noun phrases.[71] In this respect, they behave like restricted quantifiers. Following the literature, we will call expressions of the form 'That F' complex demonstratives, though in the end it will emerge that this traditional terminology is misleading.[72] Our question in this chapter is how to accommodate such cases within a truth theory satisfying Davidson's Convention T.

The matter is not as simple as it might at first seem. Complex demonstratives have received considerable attention from philosophers recently. There are two main camps into which treatments of complex demonstratives fall. The first consists of those treatments which take complex demonstratives to be themselves simply referring terms. This is the majority view. These views can be classified on the basis of whether they take the nominal (1) to contribute to the truth conditions of the containing sentence but not to constrain the referent, (2) to constrain the referent of the complex demonstrative but to contribute nothing to the truth conditions of the containing sentence, (3) both to constrain the referent and to contribute to the truth conditions of the containing sentence, or (4) to contribute nothing either to fixing the referent of the complex demonstrative, or to the truth conditions of the containing

---

[70] This chapter is based on material in Lepore and Ludwig (2000).

[71] However, this does not include what we can call specialized demonstratives, demonstrative uses of the personal pronouns, 'you', 'he', 'she', 'it', 'they', etc., and demonstratives of time and place, 'then' and 'there'. We discuss these in the last section of this chapter.

[72] We will be discussing 'that' for the most part, but it will be clear that our remarks extend straightforwardly to 'this', 'those', 'these', etc.

sentence. Larson and Segal (1995) argue for the weakest alternative, (4). Likewise, Schiffer (1981: 73–4, 79–80) and Perry (1997) hold that complex demonstratives are singular terms which can contribute *only* their referents to the propositions expressed by uses of sentences in which they occur. On this view, the nominal '*F*' in 'that *F*' plays only a pragmatic role in bringing our attention to what the speaker is demonstrating with his use of 'that', an object which may still be picked out, even if the nominal fails to apply to it. In contrast, Kaplan (1989: 515) defends alternative (2), arguing that 'that *F*' contributes *no* object to the proposition expressed by a sentence of the form 'That *F* is *G*' *unless* its referent is *F*. On Kaplan's view, in uttering 'That man is a thief', if the object one tries to demonstrate with an utterance of 'that' is not a man, nothing is demonstrated. On this account, the complex demonstrative in use functions rather like a picture with an arrow attached to it; the picture filters out objects other than those that fit it in the direction the arrow points. McGinn (1981: 162), Peacocke (1981: 201), Davies (1982), Braun (1994: 209–10), Recanati (1993: 13 nn. 16,17, and 19), Borg (1999), and Higginbotham (1988, 2002) likewise adopt a view according to which the contribution of the nominal in 'That *F* is *G*' is to restrict which object 'is *G*' is evaluated with respect to. All these authors agree that the nominal in a complex demonstrative contributes nothing to the truth conditions of sentences in which it occurs. In contrast, Richard (1993) argues that, in addition to restricting what can be the referent, the nominal contributes to the truth conditions of sentences containing the complex demonstrative; in particular, the sentence 'That *F* is *G*' cannot be true unless the referent of the demonstrative is *F*, and is false if the referent is not. In effect, Richard is defending (3). So, (2)–(4) are occupied by some philosopher or other. Our own position does not fit neatly into this taxonomy, though it is closest to (1). The reason our position does not properly fall into this taxonomy is that we challenge the assumption that complex demonstratives should be treated as a unit which is a referring term.

The second camp consists of views according to which complex demonstratives are not singular terms at all but quantifier expressions. Views in this camp also usually hold that simple demonstratives, despite appearances, are quantifiers. The basis for this position is that complex demonstratives also exhibit many features more usually associated with quantified noun phrases, such as 'All philosophers', 'The king of France', and 'Someone in the rain'. Since it is difficult to see how to accommodate these features, if complex demonstratives are referring terms, some authors have been led to treat all demonstrative expressions as quantifiers in order to provide a unified account of both their simple and complex forms.

Taylor (1980), for example, endorses this view, basing his position largely on data provided by complex demonstratives, data we will review below. Barwise and Cooper (1981: 177, 184) suggest that all noun phrases are generalized quantifiers, including demonstrative constructions. More recently, Neale (1993: §9) has suggested that all *complex* noun phrases should be treated as quantificational, and that demonstratives in particular might be treated as equivalent to a certain sort of rigidified definite descriptions, in order to bring complex demonstratives into conformity with this thesis. (Davidson (2001*c* (1967): 34) may be construed as anticipating a quantificational treatment similar to Neale's.) Another recent suggestion along these lines, rather different from Neale's, is made in King (2001). We will discuss below some objections King has made to the account we give in this chapter.

The position of this chapter is that both camps have correct insights into the semantics of complex demonstratives, but each fails through failing to accommodate the insights of the other. The position we advance treats demonstratives as referring terms wherever they appear, but treats complex demonstratives, compatibly with this, as quantified noun phrases.

1. Evidence that Complex Demonstratives are Quantified Noun Phrases

We approach the problem by first considering what reasons there are to hold that complex demonstratives are quantified noun phrases. When we see the limits of the analogy with quantifier expressions, we will also be in a position to see what the correct account must be.

One of the most striking analogies between the demonstratives 'this', 'that', 'these', and 'those, and quantifier words is that they are *determiners*. Like quantifier words, and unlike other deictic terms and indexicals[73] such as 'I',

---

[73] The genitive case for both names and indexicals are exceptions to this rule, e.g. 'My hat', 'Mary's dog', etc., as well as numerical quantifiers, such as 'Three men'. We return to these constructions below. There are also some *apparent* exceptions to the rule barring the use of personal pronouns with nominals to form noun phrases, e.g. 'You children had better behave', 'We leaders of the senate have an obligation to see this bill passed', 'Everyone asks us philosophers what we do for a living'. However, these seem rather to be cases of nouns used in apposition, and not uses of them to form complex noun phrases with the personal pronouns. In any case, if these were to be treated as complex noun phrases, the account we give of complex demonstratives could be easily extended to them.

'he', 'she', 'now', 'there', etc., demonstratives combine with nominals to form complex noun phrases.[74] Thus, compare [1]–[3].

[1] Some professor bored us stiff. Quantifier word+nominal=>
       noun phrase
[2] That professor bored us stiff. Demonstrative+nominal=>
       noun phrase
[3] *John professor bored us stiff. Name+nominal≠>noun phrase

[3] is ill-formed, whereas [1] and [2] are not. A natural hypothesis for why this is so is that [2] is an instance of the same rule that leads to [1], that is, demonstratives are quantifier words and complex demonstratives are quantified noun phrases.[75]

The appeal of this hypothesis is increased by the observation that the nominal in a complex demonstrative does not appear to be semantically inert. Thus, if a determiner has existential import, as with 'some', 'few', 'the' (represented as 'Det₃'), then instances of the following inference schemas are semantically valid:

$Det_3 F$ is/are G $Det_3 F$ is/are G
So, some F is G So, something is F and G

This suggests that demonstrative determiners are quantifier words with existential import, since the inference schemata hold for them as well.

Furthermore, sentences such as [4]–[7] do not strike us as ill-formed, and it is easy enough to imagine appropriate contexts of utterance.

[4] *Someone* loathes that man to *his* right.[76]
[5] *The man in the white hat* hates that man addressing *him*.
[6] *Each woman in this room* admires that man whom *she* sees at the podium.
[7] *All of the students* hated that professor who flunked *them*.

It might be thought that in [6] 'whom she sees at the podium' is a non-restrictive relative clause but there is clearly a restrictive reading, and, in any

---

[74] It is largely this feature of demonstratives that lead Barwise and Cooper (1981) and Neale (1993) to suggest treating demonstrative expressions as quantifiers.

[75] Johnson and Lepore (2002).

[76] Adapted from an example of Taylor (1980: 195). Higginbotham (1988: 47 n. 4) says that sentences like [4] are ungrammatical, and tries to explain away the intuition as confusing a referential use of 'someone' with a quantificational use. We do not see how one could insist on this, except in the light of a theory which requires it. In any case, one could intelligibly add to [4], 'But I'm not going to say who he, or they, may be'.

case, we may modify the example slightly. Suppose we are at a bigamist convention, and each woman in the room is married to each of several men at the podium. One person remarks to another, pointing to one of the men, 'Each woman in this room admires that husband of *hers*', and, pointing to the other, 'Each woman in this room loathes that husband of *hers*'. Here 'of hers' is clearly syntactically part of the restricting nominal. Likewise, in the case of [7], we may modify the example to 'All of the students hated that professor of his who flunked him', where we may imagine that they were all in fact flunked by several of the same professors, only one of whom all of them hate, and the speaker points to the one in question.

These data are all perfectly ordinary; each case involves a pronoun in the complex demonstrative being bound by the quantifier. In this respect, complex demonstratives exhibit important similarities to quantified noun phrases. Compare [4] with [8].

[8]   Someone loathes a man to his right.

The suggestion that demonstratives are quantifier words, and that complex demonstratives are quantified noun phrases provides a ready explanation of the intelligibility of [4]–[7].[77]

In addition, pronouns outside the complex demonstrative can be anaphoric on quantifier phrases inside the nominal of a complex demonstrative, as illustrated in [9].

[9]   That shark that took a swimmer off Flager beach last summer attacked him inside the sandbar.

In [9], 'a swimmer off Flager beach last summer', which is a part of the nominal of the complex demonstrative, controls the pronoun 'him' in the predicate.

---

[77] We do not claim that these considerations about quantifying into the nominals of complex demonstratives rule out their being referring terms, but only that this together with other similarities to quantified noun phrases suggest they should be treated semantically as in the same category. In Ch. 4, §2, we showed how to treat function terms as directly referring terms, which allow quantification into them. One could offer a similar account of complex demonstrative, treating them as assigned referents when a free variables appears in them relative to an assignment of values to variables. For example, for any nominal N, for any function f, for any speaker s and time t, for any x, if x satisfies N relative to f and x is the object demonstrated by s at t, then $\text{ref}(\text{'that'}^{\frown}N, s, t, f) = x$. However, this proposal does not meet all of the desiderata we assemble for a correct account of complex demonstratives. For example, it will not explain the contribution of the nominal to the truth conditions of sentences containing the complex demonstrative, and will not explain the scope ambiguities which complex demonstratives generate, but function terms do not.

128

Clearly, we ordinarily associate these features with restricted quantifiers, as in [10] and [11].

[10]   *Every man who has a son* loves *him*.

[11]   *The woman standing beside a bus* is going to board *it*.

We would have an explanation of these phenomena if 'that' were a quantifier word.

These analogies between complex demonstratives and restricted quantifiers cast doubt on the traditional view that demonstratives are context-sensitive referring terms. In view of their grammatical role as determiners, it is not implausible that demonstratives are context-sensitive quantifier words, and not context-sensitive referring terms. But, then, it should be possible to provide a semantic treatment for demonstratives parallel to that for restricted quantifiers.

2. Demonstratives as Quantifiers

We take 'that' as a representative of the demonstrative determiners. A first approach would be to treat 'that' as a quantifier word just by reusing it in the metalanguage in giving satisfaction conditions. However, since our metalanguage must be context-insensitive, and 'that', even if a quantifier word, clearly is not, this approach fails. Instead, we take up the suggestion that it can be treated as equivalent to a kind of specialized context-sensitive definite description.

The most natural suggestion is to treat 'that' as equivalent (semantically) to 'the object actually now demonstrated by me',[78] so that a sentence such as 'That is thin' would be treated as semantically equivalent to 'The object actually now demonstrated by me is thin'. This ensures that the definite description has intuitively the right denotation when a speaker uses a demonstrative successfully, i.e., the object the speaker then demonstrates.

This proposal has the virtue of clearly delivering the right truth values for sentences in which simple and complex demonstratives are successfully used. This is not surprising since the description chosen to paraphrase the demonstrative was designed to pick out its referent when used successfully.

---

[78] For variants of this approach, see Davidson (2001c (1967): 34); Neale (1993: 107–9); Taylor (1980). 'Actually' is inserted into the predicate in order to rigidify the description, so as to accommodate sentences in which demonstratives are embedded in the scope of modal operators, e.g. 'Necessarily, that is greater than 7'.

But this is not enough for it to deliver the right semantic account of demonstrative expressions, for their semantic properties differ in several important ways from the proposed paraphrases. This can be illustrated in a number of ways. The key to understanding these objections is to recognize that this account is asking us to take seriously the idea that a language like English which has demonstrative expressions can be paraphrased in a language without demonstrative expressions. This (i) renders the account unable to accommodate vacuous uses of demonstratives, (ii) saddles our uses of sentences containing demonstratives with scope readings they do not have, and (iii) saddles our uses of sentences containing demonstratives with entailments they do not have.

(i) A referring term is vacuous when it does not have a referent, and, in consequence, an utterance of a sentence containing a vacuous term fails to have a truth value. Suppose that Macbeth, hallucinating and pointing to the empty air before him, had asserted [12].

[12]   This is a dagger I see before me.

Intuitively, Macbeth would fail to secure any object for him to go on to say something about. He has not said something false, as the description paraphrase approach would require, but has failed to say anything true or false at all. The culprit is Macbeth's use of 'this', to which no referent can be assigned. This point extends to the description paraphrase approach to complex demonstratives. Someone who gestures to his right saying, 'That philosopher is a gymnosophist', when nothing is to his right, has not said something false, but has failed to say anything at all. The description paraphrase approach would require him to have said something false about *himself.* But this is just as counterintuitive as in the case of simple demonstratives.

Since quantifiers, in contrast to referring terms, do not have vacuous uses, every quantified sentence, other linguistic infelicities aside, such as vagueness or incidental demonstratives elsewhere in the sentence, has a truth value. Quantifiers do not themselves involve any reference to individuals, so we can say all sorts of things using them without having any particular things in mind. This is in large part where their utility lies.

(ii) 'That' does not permit the same scope ambiguities as its alleged paraphrase. [13], for example, has only one reading, whereas replacing the demonstrative 'that' with 'the object now demonstrated by me' in [13] allows the non-equivalent readings [14] and [15].

[13]   John believes that that is thin.

[14]   John believes [the object now demonstrated by me is thin].

[15]   The object now demonstrated by me is such that [John believes it is thin].

In addition, if an utterance of [13] is true at t, it follows that something at t is such that John believes it to be thin. In contrast, [14] could be true even if, on the occasion on which someone uses it, he fails to demonstrate any object.[79]

Neale (1993) has suggested that such scope data could be explained on the assumption that 'that', construed as a definite description, always takes wide scope (see also Schiffer 1981: 58 for a similar suggestion). What is right is that *if* 'that' functioned like a definite description, then the data we just surveyed would compel us to treat 'that' as always taking wide scope. But we would have no explanation for why this should be so. In this sense, Schiffer's and Neale's restriction seems *ad hoc*. So the data constitute a prima-facie objection to treating simple demonstratives as quantifiers. On the other hand, treating demonstratives as referring terms readily explains why if someone truly utters [13], [15] (taken relative to the same contextual parameters) is true, where the description has wide scope, and why [13] entails that someone was believed by John to be thin at that time.

(iii) Finally, the description approach is committed to entailments the demonstrative sentences it analyzes do not have. If John said, 'That is thin' (or 'That man is thin'), then one could, if the description approach were correct, truly say, 'John said something which entails that something was demonstrated by him'. But while it *may* be true that John demonstrated something, and, if he was sincere, that he intended to, nothing he *said* (or expressed) entails that he did, anymore than anything he *said* (or expressed) entails that he was *speaking English*.

There remains the question of how in the light of this we are to explain the analogies between complex demonstratives and quantifier expressions consistently with seeing demonstratives as genuine referring terms, and, in particular, how to give a semantics for sentences containing complex demonstratives compatible with this constraint.[80]

[79] This shows also that the suggestion that every use of a demonstrative is a complex demonstrative, with apparently simple demonstratives taking 'thing' as a suppressed nominal, a suggestion made to us by Kent Bach (and assumed by Barwise and Cooper 1981), cannot be right. For if that were so, then we would find scope ambiguities even for apparently simple demonstratives. But we do not. Furthermore, it seems clear that 'that is not a thing', while false, is not logically false, though 'that thing is not a thing' is.

[80] Jeffrey King (J. C. King 2001: 43–8) offers a quantificational account of complex demonstratives that appears to avoid these objections. King treats 'that' as introducing a four-place

3. Semantics for Complex Demonstratives

In light of the difficulties encountered in treating 'that' as a quantifier word, it might seem prudent to reconsider the suggestion that complex demonstratives function as referring terms, and that the nominal in the complex demonstrative does not contribute to the truth conditions of the sentence. This might be recommended by the observation that when we use sentences of the form 'That *F* is *G*', we are clearly most interested in saying of some demonstrated object that it is *G*. In fact, it seems that we can succeed in demonstrating an object in order to say it is *G*, using 'That *F* is *G*', even when it fails to be *F* (*contra* Kaplan *et al.*). Suppose that someone says, pointing to a white horse, 'That unicorn is white'. It seems to make perfect sense to say in response, 'That's white, but it's not a unicorn'. This indicates that we think the speaker has succeeded in demonstrating something, which we in turn demonstrate, even though it is not a unicorn. The nominal, it might be suggested, plays only a pragmatic role in helping an auditor to determine which object the speaker

---

relation between properties, two of which are contextually determined. The matrix King introduces for 'that' is '___ and ___ are uniquely ___ in an object *x* and *x* is ___'. We will modify this slightly to '___ and ___ uniquely possess ___ in an object *x* and *x* has ___' so that we can uniformly substitute terms that refer to properties. Thus, 'That *F* is *G*' is represented, independently of context, as 'being *F* and ___ uniquely possess ___ in an object *x* and *x* has the property of being *G*'. The key point for the above objections is that King holds that when a complex demonstrative is used with a demonstration, the second argument place is supplied with, for an object *x* demonstrated, the property of *being identical to x*, a property that could be expressed with '= *b*', where '*b*' picks out directly the object it is the speaker's intention to talk about, and the third argument place is supplied with the property of *being jointly instantiated in w at t*, where *w* is the world of utterance (i.e. the actual world, for any actual utterance) and *t*, presumably, the time of utterance. On King's view, this is to treat complex demonstratives like other quantified nouns phrases introduced by a determiner, which he treats as introducing two-place relations between properties. (For example, 'All *F* are *G*' expresses a relation between the properties of being *F* and being *G* which holds just in case the extension of '*F*' is a subset of the extension of '*G*'.) Part of the aim here is to enable one to accommodate uses of complex demonstratives which apparently do not involve any intent to refer to a particular object, as in 'Every author loves that first book he published'. In this case, 'that first book he published' is taken to express 'being a first book he published and being a first book he published uniquely possess the property of being jointly instantiated by an object *y* and *y* has ___'. The advantage of this approach is that it enables complex demonstratives sometimes to involve direct reference to particulars, mimicking the behavior of singular terms, and at other times to act just like definite descriptions. However, whatever its attractions, it is not an approach that will recommend itself to anyone who does not think of quantifiers as introducing relations between properties. We doubt that the use of quantifiers carries the kind of ontological commitment this approach requires, and we also doubt that people who use complex demonstratives have intentions of the sort this account would require. We also think that the proposal we make, which is less ontologically committed, handles the data equally well, and is more in tune with common sense. We address below two objections King raises in his book against the account we give and argue that they are not successful.

is demonstrating to say of it that it is G. If the nominal played a semantic role as well, surely whether an object is demonstrated would depend on its being F; and, in addition, we have an explanation for the role 'F' plays that does not depend on its being semantic.

However, while an adequate account should explain the possibility, when uttering a sentence of the form 'That F is G', of demonstrating an object which fails to be F, and should accommodate the idea that the nominal plays a role in helping an auditor to determine what object is being referred to, the suggestion that the nominal plays no semantic role seems incompatible with the data surveyed in §1.

Someone who advocates that the nominal plays no semantic role would be committed to saying that all sentences of the form 'That F is G', no matter what substitutes for 'F' (for some fixed replacement for 'G'), have the same (relativized) truth conditions! This view is incompatible with semantic entailment relations into which such sentences enter (or what is expressed using them). As noted in §1, for any determiner with existential import, $Det_\exists$, any true assertion of '$Det_\exists F$ is(are) G' semantically entails what is asserted by 'Some F are G', and, hence, what is asserted by 'There are some F' (fixing contextual variables). In fact, it seems we can infer either of 'That clown is funny' and 'That is a funny clown' from the other, when the demonstrative picks out the same thing.[81] Similarly, from a true assertion of 'All Fs are Gs', the truth of 'That F is G' can be inferred, where what is demonstrated is an F, for example, 'All aviators wear sunglasses; therefore, that aviator wears sunglasses' (again, fixing contextual parameters). And while someone could say, without fear of formal contradiction, 'That is not a clown', if he says 'That clown is not a clown', he could only be understood intelligibly if we took him to intend 'clown' in different senses in the two occurrences.

Likewise, we will accept as true such necessitated conditionals as 'Necessarily, if it was that clown in the aviator sunglasses who won the prize, then some clown in aviator sunglasses won the prize', which requires us to think of the nominal of the complex demonstrative as contributing to the truth conditions of the sentence in the antecedent. This shows decisively that the nominal must contribute to the truth conditions. No account which treats it as merely constraining the referent of the demonstrative can account for the truth of such necessitated conditionals. On their account, it has the form,

---

[81] Strawson (1950a: § V (b)) claimed in a famous discussion that sentences of the form 'That F is G' and 'That is the F which is G' say the same thing. He was onto something, for if we are right (see below), the truth of an utterance of either guarantees the truth of an utterance of the other, when 'that' is used in each to pick out the same object, at the same time.

'Necessarily, if it was X who won the prize, then someone wearing aviator sunglasses won the prize', where 'X' is a directly referring term. But, so construed, it is clearly false. Further evidence, which we will not recount here, is provided by considerations involving clefting, which are discussed in Richard (1993).

It has been suggested to us that (i) 'Necessarily, if I won the prize, then some speaker of an utterance won the prize' is intuitively equally true. If so, this would suggest that in uttering such conditionals we are sensitive to the truth of the embedded sentence in all contexts of utterance, rather than strict necessity. We confess that we do not find (i) to have a true reading. But to test whether speakers respond to truth of the embedded sentence in all contexts in reacting to 'Necessarily, if it was that clown in the aviator sunglasses who won the prize, then some clown in aviator sunglasses won the prize', we can ask "Is *the proposition expressed by* a use of (iii) 'if it was that clown in the aviator glasses won the prize, then some clown in aviator sunglasses won the prize' is necessarily true?", and "Is *the proposition expressed by* a use of (iv) 'if I won the prize, then some speaker of an utterance won the prize' is necessarily true?" It seems to us that the answer to the second question is clearly no, but that the answer to the first is yes.

Furthermore, appealing again to data presented in §1, the nominal can interact with other elements in the sentence in which the complex demonstrative appears. One can quantify into the nominal, and terms in the sentence can be anaphoric on quantifier expressions in the nominal. So, it seems not to be an option to treat the nominal as pleonastic, or even to restrict its semantic role to placing a necessary condition on securing a referent for predication. We must take seriously the parallel between the treatment of sentences of the form 'That F is G' and those of the form 'QF is/are G', where 'Q' is replaced by a quantifier word.

In light of these considerations and our arguments against treating 'that' as a quantifier word, we propose the following desiderata on any adequate account of complex demonstratives.

(i) The account must exhibit 'that' as a referring term and not as a quantifier word.

(ii) The account must show how 'that' can be used in 'that F' to demonstrate an object, even though the object demonstrated is not F.

(iii) The account must explain how the nominal in 'that F' can play a pragmatic role in helping an auditor to determine what the speaker intends to be referring to.

(iv) The account must exhibit the nominal '*F*' as contributing to the truth conditions of a sentence of the form 'That *F* is *G*', and in particular the account should explain the entailment relations into which 'That *F* is *G*' may enter.

(v) The account must interpret sentences of the form 'That *F* is *G*' in a way that exhibits their structure as parallel to that of sentences of the form '*QF* are *G*', where '*Q*' is replaced by a quantifier expression, and, in particular, the account must enable us to explain how the nominal in complex demonstratives can interact with other elements in a sentence in the same way as the nominal in restricted quantifier expressions.

In effect, we meet desiderata (i) and (ii) first by assigning 'that' a reference clause (thereby treating it as a referring term) and, then, by providing a recursion clause for sentences of the form 'That *F* is *G*' in which the semantic contribution of 'that' is exhausted by its reference clause. This will meet (ii) because the reference clause will provide conditions for 'that' picking out an object independently of any nominal it is concatenated with to form a complex demonstrative. (This terminology of course is misleading if we are right.) However, as we have seen, there appears to be a tension between (i)–(ii) and (iv)–(v). In what follows, we will reconcile these four desiderata with materials needed to satisfy the pragmatic desideratum (iii).

We rejected semantically interpreting 'that' in a way exactly parallel to how we standardly interpret quantifiers in sentences of the form '*QF* are *G*' because 'that' is a referring term. On the other hand, we apparently want whatever object 'that' picks out to be, as it were, fed into the construction '*x* such that *x* is *F* is such that *x* is *G*' in a way that parallels quantification. That is, we want to represent the object which is the referent of 'that' as used by the speaker as fed into this construction in a way parallel to the way quantifiers feed objects to this construction. But to do this in full generality within a truth theory, we must invoke satisfaction, because nominals and predicates are both productive categories, that is, complex ones can be built up out of simpler ones by the usual recursive devices. Because we must interpret constructions of the form 'That *F* is *G*' recursively in terms of how we interpret '*F*' and 'is *G*', we will represent 'That *F* is *G*' as '[That *x*: *x* is *F*](*x* is *G*)'. What we want, then, is for a function f to satisfy '[That *x*: *x* is *F*](*x* is *G*)' iff a function f' differing from f at most in that f' assigns to '*x*' what is demonstrated by the speaker in using 'that', *and* which satisfies '*x* is F', is such that it *also* satisfies '*x* is *G*'. There will in fact be only one such function because of the requirement

135

that it assign to '*x*' what 'that' refers to. Exploiting this fact, we can write out our candidate satisfaction clause as in [16].

[16] For all functions f, f satisfies(S, t, u) '[That x: x is F](x is G)' iff [the f': f' differs from f at most in that $f'('x') = \text{Ref}(S, t, u,$ 'that') and f' satisfies(S, t, u) 'x is F'](f' satisfies(S, t, u) 'x is G').

For the general case, we can write:

[17] For all functions f, variables v, predicates ϕ, ψ containing a free occurrence of v, f satisfies(S, t, u) $\ulcorner$[That v: ϕ](ψ)$\urcorner$ iff [the f': f' is a ϕ/v-variant of f and $f'(v) = \text{Ref}(S, t, u,$ 'that')](f' satisfies$(S, t, u)\psi$).

[17], as a semantic proposal for how to interpret complex demonstratives, meets desiderata (iv) and (v) compatibly with (i) and (ii). Our formulation of [17] is, in fact, *essentially a more precise rewording of our desiderata*. By specifying the semantic contribution of its simple demonstrative constituent using a reference clause, we continue to treat 'that' as a referring term. However, at the same time, we capture the semantic contribution of its nominal to the truth conditions of the sentence in a way that parallels the standard treatment of restricted quantifiers. In effect, we treat English sentences of the form 'That F is G' as sharing interpretive truth conditions with sentences of the form '[The x: x = that and x is F](x is G)'.[82]

Our desiderata have led us to postulate that sentences of the form 'That F is G' are semantically equivalent to *restricted existentially quantified sentences*, the restrictive clause of which contains a referring term, to wit, a demonstrative. This view neatly handles all of the assorted data we have discussed.

It explains the similarity in form between 'That F is G' and $\ulcorner Q\,F$ are $G\urcorner$ by treating the former as having the logical form of $\ulcorner [Qx: \phi(x, \text{that})](x$ is $G)\urcorner$, where $\ulcorner \phi(x, \text{that})\urcorner$ represents a complex predicate that contains a demonstrative in an argument place. It thereby exhibits 'that' as a genuine referring term whose contribution to a sentence does not depend on the nominal to which it is conjoined. It explains why 'That F is G' is materially equivalent to 'That is F and G', since '[The x: x = that and x is F](x is G)' semantically implies 'Something is identical with that and it is F and G'.[83] And it explains how, despite

---

[82] Since, on our account, the predicate restriction contains a requirement that ensures at most one thing will satisfy it, we could instead have used, e.g. 'some', 'one', or 'all', in place of 'the' in [17]. The essential role for these quantifiers is to bind the variables in the nominal and the predicate. Perhaps this partly explains why the quantifier is suppressed: there does not seem to be a single most appropriate quantifier word to use.

[83] It has been objected to our treatment that it makes 'That F is G' and 'That G is F' equivalent. It is true that respective utterances of sentences of these two forms, where 'that' in

the nominal not semantically determining the referent of 'that' as used by the speaker, it nonetheless enters into the sentence's truth conditions. In the case of an utterance of 'That unicorn is white', we can explain how someone can demonstrate something, even though there are no unicorns, and why the utterance is false, even when someone successfully demonstrates something white. We will also be able to explain why the nominal plays a pragmatic role in helping an auditor to determine which object the speaker intends to be demonstrating (see the next section). Thus, we can accommodate all the intuitions that pull people in different directions about the semantics of complex demonstratives.

The account achieves its explanatory goals by forgoing certain traditional assumptions about so-called complex demonstratives, perhaps the chief of which is that expressions of the form 'That F' are themselves referring terms *if* 'that' is a referring term. From the perspective afforded by our account, wanting to treat 'that' as a quantifier word, or to treat the nominal 'F' in 'That F is G' as semantically inert, or at least not predicated of the object picked out, results from failing to see that combining a demonstrative with a nominal is itself a bit of semantically significant syntax, to be interpreted as a restricted existential quantifier in which a demonstrative appears in the nominal restriction.[84]

The suggestion that some noun phrases function as quantified noun phrases, even though they lack an explicit quantifier word, should be familiar. Sentences such as 'Whales are mammals' and 'Men are wicked' are treated as equivalent to 'All whales are mammals' and 'All men are wicked', though they contain no explicit quantifier word.[85] Similarly, genitive forms of proper names and indexicals that combine with nominals to form complex noun phrases, as in 'John's beagle' and 'His hat', are standardly treated as equivalent to descriptions in which the referring terms are treated as part of the predicate restriction on the article. It should not be so surprising to find a

---

each is used to refer to the same object (at the same time) would both be true or false together. But this does not mean that they are semantically equivalent, since they are assigned different semantic structures. And, of course, there would be no reason to hold that they are 'cognitively' or pragmatically equivalent either, since the order of elements in a sentence clearly can make a significant difference to the pragmatic import, even when sentences are materially equivalent, as in 'I got dressed and went to the office' and 'I went to the office and got dressed'; or, if we are right, as in 'That man is a bachelor' and 'That bachelor is a man'.

[84] This treatment of complex demonstratives supports the thesis advanced by Neale (1993) that every complex noun phrase in English is a restricted quantifier without having to give up the view that demonstratives, everywhere they appear, are genuine referring terms. Indeed, the current proposal, which is motivated independently of Neale's thesis, constitutes powerful support for it, since it shows how to reconcile it with what appears otherwise to be a recalcitrant exception.

[85] Neale (1993: 109).

similar phenomenon with complex noun phrases formed from concatenating demonstratives with nominals. Indeed, with these parallels in mind, our proposal seems like the obvious thing to say about complex demonstratives.

It is interesting to note that when we turn to plural demonstratives, such as 'these' and 'those', there appears to be an equivalence between sentences of the form 'These *F*s are *G*s' and 'All these *F*s are *G*s', which suggests that the former is an abbreviated syntactical device for expressing the same thing as the latter. The natural extension of our account to 'These *F*s are *G*s' is to say that all things that are among these and are *F* are also *G*, which is also the most natural way to interpret 'All these *F*s are *G*s'.[86]

4. Pragmatics of Complex Demonstratives

We turn now to a brief discussion of the pragmatics of complex demonstratives, with an eye both to explaining how we can meet desideratum (iii) above and to explaining away certain worries about quantifying into the nominals of complex demonstratives.

Quantification into the nominals of complex demonstratives, while supplying the data for semanticists who deny they are referring terms, also present some prima facie obstacles to their thesis. The problem is that, though we can naturally quantify *into* complex noun phrases, as in [18], this can seem quite strange in the case of some complex demonstratives, as in [19] (where we imagine the speaker pointing to some particular woman).

[18]   *Every man* loves the woman who is *his* mother.
[19]   ?*Every man* loves that woman who is *his* mother.[87]

---

[86] One might object that if someone demonstrates non-*F* things, the sentence will come out true rather than false. The grounds are that '[All *x*: *x* is one of these and *x* is *F*](*x* is *G*)' is materially equivalent to 'For all *x*, if *x* is one of these, and *x* is *F*, then *x* is *G*', which is vacuously true when nothing demonstrated is *F*. The proposal can be modified to avoid this difficulty by employing the plural definite description in place of 'all', representing 'These *F*s are *G*s' as '[The *x*'s: *x* is one of these and *x* is *F*](*x* is *G*)'. However, this will undermine the suggestion that 'These *F*s are *G*s' is equivalent to 'All these *F*s are *G*s'. This objection is founded on a view that has become prominent since Frege, namely, that 'All *F*s are *G*s' is equivalent to 'All *x* are such that if *x* is *F*, then *x* is *G*'. Intuitions about English sentences notoriously, however, fail to conform to this paradigm, and once we see that, in general, the structure '*QF* are *G*' is not paraphrasable into classical first order logic, there is reason to re-examine it.

[87] Sometimes, of course, 'that' is pressed into service as a variant of 'the', and one could imagine someone uttering [19] with that in mind. We are not concerned with such uses of 'that', but rather with demonstrative uses. Our proposal requires that there be demonstrative uses of 'that' in complex demonstratives which contain pronouns of cross-reference bound by

Some authors have gone as far as to suggest that sentences like [19] are semantically incoherent.[88] But if our treatment is correct, [19] should be semantically in order, because it is equivalent to the perfectly well-formed [20],

[20]   [For every y: y is a man][the x: $x = that$ and x is a woman who is the mother of y](y loves x).

If we are right, quantification into 'that F' is just quantification into a quantified noun phrase. So, we must defend the view that whatever may seem odd about [19] is not due to any incoherence in its construction. And, in fact, we believe that whatever oddness surrounds utterances of sentences like [19] is due solely to the difficulty in imagining circumstances in which it would be reasonable to assert it.

As Taylor (1980: 195) notes, it is not easy to see what could prevent the inference from [21] to [22] by existential generalization.

[21]   James is marrying that woman he is kissing.
[22]   Someone is marrying that woman he is kissing.

Clearly, the sentential matrix 'x is marrying that woman x is kissing' can be satisfied by an object; thus, we can surely say that some object satisfies it; or, in the material mode, something is such that it is marrying that woman it is kissing. Our account makes sense of this possibility (and it does so without the desperate expedient of treating demonstratives as quantifier words). Again, consider [23].

[23]   Mary loves that man kissing Judy.

'that' is being used as a demonstrative in [23]. From [23], [24] surely follows.

[24]   Mary loves that man kissing someone.

Indeed, one could imagine drawing attention coyly to the man one is demonstrating by using [24], rather than [23]. But is [24] not equivalent to [25]?

[25]   [Some x](Mary loves that man kissing x)

Moreover, it is easy enough to think up perfectly normal sentences in which it is acceptable to bind variables inside a complex demonstrative by a universal quantifier from outside. Our earlier [6] provides an example:

quantifiers outside the scope of the complex demonstrative. The objection we consider here is that "demonstrative uses" of complex demonstratives are not compatible with treating them as restricted quantifiers because of the oddity of such uses in sentences like [19].

[88]   See Davies (1982); Neale (1993); Taylor (1980).

[6]   *Each woman in this room* admires that man whom *she* sees at the podium.

It is easy to see that there can be demonstrative uses of 'that' in [6]. For example, there may be two men at the podium, and the speaker may be pointing at one of them. In such circumstances, [6] does not seem at all odd, and in the imagined circumstances it is clear that one could not intelligibly reinterpret 'that' as a definite article. A true assertion of [6] in the imagined circumstances would clearly involve a demonstration, although a universal quantifier binds a variable inside the complex demonstrative. No puzzle arises about its assertion because it is clear that there is a single man whom they all admire. So, there cannot be anything semantically amiss with quantifying into complex demonstratives.

Any oddity with [19], then, cannot be due to the fact that a variable in the complex demonstrative is bound by a quantifier outside it, but must attach to some pragmatic infelicity accompanying its typical utterances.[89] And it is not difficult to see why it would be odd to assert [19], given its semantics, for unless we are all very much mistaken about our ancestry, [19], interpreted literally, is absurdly false; there are no ordinary circumstances in which it would make good conversational sense to assert it.

More generally, part of the usefulness of the construction 'that *F*' is to help draw an auditor's attention to his interlocutor's belief that the object he is demonstrating falls under '*F*', in a way that renders the property it expresses salient for tracking the speaker's demonstrative intentions. Our account neatly

[89] Interesting issues are raised by cases of complex demonstratives which are apparently intended to be interpreted as variables of cross-reference. Consider utterances of sentences such as 'Every boy kissed some girl that that boy loved'. There is a reading of this sentence on which 'that boy' is used demonstratively; e.g. one may say this while pointing at a particular boy. But other utterances will naturally be interpreted as equivalent to 'Every boy kissed some girl that he loved', in which 'he' functions as a variable of cross-reference. It is perhaps not surprising to find this dual use, since 'he' and other pronouns of cross-reference also have a dual use as variables of cross-reference and as demonstrative pronouns. In the case of complex demonstratives, it is natural to suggest that the demonstrative itself is what functions as the variable of cross-reference (simple demonstratives clearly do, as in 'Everyone loses something, and that is usually just the thing he most needs at the time'). Thus, 'Every boy kissed some girl that that boy loved', where 'that' functions as a variable of cross-reference, is treated as equivalent to '[Every x: x is a boy][some y: y is a girl such that [the z: $z = x$ and z is a boy](z loved y)](x kissed y)'. The utility of using a complex demonstrative lies in the way the quantifier construction helps to draw attention to which quantifier binds the argument place occupied by the demonstrative by using the same nominal as that in the binding quantifier expression. This indicates that the values of the variable of cross-reference are intended to be restricted to objects which satisfy the predicate constructed from the nominal, making it salient as a candidate for binding by a quantifier in whose scope it falls, which likewise restricts its variables to objects which satisfy the same predicate.

explains, on the basis of the semantics of 'That F is G', why this inference is reasonable, since it requires 'F' to be true of the demonstrated object. Thus, our account handily explains the intuition that the nominal *pragmatically* helps to determine the demonstrated object. This utility would explain why someone asserts 'That F is G' in preference to 'That is an F and G' or simply 'That is G', when what is most important is that the object demonstrated is G. Thus, we satisfy desideratum (iii), as promised.

This utility is often lost when the nominal contains a variable bound by a quantifier external to it. Quantifiers normally are not in the business of singling out particular individuals, and so a relativized nominal will often fail to specify useful identifying information. Against the standard practice, quantifying into complex demonstratives will often seem odd, as it does. But that is because using such constructions normally issues in odd performances, and not because the result is semantically incoherent. This pragmatic role the nominal plays may also explain why nominals formed with a relative clause in past tense can seem not entirely natural, as in [26].

[26]   ?Mary loves that man *who kissed Judy*.

This relative clause would often fail to provide useful information about the speaker's demonstrative intentions. One cannot survey the immediate environment to see what satisfies 'man who kissed Judy' for help in identifying the object the speaker intends to be demonstrating, since no such event occurs at the time of utterance. (If there is enough discourse context to make clear what the speaker has in mind, however, a use of [26] may seem unproblematic.) Contrast [26] with [23], or [27], utterances of which are clearly unexceptional.[90]

---

[90] Further discussion of the pragmatics of complex demonstratives and responses to additional objections can be found in §6 of Lepore and Ludwig (2000). We take this opportunity to correct, however, one mistake in this paper. We discussed at length an example due to David Braun, and discussed in Richard (1993), namely, 'Necessarily, if that dog with a blue collar exists, then it has a collar'. This can seem not to have a true reading, which it may seem it should have on an account which treats the nominal as contributing to the truth conditions of the sentence of which it is a part. We argued that, in utterances of this sentence, 'that dog with a blue collar' is naturally given wide scope over 'Necessarily', as in '[The x: $x =$ that and x is a dog with a blue collar](necessarily, if x exists, then x has a blue collar)', since a speaker will be using it to identify something he wants to say something about, and this would account for the falsity of what is expressed. However, given the way we represented the narrow scope reading, 'Necessarily, [The x: $x =$ that and x is a dog with a blue collar](if x exists, then x has a blue collar)', the narrow scope reading will also be false, since the definite description has existential import. And so for this to be true, what is referred to with 'that' would have to exist and be a dog with a blue collar in every possible world, which is not so. (We are indebted to Ana Maria Andrei for bringing this difficulty to our attention.) Another reading might be urged, however, on which the 'it' in the consequent is taken to be an E-type pronoun (see Neale (1990*b*)), and so to be in effect interpreted, on our

[27]   Mary loves that man who is kissing Judy.

5. An Objection and Rejoinder

In this section, we consider a particularly interesting objection to our account based on the interaction of complex demonstratives with claims about possibility and necessity. We choose this particular objection to consider because it elicits a strong intuition which appears to run counter to our account, and diagnosing it will help to illustrate the complex interplay between pragmatic and semantic factors in our interpretations of utterances.

The objection is that our account does not give the correct results for sentences such as

[28]   It is possible that that senator from California is a crook.[91]

Let us suppose that the person who asserts [28] is demonstrating someone, H, who is not a senator from California at the time at which he asserts it. It seems that, in these circumstances, his utterance would be false. Prima facie, our account has the resources to accommodate this, since it allows for the possibility of 'that senator from California' taking wide scope over 'It is possible that', as represented in [29].

[29]   [The x: $x =$ that and x is a senator from California](it is possible that x is a crook).

Since nothing is uniquely H and a senator from California, [29] is false.

The problem, however, is that on our account, [28] should also have a true reading, namely, [30].

[30]   It is possible that [The x: $x =$ that and x is a senator from California] (x is a crook).

view, as 'the dog with a blue collar identical with that'. Then we would interpret the conditional as 'Necessarily, if the dog with a blue collar identical with that exists, then the dog with a blue collar identical with that has a collar'. In this case, we would expect a true reading, for when in a world in which there is no dog which is identical to that and has a blue collar, the conditional will have a false antecedent and so be true, and in a world in which there is a dog which is identical to that and has a blue collar, the antecedent will be true, but in that case so will the consequent. Our pragmatic account is relevant to why *this* reading is hard to hear.

[91]   This objection is due to Jeffrey King (see J. C. King 2001: 182). This example presents a problem also for views according to which the complex demonstrative is a directly referring term, for on that view a literal utterance of [28] would be true, if truth-valued at all.

This is true, it seems, provided that the person to whom the speaker refers might have been at the time a senator from California who was a crook. Since being a non-senator and being a non-crook are not essential properties of anyone, [30] would then be true in the envisaged circumstances. However, it is extremely difficult to hear an utterance of [28] as having a true reading.

Does this undermine our account? No. We can show directly that our intuitive reaction to [28] does not refute our account by considering what reaction we would have to a sentence like [28] in which we replace the complex demonstrative with a noun phrase that is equivalent to our analysis of it, as in [31].

> [31]   It is possible that the senator from California identical to that [or that man] is a crook.

Imagine, as before, that someone, in uttering this, points to a man, H, who is not a senator from California. We would, again, judge the speaker to have said something false. In this case, there clearly is a narrow scope reading, [32].

> [32]   It is possible that [the x: x is a senator from California and $x = H$] (x is a crook).

Yet, it seems as difficult to hear an utterance of [31] as true, in the imagined circumstances, as it was to hear an utterance of [28] as true, in those circumstances. We encounter the same difficulty in getting a true reading even when we change the determiner in [31] to 'some', as in [33].

> [33]   It is possible that some senator from California identical to that is a crook.

Again, if we imagine that someone who is not a senator is demonstrated, we hear an utterance of [33] as false, and we encounter difficulty in getting a true reading. This shows that our intuitions in these cases, [31] and [33], must be generated by an interplay between the literal meaning of their utterances and pragmatic factors. It shows also that the intuition we have that an utterance of [28] does not have a true reading, but only a false one, cannot be used to undermine our account, because this shows that our account, by a mechanism we have not yet identified, does produce the intuitions which we actually have in response to utterances of sentences like [28].

What then is the explanation of our intuitive response to utterances of [28]? We might first try to bring to bear our earlier remark that the point of using the complex demonstrative is to draw attention to an object to say something about it. Thus, an interlocutor will suppose that the speaker is primarily intending to say of an object that it is so and so. Then, when a sentence of the form 'That F is G' is embedded in a context such as 'It is possible that', our attention will be drawn to whether the object singled out for attention is relevantly possibly a G. This is in effect to give the complex demonstrative (or, the quantified noun phrases in [31] and [33]) wide scope.

However, this seems inadequate to explain our intuitions in the present case. For we can in effect force the nominal to take narrow scope with respect to the claim of possibility by first expressing what is expressed by the embedded sentence, and then say of it that it is possible, as in [34] and [35].[92]

[34] That senator from California is a crook.

[35] *That* is possibly true.

We imagine [34] uttered in the same circumstances as before, H, who is not a senator, again being demonstrated. Then we imagine, absent other clues, [35] being uttered, and obviously intended to be in response to the speaker's performance.

Is [35] true? We think that most people will say that what would be intended by an utterance of [35] would not be true in the described circumstances.[93] But how could we explain this? There is no question of the complex demonstrative taking wide scope over the modal operator in this case. For the complex demonstrative is in sentence [34], and the modal operator is in sentence [35].

Before we consider a diagnosis, let us first consider, once again, a parallel exchange in which we replace the complex demonstrative with an explicit definite description with a nominal restricted by a use of a demonstrative, as in [36] and [37].

[36] The senator from California identical to that is a crook.

[37] That is *possibly* true.

Here, again, in the imagined circumstances, we find that we are pulled to interpret an utterance of [37] as false! This shows, as before, that our intuitions in this case, involving [36] and [37], must be an interplay between semantic and pragmatic factors which we have overlooked. And it shows, therefore,

---

[92] This extension of the objection is due to King (2001). King notes we respond to the objection in Lepore and Ludwig (2000), but does not address the point we make there that the same intuitions are generated by clearly quantificational phrases, so that whatever is generating these intuitions cannot count against the noun phrase being construed semantically as quantificational.

[93] At least when 'that' is taken to refer to what the speaker said using [35], as opposed, e.g. to the sentence he used to say it. For it is clear that the sentence could be used to make a true assertion. This still does not isolate out what the sentence as used meant literally, as opposed to what the speaker meant in using it, and this is important for the diagnosis we offer below.

that our intuition that [35] is not true cannot be used to undermine our account. For our intuitions are the same when we substitute for the complex demonstrative in [34] our analysis of it.

The explanation of our intuitions, we believe, is that we are strongly pulled to interpret the modal claim in the present case as involving *epistemic* possibility, rather than possibility *tout court*. In this case, the utterance would, in the imagined circumstances, be false on both the wide and narrow scope readings. We are strongly pulled to interpret the modal claim as about epistemic possibility because there would typically be no point in asserting of anyone, or anyone described as an elected official, that it is *conceptually* possible that he is a crook (tell me about it!). We imagine, then, a background in which suspicion has been raised, and that the speaker is suggesting it is possible, in light of the evidence, that that senator from California is a crook. Here the epistemic position relative to which the claim is to be evaluated will be, of course, not that of the speaker himself, or of the man he points to, but of, roughly, the community at large, or some relevant subportion of it charged with an investigation. In this case, *even on the narrow scope reading*, the utterance of the sentence is false, for in evaluating it, we are to consider possibilities compatible with the public epistemic position: but since *we* know that the person demonstrated is *not* a senator, there is no epistemically possible world in which he is *a senator and a crook*. Thus, on both the wide and the narrow scope reading, as noted, we would expect, on our account, an utterance of the sentence in the circumstances to be false, given the epistemic reading of 'it is possible that'. This explains as well the intuitions about [31] and [33].

It could be objected that our intuitions would be explained by reading the possibility as epistemic possibility in this case, but that even if we interpret the possibility as possibility *tout court*, we still cannot get the narrow scope reading, so that this explanation cannot at least be the whole story. Let us then consider [38] and [39], where we aim to force a non-epistemic reading of 'possible'.

[38] That senator from California is a crook.

[39] It is conceptually possible that the proposition expressed literally by that utterance of that sentence is true.

We imagine that a man who is not a senator is demonstrated. [38] is false. But is [39] true? It seems to us that we should be cautious here. [39], which makes clear in technical terms what is wanted, is not something that we ordinarily say, and perhaps only a philosopher would ever say anything quite like it. We do not think we have any immediate ordinary intuitions about it. The answer clearly depends on exactly what proposition is expressed by [38]. And this is something which it is not easy to say, for it depends on, among other things, how the nominal contributes to the proposition expressed. We do not have the sort of confident response to the question whether [39] is true that would enable us to use a response as basic data. Thus, we should decide what to say in this case on the basis of a more global investigation into the behavior of complex demonstratives, which, we have argued, suggests strongly that they are semantically quantified noun phrases with a demonstrative in the restrictive clause. (If a reader does have a strong sense that [39] is not true, then we suggest substituting for the complex demonstrative the analysis we would give it to see whether that makes a difference: if not, then, again, the intuitions cannot be used to show that our account is incorrect.)

6. Specialized Demonstratives

We turn now briefly to the treatment of specialized demonstratives, which we postponed because our treatment of complex demonstratives is relevant to one of the options available for understanding their semantic role. By specialized demonstratives, we have in mind the demonstrative pronouns, such as 'he', 'she', 'her', 'him', 'you',[94] and demonstratives of time, 'then' and 'now', and place, 'here' and 'there' (recall our earlier discussion of 'now' and 'here', in which we argued that some uses at least seem clearly to have a demonstrative element), which introduce an understood restriction on the intended referent of the demonstrative term.

Let us consider 'he' as an example. If 'he' is a referring term, receiving in the truth theory a reference clause, then we must decide whether gender is to play a role in determining the referent of a use of 'he' (on its non-gender-neutral use). The two options are given in [40] and [41].

[40] For all objects x, if S demonstrates x at t using 'he' in u and x is male, then $\text{Ref}(S, t, u, \text{'he'}) = x$.

[41] For all objects x, if S demonstrates x at t using 'he' in u, then $\text{Ref}(S, t, u, \text{'he'}) = x$.

In [40], 'he' will not be assigned a referent unless what is demonstrated is male, while in [41], a referent will be assigned whether the object demonstrated is

---

[94] Of course, the pronouns have uses also as bound variables of cross-reference ('*Everyone* loves someone who loves *him*'), and perhaps also special uses as unbound anaphoric pronouns ('*Everyman who owns a donkey* beats *it*'), but we are concerned presently with their demonstrative uses.

male or not. On the proposal given in [41], the gender of the pronoun plays no semantic role, but is rather something conventionally implied by the use of the male pronoun which, strictly speaking, does not contribute to fixing the truth conditions of sentences containing it. On neither of these proposals would it turn out that 'He is handsome' as used by a speaker at a time implies 'Something is male', though, on proposal [40], one *could* infer from 'He is handsome' *having been asserted truly or falsely* that something is male.

But to secure the stronger requirement that the content of what is asserted in using truthfully 'He is handsome' entails that something is male, one would have to give up the view that 'he' functions simply as a referring term. Rather, we would have to treat 'he' as a restricted quantifier phrase, a fusing, as it were, of 'that' with 'male'. But since no separate lexical item plays the role of the referring term in 'he', we would have to give satisfaction conditions for 'he' in context. We want to retain the idea that no sentence containing 'he' in a position where it could only be used as a demonstrative pronoun is true or false except as used. We did this in the case of 'that' by assigning a referent to it only as it is used at a time to demonstrate something. We cannot do that for 'he' because we cannot give a separate reference axiom for 'he', if we want to secure that a necessary condition on the truth of a sentence in which it appears is that the object demonstrated is male. So we must conditionalize our satisfaction clauses of sentences containing demonstrative uses of 'he'. We illustrate this with respect to 'He is handsome', or, rather, its regimented cousin, '[He x](x is handsome)', in [42].

[42] For all objects y, if S demonstrates y at t using 'he', then for all functions f, f satisfies(S, t, u) '[He x](x is handsome)' iff some function f' that differs from f at most in that $f'('x') = y$ and $f'('x')$ is male satisfies(S, t, u) 'x is handsome'.

Trying to adjudicate between these approaches here would take up too much space. Our aim has been to note what the consequences are of different judgments about the role of the gender inflection. If one cannot say truly 'He is not male', then [41] is ruled out. If one can say truly 'that he is tall entails that some male is tall', or that sentences like 'He is handsome' and 'She is beautiful' imply, respectively, 'Something is male' and 'Something is female', then [40] is ruled out in favor of [42]. Here issues about scope may also be relevant. Thus, on the assumption that one's biological gender is not an essential feature of one (i.e. one doesn't become someone else by having a sex change operation), a (felicitous) assertion of 'Necessarily, he is male,' when 'he' is used to refer to a male, will be false—except insofar as there is the possibility of giving 'he' a wide scope reading. In that case, there should be two readings, one true and one false. If there is no reading of it on which it is true, then 'he' seems not to exhibit the scope ambiguity we would expect of a quantified noun phrase. Likewise, in the case of an attitude report such as an assertion of 'June believes that he is a surgeon', we can ask whether this is false if the person in question is someone June believes to be a woman, and whether, if there is a false reading, there is also a true reading of it, which might correspond to a wide scope reading of 'he'. Similar issues arise for other pronouns such as 'you', 'we', etc., and the demonstratives 'then', 'now', 'here' and 'there', and even for 'I', though the last does not function demonstratively.

6

The Semantics of Quotation

In quotation not only does language turn on itself, but it does so word by
word and expression by expression, and this reflexive twist is inseparable
from the convenience and universal applicability of the device.

(Davidson 2001*b* (1979): 79)

In this chapter, we take up the proper semantic treatment of quotation, which
has traditionally been treated as a device designed for reference specifically to
linguistic expressions. We discuss, refine, and evaluate Davidson's treatment,
and then briefly consider a simpler alternative account.

1. Traditional Treatments of Quotation

What is quotation? Davidson gives the following general account (2001*b*
(1979): 79; unless otherwise noted, page numbers in this chapter are for this
article):

Quotation is a device used to refer to typographical or phonetic shapes by exhibiting
samples, that is, inscriptions or utterances that have those shapes.

Perhaps to say that quotation is a device for referring to typographical or
phonetic shapes by exhibiting samples of what is referred to already contains
a prototype semantic theory, but the general idea can be put even more
neutrally. It is that quotation is a device for referring to typographical or
phonetic shapes, to linguistic expressions, that involves the appearance of
those expressions or tokens of them. The question of how to give the logical
form of quotation in the context of truth-theoretical semantics is the question
of how to represent the semantics of quotation in the axioms of one's truth

theory. To give an account of quotation in a truth theory presupposes that there is some uniform and unambiguous syntactic marker (or range of syntactic markers) for quotation. In the following, we will take this to be represented by single quotation marks. The treatment of other devices for quotation would be patterned after the treatment of single quotation marks.

To begin, we should mark, with Davidson, two different, but (perhaps) related, cases of the use of quotation marks, and of quotation devices, namely, what we will call 'pure quotation' and 'mixed quotation'. Pure quotation is illustrated in [1]. Mixed quotation is illustrated in [2]:

[1]   'Oligarchy' has four syllables.
[2]   Davidson says that he was introduced to quotation "as a somewhat shady device".

In pure quotation, an expression is referred to, but understanding the expression is not necessary for understanding a sentence in which it appears. In mixed quotation, in contrast, an expression is referred to (as in [2], the expression in the quotation marks), but understanding the expression is crucial also to understanding the sentence in which it appears. In this sense, in mixed cases an expression is both used and mentioned.[95] To indicate that this is a distinctive form of quotation, we have used double quotation marks in [2] instead of single quotation marks.

Davidson canvasses and dismisses three theories of quotation before offering his own: the proper name theory, the picture theory, and the spelling theory. We begin by a brief review of the difficulties of these theories, which serve as the motivation for the desiderata Davidson advances for any successful theory.

It is evident that quotation marks work according to a semantic rule, for we know what expression is referred to when we find an expression enclosed in quotation marks without having to learn any new semantic primitives of the language. This rules out the proper name theory of quotation, according to which expressions of the form $\ulcorner`\phi'\urcorner$ are unarticulated proper names to which no semantic rule is attached, and it is an accident of spelling that they actually contain an instance of the expression to which they refer. As Davidson says,

---

[95]   There are different senses we can give to 'use'. The thinnest sense of the use of an expression is just that in which the string of symbols constituting the expression appears in the string of symbols representing the type of the speech act, as 'cat' and 'log' are used in 'catalog'. A sense of intermediate thickness is that employed here in the text, in which the expression is understood to be a word, a semantic unit, in the sentence and understood in one of its senses. But note that this is still thinner than the sense in which the expression is understood as a semantic unit and treated as contributing its extensional properties to the truth conditions of the sentence in which it appears.

In an adequate theory, every sentence is construed as owing its truth or falsity to how it is built from a finite stock of parts by repeated application of a finite number of modes of combination. There are, of course, an infinite number of quotation-mark names, since every expression has its own quotation-mark name, and there are an infinite number of expressions. But on the theory of quotation we are considering, quotation mark names have no significant structure. It follows that a theory of truth could not be made to cover generally sentences containing quotations.   p. 83)

The picture theory appeals to a kind of metaphor, picturing the quotation marks as a frame and what appears within as a picture of what is referred to. In Davidson's words, "According to this view, it is not the entire quotation, that is, expression named plus quotation marks that refers to the expression, but rather the expression itself" (ibid.). As Davidson is interpreting the picture theory, then, that an expression appears within the frame of quotation marks indicates that it is a referring term, and that it refers to itself. The quotation marks function like punctuation that helps us to interpret the expression within them. According to Davidson, the problem with the picture theory is that, once we recognize that its central feature is the claim that in the special context of quotation marks a word refers to itself, the special appeal to a relation of picturing drops out altogether. That is, there is no explanation of how the fact that the very expression referred to appears within the quotation marks is connected with what it refers to. Rather, what is needed is some feature of the entire expression which is to be interpreted as indicating that there is a connection between what is contained in the quotation marks and what is referred to.

This thought leads to the spelling theory (which Davidson attributes to Geach and to Quine and Tarski[96]). According to the Tarski–Quine version, the name theory is correct for quotation marks appearing around letters, for example, 'a', 'b', 'c', etc., are to be treated as primitive expressions in the language referring to the first, second, and third letters of the alphabet, and so on. Quoted expressions which are concatenations of letters (and spaces and other primitive symbols in the language) are to be treated as descriptions in the following manner. The expression [4] is an abbreviation of [5], which can also be written as [6], treating 'space' as a name for a space.

[4] 'Snakes bite'
[5] the concatenation of 'S' with 'n' with 'a' with 'k' with 'e' with 's' with ' ' with 'b' with 'i' with 't' with 'e',
[6] 'S'⌢'n'⌢'a'⌢'k'⌢'e'⌢'s'⌢space⌢'b'⌢'i'⌢'t'⌢'e',

---

[96] Geach (1957: 79–80); Quine (1960: 212); Tarski (1983 (1935): 160).

151

This proposal meets the requirement that it can be incorporated into a recursive truth theory with a finite number of primitive expressions. It treats as primitives only names of the primitive symbols of the language, which are finite in number. And otherwise it only employs devices whose contributions to truth conditions are easily given.

Davidson raises several objections to this theory. The first is that no special semantic role has been assigned to quotation marks. They are dispensable in the case of the primitives, a mere accident of their spelling, for they have no independent semantic significance there. For expressions which are concatenations of the primitives, they are just abbreviatory devices and are assigned no specific or special semantical role. The force of this objection is supposed to derive from something that is right about the picturing theory, namely, that our understanding of quotation marks is connected with the fact that the expression referred to is contained within them. This feature is lost by the spelling theory (as explained above). The second objection is that the description theory cannot give an account of cases of mixed quotation. For if it treats expressions like 'Aristotle' (that is, the quote name of 'Aristotle') as abbreviations for descriptions of the configuration of letters, then, semantically, there is no word which could be both used and mentioned in any sentence in which it appears. (Note that, implicitly, this is to assume that we need to give a uniform account of pure and mixed uses of quotation marks, that is, that no semantic ambiguity is involved.) Finally, while quotation marks can be used to introduce new primitive symbols, a new alphabet, this would make no sense on the spelling view because quotation marks around primitive expressions have no semantic function, and the expression appearing within them is not treated as having a connection with what expression is named by the complete expression.[97]

On the basis of his criticisms of opposing theories, Davidson develops three criteria any adequate theory of quotation should meet.

1. The theory "should merge with a general theory of truth for the sentences of the language" (Davidson 2001*b* (1979): 89).
2. "[T]he theory [must] provide an articulate semantic role for the *devices* of quotation (quotation marks, or verbal equivalents). When we learn to understand quotation we learn a rule with endless applications: if you want to refer to an expression, you may do it by putting quotation marks around a token of the expression you want to mention" (pp. 89–90).

---

[97] Another difficulty is presented by the observation (due to Barry Loewer) that " 'Alice swooned' will never be tokened" cannot be true, but can be true on the spelling theory.

3. The "theory must explain the sense in which a quotation pictures what is referred to, otherwise it will be inadequate to account for important uses of quotation, for example, to introduce novel pieces of notation and new alphabets" (p. 90).

The third of these desiderata plays a crucial role in the justification of Davidson's proposal.

2. Davidson's Proposal

The account Davidson provides of the logical form of quotation employs a strategy which we will see, in subsequent chapters, that Davidson applies also to two other problem cases. The strategy is to treat sentences in which quotation appears as decomposable into two distinct sentences or expressions, one of which refers to the other, or, rather, in use, to an instance or token of the other. Davidson motivates this move by the following reflection:

The main difficulty springs . . . from the simultaneous demands that we assign articulate structure to quotations and that they picture what they mention. For articulate linguistic structure here must be that of description, and describing seems to forestall the need to picture. The call for structure is derived from the underlying demand for a theory of meaning, here thought of as a theory of truth; all that is needed is enough structure to implement the recursive characterization of a truth predicate. Still, enough structure will be too much as long as we regard the quoted material as part of the semantically significant syntax of a sentence. The cure is therefore to give up this assumption.   (ibid.)

Accordingly, Davidson suggests that the quotation marks are the singular term in a sentence such as [1] or [4], and that the material inside the quotation marks "does not refer to anything at all, nor is it part of any expression that does" (ibid.). The quotation marks "help refer to a shape by pointing out something that has it" (ibid.). For this reason, Davidson calls his theory the "*demonstrative theory* of quotation" (ibid.). The quotation marks, he says, "may be read 'the expression a token of which is here'" (alternatively, 'the expression with the shape pictured here') (ibid.). (This indicates that the suggestion is not that quotation marks function as a pure demonstrative, but rather that they function as a description with a demonstrative in its nominal restriction.) As a heuristic, Davidson suggests we can better exhibit the semantic role of quotation by rewriting a sentence such as [1] as [7] (ibid. 91).

[1] 'Oligarchy' has four syllables
[7] Oligarchy. The expression of which this is a token has four syllables.

In the second of these, the role of the quotation marks in the first is played by the definite description 'the expression of which this is a token'. The expression 'Oligarchy' is not treated semantically as a part of the sentence at all.

How would this suggestion be integrated explicitly into a truth theory? Since the proposal holds that the expression within quotation marks is not part of the sentence semantically, and, in particular, is not part of the subject term in the sentence, it is difficult to see how to integrate the suggestion into a truth theory in a way that directly makes use of the material contained within the quotation marks. Thus, it appears that to implement the proposal, one would have to treat 'The expression of which this is a token has four syllables' as the canonical form of ' "Oligarchy" has four syllables', and then apply the truth theory to the canonical form.

Does the suggestion meet the criteria which Davidson lays out? It clearly meets the first criterion. As Davidson puts it, "the demonstrative theory assigns a structure to sentences containing quotations that can be handled in a straightforward way by a theory of truth—assuming of course that there is a way of accommodating demonstratives at all" (p. 91). And, since it assimilates quotation marks to demonstrative descriptions, it gives quotation marks an articulate semantic role, meeting the second criterion. And it also appears to meet the third criterion, that of explaining, or, at any rate, making sense of, the sense in which quotation involves picturing what is referred to, since it treats quotation (when successful) as involving a token of what is referred to, and, in this way, it also accommodates the possibility of introducing new notation using quotation.

That leaves the question of how well it can be extended to cases of mixed quotation. Here the suggestion is that mixed quotation involves a use in a sentence of words which are semantically a part of it, and, at the same time, by way of the use of quotation marks, a reference to the words which are used. Thus, using our earlier example, [2] could be paraphrased as [8].

[2] Davidson says he was introduced to quotation "as a somewhat shady device".

[8] Davidson says, using words of which these are a token, that he was introduced to quotation as a somewhat shady device.

The idea here is that 'these' in an utterance of [8] is to be taken to refer to the token of 'as a somewhat shady device' used in an utterance of [8]. This does exhibit mixed cases as having something semantically in common with pure quotation, since in both cases the quotation marks are taken to involve a demonstrative description. However, it should be noted that the treatment cannot be completely semantically uniform, since we cannot arrive at the paraphrase of [2] by an application of the semantic function assigned to quotation marks in pure quotation. Rather, what we have are two distinct uses of quotation marks, which are semantically related. Thus, pure and mixed quotation involve an ambiguity in the use of quotation marks. That this is so is brought out by the possibility of using quotation marks in indirect discourse in the pure sense, as when one asserts [9] when reporting Amy's utterance of 'That's a funny name' after Albert told her his name. In this case, [10] would not be an adequate paraphrase of [9].

[9]   Amy said that 'Albert' is a funny name.
[10] Amy said, using this very word, that Albert is a funny name.

This last observation suggests a way of handling mixed quotation for the spelling theory. If quotation marks must be treated as ambiguous in pure and mixed cases, then the spelling theory can maintain that in indirect discourse, on one reading, [2] is equivalent to [11].

[2]   Davidson says he was introduced to quotation "as a somewhat shady device".

[11] Davidson says that he was introduced to quotation as a somewhat shady device, and Davidson used 'as a somewhat shady device' in doing so.[98]

The spelling theory could then be applied directly to the quoted material in the paraphrased version. In light of this possibility, the other arguments against the spelling view take on greater importance. It is worth noting that this treatment of mixed quotation is available to any account of pure quotation.[99]

3. Evaluation

We turn now to evaluating Davidson's suggestion. We consider objections one might raise to Davidson's proposal, and an alternative in §4.

---

[98] This suggestion is incomplete as it stands. A fully general account would have to accommodate multiple distinct uses of quotations in the complement clause of indirect discourse and allow for the possibility that the same word is quoted in different places. So, a fully general account has to pay attention to the possibility of any number of instances of quoted expressions and the grammatical position occupied by them. One way of handling this is illustrated in Ch. 11.

[99] Additional objections are raised to this strategy in Cappelen and Lepore (1997), though one of the present authors (Ludwig) remains unconvinced that they are successful.

One might object that Davidson's account of the semantics of sentences containing quotation marks does not preserve all of the semantic information contained in these sentences. It appears, for example, that on Davidson's account it would be possible for an utterance of a sentence such as [1], repeated here,

[1]   'Oligarchy' has four syllables,

to be false because the demonstrative description, represented by the quotation marks, might have been used to denote a word other than 'Oligarchy', even though, intuitively, the reference of ' "Oligarchy" ' is semantically fixed as 'Oligarchy'. This prima facie failure of the paraphrase is directly traceable to the demonstrative strategy, which treats 'Oligarchy' as no part, semantically, of the sentence. This allows the subject term of the sentence to refer to something other than 'Oligarchy'. The treatment of quotation as involving even the constrained demonstrative element Davidson suggests thus appears to provide too much freedom in what the referent of the quotation device can be.

In response, one might try to further constrain the denotation of the description. For example, we might treat the quotation marks as introducing the description 'the expression of which a token appears between tokens of quotation marks in this sentence I am now uttering'. Yet, this will not do as it stands, because one may use more than one quotation name in a sentence. It is also a shift away from the spirit of Davidson's proposal, for there the demonstrative would be intended to refer to a sentence rather than a token expression in quotation marks. And, even apart from this, it does not yet meet the difficulty, since, given our account of complex demonstratives, 'this' could still be used to refer to something else, and, indeed, might even fail of reference altogether.

One suggestion to get around this difficulty is that we treat the quotation marks not as involving a demonstrative, but rather an indexical, which is constrained to refer to the material inside the quotation marks. (This is even suggested by Davidson's paraphrase of quotation marks as 'The expression a token of which is here', if we take 'here' to function indexically rather than demonstratively—though this appears not to have been the way Davidson was thinking of it.) We would think of the quotation marks as semantically equivalent to a description which denotes an expression a token of which was contained between them (if anything). The trick is to say how exactly to represent this in a truth theory. We will not pursue this suggestion further here, but only note that it points in the direction of the suggestion which we make in the next section.

A second objection one might raise against the proposal is that, by treating quotation names as equivalent to definite descriptions, it is committed to statements employing quotation names having entailments that they do not have, and is committed to there being readings of sentences containing quotation names, due to scope ambiguities, that they do not have.[100] Thus, if Davidson's proposal were correct, then a true assertion of [1] would entail [12].

[12]   There are expression types and some expression type has been tokened.

But while this must be true if [1] is uttered truly or falsely, it is not intuitively part of what is meant in uttering [1]. While one talks about an expression in uttering [1], one does not say anything that commits one to there being expressions in uttering it, any more than when one says 'That is white' pointing to a horse, one says that there are horses.[101] On the second point, consider again [9] as a report of Amy's saying 'That's a funny name'. If Davidson is right, it should have in effect two readings, namely, [13] and [14].

[13]   Amy said that [the x: x is an expression of which *this* is a token](x is a funny name).

[14]   [The x: x is an expression of which *this* is a token](Amy said that x is a funny name).

Even granting that 'this' as used on the appropriate occasion picks out the right token in the vicinity, [13] is clearly false in the imagined circumstances. But there does not seem to be a false reading of the original. This would therefore have to be explained away on Davidson's account.[102]

Davidson's solution to the problem of giving the logical form of sentences containing quotation is to assimilate them to more familiar devices for which we know how to give a truth theory. The motivation is to accommodate the felt tension between the need to accommodate the essential role of the

[100] This assumes definite descriptions are quantified noun phrases, something not universally accepted. See Neale (1990*a*) for the brief in favor.

[101] See Cappelen and Lepore (1999) for an alternative construal of Davidson's proposal, which might avoid this objection.

[102] An option here would be to treat the description not as semantically equivalent to the quotation marks, but rather as their character, in Kaplan's sense, i.e. rather as a rule for determining the referent of the quotation marks. Then the quotation marks would have as referent what the description denotes relative to a context, but would be a directly referring term, and so not exhibit any scope ambiguities. This leaves the problem that treating the quotation marks as demonstratives leaves too much freedom in what a speaker can refer to. See n. 105, however, for a further suggestion along these lines which removes this last difficulty.

appearance of the expression that is being referred to between the quotation marks, and the need to treat the quotation marks as indicating in some way which expression is to be referred to. Davidson's own attempt to resolve this tension, while it gives quotation marks an indicating role, might be seen as weakening their connection with the material contained within them too much, and at the same time failing to respect their special character as referring terms by assimilating them to quantified noun phrases.

4. A Simple Alternative Reference Rule

There is a simpler suggestion that can be gleaned from the informal rule Davidson himself gives for quotation, which appears to avoid the difficulties we have just canvassed:

if you want to form a quotation-mark name of an expression, flank that expression with quotation marks; and, a quotation-mark name refers to 'its interior' (as Quine puts it). (p. 83)

The most straightforward way to implement this in a truth theory is to give a reference clause for all expressions of the form $\ulcorner`\phi'\urcorner$ that indicates that they are to refer to the expression that appears between the quotation marks, as in [15], where the quantifier ranges over whatever entities can be referred to by the use of quotation marks (expressions, let us say).[103]

[15] For any expression ϕ, $\text{Ref}(S, t, u, \ulcorner`\phi'\urcorner) = \phi$.

This treatment integrates with a general truth theory for the language, it assigns a semantical role to the quotation marks, and, in the most straightforward way possible, it explains why there is a special relation between what is referred to in quotation and the expression appearing between the quotation marks, and thus accommodates the intuition that quotation is akin in some sense to picturing. It does so, however, without treating the semantical content of quotation marks as a kind of explicit description or as involving, counterintuitively, any kind of demonstrative element.

If a rule for a referring device enables one who understands it to understand any sentence he is presented with in which the device is used, then there cannot be anything about its semantic function that remains hidden. Should

---

[103] This reference clause is suggested in Wallace (1975: 237–8), which originally appeared in 1971. More recently, Mark Richard has made the same suggestion in Richard (1986: 390).

we, then, grant that [15] provides an adequate account of the semantic function of quotation marks?

One concern here is whether the T-theorems we derive from such reference axioms will be interpretive. The difficulty is that we may instantiate [15] to a proper name of an expression. Thus, if we use 'Bob' as a name for the ampersand, we might derive a T-theorem such as [16] (ignoring for the moment context-sensitive elements).

[16] ⌜'&' is a logical connective⌝ is true iff Bob is a logical connective.

It might be thought that the metalanguage sentence used here, while it expresses the same proposition as the object language sentence described, yet differs in meaning because the referring term in the metalanguage functions differently from that in the object language. However, if we wished to, we could require in our canonical proof procedures that [15] be instantiated only to quotation names of the expressions, which would ensure that the T-theorem we arrived at would use in the metalanguage a quotation name of the expression denoted by the object language quotation name in question.

Another concern may arise from reflection that there is no way to recursively generate the class of quotation names. For to accommodate the possibility of introducing new symbols into a language using quotation names, it is necessary that we allow the quantifier in [15] to range over all symbols. Given that, plausibly, there are at least a denumerable infinity of simple symbols (symbols which are not concatenations of simpler symbols), it follows that the class of quotation names, though it can be described, cannot be generated by a rule from a finite stock of primitives.

It does not follow from this, however, that language contains an infinity of *semantic* primitives. For recall Davidson's original characterization of a semantic primitive (see Chapter 1, §1). An expression is a semantic primitive if you cannot understand the sentences in which it appears on the basis of understanding sentences in which it does not. Given this characterization of a semantic primitive, distinct quotation names, given the reference clause in [15], do not count as distinct semantic primitives. The quotation marks are semantic primitives, but not the referring terms formed with them. If one understands an expression formed from quotation marks in one sentence, then, given that identification of a sentence (or token of a sentence) containing a quotation name requires being able to identify any symbol in quotation marks in it, one will be able to understand any new sentence one is presented with using quotation marks without having to learn any new semantic facts. That is, one can understand the expression formed using the quotation marks and the symbol enclosed within them on the basis of understanding other sentences in which that expression does not appear. And, therefore, referring terms formed from quotation marks, as opposed to the quotation marks, are not semantic primitives.

However, there is a connected worry about the implications of [15] for the possibility of giving a truth theory of the sort we have been considering. This is that a theory accepting [15], and so accepting that any expression consisting of some expression enclosed in quotation marks is a term of the language, will not formally entail all *T*-sentences. This is because to entail formally all *T*-sentences, there has to be a formal way of identifying all the well-formed formulas of the language. Allowing quotation names of arbitrary symbols, which are not symbols of the language, means that the grammar is not recursively specifiable. It is not clear how significant a concern this is.[104] For we still get a theory which is finitely statable, and which enables one to produce a *T*-sentence for any sentence of the language *one is presented with*, and so, in that sense, it meets the original constraints.[105] We could also introduce an axiom schema in the place of [15], as in [17], with 'ϕ' serving as a schematic letter that may be replaced by any symbol.

[17] $\mathrm{Ref}(S, t, u, \ulcorner`\phi'\urcorner) = `\phi$'

The truth theory could then formally entail all *T*-sentences, but at the cost of our not being able to grasp all of its axioms. As before, however, this would not prevent us from using the theory to interpret any sentence we were presented with, since as soon as we are presented with a sentence containing a quotation name, we can produce the appropriate instance of [17].[106]

It should be remarked that not all devices which Davidson treats informally as quotation devices will turn out to be quotational devices on this account.

---

[104] One of us (Lepore) once thought this is a significant concern. See Lepore (1999).

[105] To try to avoid this problem, one might treat the quotation marks themselves as the referring term, as on Davidson's suggestion, rather than the quotation marks plus what is in their interior, but retain the idea that there is a rule that takes one from quotation marks and a context to a referent, where the material in the quotation marks is treated as part of the context. Thus, one might suggest the reference axiom, 'for any speaker S, time t, speech act u, token expression x, for any consecutive pair of token quotation marks y used in u, if y encloses x, then for any z such that z is the expression x is a token of, y refers to z.' We would here need to understand 'consecutive pair of token quotation marks' so that consecutive pairs were ordered in non-overlapping pairs from the beginning of the sentence. However, while this might work, it would also appear to require us to introduce token expressions as semantically relevant features of the context of utterance, and so to add them to the features of context we quantify over in our axioms.

[106] For further discussion, see Cappelen and Lepore (1999) and Ludwig and Ray (1998).

But quotation marks are a quite special way of referring to expressions, and not all ways of referring to expressions should be assimilated to them.

Quotation, as opposed to mentioning expressions more broadly, is specially suited for written inscriptions of sentences, rather than spoken sentence tokens. There are verbal equivalents, as when one says "quote" and "unquote" before and after the material which one wishes to refer to. These are not exactly quotation marks, but they would receive a similar treatment in the truth theory. But often when we speak we do not indicate by any explicit sign that we are mentioning rather than using a word. If one asserts, ' "Florida" means land of flowers', what one says will sound the same as 'Florida means land of flowers'. Yet, it seems we can assert the former as well as the latter verbally. To accommodate this, we have to understand the verbal utterance as ambiguous. Context helps us then to disambiguate it. We resort to other devices or provide additional clues when context may mislead or provide insufficient indication, for example, saying, 'The name "Bob" is short' instead of ' "Bob" is short'.

How does this proposal fare with mixed cases? We have already established that pure quotation and mixed quotation are two different, though no doubt related, semantic devices. Thus, the rule for pure quotation need not by itself provide an account of the semantical role of mixed quotation (Davidson's proposal for mixed quotation does not do this either). A full solution to mixed cases may very well need to be incorporated into a solution to the problem of indirect discourse more generally, which is the subject of Chapter 11. One way, however, of attempting to combine the two would be to make use of the suggestion already bruited in defense of the spelling theory, namely, to treat mixed quotation as an abbreviatory device in which a sentence such as [2] is treated as a conjunction, one of whose conjuncts involves pure quotation, and the other of which is an unmixed case of indirect speech.

7

Adjectives and Adverbs

It is not always evident what the quantificational structure of a sentence in natural language is; ... the requirements of theory may suggest that a sentence plays a role which can be explained only by treating it as having a quantificational structure not apparent on the surface.

(Davidson 2001 (1977): 210–11)

We take up two related topics in this chapter, adjectival modification, as in [1], and adverbial modification, as in [2].

[1]   Brutus is an honorable man.
[2]   Brutus served Rome honorably.

We will be following out Davidson's well-known and influential treatment of adverbs. We begin with a discussion of adjectival modification, which will form a useful backdrop to the discussion of adverbial modification. We will treat both what we call topic independent and topic dependent adjectives; the former modify the subject independently of the noun they attach to (e.g. 'red'), the latter do not (e.g., 'tall'). In our discussion of adverbial modification, we will extend Davidson's treatment to adverbs related to topic dependent adjectives. In Chapter 9, §5, we will suggest a modification of Davidson's treatment of adverbial modification in light of our discussion of tense.

The topic of this chapter is a large one, and we cannot hope to do justice to the enormous literature on the topic.[107] Our aim is rather to indicate the kinds of tools that have been introduced in the truth-theoretic framework to deal with these kinds of modifiers.

---

[107] For entries into the literature, see Schein (1993).

1. Adjectival Modification

Adjectival modification is the modification of a noun by an adjective. Nouns in general we have treated as supplying predicative material to the truth conditions of sentences in which they appear. We likewise treat adjectives as supplying predicative material to the truth conditions of the sentences in which they appear. When complex nouns appear in the nominal of a noun phrase, as in [3], we represent this as contributing a complex predicate restricting a quantifier, as in [4].

[3]   All married men are happy
[4]   [All x: x is a married man](x is happy)

Thus, the primary construction to be treated is the modification of a noun in a predicate construction by an adjective. We will first treat topic independent adjectives, and then give a treatment for at least some topic dependent adjectives.[108] Contrast [5] with [6].

[5]   Tom is a six foot tall basketball player.
[6]   Tom is a short basketball player.

It is clear that in [6] the contribution of 'short' is understood in relation to the contribution of 'basketball player', whereas in [5] the contribution of 'six foot tall' is not understood in relation to the contribution of 'basketball player', but independently. Where the interaction illustrated in [6] between the modifying adjective and noun occurs, the adjective is a topic dependent adjective.

---

[108] For both these classes of adjectives 'x is a G' follows from 'x is an F G'. There are other sorts of adjectives we will not take up here for which this is not so. For example, 'It is a fake/toy/decoy dog' does not imply 'It is a dog'; here the intensionality is obviously connected with the intensionality of the contexts created by propositional attitude verbs. Again, though for different reasons, 'Jack is a former/future pro golfer' does not imply 'Jack is a pro golfer'. Here 'former' modifies the tense structure of the sentence. This is equivalent to 'Jack is such that Jack was/will be a pro golfer'. In the case of 'Jack is an alleged/putative murderer' we would treat this as involving a sentential operator: 'It is alleged/supposed of Jack that he is a murderer'. In none of these cases is there a corresponding comparative, which marks them out as distinct from topic dependent adjectives of the sort considered below. What about the class of adjectives illustrated by 'That was a partial filling of the tank'? It might be said that this does not imply 'That was a filling of the tank'. However, in light of our treatment of the progressive in Ch. 8, §3, it would be natural to take 'filling' here to be expressing an event type which can occur with or without its being completed, so that 'partial' here functions to specify that the event type expressed by 'is filling' was not completed. It is just that usually when we say 'there was a filling of the tank' we take the person saying it to be committed to its being completed unless he specifies otherwise. This is supported by the fact that it does not seem contradictory to say: there was a filling of the tank, but it was only partial/not completed before the gas ran out.

Topic *in*dependent adjectives contribute effectively a conjunct to the truth conditions of the sentences in which they appear. To say that something is a red apple is to say no more than that it is red and an apple. Thus, the construction Copula + Indefinite Article + Adjective + Nominal is a truth-functional recursive structure that subserves the same semantic role as conjunction in a more compact form. The satisfaction conditions, then, for this sort of construction are given as in [7].

> [7] For all functions f, for all topic independent adjectives A and nominals N, f satisfies(S, t, u) $\ulcorner x$ is a $AN\urcorner$ iff f satisfies (S, t, u) $\ulcorner x$ is $A\urcorner$ and f satisfies(S, t, u) $\ulcorner x$ is a $N\urcorner$.

Clearly, with the obvious axioms for complex predicates formed using truth-functional connectives, 'is round and hollow', 'is red or green', this will handle constructions of arbitrary complexity.

This approach breaks down when we turn to topic dependent adjectives. We will concentrate primarily on topic dependent adjectives which are derived from comparatives, as in [8]. But we will also give brief consideration to the (somewhat dubious) suggestion that the class of topic dependent adjectives is broader than those formed from comparatives, and includes examples like those illustrated in [9].

> [8] Mickey is a large mouse/rodent/animal.
> [9] That is a water bucket/boy/image.

To begin with [8], it is clear that what is being said about Mickey is to be understood in relation to the noun that 'large' modifies. If we took the approach suggested by [7], we would treat 'Mickey is a large mouse' as equivalent to 'Mickey is large and Mickey is a mouse'. But this cannot be correct, because while Mickey is a large mouse, he is not a large entertainer, and we do not want to say that Micky is both large and not large. We might try 'Mickey is large for a mouse and Mickey is a mouse', but this leaves us with the predicate 'is large for a mouse' to deal with, which employs the same two words we started with, and leaves their interaction unexplained, for 'Mickey is large for a mouse' implies 'Mickey is a mouse'. In addition, it is not clear how this proposal could be used to handle iterated topic dependent adjectives, as in 'Mickey is a smart large mouse', in which we intend 'smart' to be understood relative to large mice. For if we employ the maneuver just suggested, we get 'Mickey is smart for a large mouse', but now we cannot unpack 'a large mouse' intelligibly with 'large for a mouse', for that gives us the uninterpretable 'Mickey is smart for large for a mouse'.

The conceptually fundamental relation here is that of being larger than, since once we have specified the ordering of mice in terms of this relation, we have fixed all the facts relevant to judging whether Mickey is a large mouse. This suggests understanding the adjective in terms of the comparative, namely, 'is larger than', and that one of the relata is understood, speaking loosely, in terms of the class of things to which the predicate formed from the modified noun applies (we say 'speaking loosely' because we do not believe there is any reference to classes in such sentences).[109] The question is exactly how. Whatever the answer, it has to accommodate the fact that there is some looseness in the application of 'large mouse' to mice, that is, that it is vague. A symptom of this is that we can construct a sorites argument for 'is a large mouse' using the step premise 'if x is a large mouse, and y differs in size from x by ε, then y is a large mouse', which looks very plausible for small enough ε, to reach, by apparently impeccable reasoning, the conclusion that if there is a large mouse, every mouse is a large mouse.[110]

An attractive suggestion is that to call, for example, Mickey a large mouse is not to specify precisely his size in the range of sizes of mice, but rather to say something to the effect that he is larger[111] than most of his kindred.[112] In other words, the suggestion is to give the truth conditions as in [10].

[10]   'Mickey is a large mouse' is true(S, t, u) iff Mickey is larger than most mice at t and Mickey is a mouse at t.

The satisfaction clause for such predicates would then be as illustrated in [11].

---

[109] There is great pressure to see the comparative, e.g. 'larger than', as basic and other forms such as 'large' and largest' as understood in terms of it. In the case of 'Mickey is the largest mouse' the representation is easy: [The x: x is a mouse and [for all y: y is a mouse](x is larger than y)](Mickey = x). This explains straightforwardly why 'Mickey is larger than Minnie' follows from 'Minnie is a mouse distinct from Mickey' and 'Mickey is the largest mouse'.

[110] See Ludwig and Ray (2002) for a diagnosis of sorites argumentation.

[111] In the following we will make use of the comparative in explaining the logical form of sentences involving adjectives derived from them, but we will not be offering an analysis of the comparative itself, which arguably involves itself some important logical structure, specifically quantification over degrees. If so, then this raises the question whether in [11] the quantifier over degrees might take scope either over or under 'most', so that [11] is ambiguous. The construction '[Most y: ... y ...](...)', however, being equivalent to '... is/are such that ...', guarantees that '[Most y: ... y ...]' takes scope over '(...)'.

[112] We have previously made this suggestion in print (Ludwig and Lepore 2001). It was originally made, to our knowledge, by Langford (1942: 335). It is considered and rejected in some early work on topic dependent adjectives in the truth-theoretic framework—for reasons we will discuss below—in Wheeler (1972: 319) and Wallace (1972: 777). As will emerge, we think that they were too quick to give up on the proposal.

[11]   For all functions f, f satisfies(S, t, u) 'x is a large mouse' iff f satisfies '[Most y: y is a mouse](x is larger than y)' and f satisfies(S, t, u) $\ulcorner x$ is a mouse $\urcorner$.

This shows the argument from 'Mickey is a large mouse' to 'Mickey is a mouse' to be logically valid. It is easy to verify that it explains the validity of a number of other intuitively valid natural language arguments in a straightforward way. (1) Minnie is a large mouse; Mickey is larger than Minnie; therefore, Mickey is a large mouse. (2) All mice are larger than other rodents; Mickey is a large mouse; therefore, Mickey is a large rodent. (3) All and only opossums are North American marsupials; Oscar is a large opossum; therefore, Oscar is a large North American marsupial. The proposal also explains why the following argument is not valid: 'Mickey is the largest mouse'; therefore, 'Mickey is a large mouse'. The first is compatible with Mickey being the only mouse, in which case he is neither large, nor small, nor medium-sized for a mouse. The technique works recursively, and so will handle arbitrarily complex adjectival modifications.[113] The use of the vague quantifier 'most' looks to answer at least in part to the vagueness of the application of 'large mouse'. And this suggestion avoids treating 'large' as introducing a relation between individuals and classes (or individuals and intensions), to which intuitively there is no reference in the sentence 'Mickey is a large mouse', or at least no more than in the sentence 'Mickey is a mouse', for whose semantics there is no need for reference to classes.

It is sometimes objected that approaches like this will not work because it means that whether someone is a tall or short basketball player, for example, would depend on when he was alive. Two points should be made here. First, 'x is a tall basketball player' is true iff x is a basketball player and x is taller than most basketball players. The comparison class is picked out by the nominal of 'most', but there is no reason to hold that its extension must always be restricted to just current basketball players. In 'Most of the POWs have been repatriated', for example, it is clear that the extension of 'POW' is not understood to cover only current POWs.[114] Second, we do sometimes clearly allow that someone's status as, for example, being a large offensive lineman may change as the average size of offensive linemen goes up. So there is nothing incoherent about saying: He was a large offensive lineman

---

[113] We must allow for ambiguity in iterations of adjectives. 'Jack is a fat old man' may be interpreted as 'Jack is a fat man and Jack is an old man' ('Jack is a fat, and old, man'), as well as 'Jack is fatter than most old men'.

[114] See Ch. 10, §1, n. 175, for more discussion.

when he entered the league, but he isn't any longer (without implying that he has shrunk).

However, on another point, we can note that there can certainly be circumstances in which asserting that someone is, for example, a tall basketball player would be true on the above account, but would not be something that we would assert. If, for example, there are 100 basketball players, 80 of whom are 6', one of whom is 6'1", and the rest 7', it would be odd to say of the one that is 6'1" that he was a tall basketball player. One quick response to this would be to argue that the intuition here attaches to a conversational implicature. That is, though it is true given [11], it does not follow from [11] that it would be conversationally appropriate in the described circumstance to assert of the 6'1" basketball player that he was a tall basketball player. There is a clear reason why it would not be, namely, there is not a significant difference in the height between the one who is 6'1" and most of the others, and if we assert of someone that he is a tall basketball player, we will typically be taken to be saying something of interest. So one might say here that there is a misleading implication, or false implication, in asserting of someone not significantly taller than the others that he is tall relative to them, for this implies he is, relative to context, significantly taller.

This seems less than fully satisfactory, however. Consider 100 basketball players all of whom are nearly the same height, and among whom heights differ only by millimeters. The tallest of them may be taller than most, but it is not clear that we will say that any of them count as tall players. Some, we feel like say, are taller than others, but not so much so that any of them count as tall players. Perhaps then to say someone is a tall *F* is to say that he is an *F* and significantly taller than most F's. This could be accommodated straightforwardly in the account.[115]

Consider, however, another example, in which we have, say, 100 gremlins, 50 of whom are 3' tall and 50 of whom are 4' tall. Suppose we are challenged to sort the gremlins into two categories, short gremlins and tall gremlins. Then it is clear that the 4' gremlins will be classified as tall gremlins and the 3' gremlins as short gremlins. Indeed, if 49 were 3' and 51 4', and the same challenge were issued, we would sort the 3' gremlins into the short category and the 4' gremlins into the tall category.[116] However, in neither case would those we classify as tall gremlins be taller than most gremlins. We cannot modify the suggested account by requiring a tall gremlin to be taller than

---

[115] We are indebted to Paul Pietroski for discussion.
[116] Patterned after the example in Wheeler (1972: 319).

or equal in height to most of the gremlins, because then if there are 60 3′ gremlins and 40 4′ gremlins, all of them will count as tall. The difficulty with the classification, however, lies in its being presented to us as a forced choice. On the assumption that some are tall and some are short, there is only one classification available. Suppose that 75 were 4′ and 25 3′. There would be no difficulty in saying that the 3′ gremlins were short gremlins. But suppose we are challenged to sort them into short and tall gremlins. Then again there is only one classification available. The 4′ gremlins are the tall gremlins. And so we would have to say that most of the gremlins are tall gremlins.[117] But this last sounds extremely strained!

What is going on? We think that there are three connected things that lead to the mistaken judgment in this case. First, we assume that populations do (typically) have both short and tall members (and similarly for other categories that are opposites though not contradictories formed from comparatives). So we are predisposed to think that there must be both short and tall members of a population where there are differences in height. Second, the question, 'Which are the tall gremlins' presupposes that there are tall gremlins. In attempting to answer the question, we have a tendency to accept its presupposition, which distorts our judgments. The first and second points reinforce each other. Third, there is, in any case, a natural tendency to interpret a question in a way that allows one to give information that the questioner might be reasonably supposed to want, and, absent any special information, one may suppose that a questioner would be interested in sorting the gremlins into the taller and shorter ones. Thus, 'tall ones' and 'short ones' are treated as coding for 'taller ones' and 'shorter ones'. The combined effect is that we get mistaken results in cases in which the presupposition that there are tall gremlins is incorrect,

---

[117] Wallace (1972) gives the example of a size of lawn mower, introduced for midgets and children, much smaller than the standard size, and many fewer of which are produced, and holds that in this case most of the lawn mowers are large. But switch the example. Most human beings are not midgets or children. But are most human beings therefore large? We suggest that the use of a commodity has influenced Wallace's intuitions here. Clothing and other commodities often come labeled for size, a crude labeling scheme being 'small', 'medium', and 'large'; or if there are just two sizes, variously, depending on the marketing advantage of the designation, 'small and medium', 'small and large', or 'medium and large'. It clear that this need have no relation to the number of units of any given item produced or the usual use of 'large' and 'small'. These involve a semi-technical use of these terms, for they are keyed to certain measurements (which may differ between markets or manufacturers), and are used as labels for those. It would not be a contradiction to say that the large sized shirts in the Big and Tall shop are not large shirts there. When we hear the story about the lawn mowers, we think, 'They have two sizes, large and small'. But suppose them labeled 'standard' and 'small'; there is no inclination then to say that the standard sized lawn mowers are large lawn mowers.

as shown by the example above involving 75 4' gremlins and 25 3' gremlins. On reflection, it seems that the correct thing to say in that case is that there are, strictly speaking, no tall gremlins. The typical height of gremlins is 4', but there are some that are shorter, only 3', that is, some short gremlins; and, of course, there are taller ones and shorter ones.

We suggest that the same thing is going on in the case in which we have 50 3' and 50 4' gremlins, or 49 3' and 50 4' gremlins, and we are asked to apply 'tall gremlins'. It is less obvious in this case that the forced choice has produced a mistaken result because these are close to cases in which it would be correct to say that there are tall gremlins, that is, cases in which somewhat more of the gremlins are 3' tall. But notice that if we redescribed the case by saying that 49 gremlins were 3', 49 4' and one 5', the result of the forced classification would immediately change: one would judge there to be 49 short gremlins and one tall gremlin. This supports the suggestion, we think, that the forced choice is distorting our judgments about which gremlins are tall.

An alternative suggestion that might be made to try to accommodate the forced choice results would be to treat 'is a tall *F*' as equivalent to 'is an *F* and is significantly taller than average for *F*'s' (Quine makes a suggestion of this sort, 1960: 132). However, averages are very sensitive to statistical outliers, especially when the population is not very large. This will give rise to cases in which only one member of a population is judged to be tall, and the rest short, because the one member is so tall that the average turns out to be above the height of the rest of the population, though the heights of the rest of the population are distributed on a bell curve. One might then suggest treating 'is a tall *F*' as equivalent to 'is an *F* and is significantly taller than the median for *F*'s'. This avoids the difficulty of statistical outliers, but it does not respond to the case involving 49 3' gremlins and 51 4' gremlins, for the median in that case is 4', and then none of the 4' gremlins would count as tall. Moreover, if we are right that the forced choice cases give the wrong results, this account would likewise give the wrong results in the case of 50 3' gremlins and 50 4' gremlins, for in that case the median is the average of the middle pair, which is 3½', and plausibly the 4' gremlins are then significantly taller than the median (by enlarging the difference between the two categories, we could make the difference from the median more significant).

One could also resort to a disjunctive account of the following sort: '*x* is a tall *F*' is equivalent to '*x* is an *F* and if (#) the *F*'s sort into two roughly equal populations with respect to height which are such that there is a significant difference in height between the tallest of those in the population whose average height is the lesser of the two and the shortest of those in the

169

population whose average height is the greater of the two, then x is a member of the population whose average height is the greater of the two, and if it is not the case that (#), then x is significantly taller than most F's. This would accommodate the initial intuitions in all the cases discussed so far. However, we find it implausible that this is the rule that the practice we are introduced to by example induces on the application of topic independent adjectives to nouns, especially in the light of our having an explanation of the initial reactions to the forced choice cases on the basis of a simpler semantic account that handles the other cases.

Another worry arises for the proposal, however, when it is applied to an infinite domain of ordered items such as the numbers.[118] We do speak of large and small numbers. For example, most people would say that one googol (10^{100}) is a large number. But is one googol larger than most numbers? The set of numbers larger than one googol is of infinite cardinality, while, if we focus at least just on the natural numbers, the set of numbers equal to or smaller than one googol is finite. So one googol is not larger than most numbers. Application of 'large' to numbers does not correspond to the rule we have given. What do we intend though when we say a number is large? We intend to say something to the effect that it is large relative to the numbers used in everyday life, or larger than most numbers used in everyday life. It is not difficult to see how such a usage can arise out of the sort of rule which we have provided. There is no natural application to the domain of numbers taken as a whole. In any case, most people are quite unclear about the concept of infinity. We are apt to compare an item when considering whether to call it large or tall to those we are familiar with, taking them, as it were, to be typical of most. When we come to the numbers, of course, those we are familiar with are not typical of most! But it would be natural for most speakers to compare numbers for largeness to those they are most familiar with nonetheless, when called upon to say whether it is large or not. This is as good a method of extending the use of 'large' to the numbers as we are apt to come up with. The usage becomes entrenched, and we arguably have a variant usage of 'large' in application to the numbers in particular. Take another arguably infinite series, the series of temporal instants. Suppose time infinite backwards and forwards. What is an early time? What is a late time? These questions leave us perplexed. There is in this case nothing like 'numbers we have common concourse with' we can compare times with, for we have to accommodate speakers at any time, and speakers are not all familiar with the same times.

---

[118] An anonymous reviewer raised this difficulty.

Not all adjectives formed from comparatives can be handled in the fashion indicated above. In particular, evaluative terms, for example, 'good', that have corresponding comparatives do not involve a comparison with the class of things of the sort in question which are actually good. A knife may not be good though it is the best of the lot. Similarly, for men. Diogenes lit a lamp in broad daylight and said he was looking for a good man. When asked where there were good men to be found in Greece, he said nowhere. While he may have been pessimistic, his answer was not necessarily false. In the case of evaluative terms, it is clear that there are standards associated with items of the various kinds which we use to determine which are better than which. Whether something of a kind is good is determined relative to those standards, not in relation to whether it is better than most things of that kind or better than the average. It is, then, natural to say that a good item of a particular kind is one which satisfies most of the standards associated with it to a high degree. These remarks about evaluative terms, however, are meant merely to be suggestive. A full treatment of evaluative adjectives would require more space than we can devote to it here.[119]

Let us turn now to the examples given in [9], repeated here.

[9]   That is a water bucket/boy/image.

It is far from clear that these examples should be treated as involving compositional meaning rules, as opposed to their having uses as idioms. In the first case, it might be said, we mean a bucket for holding water, in the second, we mean a boy designated to fetch water, in the third, we mean an image which is of water. These give us interpretations other than the conjunctive one. The case for thinking that they are more than idioms rests on the fact that people often arrive at analogous interpretations readily when we substitute other container nouns, for example, for 'bucket', and other kind terms for 'water', even ones we have not combined before, and so on.

---

[119] What about modifiers of adjectives formed from comparatives such as 'very', 'much', 'rather', and so on? We will not enter into an extended discussion here, but a plausible first suggestion compatible with the approach in the text would be that 'very tall man' can be analyzed as 'man and (significantly) taller than most tall men'. Intuitively 'very' does not modify 'man' but 'tall', and so contributes only to the second conjunct; this is iterable, so 'very very tall man' would be analyzed as 'man and (significantly) taller than most very tall men', and so on. But what about 'very' in a construction like 'very white carnation'? The predicate 'is a white carnation' seems to admit of both a topic dependent and topic independent reading. Modifying 'white' with 'very' on the topic independent reading should then yield 'is a carnation and is very white', and so 'is a carnation (significantly) whiter than most white things'; on the topic dependent reading, modifying 'white' with 'very' would give us 'is a carnation and (significantly) whiter than most white carnations'.

For example, it could be said that 'That is a coffee bucket' would be used to say that that is a bucket used to hold coffee, or that 'ball boy' means a boy who fetches balls. Similarly, it might be suggested that we understand 'bird image' to mean an image of a bird just as we understand 'water image' to mean an image of water, and so on. Whatever the case with these examples, however, there are many combinations which seem not to have any natural interpretation, for example, 'tree bucket', 'bowling ball cup', 'planet boy', or 'water giraffe'—other than the conjunctive interpretation. (Perhaps '*F* image' will take any substitution for '*F*' which picks out something an image can be of.) This strongly suggests that, in some cases of what can seem to be prima facie compositional constructions, there is merely apparent systematicity that is generated by there being easy *analogies* between familiar idiomatic combinations and newly coined idiomatic usages. In this case, our understanding the new combinations as intended does not reflect a rule of the language that attaches to the categories of terms.

However, if there were rules governing this, and it were not just a matter of seeing easy analogies with familiar idioms, then this *could be* incorporated into a truth-theoretic semantics straightforwardly. We give a brief illustration. Let us suppose, for the sake of argument, that when nouns for liquids are used as adjectives in application to container nouns, we always treat the adjective A as contributing the predicate 'is for the purposes of holding'$^\frown A$. (On this view, these constructions would be ambiguous, because the conjunctive reading does always seem to be available, even if absurd in some cases ('planet boy'); often enough one reading would be the obvious one, but not always, as in the case of 'He worked in a brick factory'.) Where the pairing of an adjective in a certain category and a noun in a certain category force a certain interpretation, we can specify satisfaction clauses quantifying over adjectives and nouns in those categories to specify the right satisfaction conditions. Where there is ambiguity, we resort to our general method of regimentation, and then decide in a context of utterance which disambiguated sentence the utterance is to be associated with, for the purposes of assigning it truth conditions. But in all of these cases, once it is clear which predicate we should construct from the adjective, we employ an axiom like [7] above. To handle sentences like 'That is a water bucket' (discounting ambiguity), we would introduce the axiom [12] for the predicate construction.

[12]   For all functions f, for all kind adjectives K and container nominals C, f satisfies(S, t, u) $\ulcorner x$ is a $KC\urcorner$ iff f satisfies(S, t, u) $\ulcorner x$ is for the purpose of holding $K\urcorner$ and f satisfies(S, t, u) $\ulcorner x$ is a $C\urcorner$.

Again we emphasize that the point of [12] is not to endorse the suggestion that English works this way (we believe that 'water bucket' is an idiom when used in the sense of 'bucket for holding water'), but to head off the suggestion that a truth-theoretical semantics would have trouble with such constructions if they were systematic: for if they are rule governed, the rule can be incorporated in an axiom for the construction.

There is clearly something which our treatments of adjectival modification have in common. All of them treat adjectival modification as involving predicate modification of the subject term which amplifies what is said by the unmodified predicate. In all cases, we have represented '*x* is an *FG*' as equivalent to '*x* is *F**** and *x* is *G*'.[120] The difference between the treatment of different cases has to do with what predicate replaces '*F****'. In the simplest cases, it is a predicate built directly from '*F*' itself. We treat the contribution of 'red' in 'red hat' as the predicate 'is red'. But other cases are more complex. In the case of adjectives derived from comparatives, the predicate is one formed by quantifying into one of the argument places in the related relational predicate. Thus, for 'large horse', the predicate is 'is larger than most horses'. This shows adjectival modification to be a single semantic device, and explains in the same way for every sort of adjectival modification the entailment from '*a* is an *FG*' to '*a* is *G*'.

It will be worthwhile before closing this section to consider a claim made by Evans (1976). Evans claimed that one could provide a satisfaction clause for adjectives, including topic dependent adjectives, which does not decompose the structure in the way we have illustrated above. Adapting it to our notation, his proposal for '*x* is a large man' would be [13].

> [13] For any function f, f satisfies(S, t, u) '*x* is a large man' iff $f('x')$ is a large satisfier(S, t, u) of 'is a man'.

Two different satisfaction relations are introduced on this account: one relates functions to open sentences, the other relates objects to open sentences. We would then have an additional axiom that tells us that $f('x')$ is a large satisfier (S, t, u) of 'is a man' iff $f('x')$ is a large man—similarly for other primitive predicates. The proposal runs into trouble, however, because of its reliance on the introduction of the new satisfaction relation in which 'satisfies' is modified by 'large'. This is brought out when we consider iterations of adjectives. Consider the generalization of [13] in [14].

---

[120] *Mutatis mutandis* if the modification is to the predicate contributed by the noun.

[14]   For any function f, noun N, f satisfies $(S,\ t,\ u)$ ⌜x is a large N⌝ iff $f('x')$ is a large satisfier $(S,\ t,\ u)$ of ⌜x is an N⌝.

Consider a non-conjunctive reading of 'x is a large fat man' according to which x is large for a fat man, rather than a large and fat man. From [14] we get: f satisfies $(S,\ t,\ u)$ 'x is a large fat man' iff $f('x')$ is a large satisfier $(S,\ t,\ u)$ of 'x is a fat man'. How do we proceed from here, though? We might try a new axiom: x is a large satisfier $(S,\ t,\ u)$ of 'x is a fat man' iff 'x is a large fat man. But this won't do for we would need separate axioms for all complex predicates and so an infinity of axioms. We need to give a recursive axiom which makes use of the axioms attaching to the predicate formed from the components of the complex predicate. We need an axiom of the form, 'any x is a large satisfier $(S,\ t,\ u)$ of ⌜x is a $F\ G$⌝ iff ... ', where 'F' at least is primitive, and 'G' possibly complex'. [15] is not adequate.

[15]   For any y, y is a large satisfier $(S,\ t,\ u)$ of ⌜x is a $F\ G$⌝ iff y is a large satisfier $(S,\ t,\ u)$ of ⌜x is a F⌝ and y is a large satisfier $(S,\ t,\ u)$ of ⌜x is a G⌝.

For that would not give us the large things in the intersection of the class of Fs and Gs, but the intersection of the class of large G things and the class of large F things (the latter might be empty when the former is not). It would be natural to return to the original thought and introduce another modifier of the satisfaction relation, as in:

[16]   For any x, x is a large satisfier $(S,\ t,\ u)$ of ⌜x is a $F\ G$⌝ iff x is a large F satisfier $(S,\ t,\ u)$ of ⌜x is a G⌝.

Here the first appearance of 'F' on the right of 'iff' is to be replaced by a metalanguage term translating the object language 'F'. But this is not adequate, for it is clear that this will work only for the particular 'F' in question—for we are not treating [16] as a schema in the place of 'F'. It fails to use the axiom for the predicate 'is an F', and so fails to provide a completely general solution. A separate axiom would be needed on this approach for each adjective in the place of 'F'. An *each* of these would introduce a new satisfaction relation. In this case it is 'is a large F satisfier'. And the same problem arises in turn for each of these new satisfaction relations in application to complex predicates, resulting in the introduction of new satisfaction relations, and axioms, ad infinitum, violating a central constraint on a theory of meaning for a natural language.

2. Adverbial Modification

Davidson's well-known and influential treatment of adverbs is given primarily in two articles, "The Logical Form of Action Sentences" (2001*b* (1967)) and "Adverbs of Action" (1985).[121] Although Davidson develops the account in the context of his work on action theory, since it provides a general account of how to treat adverbs, we consider it in this chapter as a part of his work on the logical form of sentences in natural languages.

To begin, we distinguish two different cases, corresponding to those between topic independent and topic dependent adjectives, which we call correspondingly topic independent and topic dependent adverbs. Thus, consider [17] and [18].

[17] Edwin swam the English Channel at midnight in his dressing gown.

[18] Edwin swam the English Channel quickly.

In the first of these, the way in which the adverbs modify the sense of the predicate is not affected by what the predicate is. In the second of these, our understanding of how the verb is modified by the adverb depends on what the verb is. Thus, Edwin might have swum the English Channel quickly, but crossed it slowly, that is, it was quick for a swimming, but slow for a crossing. Davidson's treatment of adverbs is confined to topic independent adverbs. We will follow Davidson's treatment to begin with, and then return to the problem of topic dependent adverbs.

An account of the logical form of sentences containing adverbs must show how to derive *T*-sentences for them in a recursive truth theory for the whole language, and, in particular, exhibit them as having an appropriate recursive structure when sentences containing them are obviously complex, and it must validate our intuitive judgments about entailment relations between sentences on the basis of form. Thus, for example, [17] entails [19]–[22].

[19] Edwin swam the English Channel at midnight.

[20] Edwin swam the English Channel in his dressing gown.

[21] Edwin swam the English Channel.

[22] Edwin swam the English Channel at some time in something.

As an initial remark, we can observe that the need to accommodate the evident structure of [17], and the entailment relations it enters into, rules out treating [17] as involving a four-place predicate, '*x* swam *y* at *z* in *r*'. Treating adverbs

[121] Also relevant are "Causal Relations" (Davidson 2001*a* (1967); "The Individuation of Events" 2001*a* (1969): 167; "Events as Particulars" 2001*a* (1970): 184–5; "Eternal vs. Ephemeral Events" 2001*b* (1971): 202; "Reply to Cargile" 2001*b* (1970); and "The Method of Truth in Metaphysics" 2001 (1977)). For some recent work on events in semantics, see Higginbotham *et al.* (2000).

like this would prevent us from explaining how [19]–[22] follow from [17] as a matter of form, since '$R(a, b)$' does not follow as a matter of form from '$R(a, b, c)$'. In addition, this leaves out what is intuitively a common element in all of these sentences.[122]

There is a simple solution in what appears to be the parallel case for adjectival modification. The adjectival modifications in [23], as we have observed, can be treated as introducing additional conjuncts, as in [24], which we already know how to handle in a truth theory.

[23] The violent midnight eruption of Vesuvius lit up the night sky.

[24] [The x: x is an eruption of Vesuvius and x was violent and x occurred at midnight][the y: y is the sky and y is at night](x lit up y).

This suggests that if a suitable entity could be found in the case of adverbial modification, such sentences could be treated as asserting the existence of a unique thing that has a variety of properties.[123] Consider again [17], 'Edwin swam the English Channel at midnight in his dressing gown'. It looks as if, with some awkwardness, this can be re-expressed in English as 'Edwin's swimming of the English Channel at midnight in his dressing gown took place', in which there is a referring term.[124] There is one difficulty with this, namely, 'Edwin's swimming of the English Channel at midnight in his dressing gown took place' entails there was a unique swimming of the English Channel by Edwin at midnight in his dressing gown, while [17] does not.[125] To accommodate this, we can rephrase [17] as 'There was a swimming of the English Channel at midnight in his dressing gown by Edwin'. Once we have reformulated [17] in this way, we have an entity, namely, an event (as we will say), which can be attributed various other properties. Thus, [17] can be rendered as [25].

---

[122] See Davidson (2001*b* (1967): 119).

[123] As Davidson remarks in "Adverbs of Action" (1985: 230–1): "Seeing adjectives, common nouns, and verbs as alike in forming predicates works wonders for our ability to analyze logical form in a way that gives inference a semantic base."

[124] Davidson has related in personal communication that when he originally thought of this solution to the problem of adverbial modification, he could not believe that no one else had thought of it, and read everything he could about it. The closest proposal he came across was Reichenbach's suggestion (1947: §48) that action sentences with adverbial modification were logically equivalent to sentences containing an existential quantifier over facts. Consequently, in Davidson (2001*b* (1967)), he credits Reichenbach with the idea of introducing an existential quantifier. Yet, there are significant differences between the proposals. Reichenbach does not take his logically equivalent sentences to give the logical form of the originals; and his quantification over facts rather than events introduces troubles which Davidson's proposal avoids.

[125] See Davidson's reply to Martin (Davidson 2001 (1980): 134).

[25] There is an (event) x such that x was a swimming of the English
Channel by Edwin, and x was at midnight, and x was done in a
dressing gown.[126]

The general form of the proposal, then, is that English verbs connoting change
should be treated as having an extra implicit argument place which is bound
in ordinary use by an existential quantifier, and that adverbial modification be
represented as conjunctive predication of a variable of cross-reference bound
by the existential quantifier. That is, a sentence, for example, containing
an apparently two-place predicate of the form [26] will be represented in a
canonical notation as [27].[127] Then, for adverbial modification, as in [28], the
canonical representation is [29].

[26] $R(a, b)$.
[27] $(\exists x)R(a, b, x)$.
[28] $R(a, b)F$-ly G-ly H-ly ...
[29] $(\exists x)(R(a, b, x)$ and $F(x)$ and $G(x)$ and $H(x)...)$.

This shows [19]–[22] to follow from [17] as a matter of logical form. It is also
shows how 'Vesuvius erupted' follows from [23] as a matter of logical form.

It is worth an aside to point out how this treatment of adverbial modification,
a question of logical form, is of central importance in trying to uncover the
ontological commitments of our ordinary ways of talking about the world (see
Davidson 2001 (1977)). For if Davidson's proposal is correct, many of these
ordinary ways of talking are implicitly committed to the existence of events.
We need not worry too much at this point about the nature of events: they are
whatever satisfy open sentences such as 'x is a kicking of Shem by Shaun'. In
the end, what determines our commitments about the nature of the entities
we quantify over is revealed by the predicates we take to apply to them.

The argument for the commitment to events is that (1) sentences whose
verbs connote change that involve adverbial modification must be treated as

---

[126] We will suggest in Ch. 9, on tense, that in fact the contribution of 'at midnight' be treated
as modifying not the event introduced by the main verb, but rather the time it relates the subject
and event to. But this modification does not affect the basic form of the present proposal.

[127] The general form of the proposal should not be surprising. Many intransitive verbs are
plausibly understood as involving an implicit existential quantification of an argument place
that is explicitly occupied in its transitive cousin, as, e.g. in 'Kennedy was assassinated', which
plausibly is understood as 'there is an x such that x assassinated Kennedy', there being no
assassinations without assassins. Of course, not all intransitive verbs should be construed this
way, even when they have a transitive cousin. Though we may say, 'John ran a marathon', we
may also simply say 'John ran' without implying that there was any race, or even any distance
that he ran (he could run in place, or on a treadmill, for example).

having a compositional semantics, (2) the only workable semantics requires representing the verbs as having an extra argument place for an event which is implicitly quantified over,[128] and, therefore, (3) commitment to the truth of sentences containing verbs which connote change is commitment (extensionally) to the existence of events. If we furthermore suppose we have good reason to believe many of the sentences we use whose main verbs connote change are true, then we *ipso facto* have reason to believe that there are events. It should be noted that even if the range of sentences involving verbs that connote change did not commit us to events, we of course have referring terms that do, such as 'Caesar's death', 'The eruption of Krakatoa', 'Nixon's resignation', and so on. The question is whether these could be paraphrased away or not. If Davidson's account is right, the answer is no, since they are required to formulate a compositional meaning theory for a wide range of sentences we use.

3. Thematic Roles

Brief mention is due to one development in Davidson's program, suggested originally by Hector-Neri Castaneda (1967). This is the introduction of what are now called thematic roles into the representation of action sentences. As Davidson had originally conceived of it, [25] would be represented formally as [30].

[30] $(\exists x)$(Swam(x, Edwin, English Channel) and in-a-dressing-gown(x) and at-midnight(x)).

The main verb in [17] is treated in logical form as contributing a three-place predicate. The suggestion that we represent independently thematic roles is the suggestion that we represent the role of Edwin and the English Channel in the event independently of its being an event of swimming. Edwin is the agent of the event (it was done *by* Edwin), and the English Channel is that through which the swimming took place. We can say that the English Channel was the location or "locatum" of the event of Edwin's swimming the English Channel (here assuming he swam it just once).[129] Then we can represent [17] as in [31].

---

[128] Davidson puts it this way: "...there is a lot of language we can make systematic sense of if we suppose events exist, and we know no promising alternative. The presumption lies with events" (2001 (1980): 137).

[129] Different thematic roles would be assigned to the objects, direct and indirect, of a verb depending on how they were related to the event expressed by the verb. In 'John hit the wall', for example, the wall would be said to be the patient, that on which the agent acted.

[31] (∃x)(Swam(x) and agent(Edwin, x) and locatum(English Channel, x) and in-a-dressing-gown(x) and at-midnight(x))[130]

This is a suggestion which Davidson endorsed (1985). One of the motivations for the emendation is that it helps to explain why we can infer from [17], 'Edwin swam the English Channel at midnight in his dressing gown', [32] and [33] (ignoring tense).

[32] Edwin did something
      (∃x)(agent(Edwin, x))
[33] Something was done somewhere
      (∃y)(∃z)(∃x)(agent(y, x) and locatum(z, x))

Some additional support for this refinement is provided by the aid it gives in understanding sentences attributing joint actions, which are discussed in the next section.

4. Doing Things Together

We noted in Chapter 4, §3, that some puzzles arise about complex referring terms in sentences such as [34]. The difficulty was that this could not be treated simply as shorthand for [35], since [35] could be true if Sue and Bill ate separately from Bill and Helen, but [34] would be false in that case.

[34] Sue, Bill, and Helen ate dinner together.
[35] Sue ate dinner together with Bill and Bill ate dinner together with Helen and Sue ate dinner together with Helen.

This suggested that we might need to take seriously the idea that the subject term referred to a plural entity. We suggested that this was implausible, but we deferred further discussion until this chapter, because the introduction of an existential quantifier binding an event variable, and the introduction of thematic roles, shows the way to a solution to this puzzle.

Contrast [34] with [36]. One reading of [36] is equivalent to [37]. The other is equivalent to [34], and we may suppose in this case that it is just read as elliptical for [34].

[36] Sue, Bill, and Helen ate dinner.
[37] Sue ate dinner and Bill ate dinner and Helen ate dinner.

---

[130] For present purposes, we will ignore constituent structure in the adverbs.

The difference between [37] and [34] intuitively is that [37] can be true even if there are three independent events of eating dinner, whereas [34] can be true only if there is a single event of eating dinner in which all of Sue, Bill, and Helen are participants, or, as we may say, agents. Once we have put it this way, we can see that the difference can be expressed in terms of whether the conjunction introduced by the subject term is within the scope of a single event quantifier introduced by the verb. The reading we want for [34] can be expressed as in [38] (ignoring tense).[131]

[38] (∃x)(eating-dinner(x) and agent(Sue, x) and agent(Bill, x) and agent(Helen, x)).

As long as we understand being the agent of an event in a way that allows for multiple agents, this will get the right result. [38] entails that Sue, Bill, and Helen were all participants in one event, and an event in which they were all participants was an event of eating dinner. Thus, we can see the function of 'together' as being that of a scope indicating device: it indicates that the conjunction of the subject term is within the scope of a single event quantifier introduced by the verb. This analysis extends straightforwardly to similar cases involving other adverbs of joint participation in action, such as 'jointly', and points the way to understanding verbs such as 'coauthored' and 'are married', though we will not pursue these matters any further here. It also shows that we do not need to invoke plural entities as the subjects of action to understand sentences such as [34].

A final note is in order on the subject of plural referring terms used in these contexts, which will suggest in turn one final modification of the suggestion in [38]. From [34], we can infer [39], where 'they' picks out Sue, Bill, and Helen.

[39] They ate dinner together.

How should this be handled? The most straightforward way to handle this is to represent [39] as in [40]. This recommends [40] as the analysis of [39]. On the assumption that our understanding of their being an agent of an event is a matter of each of them being an agent of it, we could represent this in turn as in [41].

[40] (∃x)(eating-dinner(x) and agent(they, x)).
[41] (∃x)(eating-dinner(x) and [∀y: y is one of them](agent(y, x))).

---

[131] Again, for present purposes, we will ignore constituent structure of 'eating dinner'.

5. Topic Dependent Adverbs

We turn now to the treatment of two puzzle cases.

The first is the case of certain adverbs which introduce an intensional context, such as 'intentionally' and 'deliberately' and their cousins. For brevity, we will focus on 'intentionally'. What we say here should be extendable in a straightforward way to other members of the same family of adverbs. If we treat this on analogy with 'in his dressing gown', then a sentence such as [42] would be represented as [43].

[42]   John hit Bill intentionally
[43] $(\exists x)$(hit(John, Bill, x) and x was intentional)

The difficulty with this is that it represents 'intentionally' as an extensional modifier of an event. However, we cannot generally substitute coextensive terms in the context '___ intentionally' *salva veritate*. For example, let us say that John hit Bill just once, and that John's hitting of Bill was John's inciting Bill to shoot John. In this case, we may substitute 'inciting-to-shoot(John, Bill, x)' for 'hitting(John, Bill, x)' in [43], since each is true of exactly the same event. Thus, this analysis would commit us to saying that John incited Bill to shoot him intentionally. However, we may suppose consistently that, although John hit Bill intentionally, John did not intentionally incite Bill to shoot him.

Davidson's suggestion is to treat the modifier 'intentionally' as introducing essentially a propositional attitude statement.

From a logical point of view, there are thus these important conditions governing the expression that introduces intention: it must not be interpreted as a verb of action, it must be intensional, and the intention must be tied to a person. I propose then that we use some form of words like 'It was intentional of x that p' where 'x' names the agent, and 'p' is a sentence that says the agent did something.   (2001b (1967): 122)

From further discussion of the proposal, it is clear that Davidson's suggestion is that we interpret [42] as 'It was intentional of John that John hit Bill', or in an emendation suggested by Castañeda, and endorsed by Davidson, as [44] (Davidson 2001 (1980): 127).[132]

[44]   It was intentional of John that he (himself) hit Bill.

---

[132] One of the present authors thinks that there is no special self-reflexive pronoun that makes its appearance in these contexts: see Ludwig (1996b).

For (a statement made using) [44] to be adequate, it must entail that John hit Bill, since (a statement made using) [42] does. This means that [44] should not be treated as equivalent to 'John intended that he (himself) hit Bill', since it does not follow from John's intending that he (himself) hit Bill that he did hit Bill. This requires treating 'it was intentional of x that' as a factive sentential operator, similar to 'it was known by x that'. If we assimilate 'it was intentional of x that p' to 'it was known by x that p', then the entailment is not a matter of logical form, but rather of the meaning of 'intentional' as it is in the corresponding case of 'know'.[133] However, there is a difficulty in this, since 'intentional' is the adjectival form of 'intend', which is not a factive verb, in contrast to 'know'. In addition, it is not clear that we do treat 'it was intentional of x that p' as factive. Consider the claim that it *is* intentional of John that he (himself) hit Bill and the claim that it *will be* intentional of John that he (himself) hit Bill. We do not take either of these claims to entail that John hit Bill. The change to 'it was intentional of John that he (himself) hit Bill' could not change the semantical character of the operator except for where it locates John's intending. And, clearly, we get a different result in the case of 'it was known by x that p': that snow is white follows from the claim that it is known by John that snow is white and the claim that it will be known by John that snow is white.

This suggests a different way of incorporating Davidson's suggestion into an account of [42], namely, by treating 'intentionally' not as a sentential modifier, but as a genuine adverb in the sense that it makes its contribution within the scope of the quantifier introduced by the main verb in the sentence. Since this is essentially to appeal to John's having the intention of hitting Bill, we write this as in [45]. However, one difficulty with [45] is that nothing requires that John's intention to hit Bill is connected with whatever event or events makes true there being an event that was a hitting of Bill by John. This suggests then binding an event variable inside the scope of 'intended' with the initial quantifier, as in [46].

[45] $(\exists x)$(hit(John, Bill, x) and John intended to hit Bill).
[46] $(\exists x)$(hit(John, Bill, x) and John intended that hit(he, Bill, x)).[134]

---

[133] This appears to be Davidson's suggestion in "Adverbs of Action," i.e. that the inference from 'John did it intentionally' to 'John did something' should not be treated as a matter of logical form (Davidson 1985: 235).

[134] Or perhaps 'he (himself)', but see the reference in n. 132. One might wonder whether this accommodates correctly 'John didn't hit bill intentionally', an utterance of which we would typically take to be conveying that while John hit Bill it wasn't done intentionally. But note that

[46] secures the entailment from [42] to John hit Bill as a matter of logical form. This also comports well with Davidson's philosophy of action. For to perform an action intentionally, it is not enough to have an intention to perform an action of a type of which the action one performs is. This would not explain why one performed the particular action one did. Rather, one must have an intention directed at the particular action which one performs. This is secured by [46], but not by [45] or by [44] (unless it is construed as equivalent to [46]). The same approach will work for similar adverbs such as 'deliberately', 'on purpose', 'unexpectedly'. For example, we could represent 'John hit Bill unexpectedly' as '$(\exists x)$(hit(John, Bill, x) and it was unexpected of John that hit(he, Bill, x))'.

This treatment would not be extended, however, to adverbs such as 'allegedly' or 'putatively' in sentences such as 'John allegedly hit Bill' or 'John putatively hit Bill'. 'Allegedly' and 'putatively' do not express ways or modes of hitting someone. They express, rather, relations to the proposition expressed by 'John hit Bill'. Semantically, these adverbs modify the whole sentence rather than just the main verb. Thus, the main verb falls in their scope, rather than their falling in the scope of the quantifier the verb introduces. These sentences would be represented as 'It is alleged that John hit Bill' and 'It is putatively the case that John hit Bill'. Adverbs like these are typically placed before the main verb or at the beginning of a sentence rather than after the verb phrase.[135] It is a sufficient condition for 'allegedly' to be a sentential modifier that from 'Allegedly p' it does not follow that p. This is not a necessary condition for an adverb to be a sentential modifier, however. For example, from 'Surprisingly p', it does follow that p, yet 'surprisingly' clearly modifies the whole sentence. A useful, if perhaps defeasible test, is whether from 'F-ly x A-ed' one can infer 'x A-ed and x did it F-ly'. This inference is felicitous in the case of 'intentionally', 'deliberately', 'knowingly', 'with a knife', 'while eating breakfast', 'on the top of a mountain', 'on purpose', but not in the case of 'allegedly', 'putatively', 'surprisingly', 'certainly', 'possibly', and 'necessarily'.

Now we turn to the treatment of adverbs like 'slowly'. The trouble, as we noted above, is that an event can be slow described one way and fast described another. Consider an example, [47]. On Davidson's basic account, this would be rendered as [48].

---

one can say: John didn't hit Bill intentionally, because he didn't hit him at all. We usually take the speaker to be conveying that John hit Bill but not intentionally because if one wanted to deny that John hit Bill intentionally on the grounds that he didn't hit him, it would be simpler to say 'John didn't hit Bill'.

[135] Not all adverbs which are sometimes called 'sentential adverbs', however, are like this.

[47] Edwin swam the English Channel quickly.

[48] There is an event *x* such that it was a swimming by Edwin, and it was of the English Channel, and it was quick.

Suppose [47] is true. Suppose further that Edwin only crosses the English Channel when he swims it. Then 'is a swimming by Edwin and is of the English Channel' is coextensive with 'is a crossing by Edwin and is of the English Channel'.[136] It follows that if [48] is the correct representation of the logical form of [47], then Edwin's *crossing* of the English Channel was quick. But, most likely (and certainly possibly), Edwin's crossing of the English Channel was quite slow. Evidently, something about the logical form of the sentence remains hidden.

The problem is the same problem as that of adjectives such as 'quick' and 'tall'. And once we have seen how to handle it for that case, it is easy enough to see how to extend the treatment to the case of adverbs. Where we have an adverb that interacts with the verb that it modifies—a topic dependent adverb, as we have called them—we treat the adverb, as in the case of topic independent adverbs, as contributing a predicate to the representation of the logical form of the sentence, but we determine, by a rule, which predicate, by considering which verb it is modifying. In the case of an adverb which is linked with a comparative, as in the case of 'slowly', we can treat it as introducing a predicate of the same sort as is introduced by similar adjectives, namely, 'is significantly slower than average among *F*s', where '*F*' is replaced by a nominal formed from the verb the adverb modifies. This suggests the treatment in [49].

[49] There is an event *x* such that *x* was a swimming by Edwin, and *x* was of the English Channel, and *x* is significantly slower than most swimmings of the English Channel.

Does this have the right entailment relations? On this account, from 'Edwin swam the English Channel quickly', we can infer 'Edwin swam the English Channel', 'Someone swam the English Channel quickly', 'Edwin swam', as a matter of form, but not, interestingly, 'Edwin swam quickly'. Each of these judgments is validated by the above analysis. Here is an interesting test case. Does 'Edwin swam the English Channel quickly' imply 'Edwin swam the

---

[136] On Davidson's account of the by-relation, when Edwin crosses the English Channel by swimming it, his crossing is the same action as his swimming. See Davidson (2001*a* (1971)).

English Channel in less time than most swimmers of it'? The answer, we think, is 'yes', which gives us just the result we want.[137]

---

[137] In Davidson (1985), he evidently thinks there is some difficulty with proposals like this one. The difficulty is discussed in relation to adjectival modification as in 'Jones is a tall man'. The objection is that this entails 'Jones is a man', but would not on analyses of the general sort proposed here. However, it is clear that our proposal does sanction this inference as a matter of form, and that it does not take 'man' to refer to a class or property, as Davidson seems to fear.

One might worry that this account will have untoward consequences in a case in which someone is the first swimmer of the English Channel. Did the first swimmer swim the English Channel quickly or slowly? But does this question really have an answer? It is intuitively a puzzle what to say. But our account explains this, for it holds that he did not swim it quickly, and he did not swim it slowly. Since this shows that the question has a false presupposition, we are able to explain why it seems puzzling. Of course, the intended contrast class might be the class of all swimmings of the English Channel, including future ones, but in that case also we should be puzzled what to say because we could not be in a position to say after the first one whether it was quick or slow.

8

The Simple Tenses of State and Event Verbs[138]

Frege showed us how to cope.

(Davidson 2001 (1977): 211)

We now turn to a relatively neglected topic in truth-theoretic semantics, namely, tense, which is routinely overlooked in philosophical analyses.[139] We think the relative neglect of tense in philosophical analysis is a serious mistake, and that attention to the semantics of tense will show that many discussions of natural language semantics and their applications to philosophical analyses are seriously flawed. To make it more manageable, our discussion is divided into three chapters. In this chapter, we discuss the simple tenses of state and event verbs, the simple past ('loved'), present ('loves'), and future ('will love'). In Chapter 9, we discuss temporal adverbials and quantifiers. In Chapter 10, we discuss the interaction of tense with indirect discourse and attitude reports, and extend the basic treatment we give in this chapter to the perfect tenses, the past ('had loved'), present ('has loved'), and future perfect ('will have loved').

In the sense in which we are interested in it, tense is a semantic, rather than a syntactic phenomenon. Although tense is identified traditionally with

---

[138] Material on which this and the next two chapters are based is drawn from Lepore and Ludwig (2003).

[139] An important exception is Peter Ludlow's recent study of the metaphysics of time (1999), in which he argues that metaphysical disputes over the nature of time can be directly related to different theories of tense, and in which he argues for a semantic position compatible with presentism, the view that only present times are real. As will be seen from the sequel, the approach we take treats tense as involving commitment to both past and future times.

verb inflection, our concern is with linguistic devices in general used for indicating a time interval, relative to, or in which, an activity or state is to be understood to occur or obtain. The phenomenon of tense, as we understand it, occurs in languages like Chinese, which lack any verb inflection. We will press into use 'tense' to cover any verb form we use to indicate time intervals in which the event or state expressed by a verb is to occur or obtain. In English, verb inflection, such as adding '-ed' to a truncation of an infinitive, is one such device, though we use a modal verb 'will' to indicate events that take place in the future, and various tensed helping verbs for the perfect tenses.[140]

Our basic approach, which goes back to Frege (1977 (1918–19)) and Russell (1903), treats tense as an indexical device for referring to times or time intervals at which events take place or states obtain. Where the time interval picked out is not the present, tense involves what we will call *indexically restricted quantifiers*. The indexical element functions to pick out a time of utterance as a reference point for indicating quantificationally the relative location of temporally bound states and events. While the central idea is intuitively appealing, it has not been systematically explored within Davidson's truth-theoretic framework.[141] It turns out to be particularly powerful in its application to systematizing the often puzzling interaction of tense with other temporal devices. Treating tense as quantificational will enable us to give a uniform account of tense and temporal modifiers and quantifiers in English, and it can be shown to complement in a compelling way the standard event/state analyses of adverbial modification (Chapter 9, §5).

In §1, we present an account of the simple tenses of state verbs (present, past, future). In §2, we extend the account to event verbs, which exhibit, in English, one striking disanalogy with state verbs which must be noted. In §3, we discuss the so-called progressive or continuous tense, and argue that, in fact, it is a mistake to take the progressive form of a verb to be a tense modification of it.

---

[140] Though we will be concerned solely with tense in English, we are interested in it as an example of a semantic phenomenon common to natural languages. The structure of a semantic phenomenon may be expected to reflect underlying facts about the structure of our thoughts about contingent particulars. We expect that all languages share basic expressive resources, even when they are realized by diverse syntactical devices. An extensive study of the categories of tense and aspect across languages can be found in Dähl (1985). See also Gabbay and Rohrer (1979) for a comparison of the expressive resources of English and Hebrew.

[141] In contrast, there is quite a lot of work done in linguistics within the model-theoretic framework that traces back to Montague (1974).

1. The Simple Tenses of State Verbs

The most salient feature of tense is that its contribution to the meaning of utterances is sensitive to the time of utterance. [1]–[3], in present, past, and future tense,[142] respectively, may be true when uttered by a speaker at some times, but not at others.

> [1] Mary loves Bill.
> [2] Mary loved Bill.
> [3] Mary will love Bill.[143]

This indicates that [1]–[3] contain a context-sensitive element, either an indexical or a demonstrative device. From the standpoint of truth-theoretic semantics, a sentence contains a context-sensitive element iff its *T*-sentence has variables on its right-hand side bound by quantifiers which bind contextual parameters in its truth predicate. If the values of the minimal set of contextual parameters alone suffice to understand what the semantic value of a context-sensitive element is, then it is an indexical device; otherwise, it is (in part at least) a demonstrative device.

With [1]–[3], in which tense is the only context-sensitive element, knowing the time of utterance suffices for understanding its contribution. So, the simple tenses are indexicals. This requires that the propositions which [1]–[3] express in a context involve direct reference to the time of utterance. For an indexical which relies on time of utterance as the relevant contextual feature will function as a term that refers directly to that contextual feature (see [4]–[6] below). On the assumption that the proposition expressed by an utterance provides the content of the speaker's belief, every thought expressed using the present, past, and future tense is singular, since it directly refers to the time of utterance.

The case for regarding at least some tenses as quantifying over times is straightforward. When asserting [1], a speaker intends to say that Mary loves Bill *then*. When using [2], he intends to say that *at some time prior to his utterance*

---

[142] [3] is sometimes said to be untensed (see, e.g. Palmer 1974: 33, pp. 36–8), since its verb is constructed from a modal auxiliary, 'will', and an infinitive verb stem, and does not involve inflection. As we noted above, our classification is guided not by syntactic but by semantic considerations, and the semantic function of 'will' + infinite verb stem is to indicate that the action or state expressed by the verb occurs or obtains at a time later than the time of utterance, and thus it semantically functions like the present and past tenses.

[143] The future tense is also expressed by using 'is' + 'going' + the infinitive, as in 'Mary is going to love Bill'. Since these are equivalent, what we say about the modal + bare infinitive applies equally to the alternative form.

Mary loved Bill. Similarly, when using [3], he intends to say that *at some time after the time of his utterance* Mary will love Bill. In the latter two, clearly, the thoughts expressed quantify, respectively, over past and future times.

Unfortunately, in stating this we reused the tenses we intend to explain. Even if untensed verbs are used in English, they cannot grammatically replace simple tensed ones.[144] This has an important consequence for the semantics of English, namely, *its semantic theory is unspecifiable in English*. Interpretive truth theories cannot use context-sensitive elements in specifying truth conditions of object language expressions, on pain of being uninterpretive. So providing an adequate interpersonal interpretive truth theory for English requires enriching the metalanguage with tenseless verbs which express relations between objects or events and times. For this purpose, we will use the present tense form, adding a variable in parentheses for the temporal argument place; for example, 'loves(t)' is the tenseless verb in the metalanguage corresponding to 'loves' in English.

Following our practice, we will specify the form of satisfaction conditions for English tensed sentences by introducing regimented versions of them that are presented as having the same logical form, and for which it is obvious what the satisfaction conditions are. We introduce a referring term 't^*' with the following reference axiom (stipulated to be interpretive): Ref(S, t, u)('t^*') $= t$. With this as background, we can represent the logical form of [1]–[3] as in [4]–[6], respectively ('$x < y$' and '$x > y$' mean 'x is earlier than y' and 'x is later than y)'.[145]

[4] Mary loves(t^*) Bill.
[5] [There is a time t_1: $t_1 < t^*$](Mary loves(t_1) Bill).
[6] [There is a time t_1: $t_1 > t^*$](Mary loves(t_1) Bill).

Given the reference clause for 't^*', it is clear that each of [4]–[6] indexes to utterance time.

[4]–[6] treat the present tense differently from the past and future tenses. The past and future tenses function as restricted indexical quantifiers, whereas

[144] Nonfinite verbs, infinitives, participles, and gerunds are said to lack tense. However, they do not function as main verbs, but rather nominally, adjectivally, or adverbially.

[145] The truth conditions we offer, in broad outline, we believe underlie most thinking about tense in other frameworks. As far as truth-theoretic accounts go, we draw attention to the formulation using restricted quantifier notation, which we think better captures the semantic structure of the past and future tenses. While we will identify some salient differences with other approaches, we will not try to provide a systematic comparison, which would be a book-length task itself.

the present tense functions as a simple indexical. We might try to treat the present tense as requiring restricted quantification, as in [7].

[7]   [There is a time $t_1 : t_1 = t^*$](Mary loves(t_1) Bill).

But in addition to the quantification in [7] being superfluous, considerations about how simple tenses embed in complex expressions provide reasons against it (see §2).

[5]–[6] reveal that the past and future tenses are, from the perspective of truth-theoretic semantics, indexically restricted existential quantifiers. Existential quantification is required, since utterances in these tenses reveal only that some event occurred in the past or will occur in the future *at some time or other*. They are *indexical* quantifier expressions because the predicate restrictions on the quantifier in their regimented versions contain an indexical.

One important consequence of this treatment is that we can never re-express in English what we express on a given occasion using sentences like [1]–[3]. (This has important consequences for the semantics of indirect discourse and attitudes sentences. See Chapter 10, §1.) If someone were to assert 'Mary loves Bill' at t, he would express a proposition directly about t. To re-express that same proposition later, it would not do to use the present tense, since any new utterance would be about a *different* time. But using the past tense, even with an adverbial modifier, would still involve direct reference to the time of utterance, which would be later than t. Suppose someone were to utter, 'Mary loved Bill at t'. Since 'at t' determines a time earlier than *the time of utterance* at which Mary is asserted to have loved Bill, the speaker still refers to the utterance time, and hence fails to express the original.

There is nothing conceptually incoherent about re-expressing a proposition expressed by a use of one of [1]–[3]; our regimented version of English allows us to do so. But this feature of natural languages is surely no accident. Our access to time in thought involves reference to the present time. We step into the river of time only at that point at the bank on which we stand, the perpetual present, and locate other times fundamentally by reference to that standpoint. Re-expressing the same proposition twice in our regimented English would involve using a directly referring term to pick the time out rigidly. But we would secure the referent of directly referring terms in thought only by describing its relation to the present time.[146]

As we represent tense, the future and past tenses involve quantification. However, importantly, unlike explicit quantification, quantification in tense,

---

[146] See Ludwig (1996*b*) for a general argument for this view.

because it is introduced with the verb,[147] will be invoked after clauses for explicit quantifiers have been invoked, and, therefore, its scope with respect to other quantifiers is determined by the scope assigned to those other quantifiers, and is not itself ambiguous; typically, this will result in the quantifier introduced by the tense taking narrow scope with respect to explicit quantifiers.[148] Sentences with explicit quantifiers receive recursive clauses in the truth theory, as in [8] (treating 'everyone' and 'someone' as unrestricted quantifiers for the moment).

> [8] For any function f, f satisfies(S, t, u) '(Everyone x)(someone y)(x met y)' iff every 'x'-variant f' of f satisfies(S, t, u) '(someone y)(x met y)'.

In the sort of truth theory we are envisaging, both explicit quantifiers in '(Everyone x)(someone y)(x met y)' would be unpacked before the axiom for its verb could be invoked, forcing the quantifier involved in tense to take narrow scope in this case, as in [9] and [10].

> [9] For all functions f, f satisfies(S, t, u) '(Everyone x)(someone y)(x met y)' iff every 'x'-variant f' of f is such that some 'y'-variant f'' of f' satisfies(S, t, u) 'x met y'.
>
> [10] For all functions f, f satisfies(S, t, u) '(Everyone x)(someone y)(x met y)' iff every 'x'-variant f' of f is such that some 'y'-variant f'' of f' is such that f'' satisfies(S, t, u) '[There is a time t_1: $t_1 < t^*$](x meets(t_1) y)'.

This appears to be the intuitively correct result. Suppose someone says, 'Everyone who came to the party met someone there'. While this is compatible with everyone who came to the party meeting someone there *at the same time*, there does not appear to be a reading that would require this for the truth of the claim.

---

[147] This neatly handles the need for a potentially arbitrarily large number of independent event times in subordinate clauses, e.g. 'John saw the man who kissed Mary, who bought a farm from the woman Bill divorced'.

[148] In the case of quantifiers which may take wide or narrow scope with respect to an attitude or indirect discourse verb, we can find the quantifier introduced by a verb taking wide or narrow scope with respect to an explicit quantifier. For example, the two readings of 'John said that everyone has smoked a joint at some point or other', namely, (i) 'Everyone is such that John said he has smoked a joint at some point or other' and (ii) 'John said everyone is such that he has smoked a joint at some point or other', show that the tense introduced by the main verb can be either outside of or within the scope of 'everyone'. Still, what scope it has is determined completely by the scope assigned to explicit quantifiers.

As we remarked earlier, metalanguage verbs are tenseless. Object language quantifiers range over every extant object, taken tenselessly, i.e. not relativized to any time. If natural language quantifiers were evaluated relative to the time of utterance, so that their domains were restricted to what existed at that time, this would have to be represented in our semantics by restricting the domain to objects existing at the time of utterance. This is not, however, how quantifiers are used in English: 'Everyone who lived in the 19th century suffered from gout' is not vacuously true but rather factually false. As we note below (Ch. 10 n. 175), for restricted quantifiers, we can interpret the restriction as in a tense other than that of the predicate to which it is attached. We anticipate some discomfort due to the reflection that a sentence such as 'Everyone was at the party' will be false on this view, because the quantifier will range over people at all times. But this is no more puzzling than that the quantifier is used with an implicit restriction on the domain of people at the present time.

How does negation interact with tense? Consider 'John did not sleep last night'. If negation can take different scopes with respect to tense, then there should be two readings of this. On one, it would be true iff for every past time last night, it is not the case that John slept at that time. That is, this reading requires wakefulness the whole night. On the other, it would be true iff there is at least one time last night at which John did not sleep. This reading would be true if John woke momentarily in the middle of the night, but fell asleep again quickly without waking until morning. Is there, then, a reading on which an assertion of 'John did not sleep last night' would be true if he woke momentarily in the middle of the night? We might try to imagine a situation in which what is at issue is the effectiveness of a certain sleeping pill. We give it to John at bedtime, and wish to know whether it was effective in giving him a good night's sleep. Can John report its failure in the morning by saying, 'I did not sleep last night', if all he means to report is that there is at least one time last night at which he was not asleep? Even in this context it seems to us we would take John's report to be false. In addition, if negation could systematically take narrow or wide scope with respect to tense, we would expect 'That will not turn red' to have a reading on which it is true even if it is also true that it will turn red, so that 'That will not turn red and that will turn red' would not be necessarily false, on one reading, even when 'that' picks out the same thing in both its uses. But there does not appear to be any such reading. We therefore tentatively conclude that negation does not insert itself between the quantifier introduced by tense and the verb.

Some authors (e.g. Burge 1974; Partee 1973) suggest that simple tenses are implicitly demonstrative. An utterance of 'I didn't turn off the stove' is usually understood to involve a specific past time interval, and not just any past time. Space constraints prevent us from discussing this suggestion fully. While a truth-theoretic approach can easily incorporate devices that worked this way, we believe these phenomena are pragmatic and not semantic. It is easy to see how the pragmatic implicature works given the literal meaning we assign to this. On the literal reading, in the schematic conversational setting we imagine it spoken in, we would suppose it pretty clearly false, since the person speaking may be supposed to have turned off the stove on a number of past occasions. We therefore assume, in our schematic scenario, that the speaker means more or something other than what is literally said. An obvious solution is to suppose the speaker intends a restriction to some past time interval that is conversationally salient, such as last night or earlier this evening, which would give point to the utterance in the context.

2. Simple Tenses and Event Verbs

In contrast to state verbs, event verbs apply to an object at a time only if it is undergoing some change. Neither 'Bill loved Mary' nor 'Bill weighed 145 lbs.' implies Bill has undergone change. But 'Bill left' implies that Bill underwent a change, minimally, of position. Also, event verbs, in contrast to most state verbs, take a progressive form by concatenating 'is' with the present participle morpheme. Corresponding to 'leave' is 'is leaving'. The same operation on state verbs is generally ill-formed; no form 'is knowing' corresponds to 'know'. (This is not uniform, as is shown by 'block', 'stand', and 'occupy'. But these have uses as event verbs as well.)

It is natural to suppose that the simple tenses function uniformly independently of the semantic category of a verb. If so, we should be able to provide a uniform treatment for state and event verbs. While this works smoothly for the past and future tenses of event verbs, it does not for the present tense. Compare [11] with [12] and [13].

[11]   Mary loves Bill.
[12]   Mary leaves.
[13]   Mary opens the door.

An utterance of [11] is true if Mary loves Bill at the time of utterance. But it is difficult to find circumstances under which we comfortably assert [12] or [13] unembedded or unmodified (in contrast to, for example, 'If Mary leaves, I will

too', or 'Mary leaves on the 23rd of this month').[149] Even though events typically require more time to complete than utterances of sentences with present
tensed event verbs, this hardly explains the data. [12] is no less odd when said
slowly enough for Mary to leave during its utterance. Moreover, many events
require no more time than would an assertion that they were occurring, for
example, 'Bill speaks', but their present tense utterances are no less odd. (We
will consider sentences like 'Bill works for a living' in Chapter 9, §4. These typically express generality.) We know of no adequate explanation of this aspect
of present tense event verbs in English. It is not shared by all languages.[150]

There is not anything conceptually incoherent about a semantics for present
tense event verbs that parallels our semantics for present tense state verbs.
This strongly suggests that whatever oddity attaches to utterances of present
tense unembedded and unmodified event verbs, it is not due to its expressing
the occurrence of an event, rather than a state. But, then, there should be an

---

[149] There are two exceptions. First, there is the so-called narrative or historical present (or,
sometimes, 'vividly reporting present'), as in live broadcasts of a sporting event, in which the
announcer attempts to convey a sense of immediacy by reporting events in the simple present:
He hits a terrific serve, approaches the net, and hits a winner down the line to win the game.
(See Visser 1972: 724), for a wealth of other examples.) We can also use the naked present in
chronological tables, '579 BC Nebuchadnezzar takes Tyre', and in vivid narration of past events
where the anchoring time is clear from the context: 'It is early morning, June 14, 1800. The
Austrian troops under the command of Lieutenant General Michael Melas are crossing the
Bormida River. They attack some isolated French divisions of the French Army commanded by
Vice Counsel Napoleon Bonaparte, who has sent away part of his strength to the north and south,
in the belief that Melas would attempt to outflank the French Army.' These are so specialized
that we are unsure what weight to grant them. Their aim is clearly to achieve a kind of vividness
in reporting that a past tense report would fail to convey (a you-are-there look at the past). The
present tense of event verbs, so oddly used in the present, lies ready to hand: it is no wonder it
is pressed into use for such an effect, even if there is something odd about it. But it does seem
to be a kind of play with words recognized as a bit odd or out of place, and partly effective for
that reason. We are inclined to say this is an *extended* and not a *core* use of the present, despite its
appearing throughout the history of English.
The second case is the use of the present tense of event verbs in issuing performatives, as in 'I
promise to meet you there', or 'I warn you not to do that'. It is unclear what to say about such
uses. It would be odd to interpret them as anything other than promises or warnings, though it is
tempting to say that one promises or warns, etc., by way of asserting one is doing so. But contrast
'I promise to meet you there' with 'I am promising to meet you there'. The latter is not ordinarily
usable to make a promise. So, no performative is accomplished by asserting one is perform*ing*
the act in question as one speaks. It seems, rather, that utterances of 'I promise to meet you
there' intended as promises are implicitly self-referential, i.e. are interpreted as 'I hereby promise
to meet you there', where 'hereby' makes implicit reference to the utterance; we may treat this
modification as introducing a reference to the time of utterance. We will discuss these cases in
Ch. 11, on opaque contexts and indirect discourse.
[150] Accomplishment and activity verbs (like 'eat an apple' and 'run') in Romance languages
or the other Germanic languages can be used in the present tense to express an ongoing process.

account of that oddity within a compositional meaning theory, since it is not based, if this is correct, in any difference between events and states. If we are right, present tense event verbs do not index to the time of utterance. Yet, from our treatment of past and future tenses, which parallels that for state verbs, it is clear that event verbs express a relation between one or more things and a time. If the implicit argument places for time in present tense event verbs were bound by a quantifier in sentences containing them, there would not be a puzzle about their utterances. We suggest, then, that the argument place for time in present tense event verbs is unbound in unembedded and unmodified uses, and that the oddity in uttering [12] and [13] is due to their being open sentences, and thereby truth-valueless. If we are right, [12] will receive [14] as its canonical representation, where 't'' is a free variable. The past and future tenses for 'leaves', in contrast, are represented in the same way as for state verbs, as in [15] and [16].[151]

[14]   Mary leaves(t').
[15]   [There is a t_1 : $t_1 < t^*$](Mary leaves(t_1)).
[16]   [There is a t_1 : $t_1 > t^*$](Mary leaves(t_1)).

The asymmetry in treatments of past and future tenses of event verbs, on the one hand, and present tense, on the other, might be regarded as a defect. But

[151] An interesting alternative explanation is given by Giorgi and Pianesi (1997). This was drawn to our attention by a reader for OUP. Their suggestion is that speech time is punctual in the sense that it is conceived as not having internal temporal structure, but that the event type expressed by event verbs has internal structure, a process with a boundary, and that processes are conceived of as having internal structure. If the speech time is conceived of as punctual and so lacking internal structure, the event type expressed by an event verb as occurring at the time of utterance would be incompatible with the way the time of utterance is conceived. Giorgi and Pianesi also offer an explanation for the difference between English, on the one hand, and Italian and German, on the other. The explanation hinges on an argument that English "associates the feature value [+ perf] to all eventive predicates" and that "this is necessary in English but not in Italian . . . and German . . . due to morphological properties of the English verb" (p. 163). One worry we have about the proposal attaches to the assumption that utterance time is always conceived as punctual and so without internal structure. As we've observed (see Ch. 4, §3), we can interpret such sentences as 'Now you see it and now you don't' as true, and it often seems that to understand utterances we have to acknowledge that they are temporally extended and have parts that can be interpreted relative to different times. Even in an atomic sentence it seems that we recognize the utterance time as a structured interval in sentences such as 'Now is not *now*'. There seems to be a coherent interpretation of this sentence which is true, i.e. in which we take the speaker to be denoting the times of utterance of each occurrence of 'now' within the utterance of the sentence as a whole. However, this is not decisive, for it may be argued that appearances here are misleading, or that the punctual interpretation attaches only to sentences which don't employ other temporal referring devices or temporal adverbs or modifiers. We cannot pursue further comparison with this alternative here, but will rather develop our own proposal.

it explains the oddity of utterances of [12] and [13], which an account treating them as parallel to state verbs would fail to do. Whether the proposal is satisfactory depends on how well it integrates into an account of how present tense event verbs interact with temporal adverbials and quantifiers, and on whether a simpler account of the data can be given. While we cannot show no simpler account is available, we will show in Chapter 9 how to integrate our treatment with one for adverbials and temporal quantifiers.

3. The Progressive

The progressive is formed by adding '-ing' to (the truncation of) the infinitive of an event verb. The concatenation of 'is' with a participle (e.g. 'leaving') has traditionally been treated as a tense of the relevant event verb (e.g. 'leave'). From our perspective, however, classifying the progressive as a tense is a mistake.[152] While 'is leaving' is tensed, since it indexes to the time of utterance, its treatment in a truth-theoretic semantics should not distinguish it from the present tense state verbs. The contribution of tense to 'is leaving' (the dimension of variation among 'is leaving', 'was leaving', and 'will be leaving') is represented by the tenseless verb 'is leaving(t)'. So represented, the present progressive picks out the time of utterance relative to which an implicit argument in the verb is evaluated, just like present tense state verbs. (However, progressives behave like event verbs in their interaction with future looking or neutral adverbials, like 'noon', or 'on Tuesday'; this looks to be because of the pull of the analogy of form with the future formed from 'to be' plus 'going' plus the infinitive.)

Treating 'is leaving' as a tense of 'leave' requires exhibiting its satisfaction conditions as derived from those for the untensed verb 'leaves(t)'. This may seem intuitively the right thing to do, since 'is leaving' is clearly related to the infinitive 'to leave'. But this is insufficient to settle whether the connection is conceptual or structural. A virtue of the truth-theoretic approach is that it provides a precise way of distinguishing conceptual from structural connections.

When two verbs are *structurally* related, the same (or a synonymous) metalanguage verb is used in their satisfaction conditions, and the only variation between the satisfaction conditions will be variations in the quantificational apparatus invoked by tense. If the connection is not structural, distinct metalanguage verbs will be used in giving satisfaction conditions.

---

[152] Though denying that the progressive is a tense is not novel, it is not universally accepted. See Comrie (1985).

Put this way, 'is leaving(t^*)' represents appropriate satisfaction conditions for 'is leaving' only if the relation expressed by 'is leaving' ('was leaving' and 'will be leaving') is distinct from what is expressed by 'leaves', 'left', and 'will leave'. That they are distinct, however, is shown by the fact that someone can be leaving, and not leave, or will be leaving, and never leave. Someone leaving the room may never make it out the door. In this case, he was leaving, even though he never left. The point is even more transparent with other event verbs: someone may be *writing* a book, but never *write* a book. These examples help clarify the relation between 'was leaving' and 'left': the former relates an agent to a time interval in which he is *engaged* in an activity which may lead to the kind of event the latter relates an agent to.

If correct, this dissolves the so-called imperfective paradox.[153] This paradox arises on the assumption that the progressive of an accomplishment verb like 'leaves' is a tense. 'leaves(t)' applies to an object x at a time t only if after t, 'x left' applies to it. If 'is leaving' were a tense of 'leave', then 'is leaving' would apply at t to something only if after t, 'left' applied to it. This is obviously incorrect. But the pressure to accept the paradoxical result dissipates once we deny that the progressive form of 'leaves' is a tense of it.

Progressives are neither state verbs nor event verbs. They express the occurrence at a time of a portion of a process which, if completed, constitutes an event of the type expressed by the verbs from which they are lexically derived.[154] We shall, following common sense, and an earlier tradition, call them process verbs.[155]

---

[153] For discussion, see Dowty (1977); Parsons (1990: ch. 9). It is called the 'imperfective paradox' because 'imperfect' in grammatical usage means 'uncompleted'. The puzzle is how a verb which expresses essentially a complete event can have an imperfect tense, i.e. a tense which implies that the event has not been completed.

[154] This does not speak to the question when someone is engaged in a process of the sort completion of which would be an event of the type expressed by the verb from which the progressive is lexically derived. One process may be compatible with several different kinds of completion. One may take the on ramp to I-75 from Gainesville in Florida with the intention of driving to New York, or to Memphis. In this case, we would usually say that one was driving to New York in the first case, and Memphis in the second, even if one's trip is interrupted in Lake City, a portion of the trip which would be identical for each process. Not all cases are so clear. But answering the question when one is engaged in one process or another which is not completed is to be decided by conceptual analysis rather than analysis of logico-semantic form.

[155] See Vendler (1967) for a classic discussion of verb classification. According to Vlach (1993: 241–3), progressives are state verbs. So, to say that John is leaving is to say that John is in the state of a process of his leaving being in progress.

9

Temporal Adverbials and Quantifiers

In this chapter, we turn to the interaction of the account of the simple tenses we have presented with temporal adverbials and quantifiers. We discuss certain relational temporal adverbs and adverbials in §1, the interaction of tense with 'before' and 'after' in §2, temporal quantifiers in §3, habitual sentences and frequency adverbs in §4, and the relation of this account of temporal adverbials to the event analysis of adverbial modification introduced in Chapter 7, in the final §5.

1. Temporal Adverbs and Adverbials [156]

In this section, we discuss relational temporal adverbials such as 'at midnight', 'before noon', 'two days hence', 'yesterday', 'tonight', 'between 2 and 3 p.m.' Temporal adverbials may be forward looking ('tomorrow', 'next week'), backward looking ('yesterday', 'a month ago', 'last week'), about the present ('now', 'at this moment', 'currently'), or neutral ('on Tuesday', 'in May'). We will call these future, past, present, and unanchored adverbials, respectively. [157]

---

[156] There is a class of adverbials whose members are used routinely to connect sentences in narratives, which we will not discuss. These are exemplified by 'three hours later' in the following passage, borrowed from Hinrichs (1986): 'They wheeled me into the operating room and put me under sedation. Three hours later I woke up.' The reference time for 'later' here is understood to be the time the narrator was put under sedation. Examples of this sort, as well as the conventions of narrative more generally, in which times of narrated events are understood to occur in an order indicated by the order of narrative, have suggested to many that the proper unit for semantical analysis is larger than the sentence, and that the traditional focus on sentential semantics distorts the semantic structures of natural languages.

[157] We borrow this terminology and classification scheme from Smith (1978).

A verb's tense restricts what modifiers it can comfortably take.[158] We use simple past with past adverbials or unanchored adverbials, but neither present nor future adverbials. 'John slept last week' and 'John slept through May' are fine, while 'John slept right now' and 'John slept in three days' are not. We use the future tense with unanchored, present, or future adverbials, but not past adverbials. 'John will sleep on Tuesday', 'John will sleep now', 'John will sleep tomorrow' are all acceptable, but 'John will sleep last week' is not. We use an event verb in present tense with unanchored or future adverbials, as in 'John leaves on Tuesday' and 'John leaves next week', and perhaps present adverbials, for example, 'John leaves now', but not with a past adverbial, as in 'John leaves yesterday'. In contrast, present tense state verbs (in atomic sentences) are used only with present adverbials. 'I am tired right now' is fine, but 'I am tired next week' and 'I am tired last year' are not.

We begin with adverbial modification of sentences in the simple past. We propose a uniform treatment of relational adverbs that will secure entailment relations like those in [1] (assuming all the sentences are evaluated relative to the same utterance time).

[1]   Bill loved Mary yesterday.
      Therefore, Bill loved Mary sometime.
      Therefore, Bill loved Mary.

We are already committed to quantifying over times due to our treatment of simple tenses. 'Bill loved Mary' is equivalent to '[There is a time t_1: $t_1 < t^*$](Bill loves(t_1) Mary)'. Modifying 'Bill loved Mary' with the adverb 'yesterday' has the effect of specifying the time interval in the past relative to the present when Bill loved Mary, that is, that it is identical with, or included in, yesterday. This recommends assigning 'Bill loved Mary yesterday' satisfaction conditions equivalent to [2],

[2]   [There is a t_1: $t_1 < t^*$ and $t_1 \subseteq$ yesterday](Bill loves(t_1) Mary),

where '$\subseteq$' is read as 'is included in or identical with'. We include the adjunct in the restriction on the quantifier because the adverb is intuitively modifying the element contributed by the tense.

Adverbial phrases formed by combining a preposition with a temporal designator receive similar treatment. What varies is the temporal property

---

[158] We refrain from saying that these combinations which are not used are ungrammatical. On the account we give of adverbial modification of tense, the combinations which are not used turn out to express necessarily false propositions. This is enough to explain why we do not use them.

expressed by the prepositional phrase. 'Bill loved Mary for two hours' is equivalent to '[There is a t_1: $t_1 < t^*$ and the duration of t_1 is two hours](Bill loves(t_1) Mary)'. 'Bill loved Mary before midnight' is equivalent to '[There is a t_1: $t_1 < t^*$ and t_1 is before midnight](Bill loves(t_1) Mary)'. 'Bill loved Mary in June' is equivalent to '[There is a t_1: $t_1 < t^*$ and t_1 is in some/this June](Bill loves(t_1) Mary)' (where the choice between 'some/this' indicates a standard ambiguity).

The satisfaction conditions in [2] underwrite the entailments in [1]. In addition, our treatment correctly predicts why certain modifiers are not used with verbs in the past tense. Future or present adverbials will require the time of an event to be in the future or the present, but the tense of the verb requires it to be in the past. Unanchored adverbials are treated as existentially quantified or implicitly context-sensitive, where neither requires the times of which they are predicated to be in the future, past, or present *vis-à-vis* the time of utterance.

The future tense receives a parallel treatment (with '$>$' substituted for '$<$'). However, we must say something about the use of 'now' with a future tense verb; to avoid incoherence, this should be understood as sentential and not adverbial modification. 'John will sleep now' should be read as 'It is now the case that John will sleep'. Our discussion in Chapter 10 of tense in complement clauses will cover this case. For present tense state verbs, satisfaction conditions are illustrated for 'Bill loves Mary now' in [3].

[3]   Bill loves(t^*) Mary and $t^* \subseteq$ now.[159]

Our treatment of past and future tense event verbs parallels exactly that of present and past tense state verbs, but the situation is more complex with present tense event verbs, such as 'leaves' or 'speaks'. One can modify a state verb with a present adverbial, but not with future, past, or unanchored adverbials. In contrast, while present tense event verbs, like present tense state verbs, cannot be modified by past adverbials, they can be modified by future adverbials, and, arguably, present adverbials, though in contrast to state verbs it is awkward to do so. [4] is unexceptional, [5] unacceptable—no competent speaker would use it—while [6] is awkward.

[4]   John leaves tomorrow.

---

[159] Is this compatible with 'Bill loves Mary, just not right now!' uttered when Bill is upset with Mary? One should not be too flat-footed. We just mean that Bill's love for Mary is not being manifest at the moment, not that he does not love Mary now. This is a matter of the play of language.

[5]   John leaves yesterday.

[6]   John leaves now.

We suspect that anyone who finds [6] acceptable is imagining it as a reply to 'When does John leave?', where the reply is expected to indicate a future time, while in fact John's departure is scheduled for the present.[160]

If 'John leaves' is an open sentence, adding a modifier binds the free argument place for time. If [5]–[6] are unacceptable, the quantifier is restricted to future times; if [5] alone is unacceptable, the restriction is to times contemporaneous with the utterance or later. We tentatively assume [6] is acceptable. 'John leaves tomorrow' then receives satisfaction conditions as in [7].

[7]   [There is a $t_1 : t_1 \geq t^*$ and $t_1 =$ tomorrow](John leaves(t_1)).

The restriction to present or future times explains the restriction on which adverbials can comfortably modify a present tense verb. Present tense verbs modified by unanchored adverbials, such as 'on Tuesday', are likewise interpreted as future looking.

This account treats non-quantificational temporal adverbials as predicates of an implicitly quantified temporal variable. Our failure to use certain combinations of tense and adverbs is due not to a structural or logical defect, but rather to semantic incompatibility. Even for unused forms, there is no difficulty in identifying logical form. What renders them unacceptable is a conflict between the requirement imposed on the event time by tense and what the meaning of the adverb requires.

2. 'Before' and 'After'

We devote a separate section to 'before' and 'after' because they appear not just in adverbials, as in 'before tomorrow' and 'before Mary', or as components in relational predicates flanked by event or temporal designators when concatenated with the copula, as in 'Midnight is before noon', but are also used to conjoin sentences, as in 'Brutus hailed Caesar before he killed him'. An adequate semantic account of 'before' and 'after' should exhibit them playing the same semantic role in each of these constructions.

A simple unified account is suggested by our approach. A sentence such as 'Brutus hailed Caesar before he killed him' will be represented as involving two existential quantifiers over past times relative to the present. 'before'

---

[160] One can also imagine it being used as stage directions, 'Sue opens the door', 'John leaves *now*'.

naturally modifies the verb in its preceding clause by relating its time to that of the verb used in its succeeding clause. So, 'before' is exhibited uniformly as a relational predicate of times. Satisfaction conditions for 'Brutus hailed Caesar before he killed him' would then be represented as [8].

[8]   [There is a time t_1: $t_1 < t^*$](Brutus hails(t_1) Caesar and [there is a time t_2: $t_2 < t^*$](Brutus kills(t_2) Caesar and t_1 is before t_2)).

This suggestion extends to 'after' and other temporal relational terms, such as 'at the same time as' (or simply 'as'), 'until' ('before but not after') and their modifications, such as 'a few minutes before' ('since', which is used with the perfect tenses, is more complicated, but the same idea applies—we return to this in Chapter 10, §3). Some relational terms are themselves complex. But there appears to be a uniform contribution of the modifiers of simple relational terms. 'x is M before y' can be unpacked as 'x is before y and INT(x, y) = M', where 'INT(x, y)' means 'the interval between x and y'. This licenses general satisfaction conditions for sentences of the form $\ulcorner \phi MR\psi \urcorner$, where '$R$' is replaced by a simple temporal relational predicate and 'M' by its modifier. This treatment explains why 'before' and 'after' are not truth-functional connectives, for the underlying logical form exhibits 'before' and 'after' as contributing temporal relational predicates.

Occurrences of 'before' and 'after' in adverbials function to relate times as indicated in the previous section. Satisfaction conditions for [9] are given by [10].

[9]   John will leave before tomorrow.
[10]   [There is a t_1: $t_1 > t^*$](John leaves(t_1) and t_1 is before tomorrow).

Sentences of the form $\ulcorner \phi$ before $\alpha \urcorner$, where ϕ is a sentence and α a noun phrase, but not a temporal designator (for example, 'John arrived before Mary' or 'John paid before leaving'), will be treated as having the underlying form $\ulcorner \phi$ before $\psi \urcorner$, where ϕ and ψ are sentences. If α is a predicate nominalization, for example, 'being fined', then $\psi = \alpha \frown$ UNOM(α, T), where UNOM(x, y) yields a predicate, of which x is a nominalization, with the tense marker y, where y will be the tense of the main verb. UNOM('being fined', future) = 'will be fined', while UNOM('being fined', past) = 'was fined'. Thus, for example, 'John paid before leaving' is treated as equivalent to 'John paid before he left'.[161] If α is a referring term or quantified noun phrase, $\psi = \alpha \frown$ PRED(ϕ), where PRED(x) is the predicate of x. PRED('John will leave') = 'will leave'.

---

[161] Here is an objection. 'John left before paying' implies 'John never paid' (or at least does not imply 'John paid'), but 'John left before he paid' implies 'John paid'. However, some speakers

Thus, for example, 'John arrived before Mary' is treated as equivalent to 'John arrived before Mary arrived' and has satisfaction conditions represented by [11].

[11] [There is a time t_1: $t_1 < t^*$](John arrives(t_1) and [there is a time t_2: $t_2 < t^*$](Mary arrives(t_2) and t_1 is before t_2)).

In effect we have treated 'before' and 'after' as inverses of each other. However, 'before' will take negative polarity items comfortably while 'after' seems to resist this. Compare 'John left before anyone sang' and 'John left after anyone sang'.[162] This suggests that 'before' and 'after' should be treated differently after all. However, it does not appear that 'after' strictly excludes negative polarity items, as shown in these sentences:

The crisis in Taunton has put a renewed emphasis on mill pond dams, vestiges of New England's manufacturing history that have kept holding water back long after anyone needed them for power.

Using a needle after anyone else has used it is dangerous.

After anyone repeats something fifty times, we are apt to get the message as well as get tired of hearing it.

hear 'John left before he paid' as also implying 'John never paid' (or at not implying 'John paid')! Either result is in conflict with our analysis. But these contrast strongly with the example in the text: 'John paid before he left' and 'John paid before leaving'. Native speakers find both of these to imply 'John left'. Similarly speakers take 'John laughed before paying/he paid' to imply 'John paid', and 'John left before Sue paid' to imply 'Sue paid'. Consider further 'John left after he paid' and 'John left after paying'. Our informants find these both to imply 'John paid'. The implications, if semantic, must be carried by form. Not all of these intuitions, then, can be intuitions about what is implied by semantic form, and some must attach rather to what we take to be typically conveyed by a use of the sentence where that departs from semantic content. It seems clear that the special case which needs an explanation in terms of pragmatics is 'John left before paying'. Certainly the implication that John never paid can be explicitly canceled: 'John left before paying but went back to pay as soon as he realized his mistake'. We suggest that the default conversational context we imagine for this sentence involves thinking of John as having an obligation (or being expected) to pay before leaving, and imagining a speaker one of whose main purposes in using this sentence is to convey that John failed to do what he was obligated (or expected) to do before leaving. We then take the speaker not really to be committed to John's ever paying, because the point being conveyed is really that at the time he was obligated (or expected) to he did not. The speaker is committed only to what is expressed by 'John left without paying'. This is supported by noticing that this provides us with a prescription for generating similar examples, such as 'The minister quit before preaching his sermon'. We are indebted here to comments from and discussion with the Lepore 05/06 reading group.

[162] 'John left before everyone [there] sang' implies 'Everyone [there] sang', while 'John left before anyone [there] sang' is compatible with no one singing. The difference is due, we suggest, to 'sang' functioning as a restriction on 'anyone' but not on 'everyone'. That is, the first is analyzed as '$[\exists t: t < t^*]$(left(John, t) & $[\forall x: \text{there}(x)][\exists t': t' < t^*]$(sang($x, t'$) & before($t, t'$)))' and the second as '$[\forall x: \text{there}(x) \ \& \ [\exists t': t' < t^*]\text{sang}(x, t')]([\exists t: t < t^*]$(left(John, t) & before(t, t')))'.

Something that complicates the diagnosis is that 'after' differs from 'later than' in that the latter is comfortable with some negative polarity items in contexts in which 'after' is not. Thus, we do not say 'He left after anyone else' but we do say 'He left later than anyone else'. This suggests that the trouble is not with the sense of 'after', for it seems to be the same as 'later than', as that of 'before' is with 'earlier than'. Except for interaction with negative polarity items, 'after' and 'later than' seem fully interchangeable. This makes it looks as if the source of this syntactic restriction, if that is what it is, is independent of the truth conditional role of 'before' and 'after'. For this reason, and because any investigation into this difference would have to examine the licensing of negative polarity items in general, we will not pursue this difference between 'before' and 'after'.

3. Temporal Quantifiers

Natural languages provide a large variety of temporal quantifiers. In English, these include, for example, (i) unrestricted temporal quantifiers, such as 'always', 'anytime', 'sometimes', 'once', 'twice'; (ii) restricted interval temporal quantifiers, such as 'someday', 'everyday', 'daily', 'weekly', 'monthly', 'yearly', 'two times a day', 'twice a week', etc.; (iii) non-specific frequency quantifiers, such as 'seldom', 'often', 'infrequently', 'frequently', 'regularly', and 'intermittently', which do not specify a particular interval, and some of which exhibit topic dependence; and (iv) unrestricted temporal quantifiers, such as 'when' and 'whenever', which, though adverbs, introduce subordinate clauses, and function syntactically as sentential connectives. All of these quantify over times, binding unarticulated argument places in one or more verbs.[163] We treat these four classes in order. This is intended to be an illustrative, rather than exhaustive, treatment of temporal quantifiers in English.

---

[163] Some uses of temporal adverbs suggest that they are not always used to quantify over times, as, e.g. in the sentence 'Even numbers are always divisible by 2'. On such grounds Lewis (1975*a*) argues that they should be treated as quantifying over "cases". This desperate expedient should be resisted. Given that forms of 'to be' in English will have a suppressed temporal argument place, there can be no difficulty in including a temporal quantifier even in sentences which are about abstract objects. Indeed, not supplying a universal quantifier for a sentence such as 'Even numbers are divisible by 2' might be thought to be misleading when a speaker intends to be conveying that this is so necessarily or by definition. The effect of introducing 'always' is to emphasize the non-contingency of the claim, although what is said, strictly speaking, falls short of what is intended.

(i) The past and future tenses interact with temporal quantifiers differently than the present. We begin with the present tense. [12] (typical uses of which would be hyperbole) means roughly that John's hair is a mess at all times, and it can clearly be used on different occasions to express the same proposition.

[12]   John's hair is always a mess.

Although [12] is in the present tense, when modified by a temporal quantifier, the verb does not function indexically. In representing its truth conditions, then, we should treat the unarticulated argument place as bound by the temporal quantifier, rather than functioning indexically. This leads to [13] (*mutatis mutandis* for other temporal quantifiers).

[13]   [For all times t_1](John's hair is(t_1) a mess).

[12] is, therefore, in Quine's terms, an "eternal sentence." In contrast, utterances of [14] at different times express different propositions.

[14]   John's hair was always a mess.

An utterance of [14] yesterday would be true iff at every time before it John's hair was a mess, but its utterance today would require also that in the intervening time his hair remain unkempt. Similarly for the future tense. Thus, whereas by modifying a present tense verb we can transform a context-sensitive sentence into a context-independent one (other deictic terms aside), past and future tense verbs remain deictic when so modified. This is one reason not to treat the present tense as involving quantification like the past and future, for it would mean treating it as combining with quantificational adverbs differently from the past and future, although they would share underlying structure. The effect of the modification is to replace the default existential quantification over past times with quantification appropriate for the modifier. The satisfaction conditions of [14], then, would be represented as those of [15].

[15]   [For all times $t_1 : t_1 < t^*$](John's hair is(t_1) a mess).[164]

[164] Consider the sentence 'John's hair is sometimes a mess'. We treat this as about some interval centered around the present. If John's hair has never been a mess, but we know it will be in the distant future, we do not say 'John's hair is sometimes a mess', and, likewise, if John's hair was sometimes a mess in his 20s, but he is in his 40s now and bald, we do not say 'John's hair is sometimes a mess'. It is unclear, however, that this is a matter of what the sentence means, as opposed to in what situations it would be misleading to assert it. For if we know his hair will be a mess in the future, though it has never been so, or that it was in the past, but that he is bald now, we can certainly report the facts more perspicuously, and should do so, if we intend to be

(ii) Adverbs such as 'someday', 'everyday', 'daily', 'weekly', 'monthly', and 'yearly' quantify over specific intervals, and indicate that the event expressed by the verb they modify occurs in, as appropriate, some or every (etc.) interval of the appropriate kind. Thus, they supply two quantifiers over time intervals. The first is restricted to quantification over time intervals of a type indicated by the noun from which the quantifier is formed. The quantifier is existential in the first example, and universal in the other examples above, which is indicated by the 'ly' in the last four. The second quantifier is an existential quantifier which binds the argument place for event time in the modified verb, which is restricted to fall within the interval picked out by the first quantifier. Thus, we represent [16] as [17].

[16]   John goes to the barber monthly.
[17]   [For all months m][there is a time $t: t \subseteq m$](John goes(t) to the barber).

We extend this to the past and future tense as indicated in the shift from [13] to [15], that is, the months would be restricted to times in the past, or future, of the utterance. This treatment extends to complex restricted interval temporal quantifiers as well, as in, for example, 'Most years he vacations in France', that is, this means that there is a time interval contained in most years during which he vacations in France. A complex restricted interval quantifier like 'twice a week' introduces two quantifiers. If John washes his car twice a week, then each week there are two times at which John washes his car. Thus, we would represent 'John washes his car twice a week' as in [18].

[18]   [For all weeks w][there are two times $t: t \subseteq w$](John washes(t) his car).

(iii) Non-specific frequency adverbials, such as 'regularly', 'intermittently', 'frequently', 'often', 'seldom' and 'infrequently', intuitively indicate that the event expressed by the modified verb recurs at intervals of time. In the case of 'regularly', this seems simply to involve intervals of at least roughly the same length. The core meaning of 'intermittently' is *not continuously but at intervals*, with the implication often of irregularity, though to say something is intermittent but regular is not a contradiction. These adverbs can be treated like 'sometimes' and 'always', that is, as introducing a simple quantifier: 'John woke up intermittently/regularly last night' can be represented as '[There are intermittent/regular times $t: t < t^*$ and $t \subseteq$ the night before t^*](John wakes up(t))'.

cooperative conversational partners; and so, if we do not use a past or future tensed verb, we will be taken to be supposing that there are times in the near past which make true the sentence.

206

For our other examples, the length of the interval is understood relative to the modified verb.[165] For example, someone may fly frequently (twice a week), and comb his hair frequently (every five minutes), though if he combed his hair only as often as he flies, he would not be said to comb his hair frequently. This topic relativity appears to attach to those frequency adverbials from which one can form a comparative, 'more frequent/often than' or 'less seldom/infrequent than'. Thus these frequency adverbials exhibit a topic relativity similar to that of adjectives or non-temporal adverbs formed from comparatives, such as 'large' or 'tall'. In Chapter 7, we suggested that to say that Mickey is a large mouse is to say that Mickey is significantly larger than most mice. This suggests treating topic dependent frequency adverbials as involving a comparison of the intervals at which an event recurs to intervals in some appropriate comparison class indicated by the modified verb. In our sample case, 'John combs his hair frequently', we want to compare the frequency with which John combs his hair with that for most hair combers. (It may be that some subset of all the hair combers is typically intended, though, since this seems to be something that can shift in context independently of any features of the sentence, it is natural to think this is the effect of pragmatic factors on interpretation of speaker's meaning.) Since it follows from John's combing his hair frequently that there are times at which he combs his hair (or that John combs his hair—see the next section for discussion of habituals), we want this to be reflected in the representation as well. Thus, we suggest representing 'John combs his hair frequently' roughly as 'There are times at which John combs his hair, and his hair combings are significantly more frequent than hair combings for most of those who comb their hair'. More formally, where we make use of plural definite descriptions and plural temporal variables, represented by 'τ', we have

[19]   [There are times t](John combs(t) his hair) and [the times τ: τ are times of John's hair combings][most x: x are hair combers][the times τ': τ' are of x's hair combings](τ are significantly more frequent than τ').

We use 'most' because its vagueness matches that of 'frequently'. 'Seldom' and 'infrequently' are handled in a similar manner. One does F seldom/infrequently if one does it but less frequently than most do.[166]

---

[165] We are indebted to comments from Samuel Wheeler here.

[166] This may be too rigid an account of how the comparison class is determined. Suppose someone says: The United States frequently checks its nuclear reactors. It is not clear that we

(iv) The adverbs 'when' and 'whenever' are syntactically sentential connectives, but should likewise be treated semantically as quantificational. In [20], 'when' and 'whenever' are interchangeable.

[20]   John blushes whenever/when Mary looks at him.

For this reason, we will treat 'when' in such contexts as abbreviating 'whenever'. They are not interchangeable in [21], which requires a separate treatment.

[21]   I did it when he wasn't looking.

The difference is that between a universal and an existential quantifier. [20] is true iff at every time Mary looks at John, John blushes, that is, [20] is roughly equivalent to a universally quantified conditional with 'whenever' functioning as a quantifier with wide scope binding the unarticulated argument place for time in both verbs. Employing restricted quantifiers, we need not represent [20] counterintuitively as containing sentential connectives, but may represent its satisfaction conditions as in [22]; treating 'when' as a restricted existential quantifier in [21] yields [23].

[22]   [For all times t_1: Mary looks(t_1) at John](John blushes(t_1)).
[23]   [There is a time t_1: $t_1 < t^*$ and he is(t_1) not looking](I do(t_1) it).

As above, the past and future tenses remain deictic, though the present of state verbs does not.

It may seem natural to treat 'when' in some contexts as a definite description. For example, if one says, 'We will go to lunch when he gets here', it seems clear that we have in mind the time of his next arrival, though there may be many more in the future. Similarly, perhaps, when we say, 'Caesar defied the Roman senate when he crossed the Rubicon', we have a particular time, and so crossing, in mind. In contrast, if A asserts [21] referring to B with 'he', it seems clear that he would not be taken to imply that B wasn't looking only once and that at that time he did it, but that at a time B wasn't looking A did it. One response is to hold that 'when' is ambiguous between an indefinite and definite reading, and hold that in the two cases above we

interpret this to mean that the United States checks its nuclear reactors more frequently than most countries which check their nuclear reactors check theirs. It is more natural to take the comparison class to be checkings of other sorts of facilities by the United States. The positioning of 'frequently' in the sentence may be important here to how we interpret this. For we are more inclined to hear 'The United States checks its nuclear reactors frequently' as expressing the claim that the US's nuclear reactor checkings are more frequent than those of most other countries checking their nuclear reactors.

have incomplete definite descriptions which the interlocutor is invited to complete in some appropriate fashion. However, invoking Grice's maxim not to multiply senses beyond necessity, if we can accommodate the data without postulating an ambiguity, we should do so. There seems no hope of accommodating [21] on the definite description reading, so we should take the existential reading as basic and seek to understand the implication of uniqueness as a product of the interaction of the literal meaning with standard context of utterance. This is not difficult, and the strategy, which should be generally applicable, can be illustrated with respect to the two examples under discussion. In the case of 'We will go to lunch when he gets here', even on the suggestion that 'when he gets here' is a definite description, we would need to supplement the restriction with 'next' or something similar to secure a unique denotation. But with that included, the implication of uniqueness is secured even if we interpret the quantifier as just an existential quantifier. In the case of 'Caesar defied the Roman senate when he crossed the Rubicon', since Caesar crossed the Rubicon many times, we must again take the restriction to be supplemented to secure a denotation if we interpret 'when' as introducing a definite description, and once again the implication of uniqueness can be carried by implied restriction.

Let us consider briefly other combinations of simple tenses grammatically conjoined by 'when' or 'whenever'. The possible combinations are:

past/past	John blushed when/whenever Mary looked at him
future/future	?John will blush when/whenever Mary will look at him
past/future	*John blushed when/whenever Mary will look at him
future/past	*John will blush when/whenever Mary looked at him
present/future	*John blushes when/whenever Mary will look at him
future/present	?John will blush when/whenever Mary looks at him
present/past	*John blushes when/whenever Mary looked at him
past/present	*John blushed when/whenever Mary looks at him.

An asterisk indicates that the combination seems intuitively to be unacceptable; a question mark indicates that it is questionable, a form that is at least awkward or infelicitous, though not so strongly felt to be unacceptable. As we have interpreted the present/present combination, the clause introduced by 'when' or 'whenever' introduces a quantifier that binds the event time of both verbs. When the tense of the 'when'/'whenever'-clause is the past or future, we interpret it as quantifying over all times in the past or future of the time of utterance. The quantifier introduced must bind across both clauses. We assume it is intended to restrict the two event times introduced by the verbs to occur at the same time.

The past/past combination is the only one, besides the present/present combination, which is clearly acceptable. It is most natural to interpret 'John blushed whenever Mary looked at him' as '[For all times t_1: $t_1 < t^*$ and Mary looks(t_1) at John](John blushes(t_1))'. (*Mutatis mutandis* for 'when' throughout.) This representation, however, does not give the past tense of 'blush' any work to do. This recommends representing this instead as '[For all times t_1: $t_1 < t^*$ and Mary looks(t_1) at John][There is a t_2: $t_2 < t^*$ and $t_2 = t_1$](John blushes(t_2))'. This is further supported by the observation that it helps to explain why some of the other combinations are clearly not acceptable.

The past/future combination, 'John blushed when/whenever Mary will look at him' would be interpreted, on the model just introduced, as '[For all times t_1: $t_1 > t^*$ and Mary looks(t_1) at John][There is a t_2: $t_2 < t^*$ and $t_2 = t_1$](John blushes(t_2))'. No utterance of this could be true, however, since its truth would require a time in the future of the utterance time to be identical to a time in the past of the utterance time. The future/past combination introduces a similar problem, requiring a time in the past of the utterance time to be identical to a time in the future of the utterance time.

However, the present/future combination, 'John blushes whenever Mary will look at him', looks as if it should admit of a coherent interpretation, namely, '[For all times t_1: $t_1 < t^*$ and Mary looks(t_1) at John](John blushes(t_1))'. Why does it seem unacceptable then? There does not seem to be an explanation of this in terms of the natural projection of the semantics for acceptable uses to this case. If we wished to express what '[For all times t_1: $t_1 < t^*$ and Mary looks(t_1) at John](John blushes(t_1))' expresses, we would rather say, 'In the future, whenever Mary looks at John, he will blush'. Here 'in the future' apparently does play the role of restricting the quantifier introduced by 'whenever' to times in the future of the utterance, and we interpret the whole as '[For all times t_1: $t_1 > t^*$ and Mary looks(t_1) at John][There is a t_2: $t_2 > t^*$ and $t_2 = t_1$](John blushes(t_2))'. This parallels what we said in the case of the past/past combinations. Similarly, 'John blushes whenever Mary looked at him' should admit of a coherent interpretation, but is not acceptable.

Again, we find no explanation of this in terms of the natural projection of the semantics for acceptable uses to this case.

Before we consider the past/present combination, let us consider the future/present combination, 'John will blush whenever Mary looks at him'. This appears to have a reading (and we stress 'appears to') which might be made clearer by 'John will blush subsequently whenever Mary looks at him'. Thus, this is to interpret the future/present combination so that the quantifier introduced by the 'whenever' clause binds the reference time for the quantifier introduced by the tense of 'blush', as represented here: '[For all times t_1: Mary looks(t_1) at John][There is a t_2: $t_2 > t_1$](John blushes(t_2))'.

In light of this, why is there no parallel acceptable interpretation of the past/present combination? We can explain this as arising from the fact that there is the suggestion that Mary's looking at John is causally responsible for his blushing. But since causation works forward in time, this cannot be the case with the past/present combination interpreted in a fashion parallel to the future/present combination.

This leaves the future/future combination to consider, 'John will blush whenever Mary will look at him'. This seems acceptable if we imagine someone emphasizing 'will' in each clause. In this case, however, it is natural to treat what is said as equivalent to 'John insists on blushing whenever Mary insists on looking at him', that is, we interpret 'x *will* do y' as 'x will insist on doing y', and take this to express an event type of insisting on doing something. Still, the future/future combination should admit of a coherent interpretation parallel to that for the past/past combination, namely, '[For all times t_1: $t_1 > t^*$ and Mary looks(t_1) at John][There is a t_2: $t_2 > t^*$ and $t_2 = t_1$](John blushes(t_2))'. However, as we have noted, we do not use the future/future combination to express this, but rather, 'In the future, whenever Mary looks at John, he will blush'.

4. Habitual Sentences and Frequency Adverbials

So-called habitual sentences are interpreted as about events that occur at (more or less) regular intervals. Many habitual sentences are simply sentences whose event verbs are modified by a restricted interval or frequency adverbial, as in examples [24]–[26].

[24] Mary often smokes in her office.
[25] Bill complains frequently.
[26] Mary lectures three times a week.

If our discussion in the previous section is correct, then the classification of these as habituals just comes to their being sentences with restricted interval or frequency adverbials, which can be treated straightforwardly as contributing temporal quantifiers, and, in the case of the topic dependent adverbs, a comparative and quantification over members of a comparison class. If the proposals of the previous section are correct, it is easy to see why these are called 'habituals', since their truth would typically be grounded in a habit of smoking in the office, or complaining, or lecturing.

However, not all sentences with habitual interpretations contain explicit frequency adverbials modifying the main verb. [27] and [28], for example, are classified as habituals.

[27]   John works for a living.
[28]   Rover barks.

In these cases, though, it is natural to say that we understand speakers to be intending that we read in a contextually appropriate frequency adverbial, more or less specific, perhaps, depending on context. In saying this, though, we do not mean to imply that the speaker must have a particular frequency adverbial in mind. In fact, usually it will not matter for practical purposes which frequency adverbial within a range is supplied, and so it will typically be, to use Arne Naess's phrase, below level of definiteness of the speaker's intention which specific frequency adverbial is read in. This need not be viewed as merely a matter of laziness, for often the speaker may not be in an epistemic position to say anything very precise about the frequency, even to the degree to which it would be appropriate to use one rather than another frequency adverbial in a certain range. With [27], the adverbial 'for a living' together with the present tense event verb tells us that it is to be understood as quantified. A living cannot be earned from a single event of working, wages being what they are, and the present tense of an event verb typically has no use unless modified by a temporal adverb. Thus, [27] might be interpreted roughly as [29]—with the caveat that in different contexts, different frequency adverbials would be appropriate, for example, 'now and again', etc., and that the speaker will not typically even then have any specific frequency adverbial in mind.[167]

---

[167] Obviously, one may say, 'John works for a living, but not regularly', or 'Rover barks, but not often'. This does not show that we do not read in an adverbial in interpreting the speaker, but that there are a lot of options to choose from. Adding a qualifying clause, as in these examples, can help to point a speaker away from a mistaken interpretation.

[29]   John works *regularly* for a living.

The use of present tense in [28] likewise requires a modifier, and since it is not future or past directed, it is naturally taken to be a frequency adverb of some sort, 'often' or 'frequently', or perhaps a vague cardinality quantifier, 'a lot [of times]' or 'from time to time' (the speaker could not be intending to convey that Rover barks all the time). Thus, [28] might be interpreted roughly (again, though, depending on context, etc.) as [30].

[30]   Rover *often* barks.

These would receive satisfaction conditions appropriate for the implicitly understood adverbials on the model exhibited above. In practice, as we have said, what adverbial is intended will be no more precise than the context requires.

We emphasize that it is not our suggestion here that it is a semantic fact about a sentence such as [27] that, in a context of use of an appropriate sort, it is to be interpreted as if it had included explicitly a frequency adverbial. Rather, the suggestion is that it is an instance of abbreviated speech, where we intend our interlocutor(s) to have the wit to understand our intent, though we do not speak it fully, as when we say, for example, 'glue pot' when asking a helper to hand us something needed at the moment. That is, the import roughly conveyed is arrived at on the basis of pragmatics, and is not a matter of the literal interpretation of the utterance.[168]

Although [29] and [30] employ present tense verbs, it is clear that their future and past analogs may be interpreted habitually as well: in these cases, however, there is an alternative reading of the sentences as existentially quantified, compatible with their modifiers. Discussing Rover's laryngitis, you may remark, 'Don't worry, Rover will bark again'. This would receive

---

[168] This helps explain why we would not want to claim that, e.g. [27] and [29] are equivalent under negation. For when we consider the negation of [29] even with a wide scope negation, we focus on the possibility of John's working for a living, e.g. from time to time, though not regularly, and it is certainly possible that a use of [27] in a context would be more appropriately captured by 'from time to time' than 'regularly'. But our claim has not been that [27] is semantically equivalent to [29] but that it is semantically incomplete, and that in use it is clear the speaker intends some frequency quantifier or other in some vaguely indicated range to be more or less appropriate for the purposes of the talk exchange. Even fixing the context, we would not want to insist that a particular frequency quantifier is indicated. A better test of the account is to ask whether, if someone does not work either regularly or irregularly or anything in between, an utterance (pertaining to him) of 'He works for a living' would be interpreted as true. We think the answer is 'no'. We are indebted to members of Lepore's 05/06 reading group for helpful discussion on this issue.

the habitual reading. However, if *A*, after remarking to *B* that Rover always barks three times before going to sleep, continues, 'I've counted two barks only so far. Rover will bark again', this does not receive an habitual reading. Sometimes an adverbial will force an habitual reading, since it is incompatible with the existential reading, given what we know about how things work. This is so for 'will work for a living' and 'worked for a living'. Both would receive the habitual reading, because making a living by working requires, for most, regular application, or at least application from time to time.[169]

We end this sketch of our treatment of habituals by considering three uses of habituals which might be thought to present counterexamples to our account. We will argue that in these cases the readings which looks as if they conflict with our account are in fact pragmatic implicatures that arise from the use of habituals. This will serve as a sketch of our strategy more generally for dealing with uses of habituals which seem to depart from the account we have developed.

The first is the so-called dispositional use of habituals, as in Quine's example, 'Tabby eats mice', to be construed as meaning that Tabby is regularly disposed to eat mice (Quine 1960: 134). We agree that 'Tabby eats mice' would typically convey that Tabby is regularly disposed to eat mice. But this can be seen as arising from a pragmatic implicature of the utterance. To see this, let us ask: Would it be true to say that Tabby eats mice if Tabby had *never* eaten mice, and

---

[169] Vlach (1993: 231) claims that "[n]o existing framework for temporal semantics provides a general treatment of durative...and frequency...adverbials," and that, in particular, none can deal with a sentence such as:

    (i)   Allen worked out regularly for two weeks last month.

Our account handles this straightforwardly. The frequency adverb is a quantifier that replaces the existential quantifier of the tense of 'worked out', keeping the past time restriction. The duration adverbial 'for two weeks last month' (where 'last month' modifies 'two weeks') modifies the time so bound, which is understood to be within the time so designated:

    (ii)   [Regular $t_1 : t_1 < t^*$ and $t_1 \subset$ two weeks last month](Allen works(t_1)).

Vlach's account of tense (or, more properly, tense inflection) is that it makes no truth-functional contribution to sentences in which it occurs, but is like the gender of pronouns, which, he assumes, does not contribute to truth conditions. English users are supposed to follow the convention to use 'he' when talking about a male and 'she' when talking about a female, but one may, he asserts, say truly of a woman, 'He is tall'. Similarly, one is supposed to obey a convention to use present and past when talking about the present and the past, but this is no part of the truth conditions of the utterance, taken literally. All the work of semantic temporal reference, Vlach says, is really done by adverbial modification. This is an interesting suggestion, but certainly swims against the tide! It hardly comports with our intuitive judgments about the truth of utterances using tensed verbs. If one asserts, 'John was elected to the Senate', but John has not acceded to that august body, one offends, it seems, not just against usage, but against the truth.

never will? It seems not. So to say 'Tabby eats mice' presupposes that Tabby has eaten some mice. But suppose that Tabby had only eaten one mouse, and that her regular diet is parakeets. Is it true that Tabby eats mice? It seems it is not true. But plausibly Tabby is disposed to eat mice regularly, and has just not had the opportunity. Tabby would eat mice if she had the opportunity, but she does not, so she does not eat mice. Thus, 'Tabby eats mice' does not literally mean 'Tabby is (regularly) disposed to eat mice'. We suggest that in saying 'Tabby eats mice' we say something, varying perhaps with context, in line with remarks above, to the effect that Tabby regularly/sometimes/from time to time eats mice, and that this in turn implies pragmatically (in a typical conversational context) that Tabby is disposed to eat mice, for that would be a natural explanation of her regularly eating mice. That the effect is pragmatic is confirmed by the fact that the implication can be contextually canceled. For example, the following is perfectly coherent: "Tabby eats mice. However, she doesn't like to. She will only eat a mouse when she is very hungry, and has no other choice. She is very different from most cats in this respect."

The suggestion here can be extended to the standard import of an utterance of 'Cats eat mice' to the effect that cats are a sort of animal in whose nature it is to eat mice. The plural calls for a quantificational determiner. Since none is explicitly supplied, plausibly the interpretation will depend in part on the context, both the sentential context and the conversational context. 'Most' would be a reasonable choice for interpretation in most conversational contexts, and 'from time to time' or 'the times at which they are available' would be plausible candidates for the quantifier understood to bind the argument place in 'eats': the implication that it is in the nature of cats to do so then is very natural, since that would be a natural explanation of the fact stated. Again, that this is pragmatic is supported by the fact that it is easy to think of contexts in which the implicature is canceled.

Another use of the habitual which can be accounted for as a pragmatic effect is illustrated by 'June sells dresses and Bill sells linens', used in a department store to explain who is assigned to selling which items. We may assert 'June sells dresses and Bill sells linens' even if we know in fact June has never sold any dresses and Bill has never sold any linens. The point of the utterance is to communicate what June's job is and what Bill's job is. Of course, no one would take either sentence to be literally about what their jobs at the department store are. 'Sells' means the same here as it does in 'June sells 10 dresses every Sunday afternoon'. The import in the context then is clearly a pragmatic implicature. The implicature can be true even if the sentence uttered is not. Usually, when people are assigned to sell an item at the department store, they in fact sell such items regularly, and if they sell them regularly, that is typically because it is one of their assignments to sell items of that kind. Thus, 'June sells dresses' goes proxy for saying what June's job is, and can serve to communicate this against this more or less standard use of the sentence to communicate what June's job is even when she has never sold any dresses.

5. Relation to the Event Analysis

Finally, we consider how our account interacts with Davidson's event analysis of adverbial modification, discussed in Chapter 7. The event analysis assigns [31] the logical form of [32] (separating out here the thematic roles—see Chapter 7, §3).

[31] John walked up the hill last night in his dressing gown.
[32] There was an e such that e was a walking, and John was the agent of e, and e was a going up the hill, and e occurred last night, and e occurred with John in his dressing gown.

On the Davidsonian account, the temporal adjunct is a predicate of an event, not a time.

However, [32] does not really avoid treating adjuncts as introducing a predicate of times, because 'e was a walking, and John was the agent of e, and e was a going up the hill, and e occurred last night, and e occurred with John in his dressing gown' is tensed. Consequently, its satisfaction conditions must be unpacked by tenseless verbs in the metalanguage. (One might insist on rewriting [32] using tenseless predicates, but then it would not be equivalent to [31] because [31] is context sensitive.) When we spell out the contribution of the tensed predicates to the truth conditions, we get [33], in which we can see that 'last night' introduces a predicate of times.

[33] [There is an e]([there is a t_1: $t_1 < t^*$](e is(t_1) a walking) and [there is a t_1: $t_1 < t^*$](e is(t_1) by John) and [there is a t_1: $t_1 < t^*$](e is(t_1) a going up the hill) and [there is a t_1: $t_1 < t^*$ and $t_1 \subseteq$ last night](e occurs(t_1)) and [there is a t_1: $t_1 < t^*$](e occurs(t_1) with John in his dressing gown)).

[33], however, is inadequate, because it does not require each conjunct to be made true by the same time. For any event in which more than one agent could participate at different times, for example, building a house, satisfaction conditions modeled on [33] would be incorrect. We need a single quantifier

over temporal argument places for every modifier introduced by an adverbial phrase. So, we should treat the main verb as introducing an existential quantifier over times which binds the temporal variable in the main verb and in any other verb introduced by its adverbials. This has an unexpected benefit. Because two quantifiers bind the adjuncts to the main verb (represented as having three places), it becomes possible to treat some adjuncts as modifiers of the agent of the act, and not the event he performs. The result is illustrated in [34].[170]

> [34]   [There is an e][there is a t_1: $t_1 < t^*$ and $t_1 \subseteq$ last night](e is(t_1) a walking and John is(t_1) the agent of e and e is(t_1) a going up the hill and John is(t_1) in his dressing gown).

Similarly, we are now able to treat what are intuitively adverbials of place, for example, 'on a mountain top', or of condition, for example, 'in top form', as modifying objects rather than events (or states). This allows us to treat inferences such as 'John was in his dressing gown at midnight; John was brushing his teeth at midnight; therefore, John was brushing his teeth at midnight in his dressing gown' as valid in virtue of logical form (fixing contextual parameters), since in the first and third sentences 'in his dressing gown' is being predicated of the same thing, namely, John, instead of John in the first sentence and an event in the third. This option is available only if we treat tense as introducing a quantifier binding argument places in each adjunct introduced by an adverbial.[171]

In closing, we consider briefly an alternative proposed in Higginbotham (1995), which aims to accommodate tense using a quantifier over events, and not times. The difficulty is to anchor reference to events to the time of utterance. The only way to do this is to force every utterance to refer to itself, since each utterance is guaranteed to occur at the time of speech. For the past tense, we might treat, for example, 'John kissed Mary' as equivalent to

---

[170] Some economy might be urged here. We could simply have a conjunct that relates e to a time, e.g. 'at(e, t_1)', and then drop the temporal argument place from other predicates of the event. It seems more natural to us, however, to think that the verbs in logical form have argument places for times, and there may be cases in which this turns out to be important. For example, if Jack and Jill build a house, it need not be that they are agents of the building at the same time, or that either of them are agents the whole time the building goes on. So we seem to work with the concept of someone's being an agent of an event at a time in thinking about action. It seems also we may think certain events, e.g. a journey, may be a walking for part of the time, a flying for part of the time, and so on, for the whole time of the journey.

[171] Davidson was aware that his analysis of action sentences abstracted away from tense, and it is reasonable to think he would regard its inclusion here to be an advance over his treatment (2001 (1980): 123).

'[There is an event e: $e < u^*$](Kissing(e, John, Mary)'. Then 'u^*' would index to the speech act in which it was used. It seems counterintuitive, however, to treat every utterance as self-referential. This comes out when we consider in which counterfactual circumstances the various things we say are true. For example, it seems that what one says in uttering 'It will rain this afternoon' could have been true even if there had been no utterances. However, on the approach sketched by Higginbotham, this is not so. Each utterance of a tensed sentence on that account is about *inter alia* its utterance. Just as an utterance of 'I am hungry' by x expresses a proposition which is not true at a possible world where x never exists, so on Higginbotham's account no utterance of any tensed sentence expresses a proposition true at a world in which there are no utterances. Our approach encounters no difficulties on this score, since it allows that what we say could have been true even if there were no utterances, and no parallel difficulty arises about times, because what one expresses in saying 'It will rain this afternoon' could not have been true if there had been no times.

10

Tense in Sentential Complements and the Perfect Tenses

We take up now two final topics on tense. The first is the interaction of tenses in the main and subordinate clauses of indirect discourse sentences and propositional attitude sentences, and the related phenomenon of tense sequencing in English. We take this up in §§1–2. The second is the extension of the quantificational approach sketched for the simple tenses to the perfect tenses. We explain the extension in §3, and discuss briefly in §4 its relation to Reichenbach's (1947) account.

1. Thought and Tense

Sentences we use to describe particulars are often indexed to the time of their utterance, and the contents of thoughts we express using them are determined by what they express. Consequently, the thoughts we so express about particulars are thoughts directly about the times of the thoughts themselves. Since sentences we use to express thoughts express them only once, when we want to attribute thoughts or speech acts to others, or to ourselves at times other than the time of attribution, which sentences we use to articulate their contents must be indexed to the time of the reported thought or speech act. In this section, we consider how this is reflected in the interpretation of tense in complement clauses of indirect discourse and attitude sentences. This treatment extends generally to sentential complements.

We will approach the topic of tense in attitude sentences and indirect discourse as a design problem for constructing reports of attitudes and speech acts, given a straightforward semantics for unembedded tensed sentences. Consider John's potential assertions at t_0 of $[1a]–[3a]$, and their corresponding canonical representations interpreted relative to t_0 in $[1b]–[3b]$.

[1]   (*a*) Mary was tired.   (*b*) [There is a t_1: $t_1 < t_0$](Mary is(t_1) tired).

[2]   (*a*) Mary is tired.   (*b*) Mary is(t_0) tired.

[3]   (*a*) Mary will be tired.   (*b*) [There is a t_1: $t_1 > t_0$](Mary is(t_1) tired).

We may report John's assertion (or the belief he thereby expresses) either before or after it occurs, or even simultaneous with it. Our temporal position with respect to John's utterance determines the tense of the main verb in our report; the tense of the complement clause, however, must be sensitive to the tense John used to express his belief. Let us consider first a report of what John said from the perspective of a time later than his assertion. The main verb will be in the past tense, but how do we report, given available resources, the content of John's assertion?

Context-sensitive elements in complement clauses are usually interpreted relative to the speaker's context. Thus, although in direct speech we would report that John said 'I am tired', in indirect discourse we would report the same act by 'John said that *he* was tired'. However, unlike demonstrative pronouns and indexicals, which are always interpreted relative to speaker context, just as they are when not embedded in a complement clause, tense is more complex. In reporting an assertion by John of any of $[1a]–[3a]$ at t_0 from the perspective of a later time, it would be inappropriate to interpret a tense in the complement clause relative to speaker context, for that would attribute to the subject an assertion about the speaker's time and not his own. Thus, the tense in the complement clause must have its reference time, the time with respect to which tense of the complement clause verb indicates the time of the occurrence of the event it expresses, fixed by the tense of the main verb. That is, the argument place that functions indexically when the sentence is unembedded must be bound by the quantifier introduced by the main verb when embedded in indirect discourse. Then the verb in the complement clause must indicate that the event expressed occurred before, at, or after the time of the reported utterance.

From the design standpoint, it would be simplest to reuse in the complement the tense used by the subject. If the argument place that usually functions indexically were bound by the quantifier the main verb introduces, this would capture the relative present, past, or future directedness of the content of the original assertion. However, while some languages work like this (for example, Russian and, though without verb inflection, Chinese and Japanese[172]), English does not: in indirect speech, if the main verb is in the past, the tense of the complement clause shifts to the past perfect, past or past future, respectively, as the tense of the main verb in the reported utterance is past, present or future. This tense sequencing rule[173] is illustrated in Table 1.

Table 1

Sentence uttered by John	Tense shift in complement clause with past tense main verb
Mary was tired.	John said that Mary had been tired.
Mary is tired.	John said that Mary was tired.
Mary will be tired.	John said that Mary would be tired.

These would be interpreted respectively as [4]–[6].[174]

[4] [There is a t_1: $t_1 < t^*$](John says(t_1) that [there is a t_2: $t_2 < t_1$](Mary is(t_2) tired)).

[5] [There is a t_1: $t_1 < t^*$](John says(t_1) that Mary is(t_1) tired).

[6] [There is a t_1: $t_1 < t^*$](John says(t_1) that [there is a t_2: $t_2 > t_1$](Mary is(t_2) tired)).

The tense of the main verb controls the temporal argument place of the verb in the complement clause, which functions indexically when unembedded. For in order to articulate what John said using [1*a*], we must represent him as saying at some past time that at some prior time Mary was then tired; this is

---

[172] See Comrie (1985: 109); Kondrashova (1998); Kusumoto (1999); Philippe (1999); Stowell (1995) for Russian; and also Ogihara (1996). However, for a recent argument that the no sequence of tense view is empirically inadequate for Russian, see Altshuler 2004. Thanks go to Daniel Altshuler for bringing the contrary data to our attention. Apart from the empirical issues, one could write down rules for a language which provided for appropriate interpretations of complements without sequence of tense, so as a conceptual matter, sequence of tense is not necessary.

[173] This terminology is not used consistently in the literature. Sometimes it is used for the semantic phenomenon of the tense in one clause controlling that in another, sometimes to refer to the syntactic phenomenon of back shifting of tense markers. We use it here in the latter sense.

[174] We are following traditional rules for sequence of tense in reporting indirect discourse and attitude sentences. One would expect some variations in speech, and the simple past to sometimes be used for both the simultaneous reading, [5], and the past relative to the time of the reported speech, [4], especially since the tense sequencing rules do not represent any deep fact about language. Higginbotham (1995) assumes this, as does Abusch (1997), who offers examples in which reading [4] would be forced by the narrative context: 'John mostly slept through the sixties. But Joan later claimed that he was active in the anti-war movement' (our example). Locating the saying in the discourse at a time later than the time the mentioned speaker intends to comment on forces an auditor to interpret the indirect discourse as in [4].

represented by [4]. This has been identified traditionally as the function of the past perfect, that is, to pick out a time prior to some past time indicated by a verb in the sentence. Were the verb in the complement clause to be interpreted relative to the speaker's time, the report would be false of John, since he said nothing about the time of the speaker's utterance. Likewise, to capture what John said using [2a], we must say that there is some time such that John said at that time that Mary was then tired, which is what [5] expresses. To report that in the past John said that in the future relative to the time of his utterance Mary would be tired, the reference time of the embedded verb must be fixed by the time of John's utterance, as shown in [6].[175] If we are right, therefore, most indirect discourse and attitude sentences quantify into the complement clause.

There are apparent exceptions to the rule illustrated in Table 1, for example, reports of certain states which continue into the present, as in 'I heard last night that Mary is sick' or 'The Egyptians knew that the earth is round' (borrowed from Smith 1978: 66). In this case, the present tense is interpreted relative to the speaker's context, rather than that of the event or state being reported. This seems acceptable only when the verb is factive or a verb of indirect discourse. One cannot say, e.g. 'I thought that the earth is round'. We suspect that, in this case, the present tense is used to indicate that what is being reported was not something the content of which was relativized simply to the time of the reported event or state, but rather was intended to express a state that would extend into some future indefinite time that at least includes the time of utterance. Abusch (1997) gives a different account which makes the appropriateness hinge on what the speaker believes, but if we wish the reports to be possibly true, the right account should focus on what the reportee knows, hears, says, etc.; one of Abusch's examples, 'John believed that Mary is pregnant', we find hard to interpret!) A related case is 'I asked him who that lady in the tiara is'. Here there is the pull of the demonstrative construction, interpreted relative to the speaker's time, as well as the assumption, forced by the use of the expression in the nominal modifying the demonstrative, that the lady in question is still wearing a tiara. (The example is borrowed from

[175] Tense sequencing shows up even without an explicit tense marker governing it, as in Abusch (1997: 29): 'Mary's desire to marry a man who resembled her is bizarre'. The past shifting of 'resemble' indicates that the desire is located prior to the time of utterance. This tells us that in its canonical paraphrase, '[The x : x was Mary's desire to marry a man who resembled her](x is bizarre)', the appropriate tense for the copula in the restriction on the quantifier is the simple past. This also points to an account of the acceptability of 'The fugitives are all in jail now' (borrowed from Vlach (1993: 259), which, while perfectly acceptable, might seem odd because prisoners are not fugitives. By understanding the predicate introduced by 'fugitives' in the past tense, this unwelcome conflict is resolved.

Visser (1972: 779), a rich source of examples from Old to Modern English. Visser notes (p. 827) that the use of the present in the complement has been common in all periods of the language, though more recently neglected by grammarians. The examples all seem, however, to fit the diagnosis here given. An event or process definitely located only in the past relative to the time of speech is quite unhappily reported in the present in the complement for example, 'He said that he is tired yesterday'.)

The tense sequencing phenomenon occurs only with the main verb in the past. So, reports of John's future speech act will use the tense John would use, as in Table 2. Their interpretations would then be represented as in [7]–[9].

Table 2

The sentence that will be used by John	Complement clause tense with future tense main verb
Mary was tired.	John will say that Mary was tired.
Mary is tired.	John will say that Mary is tired.
Mary will be tired.	John will say that Mary will be tired.

[7] [There is a t_1: $t_1 > t^*$](John says(t_1) that [there is a t_2: $t_2 < t_1$](Mary is(t_2) tired)).

[8] [There is a t_1: $t_1 > t^*$](John says (t_1) that Mary is(t_1) tired).

[9] [There is a t_1: $t_1 > t^*$](John says (t_1) that [there is a t_2: $t_2 > t_1$](Mary is(t_2) tired)).

The tense of the main verb, again, controls the temporal argument places of the verb(s) in the complement clause which, when unembedded, index to the time of utterance.

As we remarked earlier, there is a clear reason not to interpret the tense of the complements of the sentences in the right-hand column in Table 2 relative to the speaker's context: this would guarantee that the reports were false, since the reportee will not say anything in the future directly about the present time (that has the right structure). We are treating indirect speech as a model for attitude sentences. But with attitude sentences, there appears to be a counterexample to our analysis, in a sentence noticed by Parsons (reported in Dowty (1982: 50)):

(i)   One day John will regret that he is treating me like this.

In (i) the tense of the complement verb 'is treating' is independent of that of the main verb, i.e. it indexes to speaker time. Is this loose talk or a counterexample?

If what one intends to say by (i) is true, John will one day be disposed to report himself by, 'I regret that I treated him like that'. But interpreted relative to their respective contexts, the sentences in the complement clauses do not express the same proposition, being directly about different times. How then could (i), interpreted as intended, be true? What one intends to convey could have been reported by (ii).

(ii) One day John will regret that he (has) treated me like this.

This gets it just right. We suggest the following account of the use of (i). A speaker, resentful of John, wishes to emphasize John is mistreating him, and to emphasize its objective wrongness by asserting that John will regret (someday) his mistreatment of him (his treating him like this). Our speaker could say, 'John is treating me like this and one day he will regret his treating me like this', but this is a mouthful, and in the heat of the moment, out comes a fusion of the two, natural enough, given that 'his treating me like this' is the nominalization of 'he is treating me like this'. We so interpret him because 'this' is used to pick out a current activity of John's, which requires the tense of 'is treating' to index to the present, and not to the time of John's regret. We understand what he intends well enough, though he issues an inaccurate report and violates some (well-grounded) rules of usage.

Reports of present sayings use the same tense as used by the person whose speech act is being reported, but employ the present progressive for the main verb, as is illustrated in Table 3. Here the main verb does not express quantification over times, and, hence, in complement clauses verbs are simply interpreted relative to the utterance time, which gives correctly the content of John's assertions, if he uses those or synonymous sentences. The interpretations are [10]–[12].

[10] John is saying(t^*) that [there is a t_1 : $t_1 < t^*$](Mary is(t_1) tired).
[11] John is saying(t^*) that Mary is(t^*) tired.
[12] John is saying(t^*) that [there is a t_1 : $t_1 > t^*$](Mary is(t_1) tired).

Table 3

Sentence used by John	Complement clause tense with present tense main verb
Mary was tired.	John is saying that Mary was tired.
Mary is tired.	John is saying that Mary is tired.
Mary will be tired.	John is saying that Mary will be tired.

(This provides further support for rejecting the treatment of the present tense given in [7] in Chapter 8.)

There is no deep reason why English must employ a tense sequencing rule for indirect discourse and attitude sentences when the main verb is in the past tense. Not all natural languages do—Russian, for example. Furthermore, the tense sequencing rule appears to prevent unambiguous reports of certain past speech acts. If a speaker uses a sentence in the past perfect, for example, 'Mary had been tired', or in the present perfect, for example, 'Mary has been tired', no tense can be used unambiguously to report him indirectly, since the past perfect has already been allocated to reporting utterances of sentences in the simple past. Our practice is to use the past perfect to report speech in the past perfect and the present perfect as well as the simple past, and to rely on context for disambiguation. This limitation can be got around to some extent by employing adverbial modifiers. We can say, 'John said then that Mary had been tired before some previous time'. This fails to assign content correctly, even if the quantifiers take wide scope, since the modifier is still represented as a conjunct. But such peculiarities of English cannot be philosophically significant, since languages can plainly be designed so as to avoid them.

2. Adverbial Modifiers in Complement Clauses

In this section, we briefly consider adverbial modifiers in complement clauses. We take indirect discourse again as our model. By and large, we use the same modifiers as those in the reported utterance. John's assertion of 'Mary left before Jim' would be reported as 'John said that Mary had left before Jim'. This would be represented as '[There is a time t_1: $t_1 < t^*$](John says(t_1) that [there is a t_2: $t_2 < t_1$](Mary leaves(t_2) and [there is a t_3: $t_3 < t_1$](Jim leaves(t_3) and t_2 is before t_3))'. Adverbials that contain deictic referring terms such as 'now' and 'today', however, are evaluated relative to the time of utterance, which forces a shift from the adverbial originally used. Thus, if John said yesterday, 'Mary will leave before the day after tomorrow', he would be reported indirectly today as in [13], which is interpreted as [14].

[13] John said that Mary would leave before tomorrow.
[14] [There is a time t_1: $t_1 < t^*$](John says(t_1) that [there is a t_2: $t_2 > t_1$](Mary leaves(t_2) and t_2 is before the day after t^*)).

Unanchored adverbials, which seem to function indexically when unembedded, such as 'at midnight' and 'by noon', are an exception. In [15], the referent of 'midnight' is determined relative to the time of John's saying, not the time of utterance. Similarly, for other expressions which pick out times relative to a day or other standard unit. [15] would be interpreted as [16].

[15]   John said that Mary had left before midnight.

[16]   [There is a time t_1: t_1 < t^*](John says(t_1) that [there is a time t_2: t_2 < t_1](Mary leaves(t_2) and t_2 is before the midnight of t_1).

This fits in with our earlier suggestion that unembedded uses of unanchored adverbials are implicitly indexical or quantified.

The account generalizes straightforwardly to iterated attitude and discourse sentences. In [17], the tense of 'said' governs 'had told', which in turn governs 'would be leaving'.

[17]   John said last week that Mary had told him three days earlier she would be leaving tonight.

'last week' indexes to the present, as does 'tonight', but 'three days earlier' expresses a relation whose second term is suppressed, yet is evidently the time of John's report. [17] is represented as [18].

[18]   [There is a t_1: t_1 < t^* and t_1 ⊂ the week before t^*](John says(t_1) that [there is a t_2: t_2 < t_1 and t_2 ⊂ the day three days earlier than t_1](Mary tells(t_2) him that [there is a t_3: t_3 > t_2 and t_3 = tonight](Mary is(t_3) leaving))).

If 'would say' is embedded in a report with a main verb in the past, the verbs it governs are also governed by the sequencing rule. In [19], the tense of 'would tell' governs 'loved', but 'loved' indexes to the time of the telling, not to a prior time. [19] would be represented as in [20].

[19]   John said that he would tell Mary that he loved her by next week.

[20]   [There is a t_1: t_1 < t^*](John says(t_1) that [there is a t_2: t_2 > t_1 and t_2 < next week](he tells(t_2) Mary that he loves(t_2) her)).

Earlier we noted that present tense event verbs true of speech acts may be used performatively, as in 'I promise I won't be late' or 'I promise to be there'. We suggested that these are understood to be modified implicitly by 'hereby', which refers to the utterance act itself, and that this modifier provides a quantifier to bind what would otherwise be a free variable in the main verb. We can now suggest a representation of the logical form of such sentences in light of our discussion of indirect discourse. We will take 'I promise I won't be late' as our example, which we represent as in [21].

[21] [There is time t_1: $t_1 = t^*$](I promise(t_1) by this act that it is not the case that [there is a t_2: $t_2 > t_1$](I am(t_2) late)).

We likewise suggest that sometimes 'now' modifies a sentence, not a verb, as in 'Now he will resign for sure', which is equivalent to 'It is now the case that he will resign', and might be represented as in [22].

[22] [There is a t_1: $t_1 = t^*$ and $t_1 = $ now](it is(t_1) the case that [there is a t_2: $t_2 > t_1$](he resigns(t_2))).

The chief moral here is that our reports of others' attitudes at times other than the present do not completely report the content of their attitudes, since they involve quantifying into the complement clause. What we learn is that some completion of the complement clause gives the content of the speaker's assertion (belief, etc.). There appears to be no way in English to be more precise, since even adding an adjunct does not eliminate quantifying into the complement clause, because the main verb's tense must control the reference time of the verb(s) in the complement clause.

Similar binding phenomena occur between the tense of verbs, generally, in superordinate and subordinate clauses, where we find the past shifting of tense as a marker of this binding as well. Consider the contrast between [23] and [24], discussed in Kamp (1971), in which they form part of his motivation for a two-dimensional tense logic.

[23] A child was born who would be king.
[24] A child was born who will be king.

The effect of the past shifting is to introduce the same kind of binding relation between the tense of the main verb and the subordinate clause that we find in complement clauses of indirect discourse. Whereas in [24], the tense of the verb in the subordinate clause is interpreted relative to the speaker's context, in [23], it is interpreted relative to the time bound by the past tense of the main verb. This can be represented as in [25] and [26], respectively.

[25] [There is a time t_1: $t_1 < t^*$][there is a time t_2: $t_2 > t_1$](a child is(t_1) born who is(t_2) king).
[26] [There is a time t_1: $t_1 < t^*$][there is a time t_2: $t_2 > t^*$](a child is(t_1) born who is(t_2) king).

([23] is true even if a child was born who at some time after the speech act is king, although, given the availability of [24], it would be pragmatically misleading to use [23], except when the time of the child's being king precedes the time of speech.) Similarly, the use of the simple past in the superordinate and of the past perfect in the subordinate clause signals that the tense of the main verb controls that of the subordinate. In 'A president was elected who had been jailed', the natural interpretation requires that the event expressed in the subordinate clause occur prior to the event expressed in the superordinate. It is not clear that we find the same effect with the simple past in the subordinate clause, however, which, if it followed the pattern of indirect discourse, would index to the same time as the event expressed by the main verb. 'A president was elected who was jailed' does not suggest that the jailing and the election occurred simultaneously; rather, the restriction seems to be that both occurred prior to the time of utterance. The phenomenon occurs with other tenses. Consider 'John will meet a man who has been/is/will be/king'. In appropriate contexts, we can force readings in which the tense in the subordinate clause either is independent of the main clause, and indexes to speaker time, or is controlled by that of the main clause. It is clearly useful to have both readings, but lamentable that English, in this as in many other cases, provides no means of systematic disambiguation. Using back shifting of tense for verbs in subordinate clauses whose main verbs are in the past can be seen as a half-hearted attempt to disambiguate, which when employed in discourse and attitude sentences leads regrettably to the difficulties we noted with reporting unambiguously past speech acts employing the past and present perfect.

A word is in order about the implications of our treatment of tense in complement clauses for certain argument forms given in natural language. Consider the argument: John thought that Mary loved him, and he still thinks that; therefore, John thinks that Mary loved him. (The genre we treat here was brought to our attention by Richard (1981).) The argument is intuitively valid (relativizing both sentences to a set of contextual variables), but what is the function of 'that' in the second conjunct of the first sentence? If it is a referring term, then it cannot be taken to pick out a proposition referred to in the first conjunct, since the only proposition expressed there is that expressed by the full sentence, since the complement clause semantically contains variables bound from outside it. Thus, we must treat it either as something like a pro-sentence, which is to be replaced by 'Mary loved him', or, if we treat it as a referring term, it looks as if it must refer to the sentence 'Mary loved him'. In favor of the first alternative, perhaps, is the naturalness of replacing 'that' with 'so'. The second alternative, however, could be made to work as well in a sophisticated sententialist account (see Ludwig and Ray (1998) and Ch. 11).

228

3. The Perfect Tenses

In this section, we discuss the perfect tenses (or the perfective aspect, as it is often called), and how they differ from simple tenses. Table 4 gives the forms of the perfect tenses.

Table 4

Tense	Form	Example
Future Perfect	'will'/'shall' + 'have' + past participle	John will have seen it.
Present Perfect	present of 'have' + past participle	John has seen it.
Past Perfect	past of 'have' + past participle	John had seen it.

The perfect expresses a completed event. The present perfect is used to indicate that an event has been completed as of the present. It differs from the simple past in allowing that the event's terminal point coincides with the time of utterance. One can say, 'John has finished swimming now', but not 'John finished swimming now'. Likewise, one can say, 'John has worked here since 1980', which means that from 1980 to the present John has worked here, but not 'John worked here since 1980', because the simple past requires the time of the event expressed by the verb to be in the past. (Adverbials of the form 'since'⌢δ, where δ is a temporal designator, are acceptable only with perfect tenses, though there is the idiomatic, 'It is a year since we left'.) However, contrary to what some philosophers and linguists claim,[176] the event need not extend into the present, as is shown by the acceptability of 'John has been a lifeguard, but isn't any longer'. The future perfect is used to indicate something has been completed as of some future time. The past relative to the future reference time may be past relative to the speaker's time of utterance, or it may be completed at any time up to and including the future reference time. If it is true now to say John sat down yesterday, it is true to say John will have sat down by tomorrow. Likewise, if tomorrow one says truly, 'John has finished swimming now' at 3 o'clock, it would be correct to say today, 'John will have finished swimming by 3 o'clock tomorrow'. The past perfect is used to say something has been completed by some past time. So if John finished swimming at 3 o'clock yesterday, it would be correct to say today, 'John had finished swimming by 4 o'clock yesterday'.

The effect of projecting these future, present, or past reference times relative to which an event is said to have been completed can be accommodated within

---

[176] See Dowty (1982: 27), who also provides references.

229

our framework by introducing another quantifier and a relation restricting the relations among the bound temporal variables.[177] The past perfect of [27a] is illustrated in [27b], and the future perfect of [28a] in [28b].

[27] (a) John had seen it.
  (b) [There is a t_1: $t_1 < t^*$][there is a t_2: $t_2 \leq t_1$](John sees(t_2) it).
[28] (a) John will have seen it.
  (b) [There is a t_1: $t_1 > t^*$][there is a t_2: $t_2 \leq t_1$](John sees(t_2) it).

For convenience, we will adopt Reichenbach's terminology[178] to distinguish among the times represented by 't_1', 't^*', and 't_2', the *reference* time, the *speaker* time, and the *event* time, respectively. The event time is the time of the action expressed by the main verb, the speaker time is the time of utterance, and the reference time is the time relative to which the event time is located. In [27] and [28], 'have' contributes a restricted existential quantifier that relates its temporal variable, the reference time, to the speaker time as before or after it, depending on whether the tense of 'have' is past or future, and the past participle contributes likewise a restricted existential quantifier binding the variable associated with the event time, which is related to the reference time as before or simultaneous with it. The present perfect of [29a] receives a parallel treatment, as in [29b].

[29] (a) John has seen it.
  (b) [There is a t_1: $t_1 = t^*$][there is a t_2: $t_2 \leq t_1$](John sees(t_2) it).

Though we could simplify [29b], it is plausible that the function of combining a tense of 'have' with the past participle is the same in every perfect tense, but

---

[177] The reader may wish to compare our account with Parsons (1990: Ch. 10), who does not analyze the perfect as a tense. Rather, more in the vein of our account of the progressive, Parsons treats what we call the perfect tenses as perfect *forms* of verbs, which are state verbs that express being in the state of having done or been something (analogous to the structure subject + tense + have + adjective + noun, as in 'John has red hair'), and which can be in the past, present, or future ('had', 'has', 'will have'). This has the same effect as our suggestion below. It is not clear that anything we say rules decisively against this alternative, which could be adopted in the framework we pursue. On the other hand, we are unpersuaded that etymological considerations show that our analysis is incorrect: English users employ these constructions perfectly ignorant of their history, and there is nothing in their dispositions which would suggest they see a strong analogy with the use of 'have' in state attributing sentences such as 'John has red hair'. Furthermore, the double quantifier approach interacts in an intuitively compelling way with adverbial modification of perfectives.

[178] See Reichenbach (1947: 287–98).

for the contribution of the tense of 'have'.[179] This leads to symmetry in the interaction of perfect tenses with various adverbials.[180]

The utility of the perfect becomes apparent when we consider its interaction with certain adverbial modifiers which (partially) fix the reference time. In 'John will have seen it by tomorrow', 'by tomorrow' modifies the reference time, that is, the future time in the past relative to which the event is said to occur. Similarly for the past perfect and the present perfect. Thus, for 'John will have finished swimming by tomorrow', we have [30].

[30]　[There is a time t_1 : $t_1 > t^*$ and $t_1 =$ tomorrow][there is a t_2 : $t_2 \leq t_1$](John finishes swimming(t_2)).

This explains why 'John will have finished swimming by yesterday' is ill-formed, since it would require the reference time, which the quantifier restriction requires to be in the future relative to the utterance time, to be also in the past relative to the time of utterance. Similar remarks apply to the past perfect. One cannot say, 'John had seen it by tomorrow'.

The perfect tenses are useful, particularly the past and future perfect, because they allow us to set time boundaries other than the present for events. This is accomplished by adverbial modification on the past or future reference time in the past of which another event is to have occurred. This explains why unembedded and unmodified uses, or context-free uses, of the perfect can seem odd, for example, an unadorned use of 'John had been there'. The perfect tenses are almost never used without adverbial modification,

---

[179] In this we differ from Taylor (1977), who treats the present perfect as semantically equivalent to the simple past. We already noted it cannot be equivalent to the simple past, which requires the event expressed to occur strictly in the past, while the past perfect does not. We also depart from Taylor in taking syntactic structure as a guide to the semantic structure of the present perfect. Taylor's paraphrases of the perfect tenses employ demonstratives for reference times, for which there is no sanction in the original, i.e. to say that e.g. John had been a major in the army, one does not *need* to have any specific past time in mind relative to which John, before that time, had been a major in the army, although, of course, one may. Taylor also errs in his treatment of the future perfect in supposing that the event time must lie strictly in the future. This is not so, as our example in the text shows.

[180] An oddity about which adverbials the present perfect will take comfortably is that it does not happily accept adverbials that specify precisely the event time when the time is clearly in the past, though this is not so for the past or future perfect. Although one can say felicitously, 'I have seen her today', one cannot say, 'I have seen her yesterday'. (These data are discussed in Mittwoch (1988: 218).) Our account presents no semantic barrier to this, though it would be pragmatically odd, since given the difference between the present perfect and the past, when an adverbial definitely locates the event time in the past, using the present perfect will seem pointless.

231

or without an appropriate context in which there is an implicit adverbial modification provided by the surrounding discourse.

Not all adverbials modifying verbs in a perfect tense modify the reference time; some modify the event time. In 'John had arrived on Tuesday', 'on Tuesday' modifies only the event time. Generally, it appears that adverbials introduced by limiting prepositions, like 'by', 'before', and 'after', modify the reference time. Adverbials that indicate a specific date are used to specify the event time. Often, such modifications will sound odd, as in 'John will have arrived Tuesday next week'. They sound odd because using the perfect tense when the adverbial modifies the event time is usually pointless. 'John had arrived on Tuesday' seems less strange because it is easy to imagine a narrative in which the use of the past perfect would have a point, for example, 'Mary, who arrived on Wednesday, thought she had arrived before John. But John had arrived on Tuesday.'[181]

An interesting test of our proposal is whether it can explain the interaction of adverbials introduced using 'since' followed by a temporal designator with the various tenses, which seem acceptable only with perfect tenses. While we can say, 'John has/had/will have worked since 1980', we cannot say felicitously, 'John worked/works/will work since 1980'. With the past perfect and the future perfect, 'since 1980' adds that the activity expressed by the verb has taken place in the period from 1980 to the *reference* time; with the present perfect, 'since 1980' adds that the activity expressed by the main verb has taken place in a period from 1980 to the present,[182] but since this is the reference time, we can represent 'since 1980' requiring for all three that

---

[181] Reichenbach (1947: 294) incorrectly suggests that such modifiers modify the reference time. In 'John had arrived on Tuesday, a day before Mary', it is not reference time but event time that is in question. Likewise in Reichenbach's example, 'I had met him yesterday', 'yesterday' does not modify the reference time, but rather the event time. For we can likewise say, 'I had met him yesterday, but Mary did not meet him until this morning'. So, when Reichenbach claims that modifiers modify the event time only when the event and reference time coincide, he is mistaken. Rather, different modifiers should be taken to modify different times, according to their character.

[182] There is another, though less natural, reading, according to which to say that 'John has worked here since 1980' is to say that at some time between 1980 and now, John has worked here. It may be that 'since' is ambiguous. On the other hand, it may be that there is a univocal reading that in standard contexts generates the reading we offered in the text. Three possibilities suggest themselves. First, the sense of 'since 1980' is univocally 'between now and 1980', and it is usually understood as elliptical for 'ever since 1980'. Second, '=' should be replaced with '⊆' in [31]–[33] in the second quantifier, and the implication that the period is equal to the whole is pragmatically generated as the most salient period in the conversational context. Third, the latent sense is generated by the possibility of using 'since' in a context in which an implied numerical quantifier modifies it, as in answering, 'Has John worked here at any time since 1980?', by saying, 'Yes, he has worked here since 1980'. Nothing fundamental hinges on resolving this.

the activity take place between 1980 and the reference time, as illustrated in [31]–[33] (where '$t - x$' means 'the time interval from x to t)'.

[31]   [There is a t_1: t_1 = t^*][there is a t_2 : t_2 ≤ t_1 and t_2 = t_1 − 1980](John works(t_2) here).

[32]   [There is a t_1: t_1 < t^*][there is a t_2 : t_2 ≤ t_1 and t_2 = t_1 − 1980](John works(t_2) here).

[33]   [There is a t_1: t_1 > t^*][there is a t_2 : t_2 ≤ t_1 and t_2 = t_1 − 1980](John works(t_2) here).

So, modifying a verb in a perfect tense with 'since 1980' is to say that the *event* time is equal to the time interval between 1980 and the *reference* time. We can see why 'since 1980' does not sit comfortably with the simple tenses. It designates a time interval identified with the event time. But for the simple tenses, the anchor time for determining the time interval would be the time of utterance (that is, the event time would be identified with $t^* - 1980$); yet, the requirements imposed on the event time by the simple tenses are incompatible with this. Notice how nicely the account adapts to the embedding of 'since' in other modifiers, for example, 'several times since 1980'. 'since 1980' modifies 'several times', which quantifies over the event time. So, 'John has worked several times since 1980' is represented as '[There is a t_1: t_1 < t^*][several t_2: t_2 ⊂ t_1 − 1980](John works(t_2))'.

Adverbs of quantification, and 'before' and 'after' used as sentential connectives, likewise modify the event times. Consider [34] and [35].

[34]   John had loved Mary long before he said it.
[35]   John had never been to Arizona.

'Before' relates event (or state) times, that is, it relates the argument places in the main verbs of the sentences flanking it. In [34], 'long' modifies the state time. [34] is paraphrasable as [36].

[36]   [There is a t_1: t_1 < t^*][there is a t_2: t_2 ≤ t_1](John loves(t_2) Mary and [there is a t_3: t_3 < t^*](John says(t_3) it and t_2 is long before t_3)).

The extra quantifier effectively is inert, which explains why [34] and [37] express the same thing.

[37]   John loved Mary long before he said it.

The past perfect in [34] serves mostly as a way of emphasizing John's love was past relative to a relevant time also in the past. The quantifier 'never' in [35] binds the temporal argument place in its main verb. [35] conveys that at no time prior to some former time had John been to Arizona, which does not entail John has never been to Arizona. [35] is paraphrased as [38].

[38]   [There is a t_1 : t_1 < t^*][for no t_2 : t_2 < t_1](John is(t_2) in Arizona).

'when' may be used with the past perfect, but apparently only if the 'when'-clause is in the simple past. [39] is acceptable, [40] is not.

[39]   He had gone when Bill arrived.
[40]   He had gone when Bill had arrived.

In [39], 'when' binds the event time for the restricting clause, and the reference time for [39] is in the past perfect, as shown in [41].

[41]   [There is a time t_1 : t_1 < t^* and Bill arrives t_1][there is a time t_2 : t_2 < t_1](he goes(t_2)).

When we assigned satisfaction conditions to sentences of the form $\ulcorner\phi$ when $\psi\urcorner$, when ϕ and ψ were in the past tense, we saw that semantically ϕ shifts to present tense. Now we see that when ϕ is in past perfect, it effectively functions like the past with the argument place which usually functions indexically being bound by 'when'.[183] The problem with [40] is that for 'when' to bind across both sentences, it must bind the reference time in 'Bill had arrived' and what would be the indexical reference to speaker time in 'He had gone' when unembedded. This yields [42], which conveys no useful information about the temporal relations between the two event times.

[42]   [There is a time t_1 : t_1 < t^* and t_2 < t_1 and Bill arrives t_2][there is a time t_3 : t_3 < t_1](he goes(t_3))

'whenever', like 'when', is comfortable with the past perfect only when the restricting clause is in the simple past, as in [43], which would be paraphrased as in [44].

[43]   He had tried to buy it whenever he had money.

---

[183] This analysis, together with our treatment of the tenses unembedded, helps explain the peculiar behavior of an adverb that seems happiest with perfect tenses, namely, 'already'. 'He has already arrived' is felicitous enough, but 'He arrived already' is odd. This is explained by combining the plausible reading of 'already' as conveying that the event time is before the reference time with our analysis. (We cannot treat it as 'before now' because it does not always relate event time to the present, as in 'By the time he had arrived, we had already finished dinner'.) We represent 'John has already arrived' as '[There is a t_1 : $t = t^*$][there is a t_2 : $t_2 \leq t_1$ and t_2 < t_1](John arrives(t_2))'.

[44]   [For any time t_1: $t_1 < t^*$ and he has(t_1) money][for a time t_2: $t_2 < t_1$](he tries(t_2) to buy it).

These examples illustrate how to combine our account of adverbial modification with perfect tenses. There is some interest in looking at the possible combinations of tenses with 'when' and 'whenever', but that would be too involved a task for the present context. Depending on its kind, a modifier will modify either the reference or event time. Quantificational adverbs which are not sentential connectives invariably modify event time. Limiting adverbs invariably modify reference time. Temporal sentential connectives like 'before' and 'after' invariably connect event times. 'when' and 'whenever' bind event time in the first clause and speaker time in the second.

4. Comparison with Reichenbach's Account

We will finish our discussion of the perfect tenses by comparing our account with Reichenbach's celebrated discussion.[184] In the truth conditions given above, the terms 't^*', 't_1', and 't_2', as we noted, play the roles of expressing Reichenbach's speaker's time, reference time, and event time, respectively. Speaker's time is the time of utterance, and corresponds to the indexical which refers to the time of the utterance. Event time corresponds to the temporal argument place of the main verb of the sentence. Reference time corresponds to the time which is modified by adverbials. Reichenbach famously argued that all tenses involve these three times implicitly. In our analysis, it is only in the perfect tenses that these *three* times are represented. For the simple tenses, the speaker's time corresponds to the indexical anchor of time reference, and the event time is the time of the event expressed by the verb, or of the holding of the state expressed by the verb, in the case of state verbs. On Reichenbach's account, in the case of the simple tenses, his reference time and event time coincide. Reichenbach's argument for there being a role for speaker, reference, and event times in the case of simple tenses rests mainly on his claims that (*a*) intuitively the narrative point of view of the simple past is the event time, and that (*b*) without postulating this additional structure for the simple tenses, we would be unable to distinguish the present perfect from the simple past. According to Reichenbach, they differ in that while for the simple past the reference time and event time coincide, in the present perfect the speaker time and reference time coincide. This is represented in Figure 2, where 'R',

---

[184]   Reichenbach (1947: 287–98).

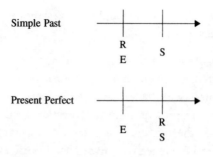

Figure 2

'E', and 'S' represent reference, event, and speaker time, respectively, and the direction of the arrows indicate future time.

Our own account distinguishes between the simple past and present perfect as well, but without postulating semantic complexity in the case of the simple past which is not syntactically or otherwise semantically justified. To see whether our account is adequate, we should survey the data Reichenbach presents to argue for a difference in intuitive point of view between the simple past and the present perfect. Reichenbach contrasts the historical narrative from Macaulay in [a], which combines the past perfect with the simple past, with the quotation from Keats in the present perfect in [b].

[a] In 1678 the whole face of things had changed ... eighteen years of misgovernment had made the ... majority desirous to obtain security for their liberties at any risk. The fury of their returning loyalty had spent itself in its first outbreak. In a very few months they had hanged and half-hanged, quartered and emboweled, enough to satisfy them. The Roundhead party seemed to be not merely overcome, but too much broken and scattered ever to rally again. Then commenced the reflux of public opinion. The nation began to find out to what a man it had intrusted without conditions all its dearest interests, on what a man it had lavished all its fondest affection.

[b]   Much have I traveled in the realms of gold
            And many goodly states and kingdoms seen;
            Round many western islands have I been
            Which bards in fealty to Apollo hold.

Reichenbach says that in [a], the reference time is 1678, and that events related in the simple past are understood to occur in 1678, and *seen from that reference point*, while those related in the past perfect are understood to have taken place prior to this date. In the present perfect, in contrast, as illustrated in [b], Reichenbach says, the point of reference coincides with the speaker's time, which is why "the words of Keats are not of a narrative type but affect us with the immediacy of a direct report to the reader" (1947: 289). In [a], it is clear that Macaulay intends the reader to infer that the events reported in the simple past took place in 1678, though he does not say this. This is of course perfectly compatible with our account. Note, however, that, contrary to Reichenbach, not all the events reported in the past perfect are to be understood to have occurred before 1678. The introducing modifier, 'in 1678', in particular, modifies event time, not reference time. Thus, the state of things changed in 1678, not at some prior time. (Compare: John had swum the English Channel in 1898 and again in 1900.) The following sentences in the past perfect are, though, intended to be understood as occurring prior to 1678, though they do not literally say this. Rather, this is something the reader infers as a matter of conversational dynamics from the way that Macaulay has constructed the narrative. While it is true that the implied point of reference for the sentences in the past perfect in [a], after the introductory sentence, is 1678, and this is also the implied time of the events narrated in the simple past, this does not in itself justify the claim that anything in the semantics of the simple past tense requires recognition of three distinct times understood by the speaker. Rather, what is going on is simply that one time is implied as both the reference time for the past perfect for some sentences, and as the event time for the simple past. This is the result of a narrative device that takes advantage of the context of discourse in which sentences appear to implicate something that is not semantically implied. And we cannot see that more is involved in the idea that the point of view of the simple past in this passage is the event time than its being conversationally implied to be the time prior to which the events reported in the past perfect (excepting the introductory sentence) were to have taken place. In the case of [b], the suggestion is that the point of reference is the present, and that coincides with the point of view from which the events narrated are supposed to be imagined as occurring, but that this point of view, though it coincides with the reference time, is yet felt to be distinct from it. However, while we are ready enough to agree that [c], in addition to upsetting the meter and rhyming scheme, conveys something importantly different than [b], the point of view in each case seems simply to be the present.

[c]   Much traveled I in the realms of gold
                    And many goodly states and kingdoms saw;
                    Round many western islands I went
                    Which bards in fealty to Apollo hold.

The difference, we suggest, lies in the fact that the present perfect does not require the time of the reported events to lie absolutely in the past, but allows that they may have finished in the present. In light of this difference, and the option to use either the past or past perfect, the choice of the past perfect, quantified as it is in [b], will tend to imply that the narrator intends to convey that the activities reported have continued into the present, and that the activities reported are a continuing practice. The use of the simple past, in contrast, would imply that the narrator had given up the activities reported. These differences in the uses of the simple past and the past perfect, then, can be accommodated within the framework we have presented, and Reichenbach's claim that, for each tense, one must admit three separate times to adequately capture its semantics is unjustified.

11

Opaque Contexts: Indirect Discourse and Attitude Sentences

'I wish I had said that.'

(Davidson 2001 (1968): 93)

In Chapter 1, we identified the semantics of opaque or oblique sentential contexts as one of the difficulties facing an extensional truth-theoretic
semantics that aims to eschew intensional entities, that is, propositions,
properties, relations, senses, meanings, and the like. An opaque context is
one in which (i) intersubstitution of coreferring or coextensive terms, or sentences alike in truth value, does not guarantee preservation of truth value,
or (ii) existential generalization on referring terms fails. In this chapter,
we first discuss Davidson's approach to this problem (§1), especially in
application to indirect discourse. Davidson's proposal, which breaks with
the tradition which treats indirect discourse as relating speakers to propositions, has been widely discussed. We consider some of the difficulties
which have been raised for Davidson's account (§2); then we look at how
far these objections can be responded to on Davidson's behalf, and suggest some modifications which are still in the spirit of Davidson's proposal (§3).

1. Davidson's Account of Indirect Discourse

Davidson sketches his approach to giving a semantics for opaque contexts in "On Saying That" (2001 (1968)), which introduces the parataxis strategy in analyzing sentences of indirect discourse, such as [1].

[1]   Galileo said that the earth moves.

The difficulty for a truth theory is that the terms following 'said that' do not appear to be making their usual contributions to the truth conditions of the sentence. We cannot in general substitute in [1] coreferring or coextensive terms for 'the earth' and 'moves', or a sentence alike in truth value to 'the earth moves', and be sure that the resulting sentence will be alike in truth value to the original. Thus, since the truth value of the whole is not determined by the extensional properties of the terms in the embedded complement sentence, the sentence appears to be, as Davidson says, "semantically inert" (2001 (1968): 96). However, there are apparently an infinite number of nonsynonymous sentences of the form [2].

[2]   Galileo said that _____

This latter observation encourages us to find some recursive structure in sentences of indirect discourse to accommodate our ability to understand any of the infinity of non-synonymous sentences represented by our schema; however, the former observation, that the embedded sentences are semantically inert, discourages this.

In developing his account, Davidson initially criticizes what he calls the "quotational approach." The quotational approach treats the context following 'said that' as a quotational context, so that [1] could be paraphrased as [3]. In "On Saying That," Davidson examines this theory in the context of the spelling theory of quotation, according to which [3] may be written as [4].

[3]   Galileo said 'the earth moves'.
[4]   Galileo said 't'⌢'h'⌢'e'⌢space⌢
      'e'⌢'a'⌢'r'⌢'t'⌢'h'⌢space⌢'m'⌢'o'⌢'v'⌢'e'⌢'s'

It might be objected to this that it erases the distinction between sentences of direct and indirect discourse. But this need not be the case, since one can take the verb in direct discourse to indicate a different relation from that of indirect discourse between the speaker and a sentence (Davidson 2001 (1968): 98). In indirect discourse, clearly what the sentence means is relevant, in contrast

240

to direct discourse; this may be captured, Davidson says, by representing the content of 'said' in [1] as in [5].

> [5]   Galileo spoke a sentence that meant in his language what 'the earth moves' does in mine.

This, though, undergoes a slight reformulation, on the grounds (in this Davidson follows Quine) that individuation conditions for languages are unclear. To sidestep this problem, Davidson suggests reformulating [5] as [6], which relativizes the meaning of a sentence not to a language, but to a speaker at a time (2001 (1968): 102):

> [6]   Galileo spoke a sentence that meant in his mouth what 'the earth moves' does now in mine.

[6] contains an important clue to Davidson's own suggestion. However, he rejects the analysis of [1] as [6] on the grounds that it fails the translation test. Note this objection, for, as we will see, it is not clear that Davidson's own subsequent, and closely resembling, proposal does not suffer from a similar defect. The translation test requires that analysis preserves translation: if one sentence is an analysis of another in one language, then the analysis of the translation of the first into a second language is the translation of the analysis of the first in the first language. The translation into French of [1] is [7].

> [7]   Galilée a dit que la terre tourne.

The translation test requires that the analysis of [7] be a translation of [6]. However, on the face of it, it is not, since [6] mentions an English sentence, while the analysis of [7] in French would mention a French sentence and not an English sentence, as illustrated in [8].

> [8]   Galilée prononça une phrase qui signifiait dans sa bouche la même chose que 'la terre tourne' signifie maintenant dans la mienne.[185]

Davidson also dismisses a popular alternative to the quotational approach, which is to appeal to propositions or meanings as entities to which the sentences in *oratio obliqua* refer, or perhaps to which expressions of the form 'that ϕ' refer. The particular form of the suggestion Davidson entertains

---

[185] It is actually of some interest in considering translation practices that the native French speaker we consulted about [6] gave us [8] as its translation! What ordinarily counts as a good translation does not respect all the strictures on sameness of meaning philosophers typically suppose.

is a modified Fregean account. We allow two semantic levels of entities, extensional and intensional entities. The suggestion goes as follows. Singular terms refer to individual concepts, and predicates refer to functions. We introduce a special function, expressed by 'the reality of', to map intensional entities onto extensional entities. In [1], 'the earth' denotes an individual concept, which the function expressed by 'moves' maps onto the proposition that the earth moves. 'Said that' maps Galileo and the proposition that the earth moves onto a truth value. Since we have said that singular terms denote individual concepts, however, we must represent the subject term of [1] as having the form 'the reality of Galileo'. Thus, [1] is represented as [9].

[9]   The reality of Galileo said that the earth moves.

Since the treatment is fully extensional, it presents no special problems for a truth theory. "With ingenuity," Davidson says, "this theory can perhaps be made to accommodate quantifiers that bind variables both inside and outside contexts created by verbs like 'said' and 'believes'," and asks, "[a]part from nominalistic qualms, why not accept it?" (2001 (1968): 100).

Davidson says, "My reasons against this course are essentially Quine's" (2001 (1968): 100). Those reasons are suspicion of the sharpness of questions about sameness of meaning which arise from commitment to the indeterminacy of translation and interpretation (see Lepore and Ludwig (2005: ch. 15). The central idea of the indeterminacy of translation (which is how Davidson frames the issue in "On Saying That") is that in communication with another speaker, there will be a number of *different* but *equally acceptable* theories for translating his words into mine. They are *different* in that each assigns to the same words in the object language (what one takes to be) non-synonymous words in one's own language. But they are claimed to be *equally acceptable* on the grounds that they serve equally well all the purposes of communication, and the facts about meaning are exhausted by what is necessary for successful communication.

. . . indeterminacy shows . . . that if there is one way of getting it right there are other ways that differ substantially in that non-synonymous sentences are used after 'said that'. And this is enough to justify our feeling that there is something bogus about the sharpness questions of meaning must in principle have if meanings are entities. (Davidson 2001 (1968): 101)

As Davidson represents it in "On Saying That," what is central to indeterminacy is the fact that in communication we can be faced with a trade-off between attributing to another speaker unusual beliefs and usual meanings, or attributing to him beliefs more closely resembling ours, but assigning different meanings to homophonic words. This results from seeing interpretation proceeding by identifying what sentences a speaker holds true. The sentences a speaker holds true result from what he believes and what (he takes) his sentences to mean. Sometimes we can make a speaker out to be more rational overall, given his behavior, by thinking of him as meaning something different than we do, and sometimes by thinking of him as believing something different than we do, though meaning the same. Indeterminacy arises when different choices about beliefs and meanings give rise to interpretations that make equally good sense of the speaker as a rational agent. The objection based on indeterminacy of translation or interpretation is that if the meaning of a sentence were an entity that it denoted, or which was associated in some way with it, then there could not be what there evidently is: a trade-off in interpreting others between what we take them to believe and what we take them to mean. In brief, the objection is the following. (1) If meanings are entities, then there cannot be indeterminacy of translation (interpretation). (2) There is indeterminacy of translation (interpretation). (3) Therefore, we cannot make sense of meanings as entities.

We have expressed doubt about whether arguments for the indeterminacy of translation or interpretation are successful elsewhere (see Lepore and Ludwig 2005: ch. 15). However, even apart from these doubts, there is reason to think this response to the suggestion Davidson considers is inadequate. For even the defenders of indeterminacy admit that a notion of synonymy can be reconstructed from reflection on what counts as success in radical translation or interpretation. If we can make sense of any equivalence relation between expressions which is meaning-based, then we can also make sense of identity conditions for a species of propositions, for propositions are just reified sentence meanings. Davidson himself, in fn. 14 of "On Saying That" (2001 (1968)), says that "radical interpretation, if it succeeds, yields an adequate concept of synonymy as between utterances."

A more telling reason to avoid the introduction of such entities would be that we can do without them, so that introduction of additional ontology would be shown to provide no additional explanatory power. Davidson says as much at one point:

We could . . . invent such entities [propositions, properties, and meanings] with a clear conscience if we were sure there were no permissible variant theories. But if we knew this, we would know how to state our theories without mention of the objects. (Davidson 2001 (1974): 154)

In addition, Davidson has said, specifically about the suggestion that we take expressions in complement clauses of indirect discourse sentences to refer to something other than what they usually do:

Since Frege, philosophers have become hardened to the idea that content-sentences in talk about propositional attitudes may strangely refer to such entities as intensions, propositions, sentences, utterances and inscriptions. What is strange is not the entities, which are all right in their place (if they have one), but the notion that ordinary words for planets, people, tables, and hippopotami in indirect discourse may give up these pedestrian references for the exotica. If we could recover our pre-Fregean semantic innocence, I think it would seem to us plainly incredible that the words 'The Earth moves', uttered after the words 'Galileo said that', mean anything different, or refer to anything else, than is their wont when they come in other environments. . . . Language is the instrument it is because the same expression, with semantic features (meaning) unchanged, can serve countless purposes.   (2001 (1968): 108)

All other things being equal, then, we should favor an account of the semantics of indirect discourse, and other opaque contexts likewise, which does without appeal to the idea that in those contexts ordinary words take on different meanings.

With this in mind, we return to the previous suggestion, in [6], which forms the basis for Davidson's own suggestion. Davidson says this is nearly right. The flaw is that if one merely mentions 'The earth moves' as a part of one's utterance, one has not used it, and so it need not mean anything in one's mouth when one utters it. This is true, for example, on the spelling theory of quotation. For this reason, he introduces the parataxis strategy, representing [1] as functioning semantically as two sentences, as in [10].

[10]   Galileo said that. The earth moves.

Each sentence is uttered by the speaker. But only the first is asserted. In the first, there is a demonstrative reference to the second sentence.[186] As Davidson puts it:

The proposal then is this: sentences in indirect discourse, as it happens, wear their logical form on their sleeves (except for one small point). They consist of an expression referring to a speaker, the two-place predicate 'said', and a demonstrative referring to an utterance. Period. What follows gives the content of the subject's saying,

[186] See the discussion in "Thought and Talk" (Davidson 2001 (1975): 165–6), esp. the use of 'paratactic': "Thus the logical form of standard attributions of attitude is that of two utterances paratactically joined. There is no connective, though the first utterance contains a reference to the second. (Similar remarks go, of course, for inscriptions of sentences.)" (p. 166).

but has no logical or semantic connection with the original attribution of a saying. This last point is no doubt the novel one, and upon it everything depends: from a semantic point of view the content-sentence in indirect discourse is not contained in the sentence whose truth counts, i.e. the sentence that ends with 'that'.[187] (2001 (1968): 106)

Thus, in the truth theory, 'said' is treated as a primitive expression that receives a base clause, and not, after all, a recursive clause, as suggested by the apparent infinity of sentences of the form $\ulcorner \alpha$ said that $\phi \urcorner$. For on Davidson's proposed analysis, what replaces 'ϕ' is not treated semantically as a part of the sentence. We can therefore give [11] as the axiom for 'said'.

[11]   For all functions f, f satisfies(S, t, u) $\ulcorner \alpha$ said $x \urcorner$ iff $[\exists t': t' < t](\text{Ref}(S, t, u, \alpha) \text{ says}(t') f('x'))$.

The T-sentence for 'Galileo said that' would be [12].

[12]   'Galileo said that' is true(S, t, u) iff $[\exists t': t' < t](\text{Galileo says}(t') \text{Ref}(S, t, u, \text{'that'}))$.

'Galileo said that' can be glossed, along the lines indicated previously, as 'There is an saying u of Galileo's, and u is the same in content as that',[188] though it is important to note that the gloss is intended merely to help explain the meaning of 'said', and is not part of the compositional meaning theory (however, since 'says' is an action verb, to indicate how it interacts with adverbs, we would have to introduce an existential quantifier over events; we suppress this additional level of complexity for present purposes—see Chapter 7).[189]

---

[187] A lovely passage: the one small point, of course, is the period, separating 'that' from what follows.

[188] See Davidson (2001 (1976): 177). We use 'saying' in place of 'utterance' to avoid worries about whether all utterances are sayings. What is involved in two utterances being the same in content, as we will see below, is important for resolving a number of questions that can be raised about the paratactic account.

[189] See "Reply to Foster" (Davidson 2001 (1976): 176–7) for a correction of a common mistake about his proposal: "The paratactic semantic approach to indirect discourse tells us to view an utterance of 'Galileo said that the Earth moves' as consisting of the utterance of two sentences, 'Galileo said that' and 'The Earth moves'. The 'that' refers to the second utterance, and the first utterance is true if and only if an utterance of Galileo's was the same in content as ('translates') the utterance to which the 'that' refers. (Foster wrongly says my analysis of 'Galileo said that' is 'Some utterance of Galileo and my last utterance make Galileo and me same-sayers'. This is not an analysis, but a rephrasal designed to give a reader a feeling for the semantics; an expository and heuristic device.)" Davidson's proposal has sometimes been criticized on the basis of taking the heuristic paraphrase as the canonical proposal, as

Before evaluating Davidson's proposal, it will be worthwhile to consider its development in the light of Davidson's treatment of quotation. For in the light of that treatment, it will be noticed that the criticism that motivates [10] relies on the spelling theory of quotation, which Davidson rejects in his own treatment of quotation. In fact, given Davidson's own treatment of quotation, it is not clear that he could not simply have adopted without modification the proposal in [6], which would have been represented semantically as in [13].

> [13]   Galileo spoke a sentence that meant in his mouth what the expres-
>   sion of which this is a token does now in mine. The earth moves.

This is essentially the same suggestion as Davidson's, except that the entities which stand in the translation relation are here sentences (interpreted relative to speakers and times) rather than utterances. This avoids the objection Davidson levels against the proposal when quotation is treated as on the spelling theory, since given the parataxis involved in his own account of quotation, there is no barrier to 'the earth moves' being used, so that it has a interpretation in the mouth of the speaker. That Davidson did not take this route is perhaps explained by the fact that his paratactic treatment of quotation was developed after his paratactic treatment of indirect discourse.

2. Objections

To begin our evaluation of Davidson's proposal, we list a number of criticisms which have been made in the literature.[190] In listing them, we are not to be taken, however, to be endorsing all of them, and we will below discuss various responses which might be made on behalf of Davidson, and also some extensions and alternatives of his proposal designed to remove difficulties.

1. The Syntactic Objection

The first objection is that the account treats what is intuitively a single sentence as two distinct sentences. The force of this objection, which is similar to an

in Lycan (1973), who criticizes Davidson's account for entailing that the speaker made an utterance.

[190] For further discussion of criticisms of the paratactic account, see Lepore and Loewer (1989); Ludwig and Ray (1998).

objection we considered to the paratactic account of quotation, is supposed to be that, intuitively, 'Galileo said that the earth moves' is understood as a single syntactical unit.[191]

2. The Understanding Objection

The account would enable someone to understand what is said in uttering 'Galileo said that the earth moves' without understanding the content of anything Galileo said. Thus, one could know that Galileo said that the earth moves, and know that Galileo said, in saying that, something true, but not be able to infer that the earth moves. This is because to understand an utterance of 'Galileo said that the earth moves', on Davidson's analysis, it is sufficient to understand 'Galileo said that', and to know that 'that' as used by the speaker refers to an utterance of his of 'the earth moves'. It is not also required that one understand the utterance demonstrated.

---

[191] Burge (1986); Hand (1991); Higginbotham (1986); Seymour (1994). We mention briefly under this head the fact that there can be syntactic interactions between the main and subordinate clauses in a sentence of indirect discourse which prima facie the paratactic account has difficulty handling, as in, e.g. 'He did not say that there was any beer in the refrigerator', a point made by Hand. It looks as if the paratactic account has to take this as referring to 'there was any beer in the refrigerator', which is not grammatical as a stand-alone sentence. It is not clear that the paratactic account runs into serious difficulty on this head, for we might say that the utterance of 'there was any beer in the refrigerator', even if of an ungrammatical stand-alone sentence, nonetheless expresses in use the same as an utterance of 'there was beer in the refrigerator'. This looks even more plausible on the account we consider below, on which we give up parataxis and the idea that demonstration is involved in indirect discourse, though retaining the idea that what a speaker is related to is an utterance. Similarly, some sentences will have complement clauses which do not contain full sentences. Any general account will have to deal with these as well. Examples are: 'He intends to finish before noon', 'He asked how to do it'. When a complement is not a sentence, it may not always make sense to say that, taken as it is, an utterance of it is the same in content as some utterance of the subject or (see our response to the extension objection below) some psychological state of the subject. But this need not be a serious difficulty for the paratactic approach. One can appeal to a more complicated relation between the utterance of the complement and the utterance or psychological state of the subject, namely, a relation that holds between what is actually uttered just in case some appropriate related expression interpreted relative to that context is the same in content as some utterance of the subject, or psychological state of the subject, as the case may be. There are difficulties also raised by elements which in surface form appear in the complement clause, but are not considered a part of the sentence that gives the content of what was said, as is the case for 'which you see underneath the ferns there' in 'Joan said that those mushrooms, which you see underneath the ferns there, are poisonous'. However, as long as we can make sense of an interrupted and then continued utterance, this should not present any insuperable difficulty.

3. The Validity Objection

A connected objection is that Davidson's account makes invalid certain inferences which are intuitively semantically and logically valid. Thus, for example, 'Galileo said in 1632 that the earth moves; therefore, Galileo said in 1632 that the earth moves' is not a formally or semantically valid inference on Davidson's account, because nothing in the form or semantics guarantees that the reference of 'that' in utterances of the premise and conclusion refer to the same thing.[192]

4. The Problem of Iterated Indirect Discourse Sentences

When we consider *iterated* indirect discourse sentences, Davidson's account encounters a difficulty akin to the difficulty the translation test raised for the analysis represented by [6]. Consider utterances of [14] and [15]. Imagine [14] uttered by Davidson, and [15] by some third person.

    [14]   Galileo said that$_1$ [the earth moves]$_1$
    [15]   Davidson said that$_3$ [Galileo said that$_2$ [the earth moves]$_2$]$_3$

Here we represent a particular use of a demonstrative by subscripting it, and the utterance it demonstrates by placing an expression of which it is a token in brackets with a corresponding subscript. We will represent these particular utterances, that is, the ones indicated by the subscripted brackets, by '①', '②', and '③', respectively. Intuitively, [14]'s being uttered by Davidson makes [15] true. However, for [15] to be true on Davidson's account, ③ must be the same in content as Davidson's utterance of [14]. The charge is that it is not, because it contains a singular term, 'that', which, as used in [15], refers to a different utterance than a singular term in [14], namely, 'that', as used in [14]. For in ③ the demonstrative 'that' is used to refer to ②, while in [14] the demonstrative used refers to ①, and ① and ② are distinct utterances. On the assumption that the *same in content* relation underlying our understanding of the 'says' of indirect discourse preserves the referents of singular terms—an assumption of the translation test which Davidson himself employs—Davidson's account gives the wrong truth conditions for iterated indirect discourse.[193]

---

[192] Lepore and Loewer (1989); Platts (1979); Schiffer (1987: 135–7); Seymour (1994).

[193] See Burge (1986); Foster (1976). Church (1950) makes a similar objection to Carnap's analysis of belief sentences.

5. The Extension Problem

It has been objected also that Davidson's account cannot be straightforwardly extended to propositional attitude sentences, since in many such cases there will be no utterance of the subject which an utterance of the speaker's can translate.[194]

6. The Counting Problem

It has been objected that Davidson's account gives the wrong results when we ask how many things Galileo said. For when we ask how many things Galileo said, we are asking how many things Galileo is related to by the 'says' relation. Since Galileo is related to as many things by the 'says' relation as there are distinct entities that satisfy 'Galileo said that', Galileo will have said as many things, in the indirect discourse sense of 'says', as there are people who have uttered a sentence which, as used, translates 'the earth moves'; in particular, this means that each time someone says 'Galileo said that the earth moves', the number of things that Galileo has said increases! So, first, it may be objected that we cannot increase the number of things Galileo said simply by repeating [1], but on Davidson's account we can. Second, it might be maintained that, intuitively, Galileo said only one thing when he said that the earth moves, but on Davidson's account, at the very least, he has said many things.[195]

7. The Demonstration Objection

As in the case of the paratactic account of quotation, use of a demonstrative as the connection between the truth-valued sentence and the sentence which appears semantically to be a part of the sentence but which, according to Davidson, is not, fails to connect them tightly enough. For it is open semantically, on Davidson's view, that someone who says in English 'Galileo said that the earth moves' is not asserting something that requires Galileo to have performed a speech act that is the same in content as a current utterance of 'the earth moves', because the speaker need not have been demonstrating his utterance of 'the earth moves'. However, it is not semantically open in

---

[194] See Blackburn (1975); McFetridge (1976); Rumfitt (1996). This difficulty is sometimes used to suggest a move to taking the complement clause to refer to a proposition, but, in fact, the difficulty has to do not with what the complement clause denotes, but with that to which it is to be related.

[195] McFetridge (1976).

English that what he asserts in asserting 'Galileo said that the earth moves' be true, though Galileo did not perform any speech act that meant what an utterance of 'the earth moves' means.

8. The Quantifying-in Problem

Davidson's account fails, it has been charged, to allow for the possibility of quantification into contexts following 'said that', but this is possible. For example, on one reading of [16], 'he' functions as a variable bound by 'everyone'.

[16]   Everyone says that he is honest.

This would not make sense on Davidson's proposal because the grammatical object of 'said' is an unstructured singular term, not a sentence, and you cannot quantify into an object whose only relation to the sentence is that it is the referent of a demonstrative used in it, even if it is a sentence, any more than you can quantify into the moon if you demonstrate it. This problem looks to be a particularly important one in the light of our discussion of tense in indirect discourse and attitude contexts in Chapter 10, in which we represented the dependence of the tense in the subordinate clauses in such constructions on the tense of the main clause as involving quantification into the complement.[196]

9. The Problem of Mixed Direct and Indirect Speech

The last difficulty we mention is how to combine Davidson's account of indirect discourse with mixed uses of quotation marks in the complements of attitude reports. The prima facie difficulty is that in a sentence such as [17], the demonstrated utterance apparently contains mentioned expressions in locations which would make literal nonsense of the sentence, so that it could not be said intelligibly to translate the speech act that was reported.

---

[196] See Higginbotham (1986); S. Schiffer (1987). Davidson acknowledges this is a problem in "Thought and Talk" (2001 (1975): 166). "It is an analysis with its own difficulties, especially when it comes to analysing quantification into the contained sentence, but I think these difficulties can be overcome while preserving the appealing features of the idea." So far as we are aware, however, he has not addressed it himself. Some initial suggestions which might be developed are contained in Hornsby (1977), though we will not discuss these in detail. We offer a response below on Davidson's behalf, and discuss another alternative still in the spirit of Davidson's proposal.

[17] Quine says that "scientific neologism" is linguistic evolution "gone self-conscious," as science is self-conscious common sense.

3. Responses

We consider in this section responses to the objections listed in the previous one. We will consider to what extent Davidson's account can respond to the objections, and also consider some suggestions for modifications which still eschew the introduction of intensional entities like propositions.

Most of the criticisms of Davidson's account, objections (1)–(3) and (6)–(7), are directly attributable to a central feature of Davidson's account, namely, the decision to treat the sentence that appears in the complement clause of a sentence of indirect discourse as not semantically a part of the sentence.

In the case of the syntactic objection (1) it is not entirely clear what Davidson's position is on the syntax of [1]. He emphasizes that, semantically, [1] functions as two sentences. At some points it looks as if he is claiming that, syntactically, we should treat [1] as two sentences. But whether he intended to claim this or not, it is not clear that there is any need for him to do so. It appears compatible with his approach that we assign truth conditions directly to 'Galileo said that the earth moves', namely, the truth conditions we would assign for 'Galileo said that' where 'that' is treated as a demonstrative.

In the case of the understanding objection (2) we can observe that it is not clear that traditional approaches are not subject to a similar objection. Take a view that treats 'that'-clauses as referring to propositions. The 'that'-clause either picks out the proposition directly or by description. If it picks it out directly, then it functions as a directly referring term. Presumably, however, it is not an accident that it picks out the proposition expressed by the sentence in the complement understood in the language as used. So we may provide the rule for determining the referent as follows: for any sentence ϕ, speaker S, time t, if the proposition expressed by ϕ in English as used by S at t is p, then Ref($\ulcorner$that $\phi\urcorner$) = p. On this account, however, it would appear that we can also understand what is said by 'Galileo said that the earth moves' without understanding 'the earth moves'. If the 'that'-clause picks out a proposition by being a description, then presumably the description makes use of the fact that the sentence in the complement expresses the proposition that is wanted. So, again, presumably the descriptive content of the 'that'-clause, for example, 'that the earth moves', is (something to the effect) 'the proposition expressed by 'the earth moves' as used in this sentence'. This, however, is open to the same objection. The understanding objection points to something important about how indirect discourse works, but it looks as if it will apply to any account which treats 'Galileo said that the earth moves' as expressing a relation between Galileo and something else, where what the something else is is determined by the semantic properties of a sentence or utterance of a sentence. One response on behalf of the propositional account would perhaps be that it is part of how we use these sentences that one is expected in part to be able to see what proposition it is which is in question by understanding the sentence in the complement. But while this may enable one to grasp the proposition, one's understanding the sentence does not itself play a role in determining what proposition someone is being related to in an utterance of an indirect discourse sentence. And Davidson could similarly claim that it is part of how we use these sentences (recall our response to the first objection) that one is expected to understand the demonstrated utterance; so, to the extent to which this response is open to the propositional account, it is equally open to Davidson.

Next is the validity objection (3). This objection presupposes that, but for treating 'that' as a demonstrative, the inference would be logically valid. However, the inference in question, 'Galileo said in 1632 that the earth moves; therefore, Galileo said in 1632 that the earth moves', is not logically valid even apart from Davidson's paratactic account. These are each tensed sentences. There is nothing in the semantics that tells one that the times which their utterances are indexed to are such that the second is a later time than the first, which is required for the truth of what is expressed by the first to suffice for the truth of what is expressed by the second. Even when the second is uttered after the first, the argument is not *logically* valid, any more than an inference from 'Bill is tall' to 'John is tall' is logically valid when Bill is John. What this shows is that often we treat arguments naively as semantically valid or even logically valid when they are not, and when our acceptance of them depends on our making certain assumptions about what values context-sensitive elements in the sentence receive. Davidson's analysis introduces an additional element of this sort. Since our practices in accepting such arguments already involve presuppositions about relations between assignments to context-sensitive terms, there is no reason Davidson cannot urge that these extend to assumptions about the assignments to the demonstratives in each of the utterances of the relevant sentences.

The problem of iterated indirect discourse sentences (4) arises from an assumption about the sameness of content relation which Davidson invokes in giving a gloss on how to understand the 'says' of indirect discourse. There is a problem here only if we insist that the sameness of content relation holds between two utterances only if, where each is about something, an utterance, what each is about is exactly the same utterance, rather than utterances which are similar in a way that abstracts from which particular utterances in each is being referred to. Davidson remarks in "Reply to Foster" (2001 (1976): 178) that good translation does not always preserve the referents of singular terms (though this is a bit in tension with his use of the translation test to dismiss the quotation theory of indirect discourse). This is the case when, for example, we translate dialogue, or when we translate a sentence that refers to itself, as in translating 'This sentence is false' into the French 'Cette phrase est fausse'. Thus, it is open to Davidson to say that the sameness of content relation can hold between an utterance ① of 'Galileo said that' followed by an utterance ② of 'the earth moves', which the use of the demonstrative in ① refers to, and an utterance ③ of 'Galileo said that' followed by an utterance ④ of 'the earth moves', which the use of the demonstrative in ③ refers to, where ② and ④ are distinct. One might say, for example, that ① and ③ are the same in content iff each says of something that Galileo said it, and what each says Galileo said is the same in content with the other. ① and ③ meet this condition, since each says of something that Galileo said it, namely, ① says this of ②, and ③ says this of ④, and ② and ④ are the same in content, in the sense that they are the same in propositional meaning, assuming 'the earth moves' is interpreted tenselessly. There is no obstacle to giving a recursive characterization of the same-in-content relation that works generally to give the intended results for iterated indirect discourse sentences.[197]

The extension problem (5) is the question of how to extend the proposal to propositional attitude sentences. The initial difficulty is that, in the case of an utterance of a sentence such as [18], we need something to which the speaker's utterance of 'the earth moves' can stand in a sameness of content relation which is not necessarily an utterance of Galileo's, since Galileo could have believed that the earth moves without ever saying so.

[18]   Galileo believed that the earth moves.

The objection is easily met, however, by appeal to a sameness of content relation between an utterance of 'the earth moves' and one of Galileo's belief states (Lepore and Loewer 1989). Thus, we can gloss [18] as [19].

[19]   There is some belief state, b, of Galileo's such that b is the same in content as that. The earth moves.

[197] See Ludwig and Ray (1998) and the proposal sketched below.

Other attitude sentences can be treated in a similar fashion. Indeed, as we have noted before, putting adverbial modification aside, we could simply appeal to a three-place metalanguage relation 'Believes(Galileo, that, *t*)'. The appeal to belief states merely serves as an explication of the intended interpretation of this three-place predicate.

Davidson suggested a slightly different approach in "Thought and Talk" (2001 (1975): 167).

If we turn to other attitudes, the situation is more complicated, for there is typically no utterance to ape. If I affirm 'Jones believes that snow is white', my utterance of 'Snow is white' may have no actual utterance of Jones's to imitate. Still, we could take the line that what I affirm is that Jones would be honestly speaking his mind were he to utter a sentence translating mine.

This suggestion could be represented by paraphrasing 'Jones believes that snow is white' as in [20].

[20]   Jones would be honestly speaking his mind if he were to utter a sentence translating that. Snow is white.

However, [20] does not seem to be the most natural way of extending the account of indirect discourse to attitude sentences, which we should expect to exhibit something like the same underlying form. [20] suggests that the logical form of 'Jones believes that snow is white' involves a conditional, and certain tense constructions, that certainly seem absent from the original, even if we could trust that [20] was always true when the original was. In any case, Davidson goes on to say,

When I say, 'Jones believes that snow is white' I describe Jones's state of mind directly: it is indeed the state of mind someone is in who could honestly assert 'Snow is white' if he spoke English, but that may be a state a languageless creature could also be in. (2001 (1975): 167)

This contains in an embryonic form the suggestion of the appeal to belief states which we have suggested in [19].

Davidson suggests elsewhere, in his "Reply to Foster" (2001 (1976)), how the account might be extended to entailment relations by appeal to logical consequence and synonymy. A sentence of the form of [21], where '*T*' is taken to refer to a theory, is treated as equivalent to [22].

[21]   *T* entails that *p*
[22]   There is a sentence *s* such that *s* is a logical consequence of *T*, and *s* is synonymous with that. *p*.

A defect of this suggestion is that the relation of 'entailment' does not track exactly that of logical consequence. If '*p*' is a logical consequence of '*q*', it follows that that *q* entails that *p*. However, the reverse is not the case, for while that John is a bachelor entails that John is unmarried, 'John is unmarried' is not a logical consequence of 'John is a bachelor'. However, this means only that we need a different metalinguistic relation, that of semantic consequence. Note that to develop this proposal for a natural language, we would have to relativize the metalinguistic relation to speakers, times, and speech acts to fix everything relevant to truth value.

We leave unresolved how to apply the account to modal statements, but it is not hard to see that following the general strategy would require treating the modal operators as indicating something broadly speaking about the semantic properties of demonstrated utterances.[198]

The counting problem (6) charges that Davidson's account has counterintuitive results about how many things Galileo said in virtue of his uttering the sentence 'La terra si muove'. On the face of it, it looks as if Davidson's account commits us to saying Galileo said many things in asserting that sentence, and more each time he is reported indirectly as having said that the earth moves. But, in fact, when we say how many things he said in asserting 'La terra muove', we say he has said just one thing. This seems to tell in favor of the view that indirect discourse sentences relate speakers to propositions, since we seem to track the number of distinct propositions Galileo expressed in his speech acts when we count the number of things he said in the sense of indirect discourse.

Contrary to initial appearances, however, this is not decisive. The crucial premise of this objection is that our ordinary counting practices with respect to indirect discourse focus on the number of particular things that the says-relation relates the speaker to. But often our counting practices do not focus on particulars, but types of particulars. It is easy to see that, when we ask how many of a certain kind of thing there are, we can have in mind either things of that kind numerically distinct, or things of that kind distinct with respect to some other implied kind. For example, we may ask, 'How many books does the library own?', meaning how many distinct titles, as opposed to volumes. Thus, the answer might be 1.2 million, though the number of items in the extension of 'is a book in the library' is 1.3 million. So we may also, when we

---

[198] See Ludwig (2006) for an account of modal contexts which builds on the proposal applied to indirect discourse and propositional attitude sentences in Ludwig and Ray (1998), the basic elements of which are sketched below.

ask how many things someone has said, have in mind how many things if we count by types rather than particulars, even if what the says-relation relates one to are particular utterances. If we imagine a language which included a device for indirectly reporting others' speech as sketched in Davidson's proposal, it would be natural for counting practices to track the number of distinct things speakers have said with respect to meaning rather than utterances, just as it is natural in considering the quality of a library's collection to consider the number of distinct titles, as opposed to volumes. Thus, 'How many things did Galileo say?' would be interpreted analogously to 'How many books does the library own?', as about types rather than particulars. Given this, our counting practices cannot be taken to be inconsistent with Davidson's proposal without further, independent, argument.

In addition, from 'Galileo said that the earth moves' it follows that 'Galileo said something' in the sense of direct discourse. Thus, in asking how many things Galileo said, we may also be construed as asking how many utterances Galileo made that were the same in content as one's own utterance of 'the earth moves'. And that number does not increase with the number of times one asserts 'Galileo said that the earth moves'.

The demonstration objection (7) focuses on what appears to be a central feature of Davidson's account, namely, the treatment of 'that' in 'Galileo said that the earth moves' as a genuine demonstrative. If the referent of a demonstrative is determined relative to a speaker's demonstrative intentions, then it appears that an utterance of 'Galileo said that the earth moves' could be true even though Galileo never uttered anything which meant that the earth moves, for the speaker could demonstrate some utterance other than that of 'the earth moves' following his assertion of 'Galileo said that', which is the same in content as some utterance of Galileo's. One could here insist that, though this is left open by the semantics, in practice we always intend, and understand others to intend, to be referring to the sentence that immediately follows 'that'. However, it is difficult to see that, even in principle, an utterance of 'Galileo said that the earth moves' could be true unless Galileo performed a speech act which was the same in content as 'the earth moves' as uttered by a speaker of that sentence. Accommodating this would require a modification of Davidson's proposal. What is needed is a way of ensuring that 'Galileo said that the earth moves' always relates Galileo to the following utterance of 'the earth moves'. This is straightforward to implement. In the clause for $\ulcorner \alpha$ said $\phi \urcorner$, we need only introduce an additional quantifier restricted to utterances of ϕ in utterances of $\ulcorner \alpha$ said $\phi \urcorner$. This is illustrated in [23], making explicit all of the quantifiers over speech acts.

[23] For any ϕ, α, for any speech act u of $\ulcorner\alpha$ said that $\phi\urcorner$, for any speech act u' of ϕ in u, $\ulcorner\alpha$ said that $\phi\urcorner$ is true(S, t, u) iff $[\exists t' : t' < t](\text{Ref}(S, t, u, \alpha)$ says$(t') u')$.

Alternatively, one could treat $\ulcorner$that $\phi\urcorner$ itself as a referring term, which, when used, refers to the utterance of ϕ in the utterance of $\ulcorner$that $\phi\urcorner$. The reference clause is given in [24].

[24] For any sentence ϕ, speaker S, time t, for any speech act u, any utterance u' of $\ulcorner$that $\phi\urcorner$ in u, any utterance u'' of ϕ in u', Ref$(\ulcorner$that $\phi\urcorner, S, t, u) = u''$.

This proposal (on either way of implementing it) preserves everything about Davidson's account except semantic parataxis and the freedom to refer to an utterance other than the one following 'that'. However, since parataxis was a device designed to remove the complement sentence from playing a role in the semantics of the sentence except insofar as its utterance was referred to, this modification of Davidson's proposal preserves the point of parataxis; and there is clearly no pull to allow an utterance of 'Galileo said that the earth moves' to be about an utterance other than that of 'the earth moves' which is a subpart of it. Thus, this looks to be a conservative refinement of Davidson's suggestion compatible with his aims which meets the demonstration objection.

We turn next to the quantifying-in objection, (8). To respond to this objection, we need to give an appropriate account of a function satisfying an open sentence such as 'Galileo said that x moves', where we give its semantics as on the paratactic approach or the refinement just mentioned. We will work with the refinement just introduced.

Let us begin with what we would want intuitively to say on this approach about a sentence such as 'Something is such that Galileo said that it moves'. We want this to be true if, for example, it is true that Galileo said that the earth moves. So, what we want is that there be some value that 'it' can be assigned in 'it moves' which will make that utterance of 'it moves' so interpreted and an utterance of Galileo's the same in content. For 'Everything is such that Galileo said that it moves', we would want there to be, for every (appropriate) interpretation of 'it' in the utterance of 'it moves', an utterance of Galileo's which was the same in content as it, so interpreted.

Let us now try to implement this suggestion in a satisfaction clause for a sentence of indirect discourse with one "free variable" in the complement. In effect, what this requires is that we introduce an additional argument place in the relation, which indicates how the free variable is to be interpreted

257

in the utterance of the open sentence, in order for someone to stand in the says-relation to the utterance.

> [25]   For any function f, for any formula with one free variable $\phi(y)$, for any α, for any speech act u of $\ulcorner \alpha$ said that $\phi(y) \urcorner$, for any speech act u' of $\phi(y)$ in u, $\ulcorner \alpha$ said that $\phi(y) \urcorner$ is true(S, t, u) iff $[\exists t' : t' < t](\text{Ref}(S, t, u, \alpha) \text{ says}(t', f('y')) u')$.

Here we would give this gloss on the 'x says(t, y) u': some saying of x's at t is the same in content as u, with the free variable in the sentence interpreted as referring to y. Then the usual clauses for the quantifiers would be left untouched.

There are some drawbacks to this proposal. First, it requires us to treat 'says' as having an extra argument place, which is apparently superfluous when we do not have a complement sentence with a free variable. Second, when we generalize to an arbitrary number of variables, we clearly do not want to add additional argument places to the says-relation for each new free variable. Thus, it looks as if what we must do is treat the argument places as taking terms that refer to the functions themselves. This, it should be admitted, seems a bit counterintuitive. It seems a mistake to read into the object language the semantic machinery of the metalanguage. Thus, though there does seem to be a technical solution to the quantifying-in problem for Davidson's account, it does not look like a completely satisfactory response.

An alternative would be to treat sentences of indirect discourse as referring not to an utterance of their complement sentences, but to the complement sentence itself. A proposal of this sort has been developed in Ludwig and Ray (1998).[199] Briefly, an utterance of 'Galileo said that the earth moves' would be treated as true just in case an utterance of Galileo's was the same in content as 'the earth moves' interpreted relative to the speaker and time of utterance (this handles sentences such as 'John said that I am a bore'), and, perhaps, the speaker's idiolect.[200] For a sentence with no free variables, we could offer the following axiom:

---

[199] For some similar approaches which appeal instead to what are called "Interpreted Logical Forms", see Larson and Ludlow (1993); see also for discussion Higginbotham (1991, 2005).

[200] Davidson notes the following objection to treating indirect discourse as referring to a sentence: "The 'that' cannot refer to a sentence, both because, as Church has pointed out in similar cases, the reference would then have to be relativized to a language, since a sentence may have different meanings in different languages; but also, and more obviously, because the same sentence may have different truth values in the same language." (2001 (1968): 165–6). This point is met once one relativizes the interpretation of the sentence to the speaker, time and speech act.

[26]   For all sentences ϕ, $\ulcorner \alpha$ said that $\phi \urcorner$ is true(S, t, u, E) iff [there is a
       $t': t' < t]($Ref(S, t, u, α) says$(t', S, t, u, \mathbf{I})$ ϕ).

We interpret 'says$(t', S, t, u, \mathbf{I})$ ϕ' as 'says(t') ϕ interpreted relative to S, t,
and u in $\mathbf{I}$'; '$\mathbf{I}$' refers to the speaker's idiolect (which we could represent as a
function of the speaker and time). We allow the possibility of $\mathbf{I}$ differing from
E to allow for correct reports using words that differ from standard English in
spelling, pronunciation, or meaning. Quantifying in, then, can be handled by
considering completions of an open complement sentence. Intuitively, what
we want for the truth of an utterance of a sentence such as [16], repeated
below, is that everyone be such that he assertively uttered a sentence which is
the same in content as a completion of 'x is honest', that is, of the incomplete
sentence in the complement, where the term that replaces 'x', for each, refers
to him.

[16]   Everyone says that he is honest.

To implement this formally, we need to provide a satisfaction clause for the
open sentence 'x says that x is honest'. Intuitively, ignoring context sensitivity
for the moment, we will say that a function f satisfies this open sentence
just in case a saying of $f('x')$ is the same in content as a sentence which is
the concatenation of a name β and 'is honest' in a language that extends the
speaker's language at most in containing β, *and in which β refers to $f('x')$*. We
appeal to extensions of the language because the language will not contain
enough names for everything. We can represent this more generally as in [27].
Here '$\phi(y)$' ranges over sentences of the object language E containing a free
variable 'y'.

[27]   For any $\phi(y)$, function f, f satisfies(S, t, u, E) $\ulcorner x$ said that $\phi(y) \urcorner$ iff
       [there is an $\mathbf{I}^+, \phi^*$: $\mathbf{I}^+$ extends I at most in that it contains a name
       β not occurring in $\phi(y)$, and β refers in $\mathbf{I}^+$ to $f('y')$, and ϕ^* is the
       result of replacing all free occurrences of 'y' in $\phi(y)$ with β][there
       is a $t': t' < t](f('x')$ says$(t', S, t, u, \mathbf{I}^+)$ ϕ^*).[201]

The approach can be extended to an arbitrary number of variables. As above,
since the modification enters in at the level of the satisfaction clauses, no
modification is needed to the standard recursive clauses for the quantifiers.
This proposal avoids introducing any of the assignment functions into the

---

[201] It is worth noting that this is not a form of substitutional quantification. The object the
function f assigns to 'y' is still used in giving satisfaction conditions, but it is displaced from the
complement clause.

semantics of the object language, and it fares at least as well as Davidson's proposal with respect to the objections considered previously (see Ludwig and Ray (1998) for further discussion).

That leaves the problem of mixed direct and indirect speech (9). A solution is presented here which builds on the approach just presented, and which could be adapted to Davidson's account more directly, though we will not attempt to do this here. The approach appeals to the general strategy introduced in Chapter 6, that is, the strategy of treating such sentences as saying that the speaker used the words in quotation marks in saying what is expressed by the sentence that results from stripping off the quotation marks, relativized to the speaker, time, and speech act. But we must also say not just that the words were used, but that they were used in a grammatical role appropriate for the quoted words in the complement of the report. To put this generally, we introduce some notation. First, let us represent the special use of quotation marks which we have been calling mixed quotation using double quotation marks, reserving single quotation marks for pure mentioning uses. Let 'UNQ(ϕ)' refer to the result of removing all double quotation marks from ϕ, and 'QUO(ϕ)' refer to the result of adding double quotation marks around ϕ. Thus, UNQ(' "scientific neologism" is')='scientific neologism is'; QUO('gone self-conscious') = ' "gone self-conscious" '. We generalize [26] as in [28].

[28] For all sentences ϕ, $\ulcorner \alpha$ said that $\phi \urcorner$ is true(S, t, u, E)
     iff
     (a) [there is a t' : $t' < t$](Ref(S, t, u, α) says(t', S, t, u, I) UNQ(ϕ)
         and
     (b) if UNQ(ϕ) $\neq \phi$, then there is a sentence ψ such that Ref(S, t, u, α) says(t', S, t, u, I) UNQ(ϕ) using ψ, and for all expressions γ and formulas ζ, if ϕ is the result of replacing 'x' in ζ with QUO(γ), then γ has the same grammatical role in ψ as QUO(γ) has in ϕ.

Clause (*a*) secures that the subject says what is expressed in the context by the complement sentence with its first layer of double quotation marks stripped off. Clause (*b*) secures that the expressions in the first layer of double quotation marks play in the sentence the subject used a grammatical role appropriate for the location of the expressions appearing in double quotation marks in the complement, no matter how many distinct appearances within the complement there are of double-quoted expressions. Where we have complements that do not introduce full sentences, we look to the role in an appropriate transform of it. Note that this allows that a speaker may use in a complement clause a term in quotation marks that might not be meaningful in English. Thus, as noted in Cappelen and Lepore (1997), we may wish to allow as acceptable sentences such as [29].

[29] My son said that I was a "philtosopher".

The speaker can be construed as using 'philtosopher' to mean what 'philosopher' means in English, but indicating that his son used 'philtosopher' instead of 'philosopher' to say it. Since the says-relation is relativized to the speaker, time, his speech act, and his idiolect at the time, there is no difficulty on the present account posed by these sorts of uses (if they are acceptable). It would also be possible to accommodate on the present approach reports such as [30], if acceptable, in which we suppose the expressions used actually have no meaning in English, or in the idiolect of the person being reported.

[30] He said that all "mimsy" were the "borogroves".

If such uses are acceptable, all that this shows is that the same in content relation extends to utterances of sentences such as 'all mimsy were the borogroves'. However, since this is a matter of how to spell out the meaning of 'says' in English, it is not something that has to be taken up for the purposes of giving an account of the logical form of indirect discourse sentences.

4. Conclusion

The main aim of this chapter has been to explain and evaluate Davidson's proposal for giving a semantics for indirect discourse, which would serve as a model for giving a semantics for opaque contexts more generally. Davidson's proposal famously treats a sentence such as 'Galileo said that the earth moves' as semantically equivalent to two sentences, 'Galileo said that' and 'the earth moves'; when someone asserts 'Galileo said that the earth moves', the utterance of 'Galileo said that' is treated as involving demonstrative reference to the utterance following, 'the earth moves'. This proposal gives indirect discourse sentences an unproblematic logical form, avoids reinterpretation of the words in the complement clause of the English sentence (preserving "semantic innocence"), and avoids appeal to meanings, properties, relations or propositions, which we might as well do without if we can. The proposal has been much discussed and criticized. We have tried to show that it has the resources to respond to many of the objections which have been made to it. Among those which are most difficult to respond to are the demonstration objection and the quantifying-in objection. We have argued that the demonstration objection can be met with what should be seen as a minor revision relative to Davidson's goals, in effect, restricting the second argument for an utterance of a sentence such as 'Galileo said that the earth moves' (what Galileo is being related to) to the utterance within it of 'the earth moves'. Quantification into the complement clause can also be handled, though at a cost. We have sketched an alternative that moves to sentences understood relative to speaker, time, and speaker's idiolect which avoids some of the discomfort of the suggestion we advance for handling quantification into complement clauses, and we have also shown that this can be extended in a straightforward way to handle mixed indirect and direct speech. This approach appears to preserve semantic innocence at least as well as Davidson's proposal, in the sense that it is crucial for its success, as for Davidson's, that the words in the complement sentence be understood in their usual way relative to the context of utterance. Our tentative conclusion, therefore, is that the paratactic account of indirect discourse can be extended or amended so as to preserve its basic insights, while avoiding what Davidson sees as the mistakes of traditional approaches that appeal to meanings and give up semantic innocence.

12

Non-Declarative Sentences

Mood must somehow contribute to meaning ... , since mood is clearly a
conventional feature of sentences. Yet it cannot combine with or modify
the meaning of the rest of the sentence in any known way.

(Davidson 2001 (1984): 117)

I say to one, come, and he cometh, and to another go, and he goeth.

(*Matthew* 8: 9)

Prima facie a serious obstacle to the program of providing a truth-theoretic
semantics for natural languages is the fact that natural languages apparently
contain an infinite number of sentences that do not appear to be truth evaluable
even in use, specifically, imperatives ('Get free stuff', 'Don't open that door',
'Stay off the grass', 'Shine my shoes') and interrogatives ('Why did you do it?',
'Are you telling the truth?', 'How did you get out?', 'What time is it?', 'Which of
them is guilty?').[202] Ordinarily, we would not suppose that it made any sense to
say of an utterance of 'Get free stuff' that it was true or false, or of an utterance
of 'What time is it?' that is was true or false. Such sentences do not apparently

---

[202] Another neglected class of expressions are exclamatives, which, though it is often overlooked, can in fact participate in the usual recursive machinery of the language. For example,
'Congratulations on ... ' may be completed by a nominal of arbitrary complexity, and the
evaluation of an utterance of it as felicitous or happy depends on the meaning of the prepositional phrase; similarly, such expressions can be embedded in complex sentences, as in 'If you
won the race and didn't cheat, as usual, then congratulations'. We neglect them here as well,
though the devices introduced later to deal with imperatives and interrogatives should suggest
some approaches to extending the scope of a compositional semantic theory to include them.
See Boisvert and Ludwig (2006) for some developments of the approach suggested here to
exclamatives.

have even context-relative truth conditions, and do not appear to have propositional meaning. Yet they are clearly meaningful and are a ubiquitous feature of
ordinary conversation. Any semantic program which cannot give an account
of the meaning and function of such sentences is obviously incomplete.

Imperatives and interrogatives therefore present a challenge to carrying
out Davidson's program in semantics. In this chapter, we consider some
responses to this challenge. We first consider Davidson's own response to
this challenge, which attempts to show that we can in fact fit imperatives,
at least, into the shoe of truth-theoretic semantics, with some perhaps minor
adjustments of fit (Davidson 2001*a* (1979)). We then consider some objections
to Davidson's attempt to fit imperatives and interrogatives into a truth
theory. On the assumption that these objections are on the right track, we
consider an alternative proposed by one of us (Ludwig). The other of us
(Lepore) has some reservations about this approach, which we will note
at appropriate points. The alternative proposal does not attempt to reduce
imperatives and interrogatives to declaratives (sentences evaluable as true or
false on an occasion of non-defective utterance), but incorporates them into
a generalization of the truth-theoretic approach, denominated the fulfillment
theoretic approach. It does this while at the same time keeping the truth
theory at the core of a compositional meaning theory by defining the more
general notion of a fulfillment condition recursively in terms of the satisfaction
relation invoked by the truth theory.[203]

In §1, we lay out Davidson's approach to imperatives and interrogatives.
In §2, we raise and consider some objections. In §3, the alternative fulfillment
condition approach is developed in application to closed sentences, including
mixed mood sentences such as 'If you are going to the store, don't forget to
buy some milk'. In §4, it is extended to a quantificational language and to
quantification into mood setters in particular, and Convention *T* is generalized
to a fulfillment theory.

1. Davidson's Paratactic Account of Mood

Davidson's basic approach to imperatives and interrogatives is to argue that
they can, contrary to appearances, be brought within the truth-theoretic fold.
His strategy for accomplishing this is to employ a device he has applied
in other areas, namely, a variant of the paratactic approach, which treats

---

[203] This approach was originally developed in Ludwig (1997). See also Boisvert and Ludwig
(2006).

imperatives and interrogatives as involving, in effect, a demonstration of, and statement about, a demonstrated token utterance whose content itself is not taken to be part of the content of the statement being made about it.

Let us review the prima facie difficulty. Consider, then, a sentence such as 'What time is it?' On the face of it, it is impossible to incorporate this into a truth theory because to do so requires that there be a true T-sentence for it. Yet, the T-form sentence for 'What time is it?' would have the form of [1], in which we would have to replace 'p' with some open sentence containing variables for speaker and time, and so represent 'What time is it?' as being true or false relative to each speaker and time of utterance.

[1] 'What time is it?' is true(S, t, u) iff p.

But we do not treat utterances of such sentences, when they are used for the their standard purpose of asking questions, as true or false. The question is how this difficulty can be overcome, if it can, within the framework of truth-theoretic semantics.

The differences between the moods are evidently connected with systematic differences in their uses. We ask questions, typically, with sentences in the interrogative mood, issue commands, make suggestions, and so on, with sentences in the imperative, and make assertions with sentences in the indicative, or, as we will say, more generally, the declarative mood.[204] This dimension of use is a matter of the 'force' with which the sentence is uttered.[205] However, since force is a feature of a speech act, and sentential mood of grammar, it is possible, and also common, that commands be issued by the use of declaratives ('Private, I think my boots need shining') or interrogatives ('Can you step this way, sir?'), and so on. Furthermore, a sentence in any mood could be uttered (for example, in practising elocution) without being uttered with any force. Likewise, of course, when we have

---

[204] The term 'indicative' is not broad enough for our uses since traditionally it is not used to cover, e.g. sentences that are said to be in the subjunctive mood; so we press into use here the term 'declarative' to classify all sentences that, as used, are evaluated as true or false (where there are no defects in the use on the occasion, such as failed demonstrative reference).

[205] See J. L. Austin (1962); Bach and Harnish (1982); Searle (1979); Searle (1969). Searle distinguishes between five basic kinds of speech acts, assertives, which represent something as being so, commissives, which commit the speaker to doing something, directives, which require of an audience that it do something, declaratives, which make something the case (e.g. someone's adjourning a meeting by saying 'I hereby bring this meeting to a close') and expressives, which express some sentiment, feeling, or emotion of the speakers (as when one says 'ouch' on stubbing a toe). Both imperatives and interrogatives are designed for use in performing directives aimed at getting an audience to provide information of some sort, with interrogatives being used to perform a more specialized sort of directive than imperatives.

embedded sentences, it is clear that they are not necessarily issued with the force that we might think appropriate for a standard use of them by themselves ('If you're going out, take the mail to the post office', 'If that's a dictionary next to you, look up "hagiography" for me', 'If you don't mind my asking, what is it exactly that you think you are doing?', 'Shut up, or would you prefer that I taped your mouth closed?') The connection between the moods and forces, then, must be indicated in an account of the sentential moods, but the connection must not be so tight that we are committed to saying that every use of a sentence in a particular mood issues in a speech act with a corresponding force. This independence of the force with which a sentence is uttered and its grammatical form will turn out to be crucial to Davidson's proposal.

As is usual, Davidson's proposal is developed to meet a set of criteria which are gleaned in part from observing the failures of rival accounts. The first point Davidson makes is the above, that linguistic meaning is what he calls 'autonomous', that is, "Once a feature of language has been given conventional expression, it can be used to serve many extra-linguistic ends; symbolic representation necessarily breaks any close tie with extra-linguistic purpose" (2001a (1979): 113). The point is directed in particular against Dummett, whom Davidson represents as holding that whether someone has made, for example, an assertion, is a matter to be determined relative to public conventions, that is, assertion is a matter of convention in the sense that there are certain conditions which are agreed by convention to be such that if an utterance of an declarative sentence (for example) is made in those conditions, the utterance is thereby an assertion. This is a matter, Davidson argues, which cannot be in the province of convention, since assertion requires at least that "a speaker ... represent himself as believing what he says" (2001a (1979): 112), and this requires certain attitudes on the part of the speaker. Whether a speaker has the attitudes cannot be a matter of convention.

While this is not a matter of central importance in Davidson's treatment of the moods, it will be worth a short digression to clarify Davidson's position, which is sometimes misunderstood. Although Davidson sometimes says things such as "mood is not a conventional sign of assertion or command because nothing is, or could be, a conventional sign of assertion or command" (2001a (1979): 114), he does not mean by this that mood is not a conventional device for indicating that a speaker intends to perform a speech act of a certain kind. What he means is that there could not be a convention that a certain overt public act, in certain publicly recognizable conditions perhaps, could constitute the performance of a certain kind of speech act. Rather, since a speech act is a certain kind of action, for it to be performed, the agent has to have appropriate intentions (though this need not be sufficient, of course). It is no defense of the conventionalist view to urge that the conditions specified by convention may include intentions of the speakers, for this is simply to subsume conditions which are necessary and sufficient independently of any conventions at all. Davidson's principal argument for his view is that any public sign that a speaker is performing a certain sort of speech act could be subverted in play or performance. Nor could the convention be repaired by the addition of a negative condition: and the speaker is not merely playing at making an assertion, etc., because the effect of this is simply to guarantee that the speaker has the right intentions, and, as already remarked, this is to admit that what makes for the performance of a particular type of speech act is independent of convention.

An important suggestion about how to treat grammatical moods, which would make them amenable to treatment in a truth theory, is to treat them as equivalent to explicit performatives which are in the declarative mood. Thus, for example, 'Let there be light' would be treated as equivalent to (or a definitional abbreviation of?) 'I command that there be light'. 'Buddy, can you spare a dime?', would be treated as equivalent to 'Buddy, I ask whether you can spare me a dime' (Lewis 1975*b*: 208). Davidson's objection to this is the following:

> … simply reducing imperatives or interrogatives to indicatives leaves us with no account at all of the differences among the moods. If any of the reductive theories is right, mood is as irrelevant to meaning as voice is often said to be. If mood does not affect meaning, how can we hope to explain the connection between mood and use, whatever the connection comes to? Reductive analyses abandon rather than solve the problem with which we began.   (2001*a* (1979): 115)

The objection is not entirely convincing. For clearly there is something which the performative paraphrase account can say about the differences between the moods. The imperative mood is an abbreviatory device to shorten a declarative sentence in which the main verb is 'command'; the interrogative mood is an abbreviatory device to shorten a declarative sentence in which the main verb is 'ask'. Their difference consists in the difference in what they are abbreviatory devices for. Mood is not irrelevant to meaning on the performative account at all, any more than 'the' would be irrelevant to meaning if it were treated as abbreviating its Russellian analysis. (Given the way Davidson develops his own proposal, through analogy with performatives, it is surprising he should level this criticism here.)

Nonetheless, the performative theory is not convincing. Intuitively, 'Can you spare a dime?' (relativized to contextual parameters) does not entail that someone is asking something, any more than 'I can spare you a dime' (suitably relativized) entails that someone is asserting something. The performative theory notices that an explicit performative can be used to perform the same function as an imperative or interrogative sentence, but this does not mean that imperatives and interrogatives mean the same as corresponding performatives.[206]

In laying out his own account, Davidson lists three "characteristics a satisfactory theory of mood should have."

(1) It must show or preserve the relations between indicatives and corresponding sentences in the other moods; it must, for example, articulate the sense in which 'You will take off your shoes', 'Take off your shoes', and 'Will you take off your shoes?' have a common element.

(2) It must assign an element of meaning to utterances in a given mood that is not present in utterances in other moods. And this element should connect with the difference in force between assertions, questions, and commands in such a way as to explain our intuition of a conventional relation between mood and use.

(3) Finally, the theory should be semantically tractable. If the theory conforms to the standards of a theory of truth, then I would say all is well. And on the other hand if ... a standard theory of truth can be shown to be incapable of explaining mood, then truth theory is inadequate as a general theory of language. (2001*a* (1979): 115–16)

The difficulty lies in a tension between the first two criteria and the third. The first two look to require that moods be treated as operators on a declarative or neutral core sentence. The last seems to require that they be treated as truth-functional operators (assuming that only in a truth theory will one be able to exhibit the moods as semantically tractable).

The key to Davidson's resolution of this tension is taken from what is suggested about the treatment of explicit performatives in the light of his treatment of indirect discourse. Consider an explicit performative such as [2]. On Davidson's analysis of indirect discourse, this is represented as semantically equivalent to two separate sentences, as illustrated in [3].

    [2]   I assert that the moon is full.
    [3]   I assert that. The moon is full.

---

[206] See Ludwig (1997: §4) for further critical discussion of the performative paraphrase approach.

268

The second sentence is referred to by the first. Since the first says that the speaker asserts the second, the first will be true iff the speaker in uttering the second sentence asserts it. On this view, presumably one explains the use of the performative as a device to indicate the speaker's intention to his audience. This picture of explicit performatives, however, suggests immediately that we treat moods analogously, particularly the imperative and interrogative moods. First, Davidson says we can leave the declarative mood alone, "we have found no intelligible use for an assertion sign" (2001*a* (1979): 119). The sentences in the imperative and interrogative moods we will treat as declarative sentences plus a mood-setter (for example, in the case of questions, among other things, the reversal of the order of the subject and main verb, 'Am I tired?' from 'I am tired', and so on). Each is assigned truth conditions. Consider an example, [4].

    [4]   Put on your hat.

The declarative core of this is 'you will put on your hat'. The mood setter is the truncation of the declarative core, the leaving out of the subject term. The declarative core is assigned its usual truth conditions. About the mood setter, Davidson says the following:

> If we were to represent in linear form the utterance of, say, the imperative sentence 'Put on your hat', it would come out as the utterance of a sentence like 'My next utterance is imperatival in force', followed by an utterance of 'You will put on your hat'.   (2001*a* (1979): 120)

But this is misleading, because, Davidson says,

> I do not want to claim that imperative sentences are two indicative sentences. Rather, we can give the semantics of the utterance of an imperative sentence by considering two specifications of truth conditions, the truth conditions of the utterance of an indicative sentence got by transforming the original imperative, and the truth conditions of the mood-setter. The mood-setter of an utterance of 'Put on your hat' is true if and only if the utterance of the indicative core is imperatival in force.   (2001*a* (1979): 120)

Thus, the proposal is that in uttering a sentence such as [4], one is understood by one's audience to have performed two speech acts, one involving as content the declarative core of the sentence (obtainable by a trivial transformation), and the other involving a claim about the utterance of the declarative core. This is, therefore, an account in which an element of parataxis is involved, in the sense that we represent the sentence uttered as semantically decomposable, even if not syntactically, into two distinct utterance acts, each with its independent truth conditions.

Does this meet the three criteria Davidson lays down for an adequate theory of mood? It trivially meets the condition of showing there is a common element of the moods: this is the declarative core. It also apparently meets the requirement that it assign a meaning to the mood-setters which distinguishes between the different moods (though, oddly, no meaning is assigned to the declarative mood—we will return to this below). Finally, by treating the contribution of the mood setter as a matter of its truth conditions, it appears to pave the way for a truth-theoretic treatment which will make it semantically tractable.

2. Difficulties for the Paratactic Account of Mood

We turn now to a number of questions about the adequacy of Davidson's account.

Despite the claim that an utterance of a non-declarative sentence can be considered as two utterances, each with its own truth conditions, it is not entirely clear how to integrate the proposal into a formal truth theory. For the formal theory must work with sentences. How, then, can we apply a truth theory to non-declarative sentences?

One suggestion would be that we treat a non-declarative sentence, such as 'Put on your hat', as primarily having as truth conditions the truth conditions of the mood-setter. Then we could represent the T-sentence as in [5].

[5] 'Put on your hat' is true(S, t, u) iff the declarative core of 'Put on your hat' as uttered by S at t is a command.

But this seems unacceptable on a number of grounds. First, an utterance of 'Put on your hat' is neither true nor false. This is something Davidson accepts, and explains as a result of the fact that it is treated paratactically. There are two independent truth conditions, but no conjunction. This seems to preclude any straightforward treatment of non-declarative sentences in a truth theory. Second, there seems to be no reason in any case to favor one of the truth conditions associated with it over the other. This might suggest treating it as a conjunction, but it is obvious that it does not have the truth conditions of a conjunction of 'the declarative core of "Put on your hat" is a command' and 'you will put on your hat'. If A says to B, 'Put on your hat', and B does not do it, it does not make sense to say that what A said was false.

If a truth theory cannot be applied directly to non-declarative sentences, then it appears that to integrate non-declarative sentences into a truth theory, we must first translate them into a regimented version of English (or whatever language we are considering) and apply the truth theory to the translation. (Indeed, it may be best to think of this as the proposal about the paratactic account in the case of quotation and indirect discourse too, to avoid the objection that these accounts get the syntax wrong.) The translation would represent 'Put on your hat' as two sentences, such as [6].

[6]   This is a command. You will put on your hat.

The truth theory would be applied independently to each sentence. An interpreter using the theory to interpret another speaker would, upon hearing someone utter a non-declarative sentence, first translate it as indicated, and then apply the truth theory.

For this to be acceptable, however, the semantic properties of the translation must be the same as those of what it translates. There are a number of reasons to think they are not. First, Davidson recognizes and agrees that an utterance of an imperative or interrogative sentence does not have a truth value. He explains this as a result of its being semantically two utterances which are not the utterance of a conjunction. In the same way, one would not say that an utterance of [7] is true or false, but rather say that the first utterance is true or false, and the second utterance is true or false.

[7]   I am tall. I am hungry.

Since there was no utterance of a conjunction, the question of the whole utterance's truth or falsity does not come up. (If a sentence in a newspaper report is false, we don't say that the report is false, we say that it is not completely accurate, and that it makes some false statements.) However, it is not clear that this is enough to blunt the force of the objection that non-declarative sentences are truth-valueless. In an utterance of [7], while the whole utterance is not true or false, one nonetheless has said two things which are truth-valued. Supposing that the utterer of [7] is both tall and hungry, he has said two things which are true. Davidson is committed to saying that in saying 'Put on your hat' one has said two things which are truth-valued, and, typically, the first of the two will be something one has asserted. If someone says 'Put on your hat' and thereby commands you to put on your hat, and then you put on your hat, Davidson's account commits us to saying that he has asserted something true, and at least uttered something else that is true. However, intuitively, when someone says 'Put on your hat', he has not *ipso facto* asserted or uttered *anything* which is true or false. There is a connected difficulty. If someone utters [7] (in English, intending his utterance literally), then he has said two things. He has said that he is tall, and that he is hungry.

He has said these things even if he has not asserted them—he has performed, in J. L. Austin's terminology, two locutionary acts. What he has said entails that something is tall, and that something is hungry. (Saying this does not require that he have said just one thing. In giving a speech that lasts an hour, one may be said to have said something that entails any number of things without implying one uttered a single very long sentence.) Similarly, given Davidson's account, it looks as if we are committed to saying that a literal utterance of 'Put on your hat' involves saying something that entails that something is a command, that you will put on your hat, that something will put on a hat, and so on. Yet, it seems, intuitively, what one says does not entail any of these things, any more than when one says 'Congratulations' one has said anything that has any entailments. Perhaps we could be persuaded, in the absence of alternatives to Davidson's proposal, that our reactions are confused or misleading, but this is, at least, a serious prima facie difficulty for the account.

Some difficulties arise specifically with respect to interrogatives that are worth noting. For a yes–no interrogative, such as 'Are you ready to go?', the paratactic account can be extended with no trouble, for this is treated as semantically equivalent to [8].

[8]   This is a question. You are ready to go.

But consider a question such as 'What time is it?' What does the paratactic account have to say about this? The difficulty is that the declarative core of this is intuitively an open sentence, namely, 'the time is x'. Using the approach just mentioned, we would represent this on the paratactic account as having the semantic form of [9].

[9]   This is a question. The time is x.

This claim that the following token expresses a question, of course, would not make sense if interpreted in the same way as in [8], so, at the very least, considerable elaboration of the account would have to be given to extend it to the various kinds of interrogatives.[207]

Another difficulty is that Davidson's account fails to treat the declarative mood on a par with the imperative and interrogative, but this seems unmotivated. Just as interrogatives are apt for asking questions, and imperatives for issuing directives, so are declaratives for making assertions, and this

---

[207] Davidson acknowledges that his account "may run into trouble when a serious attempt is made to apply it to interrogatives" (2001a (1979): 115 n. 12).

clearly has something to do semantically with the sentential mood. David-son's explanation of the function of the interrogative and imperative moods is purchased at the cost of placing beyond explanation the connection between the declarative mood and the aptness of declarative sentences for making assertions. It is clear why he must treat declaratives differently, for otherwise he would be faced an infinite regress. For then, for example, 'She is attractive' would have to be represented semantically as in [10].

[10]   This is an assertion. She is attractive.

But now we have two sentences in the declarative mood rather than just one, and we must do the same thing again, for each, and so on, which is absurd. Moreover, if we accepted this, we would also be forced to say that utterances of declarative sentences are neither true nor false, for the same reason that, on Davidson's account, utterances of imperatives and interrogatives are supposed not to be either true or false.

A final potential difficulty for the paratactic approach we wish to discuss emerges when we consider molecular sentences involving mixed moods, for arguably we do not always understand such sentences as having the force of a typical sincere literal utterance of a declarative, imperative or interrogative. One of the two authors (Ludwig) thinks such molecular sentences present a serious difficulty for Davidson. The other (Lepore) is not persuaded that we cannot treat them, after all, as simple imperatives or interrogatives, as appropriate. To see how the worry arises, consider [11].

[11]   If you stop by the post office, buy some stamps.

This does not appear to be equivalent to [12]. Someone addressed with [11] has not been told flat out to buy some stamps. If he does not buy some stamps, there is nothing he has failed to do with respect to what is required by an utterance of [11] directed at him. Is [11], though, equivalent to [13], where we indicate the imperative mood marker and its scope with 'IMP(...)'?

[12]   Buy some stamps.
[13]   IMP(if you go to the post office, then you will buy some stamps)

[13] would be used to direct its target audience to bring it about that the truth conditions of the conditional 'if you go to the post office, then you will buy some stamps' (as used on the occasion) obtain. What exactly is required will depend on how the English conditional is to be treated. We can suppose, without, we hope, any prejudice to subsequent discussion, that there are basically two ways one can bring it about that 'if you go to the post office,

then you will buy some stamps' is true, when one is the person picked out by 'you'. First, one can just not go to the post office. Second, one can buy some stamps. The second case would include the case in which one goes to the post office and buys some stamps.

An alternative reading of [11] treats typical sincere literal uses of it as issuing a conditional directive. Call this the 'conditional directive reading'. One is not, on this reading, flatly directed to do anything. Rather, the utterance has complex 'satisfaction conditions'. It is satisfied if the antecedent is false, that is, if one does not go to the post office. But it does not require any action on the part of the person addressed if it is satisfied for this reason. It does not, for example, require the person addressed to avoid going to the post office as a way of satisfying a directive issued by the utterance of [11]. It does not require the addressee to take any action with respect to going or not going to the post office. However, if the antecedent is satisfied, that is, if the person addressed goes to the post office, then for the utterance of [11] to be satisfied, he must buy some stamps with the intention of satisfying the utterance of [11]. Thus, on this reading, no simple directive is issued. No action is required of the addressee by the utterance for it to be satisfied unless the antecedent is satisfied. This contrasts with an utterance of [13], the other possible reading of [11], on which a simple directive is issued, and the addressee is required to do something with the intention of satisfying the directive issued for the utterance to be satisfied.

A special difficulty for Davidson's account arises if there is a conditional directive reading of sincere literal utterances of [11].[208] First, the difficulty, and then some considerations about whether there is the conditional directive reading. On the assumption that there is a conditional directive reading of [11], we can ask how the paratactic account could capture this. The paratactic account might try to treat the mood-setter as either covering the whole sentence [11] or its consequent. But neither case yields the right result on the intended reading. What we get is [14] and [15].

[14]   This is a directive. If you stop by the post office, buy some stamps.
[15]   If you stop by the post office, this is a directive. Buy some stamps.

The trouble with [14] is that an utterance of it involves a flat directive being issued, which is incompatible with the intended reading of [11]. The difficulty

[208] If there are such readings, then these cases show also that a taxonomy of speech acts such as Searle's (1979) is not exhaustive, and is better thought of as a taxonomy of what might be called basic or simple speech acts. For corresponding to the complex satisfaction conditions for molecular mixed mood sentences would be complex satisfaction conditions for the speech acts performed in sincere literal uses of them.

with [15] is that an utterance taken to be equivalent to successive utterances of these two sentences would not place the same intuitive requirements on someone to whom [11] was addressed (on the conditional directive reading). For if [15] is uttered, the utterance of 'buy some stamps' is either uttered with the force of a directive or not. If it is, then the conditional is true, and, independently of whether the addressee stops by the post office, he is required to buy some stamps. On the other hand, if the utterance of 'buy some stamps' is not a directive, then there is no requirement that the utterance of 'If you stop by the post office, this is a directive' places on the addressee that would require him to buy stamps, *if* he goes to the post office. It is simply true if he does not, and false otherwise. To put it in a nutshell, a conditional directive is not a simple directive whose content is given by the consequent, or a directive to make true a conditional, or something that fails to put any requirement on the speaker at all. But the paratactic account must treat it as having the force of a simple directive whose content is given by the consequent, or as a directive to make a conditional true, or as placing no constraints on the speaker's behavior at all. A connected difficulty (again, on the assumption that we give [11] the conditional directive reading), which is similar to a difficulty which the paratactic analysis of indirect discourse faces, is how to accommodate quantification into mood-setters. Consider [16], whose form can be represented as in [17]. This gets represented as [18] on the paratactic account, but we cannot make sense of the quantifier in the first sentence binding the variable in the second, independent sentence.

[16]   Invest every penny you earn.

[17]   [Every x: x is a penny you earn](invest x).

[18]   [Every x: x is a penny you earn](this is a directive). Invest x.

These difficulties arise *if* there is the conditional directive reading of [11]. The difference between the authors lies largely in their response to the question whether there is this reading. Ludwig thinks that there is such a reading. He thinks that if you say to someone, 'If it isn't an inconvenience, put this letter in the mail on your way to work', and intend it to be understood literally, it is used literally to issue a conditional directive, rather than a directive to (in effect) make a conditional true. Lepore, on the other hand, thinks the mood marker attaches to the whole. He cites examples such as a mother's saying to her daughter 'If you drive, don't drink', which he argues issues a directive that is satisfied if the daughter addressed avoids driving in order to drink. In an unpublished manuscript, Lepore and Leslie (2001) provide a positive account of the semantics of imperatives and interrogatives that adheres more closely to Davidson's original proposal, though aiming to avoid objections that have been raised to it, and offer further considerations in favor of not treating [11] and similar sentences as having a conditional directive reading. In the present context, we will not pursue these issues further.

Davidson's account of imperatives and interrogatives is ingenious. Nonetheless, there remain serious questions about whether it is adequate. Despite arguing against reductive accounts, in the end Davidson's own account forces non-declarative sentences into the Procrustean bed of truth. This is to assimilate the use of non-declarative sentences to the use of declarative sentences, that is, to assimilate them to assertions. Perhaps in the end we may be forced to this. But it would seem to be something we should accept only if we cannot find a more natural alternative. Prima facie non-declarative sentences are not truth evaluable, and, moreover, utterances of them do not constitute utterances (even two) which have truth values. In addition, *if* the satisfaction conditions of molecular mixed mood sentences like [11] need to be explained by composition of mood markers, it is unclear how one could extend the paratactic approach to successfully interpret such sentences.

3. The Fulfillment-Conditional Approach

This section and the next present an alternative approach to integrating imperatives and interrogatives into the framework of truth-theoretic semantics. One of the authors, Lepore, has reservations about this approach, and doubts it is necessary. So these sections represent an approach endorsed only by Ludwig.

The following approach assumes that imperatives and interrogatives do not have even context-relative truth conditions, and that mixed mood sentences such as [11] require composition on mood markers. This approach was first developed in Ludwig (1997), where more details and supporting argumentation are available (see also Boisvert and Ludwig 2006). The present sketch incorporates a few improvements to the earlier work.

The basic idea is to incorporate imperatives and interrogatives into a generalization of truth-theoretic semantics that gives the truth theory a central role to play. Imperatives and interrogatives admit of bivalent evaluations, relativized to appropriate contexts, just as declaratives do, but they are not evaluated as being true or false. Rather, imperatives are obeyed relative to a speaker, time, and speech act (where we treat 'obeyed(S, t, u)' as a technical term parallel to 'true(S, t, u)'), and interrogatives, we will say, are answered relative to a speaker, time, and speech act (and, similarly, we treat 'answered(S, t, u)' as a technical term parallel to 'true(S, t, u)'). These terms, 'obeyed' and 'answered', are borrowed from the terminology for evaluating speech acts of the sort typically performed using imperatives and interrogatives. But, as used here, they are not predicates of speech acts, but of 4-tuples of sentences, speakers, times, and speech acts. They bear to the terms that are applied to speech acts the same relation that 'x is true(S, t, u)' bears to the terms 'is true' and 'is false' as used of speech acts. The strategy sketched assigns context-relative "obedience conditions" to imperatives, and "response conditions" to interrogatives. These will both be classified as forms of compliance conditions. Compliance conditions and truth conditions, in turn, are treated as different forms of fulfillment conditions, as illustrated in Figure 3. In the place of a truth theory, a fulfilment theory is introduced which aims to issue in theorems of the form [F] (leaving out explicit relativization to the language).

[F] ϕ is fulfilled(S, t, u) iff p

where 'ϕ' is replaced by a structural description of an object language sentence, and 'p' is replaced by a formula of the metalanguage. A generalization of Convention T is introduced below. For atomic ϕ, the predicate 'is fulfilled(S, t, u)' is defined in terms of the truth, obedience and response predicates, as illustrated in [19].

[19]   For all atomic ϕ, ϕ is fulfilled(S, t, u) iff
if ϕ is a declarative, then ϕ is true(S, t, u);
if ϕ is an imperative, then ϕ is obeyed(S, t, u);
if ϕ is an interrogative, then ϕ is answered(S, t, u).

For molecular sentences, fulfillment conditions are given using the usual recursive clauses, until we arrive at components to which [19] can be applied.

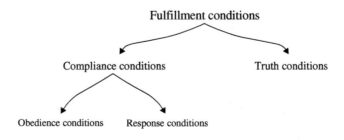

Figure 3

The key to exhibiting the truth theory as central to the fulfillment theory lies in showing how to define the predicates 'obeyed(S, t, u)' and 'answered(S, t, u)' in terms of 'true(S, t, u)'. This is taken up next. The following section shows how to extend the strategy to satisfaction predicates corresponding to each of the three varieties of fulfillment conditions, and shows thereby how to extend the account to handle quantification across mood-setters.

The basic strategy is to model the context-relativized obedience and response conditions on the corresponding bivalent evaluations of the kinds of directive that imperatives and interrogatives are designed to help us to perform. This parallels the procedure which is standardly followed for declaratives. A directive speech act is obeyed or followed just in case its intended audience does what the speaker directs, but, importantly, does it as an intentional result of his having been so directed. Thus, for example, if someone yells at the President of the United States, while he is giving a speech, not to hold his breath, we would not say that he has got the President to follow his orders, because his directive is ignored, and the President continues to speak. Thus, an imperative, such as 'Put on your hat', may be said to be obeyed relative to a speaker S, time t, and speech act u, just in case the person addressed by S at t in u subsequently puts on his hat as an intentional result of recognizing the obedience conditions of u. To generalize this, some notation will be useful. Let Core(ϕ) be a function that takes an imperative or interrogative to its declarative core, which is intuitively the sentence form or sentence from which the imperative or interrogative is derived. Let $A(S, t, u)$ be a function from a speaker S, time t, and speech act u, to an audience S is addressing at t in u. Obedience conditions for imperatives generally are given as follows.

[I]   For any imperative ϕ, ϕ is obeyed(S, t, u) iff
      $A(S, t, u)$ makes it the case that Core(ϕ) is true(S, t, u) with the
      intention of fulfilling u.[209]

---

[209] On the right-hand side of the biconditional, there is a declarative sentence, or sentence form. This then provides the truth condition for some declarative sentence. How then, it might be objected, does this approach avoid assigning truth conditions to imperatives and interrogatives? The answer is that any specification of a condition whose obtaining or not determines which of two bivalent evaluations something receives will be a specification of a truth condition for some sentence, but that it need not be that whenever such a condition is specified it functions to specify a condition for something's being true or false. Beliefs are true or false; desires are satisfied or not; intentions are carried out or not. In saying under what conditions a belief is true, or a desire is satisfied, or an intention is carried out, we use declarative sentences. But this does not entail that desires and intentions are true or false, or that in specifying their satisfaction conditions we are really assigning them truth conditions. That would be to misunderstand the function, in the context, of the sentences being used.

A few quick notes are in order. First, Core(ϕ) will yield a sentence in the future tense, so that the forward-looking character of imperatives is built into [I]. Second, $A(S, t, u)$ accommodates audiences which consist of one or more individuals. Third, though, in general, substitution of coreferential or coextensive terms in the complement of 'makes it the case' is not valid, it will be valid for all the substitutions made on the basis of a correct truth theory for the language, since if 'P' is made true in L by something, then if the truth of 'P' in L requires the truth of 'Q' in L, then 'Q' is made true in L by the same thing. Fourth, 'makes it the case' is a tenseless, and timeless, metalanguage predicate; 'x makes it the case that p' is satisfied for a value of 'x' if at some time or other it brings it about that p; the requirement that this be done with the intention of fulfilling the speech act performed using the relevant imperative guarantees it is after the speech act is issued, so no further time restriction is required. Consider the application of [I] to 'Put on your hat' with respect to a speaker $\sum$ and time τ, in a speech act μ, where $A(\sum, \tau, \mu) = \chi$, and, of course, Ref($\sum, \tau, \mu$, 'you') $= \chi$. The result is [20].

[20] 'Put on your hat' is obeyed($\sum, \tau, \mu$) iff χ makes it the case that [the x: x is(τ) a hat and x belongs(τ) to χ][there is a t': $t' > \tau$](χ puts(t') on x with the intention of fulfilling μ).

Interrogatives are in the same line of business as imperatives. They differ in being more specialized. The same template can be used in providing response conditions for interrogatives as for imperatives. Interrogatives, however, come in a variety of different kinds, which require different response conditions. The basic varieties are yes–no questions ('Do you know where you are going to?'), how and why questions ('How did he do it?', 'Why did he bother?'), and wh-questions, which are distinguished by the fact that they are formed from open rather than closed sentences ('Which of them is guilty', 'What time is it?', 'How many people were there?'). Response conditions are represented by [YN], [WHY], [HOW], and [WH].

[YN]   For all yes–no interrogatives ϕ, ϕ is answered(S, t, u) iff $A(S, t, u)$ makes it the case that ⌜you will say that Core(ϕ)⌝ is true(S, t, u) with the intention of fulfilling u or $A(S, t, u)$ makes it the case that ⌜you will say that Neg(Core(ϕ))⌝ is true(S, t, u) with the intention of fulfilling u.

[WHY]   For all why interrogatives ϕ, ϕ is answered(S, t, u) iff $A(S, t, u)$ makes it the case that ⌜you will explain why Core(ϕ))⌝ is true(S, t, u) with the intention of fulfilling u.

[HOW]   For all how interrogatives ϕ, ϕ is answered(S, t, u) iff $A(S, t, u)$ makes it the case that $\ulcorner$you will explain how Core(ϕ))$\urcorner$ is true(S, t, u) with the intention of fulfilling u.

[WH]   For all wh-interrogatives ϕ, ϕ is answered(S, t, u) iff $A(S, t, u)$ makes it the case that [there is a ψ: ψ is a completion of Core(ϕ)]($\ulcorner$you will say $\psi\urcorner$ is true(S, t, u)) with the intention of fulfilling u.

In the case of [WH], the quantification over completions cannot be discharged. Rather, to see whether someone has answered a wh-question, we must wait for a response and see whether it satisfies the existential condition.

This approach nicely handles the problem of mixed mood sentences. For consider [21]. In applying the fulfillment theory to this, we will first employ a standard recursion clause as in [22]. Then we employ the appropriate clauses of [19] for the antecedent and consequent to get [23].

[21]   If you are tired, go to bed.

[22]   For all ϕ, ψ, $\ulcorner$If ϕ, $\psi\urcorner$ is fulfilled(S, t, u) iff if ϕ is fulfilled(S, t, u), ψ is fulfilled(S, t, u).

[23]   'If you are tired, go to bed' is fulfilled(S, t, u) iff if 'you are tired' is true(S, t, u), then 'go to bed' is obeyed(S, t, u).

Supposing that $\sum$ address χ at τ in μ using [21], we can arrive at [24].

[24]   'If you are tired, go to bed ' is fulfilled(S, t, u) iff if χ is(t) tired, then χ makes it the case that [there is a t': $t' > t$](χ goes(t') to bed with the intention of fulfilling u).

This gets the right result, and does not collapse into either the requirement to make the conditional true, or no requirement on the addressee at all, or simply the requirement that would be expressed by a stand-alone use of the consequent. (For further discussion see Boisvert and Ludwig 2006; Ludwig 1997.)

The fulfillment theory requires a generalization of Convention T. We gave our generalization of Convention T for context-sensitive languages as in Chapter 1, §7. Having added an additional relativization to semantic predicates to accommodate demonstrative elements in the language, this should be generalized to [CT^*], where the corresponding M-sentence is of the form $\ulcorner s$ means(S, t, u) that $p\urcorner$ (leaving implicit the language relativization).

[CT^*]   A truth theory $\mathcal{T}$ is adequate if it is formally correct and entails all instances of schema (T)

(T) s is true(S, t, u) iff p,

where '*s*' is replaced by a structural description of an object language sentence, such that the corresponding *M*-sentence is true.

To generalize this to a fulfillment theory, which embeds a truth theory, an analog of the *M*-sentence for obedience and response conditions is needed. Suppose someone utters sincerely and non-defectively, 'Close the window', directing it at some person χ. How would we say what he meant by that utterance? It would be natural to say that in using that sentence in that way, he has requested that χ close the window. (Compare: if someone says 'The window is closed' sincerely and non-defectively, we can say that what he meant was that the window is closed.) Similarly, if someone utters sincerely and non-defectively, 'What time is it?', directing it to χ, we would say that he requested χ to say what the time is.[210] Accordingly, on this approach, we can introduce the verb 'ϕ requests(S, t, u) that' as the parallel to 'ϕ means(S, t, u) that'. Thus, substituting for 'is obeyed($\sum, \tau, \mu$) iff' the corresponding predicate 'requests($\sum, \tau, \mu$) that' in [20] yields [25].

[25] 'Put on your hat' requests($\sum, \tau, \mu$) that χ makes it the case that [the x: x is(τ) a hat and x belongs(τ) to χ][there is a t': $t' > \tau$](χ puts(t') on x with the intention of fulfilling μ).

A convention parallel to [*CT**] for a fulfillment theory can be stated as in [*CF*].

[*CF*] A fulfillment theory F is adequate if it is formally correct and entails all instances of schema (*F*)

(*F*) *s* is fulfilled(S, t, u) iff *p*,

where '*s*' is replaced by a structural description of an object language sentence, such that (1) if *s* is a declarative sentence, the corresponding *M*-sentence is true, and (2) if *s* is a non-declarative sentence, the corresponding *R*-sentence is true.

The *R*-sentence corresponding to ⌜*s* is fulfilled(S, t, u) iff *p*⌝ is ⌜*s* requests(S, t, u) that *p*⌝. This works for mixed mood sentences as well. Thus, the corresponding *R*-sentence for [24] is [26].

[26] 'If you are tired, go to bed' requests(S, t, u) that if χ is(t) tired, then χ makes it the case that [there is a t': $t' > t$](χ goes(t') to bed with the intention of fulfilling u).

---

[210] This differs slightly from the approach taken in Ludwig (1997) in using a single verb for both imperatives and interrogatives.

It should be noted that not all semantically possible mixed mood combinations are in fact found in natural languages. For example, we do not find conditionals with imperative sentences in the antecedent. There are good reasons to think that these restrictions have largely to do with such constructions being useless for any practical purpose, despite our being able to assign to them a coherent semantics.[211]

4. Extension to Open Sentences

This section sketches how to extend the fulfillment theory to open sentences. For this purpose, two additional satisfaction predicates are introduced, which are recursively defined in terms of the satisfaction predicate for declarative sentence forms; for imperative sentences it is 'satisfies^I', for interrogative sentence it is 'satisfies^Q', for declarative sentence forms it is the bare predicate 'satisfies' ('imperatives', 'interrogatives', and 'declaratives' will be used to cover open sentences of these forms, as well as closed sentences). A general satisfaction predicate, 'satisfies^F' is introduced, with the usual recursive clauses for connectives and quantifiers. The application of 'satisfies^F' to atomic open sentences is defined recursively, in terms of those for the more specific varieties of satisfaction condition, as in [27].

[27]   For all functions f, all atomic formulas ϕ, f satisfies$^F(S, t, u)$ ϕ iff
    if ϕ is declarative, then f satisfies(S, t, u) ϕ;
    if ϕ is imperative, then f satisfies$^I(S, t, u)$ ϕ;
    if ϕ is interrogative, then f satisfies$^Q(S, t, u)$ ϕ.

Usual recursive clauses for connectives will be given using 'satisfies$^F(S, t, u)$'. The satisfaction conditions for imperative and interrogative formulas will be modeled on the fulfillment conditions given in the previous section. This is illustrated with respect to the clause for imperatives.

[IS]   For any function f, imperative ϕ, f satisfies$^I(S, t, u)$ ϕ iff
    $A(S, t, u)$ makes it the case that f satisfies(S, t, u) Core(ϕ) with the intention of fulfilling u.

For interrogatives, 'satisfaction^Q' is defined in terms of satisfaction conditions appropriate for each particular kind of interrogative, as outlined in [28].

[28]   For all functions f, interrogatives ϕ, f satisfies$^Q(S, t, u)$ iff

---

[211] See Boisvert (1999) for a sustained defense of this claim.

if ϕ is a yes-no interrogative, then . . . ;

if ϕ is a why interrogative, then . . . ;

if ϕ is a how interrogative, then . . . ;

if ϕ is a wh-interrogative, then . . .

The satisfaction conditions for each variety are patterned after the response conditions given in the previous section. For example, in the case of wh-interrogatives, we have [WH*].

[WH*] If ϕ is a wh-interrogative, then f satisfies$^Q(S, t, u)$ ϕ iff $A(S, t, u)$ makes it the case that [there is a ψ: ψ is a completion of Core(ϕ)](f satisfies(S, t, u) ⌜you will say ψ⌝) with the intention of fulfilling u.

Then 'is fulfilled(S, t, u)' is defined in terms of satisfaction^F by all functions. Consider the application of [IS] to [17], repeated here, which yields [29], and then [30], and [31]—ignoring tense to keep the presentation less cluttered.

[17] [Every x: x is a penny you earn](invest x).

[29] For any function f, f satisfies$^F(S, t, u)$ '[Every x: x is a penny you earn](invest x)' iff every f' such that f' is a 'x is a penny you earn'/'x'-variant of f is such that f' satisfies^I 'invest x'.

[30] For any function f, f satisfies$^F(S, t, u)$ '[Every x: x is a penny you earn](invest x)' iff every f' such that $f'('x')$ is a penny, and Ref$(S, t, u,$ 'you'$)$ earns $f'('x')$', and f' is an 'x'-variant of f, is such that $A(S, t, u)$ makes it the case that f satisfies(S, t, u) Core('invest x') with the intention of fulfilling u.

[31] For any function f, f satisfies$^F(S, t, u)$ '[Every x: x is a penny you earn](invest x)' iff every f' such that $f'('x')$ is a penny, and Ref$(S, t, u,$ 'you'$)$ earns $f'('x')$', and f' is an 'x'-variant of f, is such that $A(S, t, u)$ makes it the case that Ref$(S, t, u,$ 'you'$)$ invests $f'('x')$ with the intention of fulfilling u.

This completes the sketch of the extension of the approach to a language with quantifiers.[212]

It should be noted that the general form in which Convention S was cast may be largely retained because most of the axioms for primitive expressions are axioms of the truth theory. It needs only to be supplemented with the requirement that axioms for the mood-setters conform to an appropriate

---

[212] See Ludwig (1997) for discussion of some further details, complications, and alternatives.

analog condition, which can be modeled on the condition given for predicates, for example, we need only introduce a 'requests' predicate that is additionally relativized to a function.

The form of the compositional meaning theory may similarly be straight-forwardly modified by replacing 'truth' with 'fulfillment', and modifying the statement about the relation between the canonical theorems of the fulfillment theory and the output of the meaning theory in accordance with [CF].

13

Semantic Structure and Logical Form

Armed with the theory, we can always answer the question, 'What are these familiar words doing here?' by saying how they contribute to the truth conditions of the sentence.

(Davidson 2001 (1968): 94)

A truth-theoretic semantics reveals the compositional structure of a natural language through an interpretive truth theory.[213] As we have seen, truth theories divide into base and recursive axioms. Recursive axioms are for terms or syntactic structures which form iterable complex expressions from simpler ones on the basis of which they are understood. The recursive structure of a sentence, and the semantic forms of the primitive expressions in it, provide its semantic form. In this chapter, we consider the relation between semantic form in this sense and logical form in the sense in which it has been used throughout the twentieth century in analytic philosophy. Following Davidson, we see the relation as basically that of identity, and provide a precise characterization in terms, first, of an interpretive truth theory, and then in the generalized framework of an interpretive fulfillment theory, of when two (initially, declarative) sentences in the same or different languages are the same in logical form. In §1, we distinguish two different conceptions of logical form, a narrower and broader notion, select the second as our target of interest, and discuss some standard positions on the notion of logical form. In §2, we proceed to offer a characterization of sameness of logical

---

[213] Much of the material in this chapter derives from Ludwig and Lepore (2001).

form for declarative sentences relative to languages in terms of the notion of corresponding proofs of *T*-sentences for the sentences in truth theories for the language. We discuss briefly the relation of this characterization to Davidson's claim that logical form is always relative to the logic of one's metatheory. In §3, we discuss the relation between our proposal and the idea of a canonical representation of the logical form of a sentence. In §4, we turn to the relation between the characterization of sameness of logical form we advance and the project of identifying logical constants in a language. We discuss two alternative approaches, one which focuses on topic neutrality as central, and the other which focuses on semantic recursion, and conclude that since both notions are projections of a pre-theoretic interest which does not clearly tell between them, each should be accepted as a conception of the notion of a logical constant, and pragmatic considerations relative to the kind of project one is engaged in should determine which one uses. In §5, we consider some questions relating to a supposed distinction between structural and logical validity, arguing that the distinction, insofar as it can be drawn, is not theoretically interesting. In §6, we sketch briefly how to extend the characterization of sameness of logical form to sentences in any mood, that is, to imperative and interrogative sentences. The appendix discusses an alternative to the approach for identifying logical constants we advance in §4.

1. What is Logical Form?

What interests us when we ask about the *logical form* of a natural language *sentence*? The logical form of a sentence is supposed to characterize something that members of a class of sentences (in a language) share. It is often connected with the pattern of logical constants or terms in a sentence, or, more broadly, with logical structure. But there are good reasons to think that focusing on the pattern of logical constants in a sentence will fail to capture adequately the broadest sense in which the term 'logical form' is used. In any case, there is the prior question of what terms or structures to count as logical.

Talk of logical form has played a central role in analytic philosophy. It has been connected with two interrelated concerns. One is a concern to identify arguments which are valid in virtue of their forms, that is, classes of arguments sharing structural features in common sufficient to guarantee their validity. A second is a concern not to be misled about the semantic structure of sentences—particularly as regards the conditions under which they are true or false—so as not to be misled about our commitments about ontology. The second is broader, since a concern to understand the semantic structure of sentences most widely construed will subsume the concern to understand the semantic structure relevant to valid argument form. It is the second concern that is expressed in Russell's famous assertion in the second of his 1914 Lowell lectures, *Our Knowledge of the External World*, that "every philosophical problem, when it is subjected to the necessary analysis and purification, is found either to be not really philosophical at all, or else to be, in the sense in which we are using the word, logical" (Russell 1993: 42). That portion of logic relevant to philosophy, which he called 'philosophical logic', he characterized as concerned with the study of *forms* of propositions, or 'logical forms'. About logical forms, he says:

some kind of knowledge of logical forms, though with most people it is not explicit, is involved in all understanding of discourse. It is the business of philosophical logic to extract this knowledge from its concrete integuments, and to render it explicit and pure.   (Russell 1993: 53)

This is a concern, at bottom, with the semantic structure of the sentences of our languages, that is, a concern with what we have above called semantic form. In what follows, we will be concerned primarily with this second and broader conception of logical form.

Russell focused on propositional form as a solution to the difficulty of characterizing logical form sententially, given that sentences alike with respect to surface form, understood in terms of the schemas which can be formed from them, can be different in logical form, as in [1] and [2], and that sentences different in surface form can be alike in logical form, as in [3] and [4].

[1]   Everyone loves someone.
[2]   John loves Mary.
[3]   The whale is a mammal.
[4]   Whales are mammals.

Appeal to propositional form renders intelligible talk of sentences similar with respect to surface form having distinct logical forms, and of sentences different with respect to surface form, in the same or different languages, having the same logical form. Sentences, on this view, can be said in a derivative sense to have logical form, namely, that of the propositions they express, that is, sentences that express propositions with the same logical form have the same logical form.

An alternative approach, more usual today, is to identify the logical form of a natural language sentence as the form of a sentence in a specially regimented (ideal), perhaps formal or semi-formal, language which is said to translate it (or, in the case of an ambiguous sentence, the logical forms it can have are associated with the sentences which translate the various readings of it).[214] For example, the logical form of a sentence with a definite description, such as [5], is sometimes said to be "given" by a sentence in regimented English such as [6], or [7],

> [5] The man in the iron mask died unknown.
> [6] $(\exists x)(y)((y$ is a man in the iron mask $\leftrightarrow y = x)$ and x died unknown).
> [7] [The $x\colon x$ is a man in the iron mask]$(x$ died unknown).[215]

A regimented language in which logical forms are "given" must contain no ambiguities and syntactically encode all differences in the logical or semantic roles of terms. A common view is to identify the logical form of the natural language sentence as the form determined by the pattern of logical constants in its regimented translation. Natural language sentences then can be said to share a logical form if they translate into the same sentence in the regimented language of choice, and to have different logical forms if they translate into different sentences. (Cf. Frege in the *Begriffsschrift*, "In my formalized language there is nothing that corresponds [to changes in word ordering that do not affect the inferential relations a sentence enters into]; only that part of judgments which affects the *possible inferences* is taken into consideration" (Black and Geach 1960: 3).)

Neither the approach we are attributing to Russell, nor the one we are attributing to Frege is satisfactory. On the one hand, any grasp we have on talk of the structure of propositions derives from our grasp on sentence structure in a regimented language which aims to express more clearly than ordinary language the structure of the proposition. Talk of propositions here is merely a reification of the similarities and differences among sentences which we wish to capture, but which are not captured by the explicit pattern of word units or structure characterized in terms of traditional grammar. On the

---

[214] This can almost be called the official view. It has made its way into the *Cambridge Dictionary of Philosophy* as the canonical account: logical form is "the form of a proposition in a logically perfect language, determined by the grammatical form of the ideal sentence expressing that proposition (or statement, in one use of the latter term)" (Audi 1995: 442). (Note that this *mixes up* the two conceptions distinguished in the text.) The author goes on to characterize sameness of logical form as sameness of grammatical form in an ideal language, but in a way that yields no characterization across languages of sameness of grammatical form, and so no characterization across languages of logical form.

[215] We ignore the fact that 'the man in the iron mask' contains a complex predicate, and likewise tense, to keep complications to a minimum.

other hand, the trouble with identifying the logical form of a natural language sentence with a sentence or structure expressible in a regimented language is that we wish to be able to speak informatively about the logical form of sentences in our regimented language as well. It is no more plausible that it is simply the pattern of expressions in the sentence in the regimented language than in natural language. Appeal to the pattern of logical expressions is of no help. First, we have not said when a term (or structure) counts as logical. Second, the pattern alluded to cannot consist of the actual arrangement of the logical terms in the regimented language, since there are clearly different regimentations possible which would be said to exhibit the same form, but differ in syntax (for example, Polish notation and standard logical notation). To present a sentence in a regimented or ideal language as the logical form of a sentence in a natural language is to present a sentence which is said to be the same in logical form, relative to its language, as the original, relative to its. But it is not to explain what sameness of logical form consists in, nor, therefore, what it is for either sentence to have the logical form it has. For that we need at least to understand the significance of the words and their arrangement in the sentence.

2. Logical Form from the Perspective of Truth-Theoretic Semantics

Our primary concern in the following will be to give a precise characterization of the notion of sameness of logical form, in the sense articulated, between any two sentences relative to any two languages, within the framework of truth-theoretic semantics. Davidson has claimed that the question of the logical form of a natural language sentence only takes on a sharp form in the context of giving a truth theory for a whole language. In revealing the logical form of a sentence *s*, we aim to identify structural elements whose contribution to the meaning and truth conditions of *s* does not depend on the denotations or extensions of primitive expressions of the language; in other words, we aim to identify structural elements of *s* which contribute to determining its truth conditions independently of whatever content is assigned to expressions in *s* by base clauses of the truth theory. A correct account of the logical form of a sentence or construction, then, must be relativized to a theory about the whole language, and the effects of a given proposal must be traced through all the sentences in the language it would affect. The guiding idea is expressed in the following passage.

What should we ask of an adequate account of the logical form of a sentence? Above all, I would say, such an account must lead us to see the semantic character of the sentence—its truth or falsity—as owed to how it is composed, by a finite number of applications of some of a finite number of devices that suffice for the language as a whole, out of elements drawn from a finite stock (the vocabulary) that suffices for the language as a whole. To see a sentence in this light is to see it in the light of a theory for its language, a theory that gives the form of every sentence in that language. A way to provide such a theory is by recursively characterizing a truth predicate, along the lines suggested by Tarski.   (Davidson 2001 (1968): 94)

Here are some other illustrative passages:

Logical form was invented to contrast with something else that is held to be apparent but mere: the form we are led to assign to sentences by superficial analogy or traditional grammar. What meets the eye or ear in language has the charm, complexity, convenience, and deceit of other conventions of the market place, but underlying it is the solid currency of a plainer, duller structure, without wit but also without pretence. This true coin, the deep structure, need never feature directly in the transactions of real life. As long as we know how to redeem our paper we enjoy the benefits of credit. (2001 (1980): 137)

...all I *mean* by saying that 'Jones buttered the toast' has the logical form of an existentially quantified sentence, and that 'buttered' is a three-[place] predicate, is that a theory of truth meeting Tarski's criteria would entail that this sentence is true if and only if there exists...etc. By my lights, we have given the logical form of a sentence when we have given the truth-conditions of the sentence in the context of a theory of truth that applies to the language as a whole. Such a theory must identify some finite stock of truth-relevant elements, and explicitly account for the truth-conditions of each sentence by how these elements feature in it; so to give the logical form of a sentence is to describe it as composed of the elements the theory isolates.   (Ibid. 143)

To give the logical form of a sentence is, then, for me, to describe it in terms that bring it within the scope of a semantic theory that meets clear requirements.   (Ibid. 144)

To know the logical form of a sentence is to know, in the context of a comprehensive theory, the semantic roles of the significant features of the sentence.   (Ibid. 146)

...to determine the logical form of a verbal expression, reduce the number of places of the underlying verbal predicate to the smallest number that will yield, with appropriate singular terms, a complete sentence. But do not think you have a complete sentence until you have uncovered enough structure to validate all inferences you consider due to logical form.   (Davidson 1985: 232–3)

Theories of absolute truth necessarily provide an analysis of structure relevant to truth and to inference. Such theories therefore yield a non-trivial answer to the question what is to count as the logical form of a sentence. A theory of truth does not yield a definition of logical consequence or logical truth, but it will be evident from a theory of truth that certain sentences are true solely on the basis of the properties assigned to the logical constants. The logical constants may be identified as those iterative features of the language that require a recursive clause in the characterization of truth of satisfaction. Logical form, in this account, will of course be relative to the choice of a metalanguage (with its logic) and a theory of truth. (Davidson 2001*a* (1973): 71)

See also the last paragraph of section 1 in Davidson (2001*b* (1973): 133). John Wallace writes in the same vein (1978: 55):

We may regard as logical that form which we read into the sentences of a language in order to see their meanings as projected by a finite number of rules, i.e., that form which a theory satisfying our test finds in sentences.

Consider all structurally truth-like properties, that is, all properties of sentences which have a recursive definition whose recursions are like those in the definition of truth except that basis clauses are allowed to differ ad lib from those in the definition of truth (we also allow the range of variables to vary ad lib, so long as it is non-empty). We find that if we define logical consequence in terms of preservation of all structurally truth-like properties—sentence S is a logical consequence of a sentence U if and only if S has every structurally truth-like property which U has—we get a relationship which serves well as a foundation for the criticism of reasonableness.

This suggestion for how to identify logical form is of considerable historical importance. Davidson's suggestion was originally made in "Theories of Meaning and Learnable Languages," at a time when no one had any criterion for the correct logical form of a sentence, and has revolutionized our understanding of logical form.

It remains to make precise a notion of sameness of logical form in light of this conception. In the following, we go beyond Davidson's own remarks, and in one respect depart from his conception. We will come back to this point below. We first discuss the notion of logical form as it applies to parts of sentences. Then we characterize sameness of logical form in terms of sameness of structure revealed by canonical proofs of *T*-sentences in interpretive truth theories, relying on a characterization of sameness of form of primitive expressions. Later we extend the characterization to *F*-sentences in a generalized fulfillment theory.

The conception of form we need to invoke applies not just to sentences, but also to significant subsentential expressions, complex and primitive. In this way, a notion of logical form associated with semantic form can be extended to include subsentential expressions, and we may talk of the logical form of a lexical item. The logical form of a sentence will be determined by the logical forms of its lexical items and how their combination contributes to determining its interpretive truth conditions. The logical form of a lexical item will be that semantic feature which it shares (at least potentially) with other lexical items, and which determines how it interacts with other vocabulary items, likewise characterized in terms of features shared with other expressions. For example, one-place predicates will interact systematically differently with quantifiers than will two-place predicates. This reveals itself in the base axioms of the truth theory, since all the axioms for one-place predicates will share a common form, and all the axioms for two-place predicates will share a different common form. The semantic type of a primitive term is given by the semantic type of the axiom it receives in the truth theory: its logical form is determined by its semantic type, that is, sameness and difference of logical form for primitive terms is sameness and difference of semantic type.

There will, of course, be a variety of different levels of classification on the basis of semantic features that expressions share in common. Context-sensitive elements can be classified together on the basis of their contributions to interpretive truth conditions being relativized to contextual parameters (speaker and time, at least). Among context-sensitive elements, we may press a further semantic division based on whether contextual parameters alone determine the contribution of the element to the interpretive truth conditions of an utterance of a sentence, or whether additional information is required, such as knowledge of a speaker's demonstrative intentions.

In general, features of the axioms for primitive expressions in the language which capture the way the expression contributes to the truth conditions of sentences can be used to classify them by semantic type. The semantic theory for the language will contain all the information traditionally sought under the heading of logical form, but much more as well. In that sense this conception of logical form is a generalization as well as a development of one strand in the traditional conception.

We said that the logical form of a sentence s is determined by the logical forms of the lexical items s contains, and how these combine to determine the interpretive truth conditions of s. This needs to be made more precise. When a compositional meaning theory for a language L is cast as a formal theory, it must include enough logic to prove from its axioms every T-sentence.[216] As

---

[216] This may involve a simplification, which should not affect the current discussion. In Ch. 6, §4, we considered one approach to quotation that gives the following reference axiom for quotation names: for all expressions ϕ, the referent of $\ulcorner `\phi' \urcorner = \phi$. Since the quantifier ranges over all expressions, including those not a part of English, if there are an infinite number of primitive symbols, there can be no finitely specifiable English syntax. This would make it impossible to prove from the axioms of the theory every T-sentence, because it would not be possible to recursively specify the symbols of the language. As we noted, one of us (Lepore), thinks this

we have said, its logic may be so circumscribed that it enables one to prove all *and only T*-sentences, or it may be more powerful. Intuitively, the contribution that elements of a sentence *s* make to its interpretive truth conditions (or the contribution of the elements of *s* to the truth conditions of an utterance of *s*) will be revealed by a proof of its *T*-sentence which draws only upon the content of axioms, that is, what we have called a *canonical* proof of the *T*-sentence. Clearly, a canonical proof of a *T*-sentence for an object language sentence *s* shows what the semantic structure of *s* is, for it shows how the semantic categories to which constituent terms of *s* belong, determined by the type of axiom provided for each, contribute to determining interpretive truth conditions for *s*. We can say that a canonical proof of a *T*-sentence for *s* reveals its logical form.

We cannot, however, say that its logical form is its canonical proof. This would be a mistake on the order of identifying its logical form with a sentence in an ideal language. A canonical proof is relative to a metalanguage and its accompanying logic, while the notion of logical form is not. The canonical proof, together with our understanding of the metalanguage, reveals the logical form, that is, the semantic form. The logical form of a sentence *s* is determined by what semantic category each primitive item in *s* belongs to, and how these combine to determine the truth conditions and meaning of *s*. The logical form of the sentence *s* for which the proof is given is a property of *s*, which is revealed by the structure of the proof and by the axioms for the primitives in *s*. This property is determined once we can characterize when two sentences, in the same or different languages, share logical form. That characterization should not depend on any particular formal theory with respect to which a canonical proof procedure is formulated. Intuitively, we want to say that two sentences share logical form when the same canonical proof *can* be given for them, adjusting for differences due to differences in the object language, and abstracting from differences between the axioms employed not based on the semantic category a term belongs to.

With this intuitive characterization as a guide, we offer a more precise characterization. First, we define the notion of *corresponding proofs* as in [8].

might be a decisive reason for rejecting this rule for quotation. The other (Ludwig) thinks that for the purposes of a compositional semantic theory that aims to exhibit how we could understand an infinity of sentences, all we need to require is that for any given sentence of the language, we be able to understand it on the basis of a finite number of rules and axioms. This is compatible with the syntax of the language not being recursively enumerable. For the rule suggested for quotation above suffices for someone who understands it to interpret the contribution of a quotation name to any sentence he encounters, provided he recognizes what token expression appears between the quotation marks in a "quotation name."

[8]   A proof P_1 of a T-sentence for s_1 in T_1 *corresponds* to a proof P_2 for a T-sentence for s_2 in T_2 iff$_{df}$

(*a*) P_1 and P_2 are sentence sequences identical in length;

(*b*) at each stage of each proof identical rules are used;

(*c*) the base axioms employed at each stage are of the same semantic type, and the recursive axioms employed at each stage interpret identically object language structures for which they specify satisfaction conditions (with respect to contributions to truth conditions).

Using [8], we define *sameness of logical form* as a four-place relation among sentences and languages, as in [9].

[9]   For any sentences s_1, s_2, languages L_1, L_2, s_1 in L_1 has the same logical form as s_2 in L_2 iff$_{df}$ there is an interpretive truth theory T_1 for L_1 and an interpretive truth theory T_2 for L_2 such that

(*a*) T_1 and T_2 share the same logic,

(*b*) there is a canonical proof P_1 of the T-sentence for s_1 in T_1,

(*c*) there is a canonical proof P_2 of the T-sentence for s_2 in T_2, such that:

(*d*) P_1 *corresponds* to P_2.[217]

[8] fixes the contributions of the recursive elements and the way in which they combine with non-recursive elements. Note that we have required sameness of interpretation up to contribution to truth conditions in [8](*c*). This qualification aims to exclude as irrelevant differences in meaning that make no difference to the way in which a recursive term determines how expressions it combines with contribute to fixing the conditions under which the sentence is true. For example, 'and' and 'but' arguably differ in meaning, but this difference is

---

[217] The requirement that the truth theory characterize a truth predicate for the language and that its axioms be interpretive are powerful constraints in this characterization of logical form. Thus, e.g. a truth theory which does not give to a semantically recursive structure a recursive axiom will not count as interpretive, and a truth theory that gives to a non-recursive structure a recursive axiom, or gives to a recursive structure a recursive axiom that invokes recursive devices which do not interpret the object language device, will not count as interpretive. We owe to Peter Ludlow the observation that the truth theory offered in Larson and Segal (1995) fails to meet both of these requirements. In particular, Larson and Segal assign to every expression an entity, which they call a semantic value, and run their recursion on semantic values, giving sentential connectives like 'and' and 'or' base clauses. A detailed comparison would be out of place here, but the reader may find it instructive to compare their approach with ours. As we have seen in Ch. 1, the idea that every meaningful expression of the language ought to be assigned some entity is fundamentally at odds with the spirit in which Davidson originally made his proposal to use a truth theory as the core of a compositional meaning theory.

irrelevant to how each determines the contribution of the sentences it conjoins to the truth of the whole sentence.

A few remarks are in order on the requirement in [8](*c*) that recursive axioms employed at each stage *interpret identically* object language *structures* for which they specify satisfaction conditions. First, we say 'structure' here because in the general case, as we note in §4, a recursive axiom applies to a pattern of expressions of various types, which may include, but need not include, a term which helps to identify the pattern. Thus, for example, the recursive axiom that would be invoked for 'Jack went up the hill and Jill went up the hill' would apply to the pattern: sentence+'and'+sentence. Here part of the pattern is determined by the conjunction 'and'. However, in 'Brutus is an honorable man', which is intuitively equivalent to 'Brutus is honorable and Brutus is a man', the pattern to which an axiom would apply is: noun phrase+'is a'+adjective+noun. Second, in saying that axioms appealed to at each stage must *interpret identically* object language structures to which they are applied, we have in mind that, on the right-hand side of the axioms, the metalanguage sentences that give satisfaction conditions should employ sentences alike in semantic structure, and use terms in those structures alike in meaning, excepting the metalinguistic terms used to pick out object language expressions. Thus, for example, we would count [10] and [11] (cf. §3) as interpreting the object language structures for which they give satisfaction conditions identically.

[10] For any sentences ϕ, ψ, $\ulcorner \phi$ and $\psi \urcorner$ is true iff ϕ is true and ψ is true.

[11] For any noun N, adjective A, name α, $\ulcorner \alpha$ is an $AN \urcorner$ is true iff $\ulcorner \alpha$ is an $A \urcorner$ is true and $\ulcorner \alpha$ is an $N \urcorner$ is true.[218]

We do not count axioms as interpreting identically object language structures if the metalanguage sentences used to give satisfaction conditions use merely logically equivalent sentences. Thus, for example, we would not count [12] and [13]

---

[218] One worry that can be raised here attaches to the fact that in [10] we have two universal quantifiers, while in [11] we have three. Thus, it appears that in any proofs of *T*-sentences, universal quantifier instantiation will have to be used twice for the first, and three times for the second. However, since the requirement is only that there be canonical proofs of both *T*-sentences the same in length using metalanguages with the same logic, [8](*a*), we can help ourselves to a logic which has a rule that allows one to instantiate any string of universal quantifiers in one step; adding this rule to a sound logic obviously will not make it unsound. We are thankful to Jim Edwards for discussion on this point.

[12] For any sentences ϕ, ψ, $\ulcorner$if ϕ then $\psi\urcorner$ is true iff if ϕ is true, then ψ is true.

[13] For any sentences ϕ, ψ, $\ulcorner$if ϕ then $\psi\urcorner$ is true iff ϕ is not true or ψ is true.

as interpreting object language sentences identically. The metalanguage sentence used to give truth conditions in [13] contains more semantic structure than that in [12].

The remaining free parameter is sameness of semantic type between base axioms in [8](*c*). There may be room here for different classifications, but in general it looks as if we will wish to classify axioms together on the basis of features neutral with respect to the extensions of predicates, though not with respect to the structure of the extensions (that is, we will treat the number of argument places as relevant for the purposes of classification). (This captures one feature of the idea that logical form is a topic neutral feature of a sentence.) Reference axioms can be divided into those for terms that are context-sensitive and those for terms that are not. For reference axioms for terms which are context-sensitive will be counted as of the same semantic type provided that they give the same rule for determining the referent relative to contextual parameters. Since we are quantifying over truth theories, we can impose a fairly strict requirement, namely, that two rules are the same provided that from one, $R(\alpha, \beta, \ldots)$, where 'α', 'β', ..., stand in for terms referring to object language expressions, the other, $R(\alpha', \beta', \ldots)$, can be obtained by replacing 'α', 'β', ..., with 'α'', 'β'', ...[219] Axioms for referring terms that are not context-sensitive can be divided into those whose referents are given directly, and those whose referents are given by a description. All those of the first class will be of the same semantic type. Likewise, all those of the second class will be of the same semantic type. In general, we wish to identify semantic categories with those such that *that* a new base term falls into the category determines how it fits into the semantic pattern of sentences in the language independently of its extension or referent. (Note that we are not supposing here that any terms, except predicates and singular terms, have extensions or referents.)

We said above that this characterization of sameness of logical form departs from Davidson's own. The departure we think is an improvement, and fully in the spirit of Davidson's proposal. In response to comments on "The Logical

---

[219] We are indebted here to some questions from Ivana Simić which helped us to clarify the notion of sameness of semantic type for reference axioms.

Form of Action Sentences," Davidson gives the characterization of logical form we began with above, but also characterizes it as a notion that is relative to a background deductive theory.

... to give the logical form of a sentence is to give its logical location in the totality of sentences, to describe it in a way that explicitly determines what sentences it entails and what sentences it is entailed by. The location must be given relative to a specific deductive theory; so logical form itself is relative to a theory. The relativ[ity] does not stop here, either, since even given a theory of deduction there may be more than one total scheme for interpreting the sentences we are interested in and that preserves the pattern of entailments. The logical form of a particular sentence is, then, relative both to a theory of deduction and to some prior determinations as to how to render sentences in the language of the theory.

Seen in this light, to call the paraphrase of a sentence into some standard first-order quantificational form *the* logical form of the sentence seems arbitrary indeed. Quantification theory has its celebrated merits, to be sure: it is powerful, simple, consistent, and complete in its way. Not least, there are more or less standard techniques for paraphrasing many sentences of natural languages into quantificational languages, which helps excuse not making the relativity to a theory explicit. Still, the relativity remains.

Since there is no eliminating the relativity of logical form to a background theory, the only way to justify particular claims about logical form is by showing that they fit sentences into a *good* theory, at least a theory better than known alternatives. In calling quantificational form logical form I was assuming, like many others before me, that quantification theory is a good theory.   (2001 (1980): 140)

There are two sorts of relativity Davidson mentions here. One is relativity to a background deductive theory. The other is relativity to an interpretation theory. The latter is connected with the thesis of the indeterminacy of interpretation, which we put aside here (see Lepore and Ludwig 2005: chs. 15 and 21). Our present concern is the claim that logical form is relative to a background deductive theory.

About this passage we should note first that Davidson is here emphasizing the role that logical form plays in helping us to systematize inferences valid on the basis of semantic form. An account of logical form of sentences in a language is not in the first instance an account of the deductive relations they enter into on account of semantic form, though it fixes what determines this. When Davidson requires that an account of the logical form of a sentence describe the sentence in a way that explicitly determines what sentences it entails and what sentences entail it, he is not requiring that one give a list of the sentences. This would be an impossible task, and uninformative. Rather,

297

what is intended is that one should make clear enough the semantic structure of the sentence to be able to determine what other sentences entail it and are entailed by it, given a similarly clear understanding of their semantic structure.

It is here that the background deductive theory comes in. For Davidson is thinking that the semantic structure relevant to entailment will be made clear by how the truth theory assigns satisfaction conditions to recursive structures, in particular, and that this will involve what metalanguage recursive structures, typically thought of as logical, will be used to give satisfaction conditions for object language recursive structures. We will illuminate the object language structures through assignments of satisfaction conditions using metalanguage devices whose semantics are already clear to us, and we illuminate entailment relations the object language sentences stand in, in particular, by having a well-worked out deductive theory for the metalanguage.

However, while it is true that, for any given theory, in explicating entailments between sentences based on compositional structure, we will employ a deductive theory specific to the metalanguage, this does not mean that the notion of logical form itself must be understood as relative to a background deductive theory. It no more follows from our using a specific deductive theory in explicating deductive relations among object language sentences that logical form is relative to that theory, than it follows from our having to use a specific language to talk about anything that what we talk about is relative to the language. The characterization of sameness of logical form can be given without treating sameness of logical form as relative to the deductive theory for any particular truth theory. We circumvent this in our formulation by appeal to existential quantification over canonical proofs in truth theories, and the notion of corresponding proofs. This allows us to say when two sentences in any two languages are the same in logical form without invoking background deductive theories for particular truth theories for the languages.

Identifying logical form in terms of how complex expressions are built up out of primitive recursive elements in the language enables us to make precise the distinction between ascribing a logical form to a complex expression and conceptually analyzing semantically primitive elements of a language. A semantically primitive expression in a language will of course not admit of decomposition on the basis of logical form, though it may not be conceptually simple in at least this sense: our understanding of its application conditions may rest on concepts which are either as a matter of fact, or necessarily, antecedently or independently acquired, or which we must at least have as part of a family of concepts acquired together or not at all. Nonetheless, these projects are not completely independent, since the conceptual analysis of a term will involve in part understanding its combinatorial role in sentences in which it occurs. Thus, for example, part of what is wanted in any analysis of the concept of belief is an account which will reveal whether to believe something is to be related to something (for example, a proposition), as the surface syntax for belief sentences might suggest, and whether, if so, belief sentences have additional unarticulated elements. For example, we will want to know whether we should treat belief sentences as implicitly quantifying over "modes of presentation," or as having an implicitly indexical component which, relative to a context, picks out a particular mode of presentation under which a proposition is entertained by the believer. These sorts of issues should be settled by an account of logical form, articulated in terms of a truth theory. But they are also important issues in the analysis of the concept of belief. The connection between the two is this: in general, an account of the logical role of an expression will be a part of the analysis of the concept expressed by it, but not a complete account. In some cases, for example, monadic predicates, the logical role is so obvious that, in analysis, attention is focused exclusively on relating the concept expressed by the predicate to other concepts. But in some cases, part of what is in dispute in a discussion of the analysis of the concept expressed by a term is the term's contribution to the logical form of sentences in which it occurs.

3. Relation to Canonical Representations

The above account does not reify logical form. The logical form of a sentence is not another sentence, a structure, or indeed anything else. Talk of logical form is talk of a complex feature of a sentence *s* of a language *L*, which is determined by what all canonical proofs of *T*-sentences for *s* in various interpretive truth theories for *L* share. The relation of sameness of logical form is conceptually basic. The expression '*x* is the logical form of *y*' should be retired from serious discussion. The basic expression is '*x* in *L* is the same in logical form as *y* in *L'*', where '... in ... is the same in logical form as ... in ...' is explicated as a unit as above. One can derivatively make sense of '*x* in *L* gives the logical form of *y* in *L'*'. The practice of "giving the logical form" of a sentence by exhibiting its paraphrase in a regimented language can be seen as a matter of replacing a sentence about whose semantic structure we are unclear with one whose semantic structure is clearer because it is formulated in a language for which the rules attaching to its various constituents and its structure have been clearly laid out. Thus, we can say that the relation

299

expressed by 'x in L gives the logical form of y in L'' is true of a 4-tuple $<x, L, y, L'>$ just in case x in L is the same in logical form as y in L', and x's syntax understood relative to L makes perspicuous the semantic structure of y in L'. A paraphrase of a natural language sentence in a regimented language may capture the semantic structure of the original more or less well, and it may be that the language does not contain the resources needed to yield a sentence the same in logical form as the original. That this occurs when a formal language is chosen as the translation target accounts for our intuition that sometimes there is indeterminacy about what the logical form of a natural language sentence is, when we are forced to try to represent its semantic form in the absence of a worked out semantic theory for the language.

Since the best understood and explored formal systems are first order systems, it is not uncommon to use first order sentences to exhibit the logical forms of natural language sentences. The relation of this practice to giving the logical form of such sentences is that noted above. There is, however, a danger in restricting oneself to first order classical logic. To assume that the logical form of natural language sentences can be given in the above sense by exhibiting a paraphrase whose logical form is familiar from classical first order logic is to assume that classical first order logic includes among its logical constants analogs of every semantically recursive element in natural language. There is no reason to believe this is so, especially since classical logic was not intended to provide the framework for an interpretive truth theory for natural languages. Thus, it would be inappropriate to insist that the logical form of natural language sentences can always be given by paraphrase in classical first order logic. As we have already seen in Chapter 2, many constructions in natural languages cannot be paraphrased into classical first order logic with unrestricted quantifiers; but this is no barrier to an account of their logical forms, provided that we can specify recursive axioms that, together with base axioms, generate T-sentences for the range of sentences in which apparently problematic constructions occur.

Some regimentation of ordinary languages for the purposes of applying a truth theory is already required because of lexical and syntactical ambiguity. Ambiguous natural language sentences lack unique logical forms. In these cases, we must disambiguate the language before we apply a truth theory to it. This makes regimentation, at least whatever is required to remove ambiguity, necessary for a useful discussion of logical form for natural languages. Additional regimentation, perhaps motivated by considerations about syntactic decomposition, may recommend applying additional transformations before applying a truth theory, but these should not be necessary, as long as some description of the sentence is possible which accommodates all the features required for applying axioms for primitive expressions to generate a *T*-sentence for it. In an account of the logical form of a sentence, of course, we would want to keep track of syntactic transformations, but, in a sense, its semantic structure would be revealed by a canonical proof of the *T*-sentence for its spruced up cousin, plus the fact that it means the same, or, on one of its interpretations, means the same.

4. Relation to Logical Constants

We wish now to consider how the notion of a logical constant, or a slight generalization of this notion, looks in light of this conception of logical form as semantic form. In the next section, we will turn to the notions of logical consequence, truth, and equivalence, and raise the question whether a distinct or narrower notion of structural consequence can be made out.

Logical constants are a subset of primitive terms of the language which are thought of as especially useful for identifying classes of argument form. The notion of a logical constant, however, conceived of as subsuming only terms, is too narrow to do the work needed for regimenting valid natural language arguments. For example, the inference from [14] to [15] is intuitively valid in virtue of its form.

[14]   Brutus is an honorable man.
[15]   Brutus is a man.

There is, however, no logical term in [14]. The term 'honorable' functions semantically to contribute a predicate to the sentence, as is shown by the fact that [14] also implies 'Brutus is honorable' (recall the discussion of Chapter 7). The effect of modifying 'man' with 'honorable' is to add to the truth conditions the requirement that Brutus be honorable, as well as a man. It is not the use of 'honorable' that signals this, but rather that it is an adjective (specifically, a topic neutral adjective) modifying the noun from which the predicate 'is a man' is formed. Thus, we need to identify here the structure,

noun phrase+'is a'+adjective+nominal,

as itself semantically significant to the semantic compositional structure of the sentence. Intuitively, modifying the nominal with an adjective does the same semantic work as adding a conjunct to the sentence—in the case of [12], of adding 'and Brutus is honorable'. Hence, our axiom [11] above. 'Brutus is an honorable man' and 'Brutus is a man and Brutus is honorable' are different

301

ways of "encoding" the same semantic information. To recognize this is to recognize that we need to talk not just about logical terms, but about logical structures. A logical structure will in general be characterized as a pattern of types of terms in a grammatical expression. What are traditionally thought of as logical constants may or may not appear in the pattern of terms. When they do, they count as part of the pattern that constitutes the logical structure. Indeed, the idea that an argument is valid in virtue of the logical terms in it is a mistake. It is rather the patterns which include the constants which make an argument valid. Logical constants are useful because they help form patterns which provide us with information about how to understand the contribution of components of the expressions in which they appear to a sentence's truth conditions. To express this notion of a logical structure, we will press into service the term 'logical syntax'.[220]

The aim of identifying logical syntax is that of identifying *syntactical* constants in sentences which help to regiment natural language arguments into classes with shared forms that account for validity or invalidity. There will be in the nature of the case a variety of different levels of abstraction at which we can identify forms which help to regiment natural language arguments. We would like to find a way of isolating out for special consideration a class of structures which are salient from the point of view of a semantic theory for the language.

The notion of logical form we have articulated is neutral on the question of what structures to count as logical. Any of the competing criteria one finds in the literature could simply be adjoined to our account of logical form. This points up an important fact about the relation between talk about logical form, if we are correct in holding that our explication tracks that use of the term that goes back to the interests expressed by Russell in the quotation in §1 of this chapter, and talk about logical syntax and the related notions of logical consequence and truth. The identification of *logical* syntax is not itself either central to or sufficient for understanding what talk of logical form comes to. Rather, it has been thought to be central because many of the kinds of terms identified as logical constants have been particularly important for understanding the semantic structure of sentences in which they appear. But identifying a particular class of terms as logical, for the purposes of identifying a class of logically valid sentences or argument forms, is not necessary to

---

[220] It should be clear that here syntax is not thought of as a purely orthographical feature of an expression, but includes some information about the semantic category of terms or places in a sentence structure.

understand the semantic structure of such sentences. The interpretive truth theory contains all the information necessary, whether or not we go on to select out a particular class of terms (or structures) for attention for more specialized interests. And, of course, the notion of the semantic structure of a sentence applies to sentences in which no logical constants, as traditionally conceived, appear.

Despite this independence, there are differences among primitive terms (and primitive terms and structures which carry important semantic information) which are particularly salient from the standpoint of an interpretive truth theory, namely, that between terms which can receive base clauses and *terms or structures which must be treated recursively*. It is natural to seize on this difference and to urge, as Davidson has, that "the logical constants may be identified as those iterative features of the language that require a recursive clause in the characterization of truth or satisfaction" (2001*a* (1973): 71).[221] Of course, we must generalize this a bit in the light of our discussion above. We will suggest that the recursive syntactical structures of the language be treated as its logical syntax. The recursive syntax of sentences gives them structure beyond that already expressed in the number of argument places in primitive predicates. It is natural to think of arguments made valid in virtue of the presence of recursive syntax in the premises and conclusion as valid in virtue of their *structure*. This gives one clear sense to the idea that in identifying logical *terms* we identify those terms that we do not replace with schematic letters in identifying the structures or forms of sentences relevant to determining what

---

[221] See "Truth and Meaning" (2001*c* (1967): 33), "In Defence of Convention T" (2001*a* (1973): 71), "On Saying That" (2001 (1968): 94).

(Interestingly, Dummett gives a similar, if somewhat less precise, criterion (1973: 22), and includes in a footnote an anticipation of the generality conception we discuss below in relation to the identity sign, which is otherwise excluded.) The requirement that a term must receive a recursive clause to be treated as a logical constant is important in this characterization, and rules out what would otherwise be counterexamples. Adjective modifiers can be given a recursive clause (but *only if* we ignore the use of connectives in adjectives, and focus only on extensional adjectives that do not interact with other adjectives—as we have noted in Ch. 7), as in the following example. 'For all nouns ϕ, and names α, $\ulcorner\alpha$ is a red $\phi\urcorner$ is true(S, t, u) iff $\ulcorner\alpha$ is a $\phi\urcorner$ is true(S, t, u) and Ref$(S, t, u)(\alpha)$ is red.' However, clearly, this is not necessary. The only feature of such constructions which must be treated recursively is the concatenation of an adjective with a noun. The contribution of the adjective can, and in fact should, be cashed out in terms of the axiom for the corresponding predicate, as in: 'For all nouns ϕ, and names α, $\ulcorner\alpha$ is a red $\phi\urcorner$ is true(S, t, u) iff $\ulcorner\alpha$ is a $\phi\urcorner$ is true(S, t, u) and $\ulcorner\alpha$ is red$\urcorner$ is true(S, t, u).' We can note in addition that the approach represented by the first of these clauses would require an axiom for each adjective, in addition to axioms for their appearances in predicates formed using the copula, though it seems clear that our understanding of the use of adjectives is of a piece with our understanding of the predicates formed from them.

other sentences, similarly identified in terms of their structures, they bear deductive relations to. The proposal rounds up many of the usual suspects, the so-called truth-functional connectives, and the quantifiers, as well as other iterative syntactical patterns that do similar work. As we have seen, the work of truth-functional connectives is not always achieved lexically, as in 'Brutus is an honorable man'. Likewise, quantification need not be signaled by an explicit quantifier word, as in 'Whales are mammals'. Verb inflection for tense, too, as we have argued, is best thought of as a quantificational device (see Chapters 8–10).

We have indicated that both terms and structures may be treated recursively. One cannot identify a recursive term or structure by a syntactic test of iterability. For example, we may concatenate 'Time is short and' with any sentence, and concatenate it with the result, and so on indefinitely. This does not mean that 'Time is short and' is a logical constant or a recursive structure. For what we need a recursive clause for is the concatenation of a sentence with 'and' with another sentence. The rule attaches to that structure, and not to particular instances of it. Similarly, though 'honorable' may be added any number of times before 'man' in 'Brutus is an honorable man', we do not suppose 'honorable' is a logical constant or itself receives a recursive clause. Again, the rule attaches to the pattern exemplified by the sentence, not to the particular terms instantiating the pattern.

These terms and structures, by and large, are also intuitively topic neutral, as we would expect, since, with few exceptions, they determine solely how the primitive predicates of the language contribute to the truth conditions of complex sentences. Exceptions in natural languages are primitive restricted quantifiers, such as 'someone' and 'anytime'. Artificial examples may be constructed as well. It seems appropriate to divide recursive terms into the logical and what we can call the purely logical. We restrict the term 'purely logical' to those recursive terms and structures whose satisfaction clauses do not (*a*) introduce terms requiring appeal to base clauses in proving *T*-sentences for the sentences containing them, other than those required for the terms to which they are applied, or (*b*) introduce non-logical metalanguage terms not introduced by base clauses for the terms to which the term in question is applied.[222] The intuitive requirement expressed by this is just that the recursive

---

[222] Modal operators *may* be counterexamples as well if they are to receive recursive clauses, for their contributions to determining the truth conditions of sentences in which they appear are not intuitively independent of features of objects picked out by the predicates in sentences to which they apply. The exclusion criterion just given would not exclude the modal operators, so they

term or structure is to be counted as purely logical only if it does not contribute any predicative material to the truth conditions.

This conception of logical syntax does leave out, however, terms which are often included, such as the identity sign. On this conception, the identity sign is treated simply as having the logical form of a two-place relational predicate and, consequently, is not singled out for any special attention. Likewise, the second order relation 'is an element of', and such relational terms as 'is a subset of', 'is the union of', will not be counted as logical on this conception; and so on.[223] These sorts of terms would be counted on a conception originally introduced independently by Tarski (1986) and Lindstrom (1966), and motivated by the idea that the "logical notions" or terms were those of greatest generality (see Sher (1996) also for a recent exposition of this line, though with some differences from the way we develop it below). This is clearly connected with the idea which we have already invoked that logical syntax is topic neutral. But it is spelled out in a way that yields different results.

The basic idea is that terms express more general notions the more stable their extensions under transformations of the universe, and those terms that express the most general notions will be those whose extensions are invariant under all permutations of the universe, that is, under all one–one mappings of the universe of discourse onto itself. For this to be applicable to all terms, of course, all terms must have extensions, and truth conditions of sentences must be given in terms of their extensions. Thus, this approach is most natural on a Fregean conception of semantics, on which sentential connectives like 'and' and 'or' are thought of as functions, and the quantifiers as second order functions (functions taking first order functions as arguments). It is not difficult to see what the upshot of this approach will be. Those terms which are associated with sets that are invariant under all permutations of the universe will be counted as logical terms.[224] Thus, for example, proper names will not be counted as logical terms because their referents (which we will treat as

---

would have to be excluded on independent grounds. Of course, if they are (implausibly) treated as quantifiers over possible worlds, as lexically primitive restricted quantifiers, the exclusion rule given in the text would exclude the modal operators as well. If the suggestion made in Ch. 11 is correct, and modal operators can be treated as essentially predicates of sentences, then they will not be treated as logical terms, since on that suggestion, they will receive base clauses in the theory.

[223] See the appendix of this chapter for a discussion of some alternative proposals.

[224] We will be assuming that there are in fact an infinite number of objects, e.g. all the real numbers, as well as spatio-temporal objects, so that concerns about the size of the universe need not affect this criterion.

their extension) will not always be mapped onto themselves. Likewise, most *n*-place first order relational terms will not be treated as logical terms. Some will, however. For example, those one-place predicates whose extensions are the universal set and the empty set, 'exists' or 'is an object' and 'is nonexistent', and those two-place predicates whose extensions are the set of ordered pairs consisting of an object and itself, and the set of ordered pairs of objects and some distinct object, that is, 'is identical with' and 'is nonidentical with'. There will be similar terms for any number of argument places. Likewise, there will be second order relations (which take extensions of first order relations as arguments) that will count as logical. If we think of the universal quantifier as having as its extension the set of the universal set, and the existential quantifier as having in its extension all subsets of the universal set except the empty set, these will count also as logical terms. Then, for example, 'Everything is *F*' will be true just in case ext('*F*') ∈ ext('everything'). What we have called restricted quantifiers may be called binary quantifiers, and can be treated as appropriate sets of ordered pairs of sets. For example, 'All' can be assigned as extension the set of all ordered pairs of sets such that the first is a subset of the second. 'All *A* are *B*' will be true provided that <ext('*A*'), ext('*B*')> ∈ ext('All'). The result of systematically extending this idea is that all the so-called cardinality quantifiers will count as logical terms, as well as the standard set-theoretic relations. With some contortions, the truth-functional connectives can be treated as logical terms on this approach as well.[225] The approach could be extended straightforwardly to our broader notion of logical syntax.

We do not think the question which of these conceptions of logical syntax (or any of the others in the literature) is the correct one has an answer. Each of them is a projection from our intuitive starting point in thinking about argument form and what sorts of constant structures we can identify to help us classify together arguments which are valid (or invalid) in virtue of those structures. Against the invariance conception, it might be said that it counts some terms as logical which do not seem very helpful in this regard, such as, for example, 'is an object' and 'is nonexistent', and 'is nonidentical with'.

---

[225] We need to assign the logical constants extensions that will be invariant under all permutations of the universe. Frege treated them as functions from truth values to truth values. If we associate The True with the universal set and The False with the empty set, then the invariance criterion will classify all the usual truth-functional connectives as logical terms. Rather than force fit truth-functional connectives to this criterion, Sher (1996) just gives a separate criterion for them. This is to admit, however, that there is not really one notion of generality which applies to all the terms we wish to count as logical.

Likewise, it might be said that if our aim is to identify intuitively topic neutral syntax, the set-theoretic relations should not count as logical terms. Likewise, one may object that to count many terms as logical on this approach, we must resort to a representation of the semantics of expressions which seems both gratuitous and misguided. On the other hand, there is no point denying that classifying terms together as logical in this way may for some purposes be useful. We are inclined to say, then, that there is no substantive, as opposed to terminological, issue here. It may well be that in the place of the term 'logical syntax' what we really need is a number of different terms whose extensions overlap. For the notions which we have been concerned with, 'recursive syntax' would do to identify the relevant notion of logical syntax, as 'semantic form' characterizes the relevant notion of logical form.

5. Logical Consequence and Structural Consequence

Once we have a characterization of logical syntax, we can extend the usual way of defining the notions of logical truth, logical consequence, and logical equivalence. However, we first need to ask whether we should make adjustments to accommodate the fact that natural language sentences are typically not true or false independently of context. Consider the following argument using context-sensitive natural language sentences, with their regimentations represented in the right-hand column, where an explicit argument place in the verb is represented and 't^*', as in Chapter 8, is an indexical that indexes to time of utterance.

I am tired	I am(t^*) tired
I am sitting	I am (t^*) sitting
Someone who is tired is sitting	Someone who is(t^*) tried is(t^*) sitting

For the conclusion to be a logical consequence of the two premises, it must be true on all interpretations of the non-logical terms which make the two premises true. It is clear that, treating the tense inflection as represented in the right-hand column, this conclusion is a logical consequence, so understood, of the premises. However, there is something misleading about this result, because 'I' and the present tense inflection here are treated as if they were referring devices like proper names. But 'I' may not have the same referent on every occasion of use, and two uses of a present tense verb will index to the same time only if they are both used at the same time. Thus, if Sam says 'I am tired' and Bill says 'I am sitting', from what they say it does not follow that someone who is tired is sitting. Similarly in the case of demonstratives. If we employ an unrelativized notion, 'That is round and red' follows from 'That is round' and 'That is red'. But in use those sentences might be used to say things about different objects (at different times). Also, 'That is that', if we treat the 'is' of identity as a logical constant, will be a logical truth if we employ an unrelativized notion, but it does not always express a truth as used. When we define 'logical consequence' for non-context-sensitive languages, we insist that the languages not harbor any ambiguous referring terms. If they did, then the syntactic relation of logical consequence would not track the semantic relation of following from. Context-sensitive terms like 'I' and 'that' present a similar problem. This suggests relativizing logical consequence, truth, and equivalence to contextual parameters which fix the contributions of context-sensitive elements.

The role of relativizing to contextual parameters is to tell us which context-sensitive terms should be reinterpreted in the same way. We do not want to fix their referents along with the interpretation of the logical syntax. For then relative to a context in which 'that' and 'I' corefer, for example, 'If I am tired, then that is tired' would count as a logical truth. (It is not that we could not extend the notion in this way, but that this would not be the closest extension of the notion from context-insensitive to context-sensitive languages, and it is a departure from the idea that logical truth and consequence is a purely formal notion, relative to fixing the interpretation of logical terms.) On the other hand, we want demonstratives appearing in different places to be reinterpreted in the same way if they corefer relative to the contextual parameters, but allow them to be reinterpreted differently if they do not corefer relative to the context parameters. So we do not want to reinterpret all appearances of a given context-referring term alike if they are of a type that can, relative to the same contextual parameters, have different referents. Let $\phi(\delta_1, \delta_2, \ldots \delta_n, \delta'_1, \delta'_2, \ldots \delta'_n, \delta''_1, \delta''_2, \ldots \delta''_n)$ be a sentence with demonstratives $\delta_1, \delta_2, \ldots \delta_n, \delta'_1, \delta'_2, \ldots \delta'_n, \delta''_1, \delta''_2, \ldots \delta''_n$, where the superscripts indicate distinct types of demonstratives (for example, 'this' vs 'that') and the subscripts represent distinct appearances of that type in the sentence. We will call the proxy of a sentence ϕ (proxy(ϕ)) relative to contextual parameters C the sentence obtained from it by replacing each demonstrative in order with a demonstrative of that type with a numerical subscript starting with '0', '1', etc., except that where a subsequent demonstrative relative to the context has the same referent as an earlier demonstrative of that type, it is replaced by a demonstrative of that type with the subscript of the earlier demonstrative with which it corefers.

308

We can now define logical truth, consequence, and equivalence relative to a set of contextual parameters. A sentence ϕ is a logical truth relative to contextual parameters C iff proxy(ϕ) is true under all interpretations of its nonlogical terms. A sentence ϕ is a logical consequence of a set of sentences $\{\psi_1, \psi_2, \ldots, \psi_n\}$ relative to a given set of contextual parameters C iff there is no interpretation of nonlogical terms under which every sentence of $\{\text{proxy}(\psi_1), \text{proxy}(\psi_2), \ldots, \text{proxy}(\psi_n)\}$ is true relative to C, and proxy(ϕ) is false relative to C; sentences ϕ and ψ are logically equivalent relative to contextual parameters C iff each is a logical consequence of the other relative to C. Essentially, this picks out those consequences as logical (relative to some contextual parameters) which are due to the meanings of the syntactical features of the language that are identified as logical.[226]

An important question is whether the perspective of an interpretive truth theory gives us the resources to identify a more restricted notion of structural consequence. Consider the contrast between inferring [14] from [15], repeated here,

[14]   Brutus is an honorable man.
[15]   Brutus is honorable.

and inferring [17] from [16].

[16]   Most men are honorable.
[17]   Some men are honorable.

The inference from [16] to [17] is supported by the meaning of 'most' and 'some', but not, it might be felt, by any structural relation holding between the sentences, that is, it does not hold in virtue of how the parts of the sentences combine to determine their interpretive truth conditions. In contrast, intuitively, the entailment between [14] and [15] is structural. Can this intuitively felt distinction be made precise?

Evans (1976) has suggested a notion of structural consequence to be distinguished from that of logical consequence. However, Evans's proposal would identify structural consequences with a subset of what we are already committed to treating as logical consequences, on the basis of a feature of them which does not seem to us to mark them out as an interestingly distinct

---

[226] We can also identify a notion of pragmatic consequence and necessity. ϕ is a pragmatic consequence of ψ iff ϕ is true in all contexts in which ψ is true; ϕ is pragmatically necessary if true in all contexts. 'I am somewhere' e.g. is pragmatically necessary. But it is best to keep these notions distinct from those of logical consequence and necessity.

class. Evans treats logical consequences as hinging on the presence of logical *terms* in a sentence. Structural consequences hinge not on logical terms, but on patterns in the construction of sentences. Thus, in [14] and [15], we recognize the validity of the argument by recognizing the forms [18] and [19]:

[18]   noun phrase+'is a'+adjective+noun
[19]   noun phrase+'is a'+noun

Understanding the semantic contribution of the adjective in a sentence of the first of these forms is sufficient to know that the corresponding sentence of the second form is true, if the first is. We have already, though, subsumed the sort of structure exhibited in [18] under the heading 'logical'. It counts as logical because it, not the terms which instantiate it, receives a recursive treatment (the terms all get their own base clauses, or terms they are derived from do). Evans does not treat the entailment from [14] to [15] as a logical one. But from our perspective, this appears to be misguided. From the point of view of an interpretive truth theory, the difference between 'Brutus is an honorable man' and 'Brutus is honorable and Brutus is a man' is merely a difference in what syntactic features of a sentence are subserving a certain semantic role. Rather than distinguish a new notion of consequence, as Evans does, it is more reasonable to extend the notion of logicality from terms to structures; indeed, as we have noted, it is not even terms, *per se*, which are logical on the recursive criterion, but the patterns the terms help to form.

If there is a notion of structural consequence to be identified narrower than the notion of logical consequence characterized above, then it must rest on a narrower base than the semantic entailments sanctioned by the logical syntax in a sentence. It will have to rest on seeing some consequences as falling out of the way the truth theory represents a sentence as being decomposed into parts. One difference between the inference from [14] to [15] and that between [16] and [17] is that a proof of a T-sentence for [14] would employ biconditionals from which the T-sentence for [15] could be derived, while that is not so for the inference from [16] to [17]. This suggests the following condition on a sentence ϕ being a structural consequence of a set of sentences $\{\psi_1, \psi_2, \ldots, \psi_n\}$: there is a canonical proof of the T-sentence for ϕ from the set of axioms required for the canonical proofs of the T-sentences for the members of $\{\psi_1, \psi_2, \ldots, \psi_n\}$. This cannot be a sufficient condition, however, because, for example, the axioms sufficient for a canonical proof of the T-sentence for a disjunction will be sufficient for a canonical proof of the T-sentences for both disjuncts. This suggests we impose the additional requirement that ϕ be a logical consequence of $\{\psi_1, \psi_2, \ldots, \psi_n\}$.

On this conception of a structural consequence, a structural consequence is a logical consequence of a (set of) sentence(s) whose *T*-sentence was provable from the same resources required for the proof of the *T*-sentence(s) for the (set of) sentence(s) in question. This will include the inference from [14] to [15], but exclude that from [16] to [17], as desired. In general, unless a sentence actually appears in the structural decomposition of another sentence, it will not be a structural consequence of it, although its appearing in the structural decomposition of another sentence is not a sufficient condition for it to be a structural consequence of it.

It is not altogether clear how useful this conception of structural consequence is. All consequence relations rest ultimately upon the meanings of expressions and the meaning of their arrangements in the sentences so related. This shows up in the notion of structural consequence we have isolated, in its reliance on the notion of logical consequence, independently characterized. The notion of structural consequence identified above requires the materials for proving the *T*-sentence for the structural consequence of a sentence be available in the proof of the *T*-sentence of the original sentence, and that otherwise the meaning of the logical syntax guarantee the validity of the inference. Thus, while 'Mermaids sing' is a structural consequence of 'It is not the case that it is not the case that mermaids sing', the latter is not a structural consequence of the former.

6. Extension to Imperatives and Interrogatives

The points made in the previous sections extend straightforwardly to the generalization of the truth-theoretic framework to a fulfillment-theoretic framework. To extend the notion of logical form so that it includes declarative, imperatives, interrogatives, and mixed mood sentences, we need to generalize [8] and [9]. We proceed to do so by replacing in [8] and [9] the notions peculiar to a truth theory with the more general notions invoked by the fulfillment theory. Thus, [8] becomes [20], letting '*F*-sentence' stand for an interpretive sentence of the form $\ulcorner \phi$ is fulfilled(S, t, u) in L iff $p \urcorner$, and [9] becomes [21].

[20] A proof P_1 of an *F*-sentence for s_1 in F_1 *corresponds* to a proof P_2 for a *F*-sentence for s_2 in F_2 iff$_{\text{df}}$
  (*a*) P_1 and P_2 are sentence sequences identical in length;
  (*b*) at each stage of each proof identical rules are used;
  (*c*) the base axioms employed at each stage are of the same semantic type, and the recursive axioms employed at each

stage interpret identically object language terms for which they specify satisfaction conditions (with respect to contributions to fulfillment conditions).

[21] For sentences s_1, s_2, languages L_1, L_2, s_1 in L_1 has the same logical form as s_2 in L_2 iff there is an interpretive fulfillment theory F_1 for L_1 and an interpretive fulfillment theory F_2 for L_2, such that

    (*a*) F_1 and F_2 share the same logic,

    (*b*) there is a canonical proof P_1 of the F-sentence for s_1 in F_1,

    (*c*) there is a canonical proof P_2 of the F-sentence for s_2 in F_2, such that:

    (*d*) P_1 corresponds to P_2.

Likewise, the notions of logical consequence, truth, etc., can be generalized in a straightforward way to include non-declaratives.

Appendix

An alternative proposal put forward by Peacocke (1976) which also draws on the resources of a Tarski-style truth theory employs an epistemic criterion. Peacocke's proposal is that a term α is a logical term just in case, with respect to a truth theory for a language containing α, from knowledge of (*a*) which sequences (or functions) satisfy formulas $\theta_1, \theta_2, \ldots, \theta_n$ to which α can be applied and (*b*) knowledge of the satisfaction clause for α, one can infer *a priori* which sequences (or functions) satisfy $\alpha(\theta_1, \theta_2, \ldots, \theta_n)$. The main idea behind this proposal is that this identifies those terms knowledge of whose contributions to satisfaction conditions does not require knowledge of the properties of any objects or the relations into which any objects enter. This is a way of trying to cash out the idea that the logical terms are topic neutral. (We can extend the proposal to terms that apply not just to formulas, but to variables and singular terms: α is a logical term just in case, with respect to a truth theory for a language containing α, from knowledge of (*a*) which sequences (or functions) satisfy formulas $\theta_1, \theta_2, \ldots, \theta_n$, and which objects sequences assign to terms $\tau_1, \tau_2, \ldots, \tau_m$, to which α can be applied, and (*b*) the satisfaction clause for α, one can infer *a priori* which sequences (or functions) satisfy $\alpha(\theta_1, \theta_2, \ldots, \theta_n, \tau_1, \tau_2, \ldots, \tau_m)$, or if it is a singular term, what object each sequence (or function) assigns to it.)

What terms get counted as logical constants on this view is sensitive to what knowledge we suppose we have about the sequences (or functions) that satisfy formulas or apply to terms. For example, knowing that sequences

312

σ_1, σ_2 satisfy 'x is F' is not in itself sufficient to know that every sequence satisfies 'x is F', even if these are all the sequences, unless we also know that they are all the sequences, which is an additional bit of knowledge. Likewise, application of the criterion to numerical quantifiers and terms like the identity sign will be dependent on whether we are supposed to know facts about the numbers of sequences that satisfy a formula, and facts about the identity and diversity of objects in sequences.

The same idea may be approached non-epistemically by appeal to entailment relations as follows: α is a logical term just in case, with respect to a truth theory for a language containing α, which sequences (or functions) satisfy formulas $\theta_1, \theta_2, \ldots, \theta_n$, and which objects sequences assign to terms $\tau_1, \tau_2, \ldots, \tau_m$, to which α can be applied, and the proposition expressed by the satisfaction clause for α entail which sequences (or functions) satisfy $\alpha(\theta_1, \theta_2, \ldots, \theta_n, \tau_1, \tau_2, \ldots, \tau_m)$, or if it is a singular term, what object each sequence (or function) assigns to it. Here too what terms are counted as logical will depend on what propositions about the sequences (or functions) that satisfy a formula we are including. To count the universal quantifier as a logical constant, we have to include propositions about all 'x'-variants of a given function or sequence.

Both of these ways of spelling out the idea suffer from a difficulty pointed out by (McCarthy 1981: §II). Indeed, it is an obvious difficulty, namely, that there are *a priori* inferences (entailments) which are not obviously grounded in the meanings of what have been traditionally taken to be the logical constants. For a simple way to see the difficulty, consider an arbitrary formula, Ω, and a operator on it, $\sum$, which has satisfaction conditions as given in,

For any function f, f satisfies $\sum {}^\frown \Omega$ iff f satisfies Ω or A,

where 'A' is replaced by any *a priori* truth, for example, '$1 < 2$'. Peacock's criterion will count $\sum$ as a logical constant, though intuitively it is not. Similarly, as McCarthy points out, if *de re* knowledge of which objects sequences or functions assign to terms includes whether they are numbers, many function signs denoting functions that take numbers as arguments, such as 'the successor of ___', or '...+___' will be treated as logical constants, though intuitively these are not topic neutral terms. Peacocke intends to exclude from consideration number-theoretic terms, but this seems *ad hoc*, and in any case, other *a priori* truths will do as well. An interesting example McCarthy mentions is the concatenation sign, '... ${}^\frown$ ___'. Knowledge of what objects sequences assign to terms which can appear in the argument places for this functor and knowledge of the satisfaction clause for it suffice for

313

knowledge of which objects sequences assign to the expression formed from those terms and the concatenation sign. Few will wish to treat '⌢' as a logical term, however. The feature that Peacocke identifies seems at best a necessary condition on a term's being a logical term, but not a sufficient one.

McCarthy's own suggestion is a version of the invariance approach which we discuss in §4. McCarthy's proposal identifies a narrower class of terms than does the invariance approach we consider above, and, in particular, fails to count cardinality quantifiers as logical terms. We will not discuss it further here. But it helps to illustrate the variety of notions of logical constants which one can identify, and to suggest, as we have urged, that there is a family of related notions, to a greater or lesser extent topic neutral, which can be classified on the basis of a number of overlapping features, and that there is little point to insisting that one is the objectively correct way of extending the practice of using the term 'logical constant' beyond the territory in which it is currently well-grounded.

14

Truth and Correspondence

> Correspondence theories rest on what appears to be an ineluctable if simple idea, but they have not done well under examination.
>
> (Davidson 2001*b* (1969): 37)

Davidson places the concept of truth at the forefront of the project of giving a meaning theory for a natural language. The use that Davidson makes of the concept of truth does not require him to say anything further about what it is for sentences, statements, utterances or propositions to be true. The central insight about truth which Davidson employs, contained in Tarski's and Davidson's Convention *T*, is so innocuous and neutral that it can be conjoined with (almost) any position on the metaphysics of truth. But it would be unnatural not to want to say something about this central concept, and what light Tarski's construction of extensionally adequate definitions for formal languages, and the prospect of extending that work to natural languages, or portions of them, might shed on it. Davidson takes up the topic in his early paper "True to the Facts" (2001*b* (1969)), and although he has apparently changed his mind about the wisdom of using the label 'correspondence theory' for the position he there adopts (see Davidson 1990: 302; 1996; 2005: chs. 1–3), he has never given up the position itself (1990 is an elaboration of the position of 2001*b* (1969)). In this chapter, we consider briefly three traditional theories of truth and their relation to Tarski-style axiomatic truth theories. In §1, we briefly discuss and set aside coherence theories of truth. In §2, we give more attention to the redundancy theory of truth, whose shortcomings point toward a Tarski-style truth theory. In §3, we turn to the prospects for a genuinely explanatory correspondence theory of truth. In the final section, §4, we discuss Davidson's views about the relation of Tarski-style truth theories and traditional correspondence theories.

1. The Coherence Theory of Truth

Two traditional rivals of the correspondence theory of truth are the redundancy and coherence theories (we leave aside pragmatism, a theory which Tarski set aside with the remark that he was not interested in that sense of the word 'true'). Coherence theorists were typically led to their views for epistemological reasons. If all we ever have direct epistemic access to are our own beliefs, but we can have knowledge of the world around us, and this requires that our beliefs be (largely) true, then it would seem that the required link between belief and truth must somehow be guaranteed by the nature of the one or the other. The coherence theorists choose the latter option, and argue that what makes for truth is simply some property of a set of beliefs, namely, coherence. Thus is born the thesis that a belief is true (or likely to be true in more timid versions of the approach—coherence theories of justification) iff it coheres appropriately with the rest of one's beliefs. However, it is not clear that the coherence theory is best understood as a thesis about truth, at least if it is motivated by these traditional epistemological worries, for relief can be obtained from these worries by a closely related maneuver which does not look as if it sheds any light on the concept of truth. What the coherence theorist needs is a link between having beliefs of certain sorts and the world being a certain way, which can be known without presupposing any prior knowledge of the world; thus, what he needs is that it can be known a priori that, given that a belief about the external world coheres with one's other beliefs, it is true or likely to be true. This link need not be grounded in the nature of truth at all. Thus, insofar as this is the primary motivation for the coherence theory of truth, to offer a theory of truth at all in response to it is a confusion. So far as the motivation goes, one's conception of truth could equally well be the redundancy or correspondence conception. Let us turn, then, to these latter two conceptions.

2. The Redundancy Theory of Truth

The basic thesis of the original redundancy theory is that 'is true' and related expressions are redundant in the sense that they can be systematically eliminated from language without loss of content. The redundancy theory of truth works best for locutions such as 'It is true that the Empire State Building is in Manhattan' and 'That New Brunswick is north of Princeton is true', which go apparently without loss of content into 'The Empire State Building is in Manhattan' and 'New Brunswick is north of Princeton'. In these examples, 'it is true that' and 'that . . . is true' function like one-place truth-functional connectives which map the truth values of sentences onto themselves. Similarly, the story goes, for 'is true' as applied to single declarative sentences (henceforth we use 'sentence' in this chapter as short for 'declarative sentence'). If every instance of the schema [P],

[P]   'p' is true iff p

is true, and, moreover, necessarily true, then we have a way of uniformly eliminating the predicate in sentences in which it appears and is predicated of a sentence in quotation marks, in favor of using the sentences to which it is applied.

But trouble is not far off. We will mention four difficulties which come up immediately. The first difficulty is illustrated in what we have just said about schema [P]. Someone who explains the redundancy theory by appeal to [P] must say that *every instance of [P] is true*. But the device we thereby introduce for eliminating the predicate is inapplicable to the sentence we use to introduce it, since there we quantify over sentences, but do not supply the infinity of sentences themselves. A similar difficulty arises if the term referring to the sentence of which 'is true' is predicated does not itself give us a sentence we could *use* in the place of saying that it is true, as, for example, in 'The last sentence of *War and Peace* is true'. Furthermore, in the case of sentences in a language other than one's own, [P] will not yield a truth, because the result of replacing both appearances of 'p' with, for example, 'La Tour Eiffel est en Paris', is not a sentence of English or of French. Finally, [P] (as we have seen) fails when applied to sentences containing context-sensitive elements. If we try disquotation with a context-sensitive sentence, we get the wrong results: 'I am sitting' is true iff I am sitting. No utterance of this represents correctly the conditions under which an utterance of 'I am sitting' is true, and unuttered it is neither truth nor false.

The simple redundancy theory must be modified, if a redundancy theory, or something like it, is to be retained. The interest of the redundancy theory for Davidson is that a modification of the theory along natural lines points toward a theory like Tarski's, as applied to a natural language. For a redundancy theory to treat cases in which we do not give the sentence or sentences of which we predicate truth, it must introduce quantification over entities to which truth is applied. The strategy is to quantify over truth bearers, and to place in our translation a variable which takes truth bearers as values, and which plays the role of a sentence used (that is, the role of the second token of '*p*' in [*P*]).

Suppose we take the most straightforward suggestion, and treat [*P*] as having a variable '*p*', and universally quantify into the places where '*p*' appears above, as in [*P1*].

    [*P1*]   For all *p*, '*p*' is true iff *p*

Here we treat ' " . . . " ' and ' . . . iff___' as functional expressions. The question is what sorts of entity '*p*' can take on as values, and, in particular, whether we can understand both appearances of the variables in the biconditional as ranging over entities of the same sort. The function '*x*' takes arguments that yield sentences as values. Since for each sentence which appears as an argument term in ' "*x*" ', the function must yield a different sentence as value, it is clear that the entities which serve as arguments must be as fine grained as the sentences which denote them, that is, any two different sentences denote a different entity. However, this need not be so for the function '*x* iff *y*', since the argument places here are extensional, in the sense that one can intersubstitute sentences freely *salva veritate*, as long as they agree in truth value. Thus, it is compatible with treating '*x* iff *y*' as a function that we treat, as Frege did, sentences as referring to truth values. This, however, leads to incoherence in [*P1*], since the variable has to range over the same entities in each of its appearances. We must treat the arguments of the function '*x* iff *y*' as the same kind of entities as those of the function '*x*'. This requires that the function '*x* iff *y*' take different arguments to the same value. There is nothing inconsistent in this. However, to be consistent, we must also take the values of the function to be entities of the same kind as its arguments; for, since the functional expression is an open sentence, its argument places take sentences as argument expressions. Thus, quantifying into [*P*] to get [*P1*] forces us to treat any two different sentences as referring to different entities. It is not easy to see how this differs from treating sentences as referring to themselves. This might be thought by itself to be enough reason for rejecting [*P1*].

We can also advance an argument against the proposal based on grammaticality. It will depend on the principle that the grammatical role of an expression reflects its semantic category as well. Thus, a first observation against the above is that it would seem to make the use of the function '*x*' superfluous, since if sentences refer to themselves (as we might as well take them to, on the above proposal) we could as well say 'snow is white is true iff snow is white'. This, however, is clearly ungrammatical. In accordance with our assumption, this shows that we do not treat sentences as referring to themselves. While it is formally consistent with this observation to maintain that sentences refer to other entities which have a one to one mapping onto sentences (perhaps the unit set of the sentence), so that the role of the function 'x' is to map such entities onto sentences, it is very hard to see what story about the semantics of the language could justify this.

Some relief from this objection might be obtained by shifting to [P2] (different entities can be chosen as truth bearers, propositions, for example, but this will do to illustrate the general strategy):

[P2] For all p, the statement that p is true iff p.

To apply this to sentences, we must first transform sentences in which 'is true' is predicated of a sentence into sentences in which it is predicated of a statement. Thus, 'The last sentence of *War and Peace* is true' goes into 'the statement expressed by the last sentence of *War and Peace* is true'. Then, we apply [P2] to obtain 'There is a statement p such that it is expressed by the last sentence of *War and Peace* and p'. Similarly, the sentence 'Everything Quine said is true' goes into 'For all p, if Quine made the statement that p, then p'.

The difficulty Davidson finds with this proposal is that it runs afoul of a variant of the slingshot argument (see Lepore and Ludwig 2005: ch. 3, §4). If sentences name anything, then all true sentences name the same thing, and all false sentences name the same thing. Thus, for all p, q, if p iff q, then the statement that $p = $ the statement that q—since the argument in each case is the same.

We can also mount an argument based on grammaticality (based on the principle, mentioned above, that the grammatical role of an expression reflects its semantic category) against taking sentences to be referring terms at all. If they are referring terms, then it should be grammatical to treat them as referring terms, but it is not. For example, whatever sentences might refer to, they would be either contingent or non-contingent entities. Thus, it ought to make sense, and be grammatical, to say such things as

Caesar crossed the Rubicon is a contingent entity.

But this is treated in English as ungrammatical, which, by our assumption, shows that sentences are not referring terms.[227]

Recent deflationary theories have instead appealed to the schema [D], restricted to instances that do not give rise to semantic paradoxes.

---

[227] See Tarski (1983 (1935): 160–3) for Tarski's discussion of this issue.

[D]   The proposition that *p* is true iff *p*,

The suggestion is that our understanding of the concept of truth is exhausted by our recognition that all instances of this schema are true. Davidson has argued that we lack an account of the semantics of 'The proposition that *p*' which can serve the deflationists' purposes (Davidson 1996, 2000). On the one hand, we may adopt a Fregean position on the definite description, treating 'The proposition that *x*' as a functional expression. In this case, Davidson argues, we may naturally take the description to map a truth value onto itself. Then 'is true' is true of The True and false of The False. We treat the sentence '*p*' as denoting a truth value. This makes instances of the schema, then, trivially true. But this cannot help explain the concept of truth, for it clearly presupposes it. On the other hand, if we adopt a Russellian account of the definite description, we must give an account of the function of the sentence following 'The proposition that'. If it is mentioned, then it must be relativized to a language, since it may express different propositions in different languages. In this case, the concept of truth is exhibited as interconnected with the concept of meaning. And, as Davidson observes, this undercuts the deflationists' attempt to show that the concept is trivial and uninteresting. However, it is not clear that the deflationists may not have available an account of the semantics of 'the proposition that *p*' which avoids at least these difficulties, which borrows a page from Davidson: namely, treating 'the proposition that *p*' in use as denoting the proposition expressed by the contained use of '*p*'. This avoids any mention of sentences or languages. See Ludwig (2004). However, notwithstanding, since propositions are just reified sentence meanings, it should be obvious from the start that schema [D] involves the concept of truth with the concept of meaning, and so with a host of other concepts with which the concept of meaning is in turn intertwined.

In any case, for the moment, our main concern is with Davidson's line of reasoning, so suppose that the approach above must be rejected for at least one of the reasons we have considered. We might have a way around the problems we have encountered in trying to eliminate uses of the predicate 'is true' by quantifying over entities associated with sentences, if we allowed quantifiers to range only over familiar entities, and perhaps entities corresponding to predicates (of any order). For example, with respect to a relational sentence '*aRb*', we might say that any sentence of the form '*aRb*' is true iff the relation expressed by '*R*' is such that the referent of '*a*' stands in that relation to the referent of '*b*'. One could, then, say, for each relational predicate in the language, what relation it expresses, and, for each referring term, what its referent is. This looks promising, but it also begins to look like the beginnings of a theory of the sort that Tarski gives. When we note that, to carry out this procedure properly, one must deal also with quantified sentences, a problem which, as we have seen, Tarski was able to solve using the notion of satisfaction, it begins to look as if pursuing this strategy will lead to something indistinguishable from a Tarski-style truth theory. Thus, given the constraints imposed here, it looks as if the redundancy theory, or its successor, is likely to look quite a bit like a Tarski-style truth theory. The question now before us is whether a Tarski-style theory in spirit is more like a redundancy theory or a correspondence theory. To that end, we turn to an examination of the traditional correspondence theory of truth.

3. The Correspondence Theory of Truth

If a sentence can be said to be true, it may seem natural to ask what makes it true, that is, to put it in a contemporary jargon, to look for truth-makers.[228] It is important that, on the traditional correspondence theory, the function of truth-makers is explanatory. If there were no truth-makers, there could be no true sentences. Thus, the truth of every sentence (or proposition, belief, statement, etc.) is explained by its relation to its truth-maker. Let us call a truth-maker a *fact*, and the relation that a sentence must bear to a truth-maker, if it is to be made true by it, *correspondence*. Then, the general form of the explanation of the truth of a sentence would be

a sentence *s* is true iff it corresponds to *p*

where what replaces '*p*' denotes a fact. As a first stab, we can note that every sentence of the form

s is true iff it corresponds to the fact that *p*

seems guaranteed to be true provided that we replace '*p*' by the sentence *s* denotes, or, more generally, a sentence the same in meaning as *s*.

Davidson gives two arguments against this traditional formulation of the correspondence theory. The first is the so-called 'Great Fact' argument (Davidson 2001*b* (1969): 42). The argumentation is exactly parallel to

---

[228] See, e.g. Armstrong (1997).

that for the claim that if sentences denote anything, then every true sentence denotes the same thing, and every false sentence denotes the same thing. Thus, the essential premises are that if a statement corresponds to the fact described by an expression of the form 'the fact that p', then it corresponds to that described by 'the fact that q', where the sentence replacing 'q' differs from that replacing 'p' only in containing a coreferring singular term, or where the sentence replacing 'p' is logically equivalent to that replacing 'q'. By an argument similar to that given in Lepore and Ludwig (2005: ch. 3, §4), one can reach the conclusion that every true statement corresponds to the same fact.

As Davidson remarks, one can deny one of the premises of the argument. What the proponent of truth-makers wants is a distinct fact for each sentence which is in some intuitive sense about something different, where it seems sufficient for two sentences (as used) to be about different facts that they be different in (propositional) meaning. This seems to be the response the correspondence theorist must make to Davidson's argument. But if he takes this route, then he is subject to the second complaint that Davidson raises (a complaint originally lodged by Peter Strawson (1949, 1950*b*) against J. L. Austin (1950, 1961)). The trouble is that if we individuate facts as finely as statements (uses of sentences to perform locutionary acts at least), then in saying what fact corresponds to a certain sentence, and so makes it true, we must use that very sentence, or one which is the same in meaning as that sentence. Thus, to refer to a fact, we must make use of a true sentence or statement. Since we have no way of picking out the facts that correspond to true sentences or statements other than by using true sentences or statements, it is difficult to see how appeal to facts can explain their truth. That is, our ability to individuate facts depends on our ability to individuate true sentences that differ in meaning, and so our understanding of what a fact is depends on our prior grasp of the concepts of truth and meaning. The trouble with the traditional correspondence theory, then, is not that we cannot give 'correspondence' a clear use—this is given by the observation that every instance of the schema

s corresponds to the fact that p iff p

is true, where a sentence that translates s replaces 'p'—but that we cannot give it a clear use which promises any illumination of the concept of truth. The correspondence theory of truth does not provide any more illumination about the nature of truth than we already get from Convention T.

4. Tarski and Correspondence

Davidson rejects deflationary theories and the traditional correspondence theory of truth—correspondence with fact. However, he does say in "True to the Facts" (2001*b* (1969)) that a correspondence theory is correct. In saying this, he treats any theory as a correspondence theory which explains the truth of sentences in terms of a relation between language and something else. If one recasts the claim of a correspondence theory this broadly, then Davidson's claim is that a Tarski-style truth theory is a correspondence theory (Davidson 2001*b* (1969): 70). To apply such a theory to a natural language, one must relativize sentences to times and speakers, to accommodate context-sensitive elements. The sense in which such a theory is a correspondence theory is that it explains what it is for sentences to be true not by relating sentences to objects, but by relating predicates and referring terms to objects, speakers, and times, via the relations of satisfaction and reference, and exhibiting the conditions under which sentences are true in terms of those relations. (This remains true even if we shift to the proposal characterized in Appendix A to Ch. 2, which avoids introduction of the satisfaction relation, for, as we saw, both approaches work by distinguishing predicates and referring terms, and make use of the idea that predicates apply to objects referring terms refer to.) This promises to be more illuminating than the traditional correspondence theory because we can exhibit, by way of the proof of a *T*-sentence from the axioms of a truth theory, how the truth conditions of the sentence are arrived at, on the basis of the satisfaction conditions for its significant parts; and for each nonsynonymous sentence, there will be a different route to its truth conditions. Moreover, it is clear that this approach affords no way of eliminating, if one is interested in the *intension* of 'truth', the concept of truth, or the closely related semantic concept(s) on which it is based, that is, satisfaction and reference, so this approach should not be thought of as a redundancy theory or a deflationary theory. It is in this sense, and only in this sense, that Davidson is a correspondence theorist. In more recent work, Davidson has rejected this label for his view as misleading,[229] though not the view itself. What is misleading about it is that the thematic heart of the traditional correspondence theory, when it was taken to be an explanatory theory, was the thought that something in the world corresponded to whole

---

[229] See Davidson (1990; 2001 (1987)).

sentences, and it was by reference to a relation between what things of that sort there were and sentences with their meanings that we could explain their truth. It is worth noting that being a correspondence theorist in the *thin* Tarskian sense is *neutral* with respect to traditional disputes between various brands of realism and antirealism, which is surely not the least of its virtues.

Davidson does not seek to provide a reductive explanation of the concept of truth. He has always taken it to be among the more primitive of the concepts which we deploy. What illumination we can gain of such concepts is provided not by a reduction of them to something more primitive, but by detailing their connections with other concepts. In "The Folly of Trying to Define Truth," Davidson puts it in this way:

Now I want to describe what I take to be a fairly radical alternative to theories I have been discussing and (with unseemly haste) dismissing. What I stress here is the *methodology* I think is required rather than the more detailed account I have given elsewhere. The methodology can be characterized on the negative side by saying it offers no definition of the concept of truth, nor any quasi-definitional clause, axiom schema, or other brief substitute for a definition. The positive proposal is to attempt to trace the connections between the concept of truth and the human attitudes and acts that give it body.   (1996: 276)

He goes on to say:

I think of truth as Frank Ramsey though of probability.... We should think of a theory of truth for a speaker in the same way we think of a theory of rational decision: both describe structures we can find, with an allowable degree of fitting and fudging, in the behavior or more or less rational creatures gifted with speech. It is in the fitting and fudging that we give content to the undefined concepts of subjective probability and subjective values–belief and desire, as we briefly call them; and, by way of theories like Tarski's, to the undefined concept of truth.... I ... see the problem of connecting truth with observable human behavior as inseparable from the problem of assigning contents to all the attitudes, and this seems to me to require a theory that embeds a theory of truth in a larger theory that includes decision theory itself. The result will incorporate the major norms of rationality whose partial realization in the thought and behavior of agents makes those agents intelligible, more or less, to others.   (Ibid. 278)

This is a summary of the technique of "The Structure and Content of Truth" (Davidson 1990), which is a résumé of Davidson's work in the theory of meaning and radical interpretation. Few philosophers have explored the interrelations between thought, language, meaning, truth, and reality more systematically and with greater subtlety than Donald Davidson.

Summary

Our aim in this book has been to clarify the foundations of truth-theoretic semantics and to illustrate its promise. To this end we have provided a general sketch of the philosophical foundations of truth-theoretic semantics in Chapter 1, dealing with the problems of theories that quantify over meanings, and showing what the role of a truth theory is in a meaning theory, and how to adapt the theory to accommodate context-sensitive elements. In Chapter 2, we showed how to extend the program in the standard way to quantified languages, and how to incorporate in a straightforward fashion restricted quantifiers into the approach, abandoning the straitjacket of classical first order logic, without, however, appealing to second order quantifiers. We have sketched briefly how this extension can be implemented in a simple truth theory for a regimented language, but have subsequently explored the extension of the framework to other suburbs of natural language more informally.

We have worked through a number of important topics having to do with referring terms and noun phrases, proper names, indexicals, and simple demonstratives, in Chapter 4. Demonstrative elements, as we saw, ultimately force a further relativization of our semantic predicates to speech acts. In Chapter 5, we argued that so-called complex demonstratives, which have been treated by a majority of philosophers as complex referring terms, are in fact quantified noun phrases in which a simple demonstrative should be seen as contributing to a nominal restriction.

In Chapter 6, we took up Davidson's treatment of the semantics of quotation, which employs the strategy of parataxis, a strategy also employed in his treatment of indirect discourse and non-declarative sentences. Davidson's proposal essentially is that quotation names, as they are traditionally known, are in fact quantified noun phrases containing a demonstrative restriction in the nominal, and, in this sense, rather like our proposal about complex demonstratives. We raised a number of difficulties for the approach, however, mostly connected with parataxis, and explored briefly a simpler alternative, namely, a simple reference rule, which embodies the common sense observation Davidson starts with, that any expression consisting of an expression enclosed in quotation marks refers to the enclosed expression.

In Chapter 7, we reviewed treatments of adjectival and adverbial modifiers, and proposed a uniform treatment for what we called subject dependent modifiers, like 'large' and 'slowly', whether adjectives or adverbs.

In Chapters 8–10, we took up the discussion of a variety of issues having to do with tense in natural languages, which have been somewhat neglected in the philosophical tradition in truth-theoretic semantics. One of the upshots of this discussion is that the metalanguage for a truth theory for a natural language like English cannot be that language itself, since we must introduce non-context-sensitive predicates that relate objects to times for the purposes of giving truth conditions, which are not present in the original language. Tense we treated as involving indexically restricted quantification, and extended the account of the simple tenses to the perfect tenses using the same devices. This approach gives system to and illuminates the workings of temporal adverbials. We also discussed some of the devices by which tense in superordinate clauses controls the tense in subordinate clauses, representing it as involving quantifiers binding temporal argument places that function in unembedded contexts as indexing to speaker time. We discussed, specifically, the relations between the tense of the main verbs in indirect discourse and attitude sentences and their complement clauses, which, if we are right, involve quantifying into those contexts—a subject typically ignored in discussions of the semantics of these classes of sentences. We extended the restricted quantifier approach to the perfect tenses, treating them as introducing two quantifiers, one of which introduces a reference time located in relation to the time of utterance, and the other of which locates the event time (and so binds the argument place in the verb) relative to the reference time. We also modified the account of adverbial modification discussed in Chapter 7 in light of the identification of an additional argument place in tensed verbs, which leads to a more natural treatment of a number of kinds of adverbials, including adverbials that intuitively modify location and objects, rather than events.

In Chapter 11, we considered how the approach could be extended to handle opaque contexts without introducing intensional entities. We reviewed Davidson's paratactic approach, which treats 'Galileo said that the earth moves' as semantically equivalent to the utterance of two sentences, 'Galileo said that' and 'the earth moves', where the appearance of 'that' in the first is used to refer to the token utterance of the second in use. We discussed a number of the difficulties which have been raised for this account in the literature, and proposed an alternative approach that hews to the spirit of Davidson's proposal, but which gives up parataxis in favor of seeing 'Galileo said that the earth moves' as a single sentence syntactically, which says, roughly, that some utterance of Galileo's is relevantly related in content to the content 'the earth moves' has in the utterance by the speaker at the time.

We next turned to another problem area for truth-theoretic semantics, namely, non-declarative sentences, imperatives, and interrogatives, in Chapter 12. We examined Davidson's proposal for incorporating imperatives and interrogatives into a truth theory by treating them as involving semantically two distinct speech acts, each of which receive truth conditions. We argued that this approach fails on a number of grounds, and, in particular, we argued that it fails to accommodate our sense that utterances of imperatives and interrogatives do not involve speech acts that are truth evaluable, and that it does not handle correctly mixed mood sentences, such as 'If you are tired, let me drive'. We introduced a generalization of the truth-theoretic approach, the fulfillment-theoretic framework, which assigns imperatives and interrogatives compliance conditions, but uses a truth theory to unpack compliance conditions in terms of a standard truth theory for the language, thereby preserving for the truth theory a primary role in exhibiting natural languages as compositional structures.

We turned in Chapter 13 to a discussion of the relevance of a compositional meaning theory in the style we have been exploring to explaining the notion of logical form traditionally at play in philosophical analysis. We used a suggestion of Davidson's to provide an account of sameness of logical from between any two sentences in any two languages, and discussed the relation of the truth/fulfillment-theoretic approach to issues of identifying logical constants, of logical entailment and equivalence, and of the supposed distinct notion of structural entailment.

In the final chapter, 14, we discussed briefly Davidson's views on the relative primacy of the concept of truth, and criticisms of traditional theories of truth, from the coherence and redundancy theories to the correspondence theory.

We do not represent ourselves, of course, as having provided anything like a complete outline of the application of the truth/fulfillment-theoretic approach to natural languages—an immense project. Our aim has been rather, as we have said, to illustrate, to discuss its general character and how the truth/fulfillment theories are related to the project of giving a compositional

Summary

meaning theory, to discuss a variety of proposals Davidson has made about handling recalcitrant portions of natural languages, and to propose in some areas solutions to what have seemed to us still outstanding problems, or problem areas where there is no clear consensus on the right approach. We hope thereby to encourage additional work within the framework and extensions of the work here presented. It is our view that this is the most philosophically sound, and practically fruitful approach to revealing the compositional structure of natural languages. It provides, with minimal resources, the illumination which we seek from a compositional meaning theory for natural languages, and connects transparently meaning with the truth conditions, or more generally fulfillment conditions, of utterances of sentences. In approaches which introduce additional ontology, the extra ontological resources provide no additional illumination about how we understand the languages we have mastered, and the connection with truth must still be made. Insofar as that is so, invoking the extra ontology as if it were needed obscures the character of our understanding of the languages which such theories are invoked to illuminate.

Bibliography

Abusch, D. (1997). Sequence of Tense and Temporal De Re. *Linguistics and Philosophy*, 20: 1–50.

Altham, J. E. J., and Tennant, N. W. (1975). Sortal Quantification. In E. L. Keenan (ed.), *Formal Semantics of Natural Language*. Cambridge: Cambridge University Press.

Altshuler, D. (2004). A Simultaneous Perception of Things: SOT in Russian. *Snippets*, 8: 5–6.

Armstrong, D. M. (1997). *A World of States of Affairs*. New York: Cambridge University Press.

Audi, R. (ed.). (1995). *The Cambridge Dictionary of Philosophy*. Cambridge: Cambridge University Press.

Austin, J. L. (1950). Truth, Part I. *Aristotelian Society Supplement*, 24: 111–28.

——(1961). Unfair to Facts, *Philosophical Papers* (pp. 154–74). Oxford: Clarendon Press.

——(1962). *How to Do Things with Words*. Cambridge, Mass.: Harvard University Press.

Bach, K., and Harnish, R. M. (1982). *Linguistic Communication and Speech Acts*. Cambridge, Mass.: MIT Press.

Baldwin, T. (1979). Interpretations of Quantifiers. *Mind*, 88: 215–40.

Barwise, J., and Cooper, R. (1981). Generalized Quantifiers and Natural Language. *Linguistics and Philosophy*, 4: 159–219.

Black, M., and Geach, P. (eds.). (1960). *Translations from the Philosophical Writings of Gottlob Frege*. Oxford: Oxford University Press.

Blackburn, S. (1975). The Identity of Propositions. In S. Blackburn (ed.), *Meaning, Reference and Necessity*. Cambridge: Cambridge University Press.

Boisvert, D. (1999). *The Semantics and Pragmatics of Mixed Mood Sentences*. Unpublished MA thesis, University of Florida, Gainesville.

Boisvert, D., and Lubbers, C. (2003). Frege's Commitment to an Infinite Hierarchy of Senses. *Philosophical Papers*, 32(1): 31–64.

Boisvert, D., and Ludwig, K. (2006). Semantics for Nondeclaratives. In E. Lepore (ed.), *Oxford Handbook for the Philosophy of Language*. New York: Oxford University Press.

Borg, E. (1999). Complex Demonstratives. *Philosophical Studies*, 229–49.

Bibliography

Braun, D. (1994). Structured Characters and Complex Demonstratives. *Philosophical Studies*, 74: 193–219.

Burge, T. (1974). Demonstrative Constructions, Reference and Truth. *Journal of Philosophy*, 71: 205–23.

____ (1986). On Davidson's 'Saying That'. In E. Lepore (ed.), *Truth and Interpretation: Perspectives on the Philosophy of Donald Davidson*. Cambridge, Mass.: Blackwell.

Cappelen, H., and Lepore, E. (1997). Varieties of Quotation. *Mind*, 106(423): 429–50.

____ (1999). Semantics for Quotation. In K. Murasugi (ed.), *Philosophy and Linguistics*. Boulder, Colo.: Westview Press.

Castañeda, H.-N. (1967). Comments on Donald Davidson's 'The Logical Form of Action Sentences'. In N. Rescher (ed.), *The Logic of Decision and Action* (pp. 104–12). Pittsburgh: University of Pittsburgh Press.

Chihara, C. (1973). *Ontology and the Vicious-Circle Principle*. Ithaca, NY: Cornell University Press.

Church, A. (1950). On Carnap's Analysis of Statements of Assertion and Belief. *Analysis*, 10: (97–9).

____ (1951). The Need for Abstract Entities in Semantic Analysis. *Proceedings of the American Academy of Arts and Letters*, 80: 100–13.

Comrie, B. (1985). *Tense*. New York: Cambridge University Press.

Dähl, B. (1985). *Tense and Aspect Systems*. Cambridge: Cambridge University Press.

Davidson, D. (1985). Adverbs of Action. In B. Vermazen (ed.), *Essays on Davidson* (pp. 230–41). Oxford: Clarendon Press.

____ (1990). The Structure and Content of Truth. *Journal of Philosophy*, 87(6): 279–328.

____ (1996). The Folly of Trying to Define Truth. *Journal of Philosophy*, 93: 263–78.

____ (2000). Truth Rehabilitated. In R. B. Brandon (ed.), *Rorty and his Critics* (pp. 65–73). Cambridge, Mass.: Blackwell.

____ (2001 (1966)). Theories of Meaning and Learnable Languages, *Inquiries into Truth and Interpretation* (2nd edn., pp. 3–15). New York: Clarendon Press. Originally published in Y. Bar-Hillel (ed.), *Proceedings of the 1964 International Congress for Logic, Methodology and Philosophy of Science* (pp. 383–94). Amsterdam: North Holland Publishing Co.

____ (2001a (1967)). Causal Relations, *Essays on Actions and Events* (2nd edn., pp. 149–62). New York: Clarendon Press. Original published in *Journal of Philosophy*, 64 (1967): 691–703.

____ (2001b (1967)). The Logical Form of Action Sentences, *Essays on Actions and Events* (2nd edn., pp. 105–21). New York: Clarendon Press. Originally published in N. Rescher (ed.), *The Logic of Decision and Action*. Pittsburgh: University of Pittsburgh.

____ (2001c (1967)). Truth and Meaning, *Inquiries into Truth and Interpretation* (2nd edn., pp. 17–36). New York: Clarendon Press. Originally published in *Synthese*, 17 (1967): 304–23.

____(2001 (1968)). On Saying That. *Inquiries into Truth and Interpretation* (2nd edn., pp. 93–108). New York: Clarendon Press. Originally published in *Synthese*, 19 (1968): 130–46.

____(2001a (1969)). The Individuation of Events. *Essays on Actions and Events* (2nd edn., pp. 163–80). New York: Clarendon Press. Originally published in N. Rescher, (ed.), *Essays in Honor of Carl G. Hempel*. Dordrecht D. Reidel.

____(2001b (1969)). True to the Facts. *Inquiries into Truth and Interpretation* (2nd edn., pp. 37–54). New York: Clarendon Press. Originally published in *Journal of Philosophy*, 66 (1969): 748–64.

____(2001a (1970)). Events as Particulars. *Essays on Actions and Events* (2nd edn., pp. 181–8). New York: Clarendon Press. Originally published in *Noûs*, 4 (1970), 25–32.

____(2001b (1970)). Reply to Cargile. *Essays on Actions and Events* (2nd edn., pp. 137–46). Oxford: Oxford University Press. Originally published as Action and Reaction, *Inquiry*, 13 (1970): 140–8.

____(2001c (1970)). Semantics for Natural Languages. *Inquiries into Truth and Interpretation* (2nd edn., pp. 55–64). New York: Clarendon Press. Originally published in *Linguaggi nella Societa e nella Tecnica*. Milan: Comunita.

____(2001a (1971)). Agency. *Essays on Actions and Events* (2nd edn., pp. 43–62). New York: Clarendon Press. Originally published in R. Binkley, R. Bronaugh, and A. Marras (eds.), *Agent, Action, and Reason* (pp. 3–37). Toronto: University of Toronto Press.

____(2001b (1971)). Eternal vs. Ephemeral Events. *Essays on Actions and Events* (2nd edn., pp. 189–204). New York: Clarendon Press. Originally published in *Noûs*, 5 (1971): 335–49.

____(2001a (1973)). In Defence of Convention T. *Inquiries into Truth and Interpretation* (2nd edn., pp. 65–75). New York: Clarendon Press. Originally published in H. Leblanc (ed.), *Truth, Syntax and Modality*. Dordrecht: North-Holland Publishing Co.

____(2001b (1973)). Radical Interpretation. *Inquiries into Truth and Interpretation* (2nd edn., pp. 125–39). New York: Clarendon Press. Originally published in *Dialectica*, 27 (1973): 314–28.

____(2001 (1974)). Belief and the Basis of Meaning. *Inquiries into Truth and Interpretation* (2nd edn., pp. 141–54). New York: Clarendon Press. Originally published in *Synthese*, 27 (1974): 309–23.

____(2001 (1975)). Thought and Talk. *Inquiries into Truth and Interpretation* (2nd edn., pp. 155–70). New York: Clarendon Press. Originally published in S. Guttenplan (ed.), *Mind and Language*. Oxford: Oxford University Press.

____(2001 (1976)). Reply to Foster. *Inquiries into Truth and Interpretation* (2nd edn., pp. 171–9). New York: Clarendon Press. Originally published in G. Evans and J. McDowell (eds.), *Truth and Meaning: Essays in Semantics*. Oxford: Oxford University Press.

Davidson, D. (2001 (1977)). The Method of Truth in Metaphysics. *Inquiries into Truth and Interpretation* (2nd edn., pp. 199–214). New York: Clarendon Press. Originally published in Peter A. French, Theodore Uehling, and Howard Wettstein (eds.), *Midwest Studies in Philosophy: Studies in the Philosophy of Language*, (1977): 244–54.

——(2001*a* (1979)). Moods and Performances. *Inquiries into Truth and Interpretation* (2nd edn., pp. 109–21). New York: Clarendon Press. Originally published in A. Margalit (ed.), *Meaning and Use*. Dordrecht: D. Reidel.

——(2001*b* (1979)). Quotation. *Inquiries into Truth and Interpretation* (2nd edn., pp. 79–92). New York: Clarendon Press. Originally published in *Theory and Decision*, 11 (1979): 27–40.

——(2001 (1980)). *Essays on Actions and Events* (2nd edn.). Oxford: Clarendon Press.

——(2001 (1984)). *Inquiries into Truth and Interpretation* (2nd edn.). New York: Clarendon Press.

——(2001 (1987)). Afterthoughts. *Subjective, Intersubjective, Objective* (pp. 154–8). New York: Clarendon Press. Originally published in A. Malichowski (ed.), *Reading Rorty* (pp. 120–138). Cambridge: Blackwell.

——(2005). *Truth and Predication*. Cambridge, Mass.: Harvard University Press.

Davies, M. (1981). *Meaning, Quantification, Necessity*. London: Routledge & Kegan Paul.

——(1982). Individuation and the Semantics of Demonstratives. *Journal of Philosophical Logic*, 11: 287–310.

Dowty, D. (1977). Toward a Semantic Analysis of Verb Aspect and the English 'Imperfective Paradox'. *Linguistics and Philosophy*, 1: 45–77.

——(1982). Tenses, Time Adverbs, and Compositional Semantic Theory. *Linguistics and Philosophy*, 5: 23–58.

Dummett, M. (1973). *Frege: Philosophy of Language*. London: Duckworth.

Evans, G. (1976). Semantic Structure and Logical Form. In J. McDowell and G. Evans (eds.), *Truth and Meaning* (pp. 199–222). London: Oxford.

——(1977). Pronouns, Quantifiers, and Relative Clauses (I). *Canadian Journal of Philosophy*, 7: 467–536.

——(1982). *The Varieties of Reference*. Oxford: Clarendon Press.

Foster, J. A. (1976). Meaning and Truth Theory. In G. Evans and J. McDowell (eds.), *Truth and Meaning: Essays in Semantics* (pp. 1–32). Oxford: Clarendon Press.

Frege, G. (1977 (1918–19)). The Thought. In P. T. Geach (ed.), *Logical Investigations* (pp. 1–30). New Haven: Yale University Press.

——(1997 (1892)). On *Sinn* and *Bedeutung*. In M. Beaney (ed.), *The Frege Reader*. Oxford: Blackwell Publishers. Originally published as Ueber Sinn und Bedeutung. *Zeitschrift für Philosophie und philosophische Kritik*, 100 (1892): 25–50.

Gabbay, D., and Rohrer, C. (1979). Do We Really Need Tenses Other than Future and Past? In R. Bauerle, U. Egli, and A. Von Stechow (eds.), *Semantics from Different Points of View*. New York: Springer-Verlag.

Geach, P. T. (1957). *Mental Acts*. London: Routledge & Kegan Paul.

Giorgi, A., and Pianesi, F. (1997). *Tense and Aspect: From Semantics to Morphosyntax*. New York: Oxford University Press.

Hand, M. (1991). On Saying That Again. *Linguistic and Philosophy*, 14: 349–65.

Higginbotham, J. (1986). Linguistic Theory and Davidson's Program in Semantics. In E. Lepore (ed.), *Essays on Truth and Interpretation: Perspectives on the Philosophy of Donald Davidson* (pp. 29–48). New York: Blackwell.

—— (1988). Contexts, Models, and Meanings: A Note on the Data of Semantics. In R. Kempson (ed.), *Mental Representation: The Interface between Language and Reality* (pp. 29–48). Cambridge: Cambridge University Press.

—— (1991). Belief and Logical Form. *Mind and Language*, 6(4): 344–69.

—— (1995). Tensed Thoughts. *Mind and Language*, 10(3): 226–49.

—— (2002). Competence with Demonstratives. *Philosophical Perspectives*, 16: 3–18.

—— (2006). *Sententialism: The Thesis that Complement Clauses Refer to Themselves. Philosophical Issues*, 16.

—— Pianesi, F., and Varzi, A. C. (2000). *Speaking of Events*. New York: Oxford University Press.

Hinrichs, E. (1986). Temporal Anaphora in Discourses in English. *Linguistics and Philosophy*, 9: 63–82.

Hornsby, J. (1977). Saying of. *Analysis*, 37: 177–85.

Johnson, K., and Lepore, E. (2002). Does Syntax Reveal Semantics? A Case Study of Complex Demonstratives. *Philosophical Perspectives*, 16: 707–34.

Kamp, J. (1971). Formal Properties of 'Now'. *Theoria*, 37: 227–73.

Kaplan, D. (1989). Demonstratives. In J. Almog, J. Perry, and H. Wettstein (eds.), *Themes from Kaplan* (pp. 481–564). New York: Oxford University Press.

King, J. (2001). Remarks on the Syntax and Semantics of Day Designators. *Philosophical Perspectives*, 16: 291–333.

King, J. C. (2001). *Complex Demonstratives: A Quantificational Account*. Cambridge, Mass.: MIT Press.

Kondrashova, N. (1998). *Embedded Tenses in English and Russian*. Unpublished manuscript, Cornell University.

Kusumoto, K. (1999). *Embedded Contexts*. Amherst, Mass.: University of Massachusetts.

Langford, C. H. (1942). The Notion of Analysis in Moore's Philosophy. In P. A. Schilpp (ed.), *The Philosophy of G. E. Moore* (pp. 321–42). La Salle, Ill.: Open Court.

Larson, R., and Ludlow, P. (1993). Interpreted Logical Forms. *Synthese*, 95: 305–55.

—— and Segal, G. (1995). *Knowledge of Meaning*. Cambridge, Mass.: MIT Press.

Lepore, E. (1983). What Model Theoretic Semantics Cannot Do? *Synthese*, 54: 167–88.

—— (1997). Conditions on Understanding Language. *Proceedings of the Aristotelian Society*, 97: 41–60.

—— (1999). The Scope and Limits of Quotation. In L. E. Hahn (ed.), *The Philosophy of Donald Davidson* (pp. 691–714). Chicago: Open Court Publishers.

333

Bibliography

Lepore, E., and Leslie, S.-J. (2001). *Mood Matters.* Unpublished manuscript.

Lepore, E., and Loewer, B. (1989). You Can Say That Again, *Midwest Studies in Philosophy,* 14: 338–56.

—— and Ludwig, K. (2000). The Semantics and Pragmatics of Complex Demonstratives. *Mind,* 109(434): 199–240.

—— and —— (2001). What Is Logical Form?, *Logical Form and Language* (pp. 54–90). Oxford: Oxford University Press.

—— and —— (2003). Outline for a Truth Conditional Semantics for Tense. In Q. Smith and A. Jokic (eds.), *Tense, Time and Reference* (pp. 49–105). Cambridge, Mass.: MIT Press.

—— and —— (2005). *Donald Davidson: Meaning, Truth, Language, and Reality.* Oxford: Clarendon Press.

Lewis, D. (1975a). Adverbs of Quantification. In E. Keenan (ed.), *Formal Semantics of Natural Language* (pp. 3–15). Cambridge: Cambridge University Press.

—— (1975b). General Semantics. In D. Davidson, and G. Harman (eds.), *Semantics of Natural Language.* Boston: D. Reidel.

Lindstrom, P. (1966). First Order Predicate Logic with Generalized Quantifiers. *Theoria,* 32: 186–95.

Ludlow, P. (1999). *Semantics, Tense, and Time: An Essay in the Metaphysics of Natural Language.* Cambridge, Mass.: MIT Press.

Ludwig, K. (1996a). Explaining Why Things Look the Way They Do. In K. Akins (ed.), *Perception* (pp. 18–60). Oxford: Oxford University Press.

—— (1996b). Singular Thought and the Cartesian Theory of Mind. *Noûs,* 30(4): 434–60.

—— (1997). The Truth about Moods. *Protosociology: Cognitive Sematnics I. Conceptions of Meaning,* 10: 19–66.

—— (2004). Davidson's Objection to Horwich's Minimalism about Truth. *Journal of Philosophy,* 101(8): 429–37.

—— (2006). *A Conservative Modal Semantics.* Unpublished manuscript.

—— and Ray, G. (1998). Semantics for Opaque Contexts. In J. Tomberlin (ed.), *Philosophical Perspectives: Language, Mind and Ontology* 12 (pp. 141–66). Cambridge, Mass.: Blackwell.

—— (2002). Vagueness and the Sorites Paradox. In J. Tomberlin (ed.), *Philosophical Perspectives: Language and Mind* 16 (pp. 419–61). Oxford: Blackwell.

Lycan, W. (1973). Davidson on Saying That. *Analysis,* 33: 138–9.

McCarthy, T. (1981). The Idea of a Logical Constant. *Journal of Philosophy,* 78: 499–523.

McDowell, J. (1977). On the Sense and Reference of a Proper Name. *Mind,* 86: 159–85.

McFetridge, I. (1976). Propositions and Davidson's Account of Indirect Discourse. *Proceedings of the Aristotelian Society,* 76: 131–45.

McGinn, C. (1981). The Mechanism of Reference. *Synthese,* 49(1): 157–86.

McKinsey, J. C. C. (1948). A New Definition of Truth. *Synthese*, 7: 428–33.

Mates, B. (1972). *Elementary Logic*. Oxford: Oxford University Press.

Mittwoch, A. (1988). Aspects of English Aspect: On the Interaction of Perfect, Progressive and Durational Phrases. *Linguistics and Philosophy*, 2: 203–54.

Montague, R. (1974). English as a Formal Language. In R. Thomason (ed.), *Formal Philosophy* (pp. 188–221). New Haven: Yale University Press.

Neale, S. (1990*a*). *Descriptions*. Cambridge, Mass.: MIT Press.

——(1990*b*). Descriptive Pronouns and Donkey Anaphora. *Journal of Philosophy*, 87(3): 113–50.

——(1993). Term Limits. In J. Tomberlin (ed.), *Language and Logic, Philosophical Perspectives* 7 (pp. 18–24). Atascadero, Calif.: Ridgeview.

Ogihara, T. (1996). *Tense, Attitudes, and Scope*. Boston: Kluwer.

Palmer, F. R. (1974). *The English Verb*. London: Longman.

Parsons, T. (1981). Frege's Hierarchies of Indirect Senses and the Paradox of Analysis, *Midwest Studies in Philosophy*, 6: 37–57.

——(1990). *Events in the Semantics of English: A Study in Subatomic Semantics*. Cambridge, Mass.: MIT Press.

Partee, B. (1973). Some Structural Analogies between Tenses and Pronouns in English. *Journal of Philosophy*, 70(18): 601–9.

Peacocke, C. (1976). What is a Logical Constant? *Journal of Philosophy*, 73(9): 221–40.

——(1981). Demonstrative Thought and Psychological Explanation. *Synthese*, 49: 187–217.

Perry, J. (1997). Indexicals and Demonstratives. In B. Hale and C. Wright (eds.), *A Companion to the Philosophy of Language* (pp. 586–612). Oxford: Blackwell.

Philippe, S. (1999). A Plea for Monsters. *Linguistics and Philosophy*, 26: 29–120.

Platts, M. (1979). *Ways of Meaning: An Introduction to a Philosophy of Language*. London: Routledge & Kegan Paul.

Quine, W. V. O. (1947). On Universals. *Journal of Symbolic Logic*, 12: 74–85.

——(1960). *Word and Object*. Cambridge, Mass.: MIT Press.

——(1980). Grammar, Truth, and Logic. In S. Kanger and S. Ohman (eds.), *Philosophy and Grammar* (pp. 17–28). Dordrecht: Reidel.

Recanati, F. (1993). *Direct Reference: From Language to Thought*. Oxford: Blackwell.

Reichenbach, H. (1947). *Elements of Symbolic Logic*. New York: Macmillan.

Rescher, N. (1962). Plurality Quantification. *Journal of Symbolic Logic*, 27: 373–4.

Richard, M. (1981). Temporalism and Eternalism. *Philosophical Studies*, 39: 1–13.

——(1986). Quotation, Grammar, and Opacity. *Linguistics and Philosophy*, 9: 383–403.

——(1993). Articulated Terms. In J. E. Tomberlin (ed.), *Language and Logic* 7. Atascadero, Calif.: Ridgeview.

Rumfitt, I. (1996). The Vagaries of Paraphrase: A Reply to Holton on the Counting Problem. *Analysis*, 74: 246–50.

Russell, B. (1903). *The Principles of Mathematics*. Cambridge: Cambridge University Press.

Bibliography

Russell, B. (1993). *Our Knowledge of the External World: As a Field for Scientific Method in Philosophy*. New York: Routledge.

Scheffler, I. (1954). An Inscriptional Approach to Indirect Quotation. *Analysis*, 10: 83–90.

Schein, B. (1993). *Plurals and Events*. Cambridge, Mass.: MIT Press.

Schiffer, S. (1981). Indexicals and the Theory of Reference. *Synthese*, 57: 43–100.

——(1987). Extensionalist Semantics and Sententialist Theories of Belief. In E. Lepore (ed.), *New Directions in Semantics* (pp. 113–42). London: Academic Press.

Searle, J. (1969). Speech Acts: An Essay in the Philosophy of Language. London: Cambridge University Press.

——(1979). A Taxonomy of Illocutionary Acts. *Expression and Meaning* (pp. 1–29). Cambridge: Cambridge University Press.

Seymour, M. (1994). Indirect Discourse and Quotation. *Philosophical Studies*, 74(1): 1–38.

Sher, G. (1996). Semantics and Logic. In S. Lappin (ed.), *The Handbook of Contemporary Semantic Theory* (pp. 511–37). Oxford: Blackwell.

Smith, C. (1978). The Syntax and Interpretation of Temporal Expressions in English. *Linguistics and Philosophy*, 2: 43–99.

Stowell, T. (1995). The Phrase Structure of Tense. In J. Rooryck, and L. Zring (eds.), *Studies in Nllt 33*. Dordrecht: Kluwer.

Strawson, P. F. (1949). Truth. *Analysis*, 9: 83–97.

——(1950a). On Referring. *Mind*, 59: 320–44.

——(1950b). Truth, Part II. *Aristotelian Society Supplement*, 24: 129–56.

Tarski, A. (1944). The Semantic Conception of Truth and the Foundations of Semantics. *Philosophy and Phenomenological Research*, 4: 341–76.

——(1983 (1935)). The Concept of Truth in Formalized Languages, *Logic, Semantics, Metamathematics* (2nd edn.). Indianapolis: Hackett Publishing Company. Originally published as De Wahrheitsbegriff in den formalisierten Sprachen, *Studia Philosphica*, 1 (1935): 261–405.

——(1986). What are Logical Notions? *History and Philosophy of Logic*, 7: 143–54.

Taylor, B. (1977). Tense and Continuity. *Linguistics and Philosophy*, 1: 199–220.

——(1980). Truth-Theory for Indexical Languages. In M. Platts (ed.), *Reference, Truth and Reality* (pp. 182–98). London: Routledge & Paul.

Tolkien, J. R. R. (1965). *The Two Towers*. New York: Ballentine Books.

Vendler, Z. (1967). Verbs and Times. *Linguistics and Philosophy* (pp. 97–121). Ithaca, NY: Cornell University Press.

Visser, F. T. (1972). *An Historical Syntax of the English Language* (vol. v). Leiden: E. J. Brill.

Vlach, F. (1993). Temporal Adverbials, Tenses and the Perfect. *Linguistics and Philosophy*, 16(3): 231–83.

Wallace, J. (1972). Positive, Comparative, Superlative. *Journal of Philosophy*, 21: 773–82.

___(1975). On the Frame of Reference. In D. Davidson and G. Harman (eds.), *Semantics for Natural Language* (pp. 219–52). Dordrecht: D. Reidel.

___(1978). Logical Form, Meaning, Translation. In M. Guenthener-Reutter (ed.), *Meaning and Translation* (pp. 45–58). London: Duckworth.

Weinstein, S. (1974). Truth and Demonstratives. *Noûs*, 8: 179–84.

Wheeler, S. (1972). Attributives and their Modifiers. *Noûs*, 6: 310–34.

Wiggins, D. (1980). 'Most' and 'All': Some Comments on a Familiar Programme. In M. Platts (ed.), *Reference, Truth and Reality: Essays on the Philosophy of Language* (pp. 318–46). London: Routledge & Kegan Paul.

Yi, B.-U. (1999). Is Two a Property? *Journal of Philosophy*, 96(4): 163–90.

Index

Index

Larson, R. 20n, 35n, 118n, 120n, 125, 258n, 294n
Leslie, S.-J. 275
Lewis, D. 118n, 120n, 205n, 267
Lindstrom, P. 305
linguistic competence 9, 18, 20, 103
  as dispositional 9, 20, 41
  as practical ability 20
  structure of 19–20, 22, 26
  see also language natural, mastery of;
    language, natural, understanding of
Loewer, B. 152n, 246n, 248n, 253
logic
  three-value 49n,
logical consequence 255, 301–2, 307–11, 327
  vs structural consequence 309–11, 327
logical constants 29, 57, 286, 288, 301–7, 312–14, 327
  epistemic criterion for 312–14
logical equivalence 301–2, 307–11, 327
logical form 7–8, 10–11, 14, 15, 201, 217, 244, 260, 285–314, 327, 327
  as relative to theory 297–8
  canonical representation of 299–301
  sameness of 11, 15, 189, 285–6, 289–307, 327
logical truth 301–2, 307–11
Lubbers, C. 3n, 74n
Ludlow, P. 186n, 258n, 294n
Lycan, W. 246

McCarthy, T. 313–14
McDowell, J. 102n
McFetridge, I. 249n
McGinn, C. 113n, 125
McKinsey, J. C. C. 66n
Martin, R. M. 176n
Mates, B. 64n
meaning
  autonomy of 266
  combinatorial aspects of 8–9
  concept of 4, 320
  nature of 1, 6, 324
  predicate
    relativized 42
  sameness of *see* synonymy
  theory of 1, 3, 6, 12, 324
    recursive 5
meaning theory 3–6, 11–13, 23, 27–50, 61, 91, 101–2, 113, 153, 264, 284, 315
  adequacy conditions for 17–19, 27–8,
  as distict from truth theory 45–7, 49–50
  axioms of 22–3, 46–7, 50
  compositional 3–5, 8–10, 11, 12, 14, 16, 17–20, 22, 27–52, 178, 245, 327–8

constraints on 5, 26
  see also Convention *T*
  form of 46–7, 52, 90
confirmation of 4
context sensitive 14, 41–52
explicit 45–6, 52, 76
knowledge of 19–20, 45
M-sentences 26–8, 42, 51, 76, 85, 280–1
theorems of 45–7,
meanings
  as entities 5–6, 9–10, 12, 28, 50, 239, 241–3, 261–2
  explanatory role of 26n
  problems for 20–6
  as proxy for equivalence classes 21–2
  structure of 10
  utility of 17, 22
means that 27–8, 42, 45–7, 50, 51, 101,
  as generating intensional contexts 27
metaphysics 1
Mittwoch, A. 231n
modal contexts 14, 100–1, 114, 255
  see also demonstratives complex, in modal contexts
modality 6, 11, 71, 129n
Montague, R. 187n
mood 263–84
  conventionalist account of 267
  fulfillment-conditional account of 276–84;
    see also fulfillment, theory
  performative paraphrase account of 267–8
  see also force; imperatives; indicatives;
    interrogatives; parataxis;
    sentences declarative; sentences,
    non-declarative; sentences, mixed
    mood

Naess, A. 212
Neale, S. 114n, 62–36, 126, 127n, 129n, 131, 137n, 139n, 141n, 157n
negative polarity 203–4
nominals 13, 91, 93, 124–8, 131–8, 131, 146, 163, 164, 184, 263n, 301
noun phrases 124, 127, 137–8, 301
  quantified 13, 53, 61, 103–4, 125–6, 126–9, 146–8, 158, 203
  referring 107–8, 325
numbers 66, 73, 74, 103–7, 126n, 170, 205n, 305n

obedience predicate 277–81
Ogihara, T. 221n
ontology 5, 8, 25n, 26, 177, 243, 286–7, 328
opaque contexts 11, 14, 100–1, 239–62